GENDER <u>IN</u> HISTORY

Series editors:
Lynn Abrams, Cordelia Beattie, Pam Sharpe and Penny Summerfield

The expansion of research into the history of women and gender since the 1970s has changed the face of history. Using the insights of feminist theory and of historians of women, gender historians have explored the configuration in the past of gender identities and relations between the sexes. They have also investigated the history of sexuality and family relations, and analysed ideas and ideals of masculinity and femininity. Yet gender history has not abandoned the original, inspirational project of women's history: to recover and reveal the lived experience of women in the past and the present.

The series Gender in History provides a forum for these developments. Its historical coverage extends from the medieval to the modern periods, and its geographical scope encompasses not only Europe and North America but all corners of the globe. The series aims to investigate the social and cultural constructions of gender in historical sources, as well as the gendering of historical discourse itself. It embraces both detailed case studies of specific regions or periods, and broader treatments of major themes. Gender in History titles are designed to meet the needs of both scholars and students working in this dynamic area of historical research.

Gender, nation and conquest in the high Middle Ages

MANCHESTER
1824

Manchester University Press

GENDER, NATION AND CONQUEST IN THE HIGH MIDDLE AGES

NEST OF DEHEUBARTH

—— Susan M. Johns ——

Manchester University Press

Manchester and New York

distributed in the United States exclusively by Palgrave Macmillan

Published by Manchester University Press
Oxford Road, Manchester M13 9NR, UK
and Room 400, 175 Fifth Avenue, New York, NY 10010, USA
www.manchesteruniversitypress.co.uk

Distributed in the United States exclusively by Palgrave Macmillan
175 Fifth Avenue, New York, NY 10010, USA

Distributed in Canada exclusively by UBC Press
University of British Columbia, 2029 West Mall,
Vancouver, BC, Canada v6т 1z2

British Library Cataloguing-in-Publication Data
A catalogue record for this book is available from the British Library

Library of Congress Cataloging-in-Publication Data applied for

ISBN   978 0 7190 8999 2   *hardback*

First published 2013

The publisher has no responsibility for the persistence or accuracy of URLs for any external or third-party internet websites referred to in this book, and does not guarantee that any content on such websites is, or will remain, accurate or appropriate.

Typeset in Minion with Scala Sans display
by Graphicraft Limited, Hong Kong
Printed in Great Britain
by TJ International Ltd, Padstow

For my family

Contents

Preface

This book has its origins in my work on Anglo-Norman women when I became intrigued by the lack of scholarly research on medieval Welsh women, particularly at a stage when my daughter was obsessed with princesses. Time has moved on, and whilst both of the former contentions are no longer true, Princess Nest of Deheubarth has remained for me a tempting figure, both because what we know of her is coloured by a dramatic and symbolic episode and because of what she represents about the rhythms and currents of medieval history and historiography. On a family visit to west Wales which included visits to Pembroke, Manorbier, Carew and Cilgerran castles, all of them distinct, dramatic ruins, I was even more convinced that the narrative of Nest's past, as represented in the popular literature of those castles, was a subject which would have much to tell historians about the place and meaning of gender in the medieval past. The focus is not therefore limited to medieval Wales, but is inspired by scholarship and study of the medieval past more generally. I had become intrigued by these ideas whilst writing on Anglo-Norman women, and was able, whilst having a career-break looking after my young children, to think about these themes and ideas more broadly. I stepped back into academic life as a part-time tutor at Sheffield University where I had the good fortune to work with Ed King and Daniel Power, whose friendly interest in the project helped to sustain it through those early years of blending teaching, writing and childcare.

I was appointed to a post as a Lecturer in Medieval History at Bangor University in 2007 and progress on Nest slowed. Living in north Wales and working at Bangor University is a great privilege: the university supports its staff in excellent teaching and facilitates research and writing. My thanks are due to the university for a sabbatical which facilitated the later research and writing which led to the completion of the book, and to my friends and colleagues in the School of History, Welsh History and Archaeology for their support. One of the benefits of working at Bangor University, apart from the glorious beauty of its location, is its long tradition of support for medievalists and for teachers, writers and researchers in medieval history and the history of Wales. I am especially grateful for the advice freely and generously given by Professor Huw Pryce. I am also grateful for the questions and comments of those who have heard various aspects of this book at numerous conferences and research seminars as my ideas developed, particularly those who attended the 2008 biannual conference held at Bangor on Medieval Wales, who heard a paper based on some aspects of this book. Parts of chapter 7 were read as a paper at the Harvard Celtic Colloquium in 2010 and aspects of chapters 1 and 2 were read at the conference in honour of Ifor Rowlands, Swansea University and at a colloquium held in honour of Professor Pauline Stafford at King's College London, both in June 2009. My thanks to all those who generously commented and whose insights enriched my understanding. The efficiency of the staff at the National Library of Wales and the archives and library of Bangor University smoothed the process of research and writing. I am very grateful for the support of Susan Reynolds, Pauline Stafford, David Bates and David Crouch and for their advice and encouragement. Any inaccuracies and defects are, of course, my own. My thanks also to the two anonymous referees for Manchester University Press: their helpful and encouraging comments and insights are much appreciated. The Press were a marvellous publisher for my first monograph, and the same has been true of this one: in particular Emma Brennan has been a supportive and highly efficient editor.

Finally, my thanks to my family for their support and encouragement, especially Carys and Gwyn who have put up with Nest hovering in the background of their early childhood, and who have supported me throughout the project. Further, without the love and support of my husband the book would not have been completed and it is to my family, my mother, in memory of my father and Lucy, that I dedicate this book.

List of abbreviations

ANS   *Anglo-Norman Studies*

BBCS   *Bulletin of the Board for Celtic Studies*

JMH   *Journal of Medieval History*

NLW   Aberystwyth, Llyfrgell Genedlaethol Cymru / The National Library
         of Wales

ODNB   *Oxford Dictionary of National Biography, Oxford University Press,
         2004*

TRHS   *Transactions of the Royal Historical Society*

WHR   *Welsh History Review*

Introduction

The twelfth century was a period of political instabilities and cultural change in medieval Europe. Twelfth-century Wales similarly underwent social, cultural, political and economic changes and was subject to an ongoing process of conquest and assimilation by the Normans following the Norman conquest of England in 1066. Historians have long debated the complexities of the fragile and fragmentary nature of Welsh political affairs in the high middle ages and this has led to the characterisation of the period *c.* 900–1282 as the 'Age of the Princes', as conceptualised by T. Jones Pierce.[1] The concept embraces the complex developments which occurred within Wales and takes account of the pre-eminence of the political affinities, dynasties and ruling elites within Wales, and the dynamic role of war. While British medieval historiography has developed interesting and new areas of historical enquiry, such as considerations of ethnicity, gender and masculinity, this book is necessary because it fills a significant gap in the historiography of medieval Wales – while women's power has been one of the most vibrant areas of historical scholarship for nearly twenty years, scholars of medieval Wales have been slow to respond.[2] It also represents a considerable opportunity to develop understandings of the interactions of gender with conquest and imperialism, and with the social and cultural transformations of the high middle ages, from a new perspective. Many studies have reconsidered these relationships, but few if any have taken women and gender as a core theme, although more recently work on ethnicity and gender has demonstrated that attention to such analytical categories can open up new questions about the way that contemporary writers constructed views on men and women which could, in some instances, be predicated on ideas about ethnicity.[3]

It is the contention of this book that the characterisation of Wales in the high middle ages as the 'Age of the Princes' is a fundamentally gendered approach which has privileged male power and action as the significant forces which shaped the history of the country: we do not have 'The Age of the Princes and Princesses'. Given that this gendered unspoken assumption about the political history of Wales underpins much of the historiography of Wales it is unsurprising that complex questions concerning the interactions between gender, power and historiography have not been addressed. This book is located within the historiographies of conquest and imperialism. Nationalist perspectives tend to emphasise conquest rather than influence, and violent and destructive conquest at that. More recently, there has been a significant tendency towards revisionism, seen in the specific context of south Wales in work on the Margam charters and work on Marcher lordships, for example.[4] This view suggests that there was no complete displacement or obliteration of existing power structures, but rather these were absorbed into new honorial structures. More broadly, in Wales and especially in Ireland, revisionists have looked at influence as being more important than brute force in the arrival of new elites.[5] More recently there has been an attempt by John Gillingham to restate the relevance of domineering and destructive conquest, if only by reconceptualising English activity as 'imperialism' and giving it a cultural context in which destructive actions were given legitimacy by the replacement of concepts of difference with those of inferiority and of non-human status for Irish (and Welsh).[6] The approach here will be to challenge this latter interpretation for Wales in the late eleventh and twelfth centuries; and to put women as actors back into the sort of exchanges described by Davies, that is to see women's roles in strategies of negotiation and integration realised through, for example, marriage. In doing so, there is the opportunity to add further to the interpretation of interaction as driven from many perspectives and not necessarily resulting in dominance and subordination. The example of Nest of Deheubarth, the core of this study, can be complemented with other examples which will be examined in more detail. One of the better known is that of Joan, bastard daughter of King John, of whom there are already some interpretations as an independent and powerful actor in Welsh politics. These tend to rely on the idea that her English royal status gave her a unique role, but this will be questioned, with other examples to suggest the extensive ways in which women were involved in power structures.[7]

Certainly the history of Wales has been written within a framework which emphasises war, conquest, resistance and change. The characterisation of the high middle ages as the 'Age of the Princes' emphasises the centrality of the ruling elite to the political, religious, social and cultural developments of Wales. It has been argued that because of the achievements of the Welsh princes, Wales enjoyed the chance to develop linguistically, culturally and socially and that the Welsh princes provided a link between two cultures – that of Welsh Wales and Anglo-Norman society.[8] Turvey accepts that the achievements of the Welsh princes must be set in context and he acknowledges that the issues surrounding the idea of Welsh nationhood are contentious. Yet this analysis is ultimately a rather old-fashioned form of writing history where men are the key players and women appear little if at all. It is unsatisfying because the significant forces shaping Wales included family feuds, at the heart of which lay dynastic links and gender roles and expectations. Further, Turvey does little to address the question of legitimacy: a question which underpins much of the disunity of the Welsh polity in the face of a strong Anglo-Norman and later English monarchy. Turvey comes close to an analysis which argues that the Welsh were in the process of becoming more Welsh. The danger of such an analysis was succinctly addressed in David Cannadine's eloquent appraisal of the 'new British history'. Cannadine argued against historical interpretations which fall into the trap of sociological teleology – that is historians must beware seeing historical developments in the British Isles as a process by which the 'British became more British'.[9]

Of course the phrase 'Age of the Princes' implies a history concerned with the political development of Wales during the crucial period in the middle ages before native ambition for territorial segregation was extinguished. Yet as a catch-all for the history of Wales in this period it is essentially unsatisfying because although it explains the history of male-centred politics, it does little to explain the wider dynamics of that power within society in a way that can provide fresh insights. For example, women are seen as the pawns in male marriage strategies, rather than as active participants in the complex world of the high political elite. The emergence of the new British History which has viewed Wales within the four nations approach is similarly gender-blind. However, there is an acknowledgement that the 'Age of the Princes' should be viewed in context, and the controversial views of Gwyn Williams that the Wales of the Princes had to 'die before a Welsh nation could be born' are unsatisfactory.[10] These approaches are an attempt to understand why Wales did not develop as a nation in the way that Scotland and England did with a polity which dominated its people through institutional, political, cultural mechanisms. This idea of the difficulties faced by Wales in its development as a nation is the key conclusion of J. Beverley Smith in a relatively recent study of Llywelyn ap Gruffudd.[11] A new interpretation is needed, which takes account of these but also properly considers the history of Wales in the light of recent historiographical developments, for example the now well-accepted view that women had significant cultural roles in areas such as the formation and transmission of oral memory, religious benefaction and literary patronage throughout the medieval period.

Gwyn Williams is one of the few historians to mention female agency: a brief mention of Nest of Deheubarth who, he argues, 'could play the role of Helen of Troy, precipitating wars over her person'.[12] Nest's significance is also that of progenitor of dynasts; in this version, for Williams, it is the ecclesiastical descendants who are significant. The role of Welsh princesses or powerful noblewomen is rarely acknowledged by any commentators of Wales in the high middle ages, while the vast cultural changes in literature, and the ethnic changes due to the impact of Norman settlements within Wales – ranging from castle building, organised religion with the monastic movement, and the economy, and placed by Williams into a European context – are generally acknowledged to be significant.[13] The implications of the immigration and settlements within Wales are discussed by R. R. Davies. Davies argued that the period 1100–1400 was characterised by ethnic tensions between Welsh people, or *Cymry* or compatriots of Wales, and the English in Wales, and that the thirteenth century was more 'ethnically vicious' than the twelfth century.[14] This work suggests the importance of ethnicity to the configuration of twelfth-century politics. Given these strands of cultural and ethnic changes it is important to consider how ethnic tensions were characterised. It is possible to explore the dynamics of these tensions through a consideration of the way ideas about gender served to create or reinforce ideas about ethnic identity. Thus, an analysis of the development of such ideas could facilitate a discussion of the ways, and the reasons behind, the portrayals of high-status women such as Nest.

Historians such as Davies have argued that the accepted role of women in Wales was as transmitters of inheritance rights and as progenitors of dynasties. Thus women's role is seen to be primarily within marriage alliances and for procreation. Genealogies in Wales and Ireland were organised around patrilineal descent groups in the high middle ages and were thus systems which privileged men. Thus Davies suggests that the predominant title to status was the 'blood . . . of men'.[15] How such ties were created, however, may have facilitated the participation of women within the often, no doubt, delicate political negotiations, as Davies, despite himself, concedes that in the native tale *Culhwch and Olwen*, Olwen had to discuss *her* marriage with 'her four great-grandfathers and great-grandmothers!'[16] Further, he implicitly acknowledges that women did have a role to play in the transmission of cultural memories when, in the eighteenth-century account of Daniel Defoe, 'stories of Vortigern and Roger of Mortimer were in every old woman's mouth'.[17] Although the comment serves to dismiss the significance of the stories, it is nevertheless a tacit admission that women were active in the oral transmission or propagation of these traditions. The formation of social memory was gendered in Wales from its inception: Gwyn

Williams, discussing the renaissance in Welsh literature and culture following the Norman conquest of Wales, noted that during the age of the
gogynfeirdd (court poets) many courts and sub-courts (although there
is no definition of what a sub-court might comprise) had their official
pencerdd (master-poet) and every household had its *bardd teulu*, the
household poet (who was a bit simpler, for the benefit of 'little fellows'
and women!).[18] In his excellent study of Llywelyn ap Gruffudd Beverley
Smith notes that genealogists 'forgot' the name of Llywelyn's mother, an
indication surely that at its inception, the way that social memory was
recorded was gendered.[19]

Domination and conquest has been seen as the key dynamic which
shaped the development of medieval Wales, and nationalists tend to
emphasise destructive, violent conquest. Professor Rees Davies saw the
history of Wales within a British context and ably demonstrated the
centrality of social, religious and economic changes within a framework
centred on the unfolding of the political chronology. His use of the
concept 'Age of the Princes' nevertheless recognised that the political
history of Wales required contextualisation. Few would disagree that the
experience of conquest was fundamentally a transformative experience,
but this is not unusual in a medieval European context. The evolution
of the 'four nations approach' – which argues that the four nations
evolved, yet interacted, in different ways at different speeds – has led to
a reappraisal of the history of Wales. There are two key problems with
the four nations approach. First, as Cannadine has pointed out, the four
nations methodology does not pay enough attention to the important
variations between and within these developments. At the heart of the
new British history lie tensions concerned with identity. Even though
the historiography of the new British History is a vibrant and important
area of scholarship, it is nevertheless still a male-dominated historiography which has yet to incorporate an awareness of the significance of
gender. For example, Hugh Kearney argues that the history of the British
Isles, the 'Four Nations' of England, Scotland, Wales and Ireland, should
be understood in a broad framework which considers the interactions,
the commonalities, between nations in broad social, cultural, economic
and political terms. In his consideration of the impact of the Norman
conquest he states that English historians have 'domesticated' the Norman
conquest since Stubbs saw the Normans as a 'masculine' race which
educated a 'feminine' race.[20] This of course echoes the comments of
twelfth-century Anglo-Norman writers such as William of Malmesbury
who saw the Norman conquest as punishment for the weakness and
femininity of the debauched English race.[21] Stubbs unwittingly reinforced

gendered categories of analysis when he noticed the elision between gender and ethnicity. Such categories of analysis need inclusion in an overall explanatory framework. As Cannadine argues, the creation of a British identity did not entail abandonment of other identities, whether Welsh, Scottish, Irish or English. Yet it is worth noting that Kearney argued that, despite strong Normanisation by the political elite through the high middle ages, local loyalties could be strong and there was cultural diversity at a local level.[22] The incorporation of gender into such an analysis facilitates an exploration of commonalities and differences in such localities. Thus a study of, for example, the memory and identity of a Welsh princess, who functioned as a focus for 'local' loyalties in the twelfth century, has much to tell us about how ideas about gender were formed in the context of the broader transformative changes wrought by conquest and political development in Wales. The way that ideas about Nest developed is a map of how ideologies were themselves developing.

Even historians who have begun to address the complexities of political relationships and developments of ideologies of empire have been willing to follow the imperialist propaganda of twelfth-century sources. For example Gillingham argues that there was a 'crucial fragility at the heart of the English empire' and the reign of Henry II is the critical turning point.[23] His view is predicated upon three suppositions. First, that the 'English invaded Ireland' – yet we know from Gerald of Wales that his relatives, 'the Geraldines', however much they had begun to identify themselves in part as English, were significant. Second, that ideological justifications for English domination were exerted through bureaucratic and administrative developments, yet there is no examination of how bureaucracy is a method of domination in itself. Third, notions of 'barbarity' had become deeply entrenched in English thought as evidenced by the appalling treatment of victims of war following the Battle of the Standard in 1138. Gillingham accepts the depiction of the enslavement of women and children by Scottish raiders and sees such activity as evidence of war as slave-hunt.[24] It would be interesting to consider the importance of gender in these portrayals of victims of male aggression to address deeper questions concerning the meanings behind the portrayal. For example, the way that ideas about gender roles informed the portrayal could be analysed for the way that they interacted with assumptions concerning ethnicity and victimhood.

Historians of women's power have shaped the debate about the historicity of women as a category of analysis so that it has moved on considerably from a view which saw women as victims of patriarchal power. Studies of queenship, women and sovereignty, gender and female power have all considerably elucidated the role and place of women in medieval society. Writings on medieval Welsh history in general have begun to take on these themes; for example, Louise Wilkinson's article on Joan (d. 1237), wife of Llywelyn ap Iorwerth.[25] There is still a lack of published scholarship on women and gender in medieval Wales when compared with medieval English or European women. The Welsh law-books have been analysed for the information they contain concerning medieval women. The publication in 1980 of a volume entitled *The Welsh Law of Women* marked a significant step forward for the subject and suggests the richness and complexity of the Welsh lawbooks for the study of Welsh medieval women. All of the essays, such as Christopher McAll's study of the contexts of women's lives as depicted in the lawbooks, laid the groundwork for future scholars, a groundwork which has yet to be built on.[26] Nevertheless, following on from these approaches, the household of the queen in the Welsh laws was briefly covered by Robin Chapman Stacey in an essay which discussed the king, the *edling* and the queen in the thirteenth-century law codes in a comparative frame-work.[27] The essay is striking in that it reveals how much more could be done on these important topics. Late-medieval Welsh women have been served by a piece by Llinos Beverley Smith which demarcated the areas of research that have been given some attention by scholars.[28] Gwenyth Richards published a volume which explored the lives of thirteenth-century noblewomen and is useful for the light it sheds on the lives of prominent noblewomen.[29] Ceridwen Lloyd Morgan discussed female authorship of poetry in an essay which appeared in a volume that explored medieval women and literature.[30] Kari Maund's biography of Nest placed her into a critical socio-political context and illustrates the resurgence of interest in noblewomen and medieval Wales generally. The approach taken here will avoid a biographical approach since Kari Maund's work discussed amply Nest's biography and political context. Further, biography as a genre is complex, and biographies are constructed fictions which raise as many questions as they answer about individuals and their lives. Angela John's work on the genre has raised interesting questions about the purpose and pitfalls of writing biography. As she contends, biographers need to be aware of the dangers of writing neat, rounded accounts and that 'jagged edges' will remain in such works. Medieval biographers were guilty of writing to a template in which their subjects were portrayed in a seamless narrative as exemplary lives.[31] The 'jagged edges' in Nest's biography are not the gaps in knowledge, for, as Maund has shown, we know very little about Nest; rather the disruptive force in the narrative of the emergence of twelfth-century Wales is the abduction of Nest. Thus the political dynamic which catalysed the history of the Normans in South Wales is centred on sexual politics. The centrality of sexual politics to the narrative of the Norman conquest is fundamental to the portrayal of the period in *Brut y Tywysogion*.[32]

Literary studies have been better served; for example, Jane Cartwright studied medieval Welsh prose to examine conceptions of virginity and chastity, and the role of women in the *Mabinogi* has generated historical interest.[33] In general, Welsh historiography has not followed the trends of 'English' and/or continental historiographies, such as the *Annales* school. Wendy Davies pointed out that there is no significant work on gender in Wales in the early middle ages, no comparable work on the Norman conquest in Wales compared to the studies of its effect on England, and further, there is little work on native aristocracies, assemblies, nor areas such as population studies, migration patterns or bondsmen.[34] There is an implicit assumption here that Welsh historiography should follow the English and continental patterns of historical enquiry and such porosity in Welsh medieval studies is to be welcomed since the absorption of new ideas and approaches can enrich the study of women in Wales. For example, Welsh women have reflected 'English' historians' approaches to the study of marriage and the legal position of women.[35] The study of women in medieval Wales has tended to follow the agenda set by nationalist historians with their emphasis on separate experience in a construct which tends to emphasise resistance to 'English' or Anglo-Norman influence. Thus an emphasis on nationality has affected the way that historians write about Welsh women. For example, Ceridwen Lloyd-Morgan in a discussion of women and literacy in Wales chose to study 'Welsh' women or indigenous women rather than women of power within the polity of Wales, whether that polity was the Anglo-Norman Marcher areas or 'Welsh Wales'.[36] This then reinforces a separatist view of the history of the place of women within Wales where ethnicity is a key element of analysis that takes precedence over gender. It privileges ethnicity at the expense of gender, seeking difference rather than commonalities.

Commonalities in the experience of conquest lie at the heart of the internal colonialism thesis advocated by Hechter, who argued that England as the 'core' territory in the British Isles used various methods of colonial rule to dominate the 'peripheries' – that is, Wales, Scotland and Ireland – based on the premise that ethnic minorities are defined against a dominant culture as an 'internal colony'. Further, national development occurs when the separate cultural identities of regions, such as Wales, become less significant and 'blurred'. In this paradigm, core and peripheral territories merge into one all-embracing culture and then, in turn, this culture becomes the 'primary identification and loyalty'. As Chris Williams has pointed out, scholars have contested the idea of an internal colony.[37] Intriguing as Hechter's views were, his model saw the middle ages as the prelude to sixteenth-century English expansion into Wales. The period's tensions and the complex multiple identities of communities and individuals within Wales were not discussed, nor did the model consider the importance of gender.

The idea of identities within communities is considered by Benedict Anderson, who argues that nations are imagined communities and can only exist when three fundamental conceptions 'lose their grip on men's minds'. These are the collapse of precepts ordering society: first, the dominance of a script language, such as Latin which is relatively inaccessible to all but a few of the educated elite; second, the belief in divinely ordained societal ordering, that is, monarchy; and third, the idea that history and the birth of the universe (cosmology) are indistinguishable. For Anderson, it is the onset of capitalism and the birth of the printing press which facilitate the beginnings of nationalism. Thus the medieval period is for Anderson a period of 'great religiously imagined communities'.[38] The emergence of capitalism, the birth of administrative vernaculars, the printing press and the Reformation eroded the hegemony of such 'great religiously imagined' communities of the middle ages. The gendered ordering of such communities and why imagined communities might sustain gender differences if incorporated into this analysis would be a fruitful way to explore, for example, the way that women were used to uphold identities concerning emergent nationhood. Race is intrinsic here, since race emerges out of concern for aristocratic descent and intrinsic to this, for example, is the notion of 'blue blood'.[39] In this interpretation the nation-state can only emerge when ideologies of class have emerged in the nineteenth century, which must also incorporate a sense of historical destiny. Such a view places the role of women squarely within a genealogical perspective based on a biologically determined functional view, and thus links ethnicity to gender as key analytical constructs.

Anderson's work is of course concerned with the complex question of identities, while Hechter is concerned with the links of identity with nationhood and the difficulties of explaining a 'Celtic fringe' in modern Britain. Richter on the other hand discussed the context for the emergence of national consciousness in medieval Wales.[40] Twentieth-century nationalist historians saw language as the locus of identity, and debates about the modern history of Wales have embraced postmodern, postcolonial, national and post-national positions.[41] The question of identity is a significant strand of Welsh historiography and yet the complex ways that such identities were created have received little attention. Huw Pryce discussed the way that the terms *Wallia*, *Walensis* came to replace the terms *Brittannia* and *Britones* as a collective noun for labelling the Welsh in twelfth-century texts and sources. Pryce argued that the adoption of English terms for the Welsh and their country should not be understood in terms of Welsh cultural domination by the English, but in terms of a broader approach which takes account of 'cultural adaptation and interaction'.[42] Such an approach is a fruitful way to explore the intricacies of the way that the history of Wales unfolded. More recent work on Marcher liberty in the Shropshire–Powys border which takes account of the elaboration of the English state similarly stresses interaction and resistance to English lordship.[43] Brock Holden also sees the developments of the English state as decisive, and his discussion of the evolution of Marcher society shows that military lordship was dominant in the March with an emphasis on the king and the role of the 'state' in contemporary society and which draws on the approach of Davies. It is a view which works within established historiographical frameworks such as debates about the role of royal lordship, aristocratic society and knightly society.[44] Identity has been a key strand of recent historiography, and the identity of Wales as a political term, or a geographical one, led R. R. Davies to argue that by the thirteenth century the Welsh were seen as, and felt themselves to be, a distinct nation.[45] The problems of defining peoples, the idea of the *gens* as a powerful force in medieval ideologies, and in turn the complexities of the terms communities, nations, nationhood, states and polities, have generated some significant and important scholarly debates. In particular the debate between Davies and Susan Reynolds on the emergence of 'states' in the medieval period demonstrates that medieval historians have become much more attentive to the ideological loads that modern concepts may carry.[46] Such concerns were also addressed by Robert Bartlett, who discussed the semantic difficulties inherent in distinguishing between sex and gender, race and ethnicity. In part this is a result of modern interdisciplinary borrowings where terms may have different meanings in those different disciplines.[47] A more complex approach was suggested by Francis James West who similarly argued that there has been a lack of consistency in the way that historians have used modern concepts such as imperialism and colonialism, which he argues are technical models not realities.[48] West nevertheless suggested that carefully applied, such concepts could facilitate a more nuanced understanding of, for example, legitimacy and land tenure in post-conquest England.

In order to address such themes, a broad range of sources will be analysed. For example, political and geographical identities are clearly discernible in the writings of Nest's grandson Gerald de Barry or Gerald of Wales in his *Journey through Wales*. Nest appears briefly in this text as 'the nobly born daughter of Rhys ap Tewdwr Prince of Dyfed in South Wales'.[49] The context in which she appears is that of mother: she is the mother of 'Henry, the son of Henry I and Uncle of Henry II . . . and Robert fitz Stephen, but by a different father'. There is no censure here: Gerald merely explains the family links with the royal house of England and Dyfed. This contrasts with the fervent condemnation of the Welsh by Gerald; he castigated them for their marital practices and accused them of incest, here meaning marriage within the prohibited degrees. Such views on the Welsh will be explored in depth in chapter 2, in order to put Gerald's presentation of Nest into a more contextualised analysis. The portrayal of Nest in the thirteenth-century *Brut y Tywysogion* or 'Chronicle of the Princes' will be explored through a discussion of Nest's functions within the text, as will the historicity of the narrative. This will then assess the traditional view of Nest as a romantic heroine and explore the origins of this view within the sources and its adaptations and continuities in later historiography. The interpretation of Nest in the nineteenth and twentieth centuries suggests the importance of ideas about the past to explain the present. Such portrayals offer a rich source for the study of the interaction of gender, nation and conquest upon the historical image of women. As such the meanings ascribed to Nest, and women in general, have much to tell us about the context in which they were created within the formation of a gendered narrative of Wales. J. E. Lloyd, for example, writing in 1935 described Nest as the 'Helen of Wales' just as he had in his earlier and pivotal work in 1911.[50] This view may owe more to his nationalistic desire to see Wales formed as a nation at this early period, and he wrote to dispel myths and to invigorate the study of the Welsh medieval past.[51] This view of Wales as linked to the classical world was a very powerful influence which affected how medieval writers constructed their texts, and this influence will be considered as part of the appraisal of Nest.

This book is therefore concerned with an exploration of the ways in which the portrayal of Nest was constructed within Welsh sources and subsequent historiography. It will consider how gender affected the portrayal of Nest and how this was implicitly woven into a narrative about the creation of a Welsh identity in the face of Norman activity. It utilises a wide range of evidence, including charters, chronicles, and literary and legal sources, to consider how the image of noblewomen was constructed within them. This can facilitate a discussion of the construction of the multiple and conflicting meanings of women's identity. Thus a study of the ways that Nest, and other powerful women of the Welsh elite, were portrayed as compared to their male counterparts has much to tell us about gender roles as well as the social and cultural transformations of the period from the twelfth through to the fourteenth century. The broader questions of if, how and why Wales became a nation and whether gender played a role in the creation of a Welsh identity within our sources can also be addressed. Key areas to be considered also include an awareness that writers created a view of key women in texts which were constrained and facilitated by genre. This will underpin an appreciation of the way that texts created and reinforced identities and consider the mutability of those identities.

These questions will be tackled through an analysis of the portrayals of Nest and other women in the twelfth century and later sources. In order to contextualise and widen the discussion, the analysis includes a consideration of the portrayal of other women, such as Nest's sister-in-law, Gwenllian, Princess Joan, daughter of King John and wife of Llywelyn ap Iorwerth (d. 1237), and Senana, the wife of Gruffudd ap Llywelyn. Contemporary or near-contemporary sources concerning Nest are sparse but still allow some access to issues at the heart of this study. Sources include charters, the writings of Gerald of Wales, Geoffrey of Monmouth, *Brut y Tywysogion*, and literary sources such as poetry and the prose tales known as *The Mabinogion*. The significance of Nest for late-medieval and early modern writers will be analysed to consider the significance of Nest in an emergent politicised Welsh identity in texts. An analysis of the portrayals of Nest from the sixteenth century onwards can add significantly to our understanding of more recent centuries of Welsh history and how standard approaches to the history of medieval Wales have arisen. This approach takes account of Nest's meaning and the role of women for later writers, and discusses continuities from and resonances of the middle ages in the nineteenth and twentieth centuries. All of this is considered within a paradigm which takes account of the historiography of medieval Wales and thereby offers an integrative analysis which has the tools to explore the identities and meanings ascribed to Nest, and other prominent women, in Welsh medieval history and historiography.

The book begins with an analysis of the portrayal of Nest in the thirteenth-century *Brut y Tywysogion* and considers how this text is key to the origination of a view about the Normans and their incursions and impact upon Wales. It also suggests how Welsh legal sources provide an insight into contemporary ideas about women, marriage and abduction. Chapter 2 contextualises views about women in contemporary texts by a close study of the work of Nest's grandson, Gerald de Barry, or Gerald of Wales, to consider the complex interplay of gender, conquest and imperialism in the portrayals of the Norman conquest of Ireland. Chapter 3 considers the way that charter evidence presents women and suggests how such evidence should be read to more fully elucidate the contexts of activity for Anglo-Norman and Welsh women. Chapter 4 examines the portrayal in the early modern period of Nest and other women through the writings of prominent Tudor gentlemen, such as George Owen and Rice Merrick. The analysis will demonstrate the centrality of the Norman conquest, understood in terms of gender and the role of women, to the political framework of early modern historiography. The way that Wales was portrayed by travel writers and later historians in the eighteenth and nineteenth centuries is considered in chapter 5; while chapter 6 discusses how Nest and other women were portrayed in the twentieth century and in more modern sources. It will consider more recent interpretations of medieval Welsh women and examine these through an analysis of the portrayal of Nest in popular histories and at heritage sites to assess how her narrative is embroidered. The mutability, or otherwise, of the image of women in various sources is thus a key theme and their incorporation into presentations of history will be assessed. Huw Pryce, integrated *some* women's history into his radio series in 1999, for example discussing a female anchorite as a point of departure in his narrative.[52] That women in the past are integrated into popular histories suggests their appeal. The way that Nest has been constructed as a great beauty is discussed in chapter 7 to draw conclusions about the importance of beauty as a key concept in the creation of a narrative about Nest.

Fundamentally, this book addresses how the study of particular high-status women in Wales in the high middle ages elucidates core themes about the trajectory of Welsh history, the role of gender, and ideas about power, in shaping a narrative of Wales. It considers how our sources should be read in a careful contextualised way with an awareness that genre played a key role in shaping content and presentation. It sets this into a historiographic context which takes account of the interactions with gender and conquest/imperialism.

Thus the approach adopted here is to suggest that an analysis of the ways that Nest was portrayed in a variety of sources, genres and contexts can illuminate ideas about ideologies and approaches to history which suggest how the history of medieval Wales was constructed in those sources. It will consider whether contemporary ideas about gender, nation, conquest and imperialism were important in that portrayal of the Welsh medieval past and its construction, and also what it can reveal about the construction of 'Wales'. Further, despite the increasing scholarly attention paid to medieval women, I shall argue that to consider women as contested sites of interpretation will shed light on the ways that narratives developed, and thus the emphasis on Nest and other women in Welsh history will facilitate reflections on this. This will be set into an analysis which takes account of the developing transformative changes wrought by conquest and its associated political development in Wales. I shall suggest that although master narratives developed, writers were capable of interpreting, adapting and reinventing the historical past and by so doing developed ideologies that were intrinsically shaped by the concerns about genre, narrative conventions and strategies deployed by sources which in turn raise questions about the importance of gender, nation and identity in that view of the Welsh medieval past.

Notes

1 J. B. Smith (ed.), *Medieval Welsh Society: Selected Essays by T. Jones Pierce* (Cardiff: University of Wales Press, 1972), pp. 19–38.
2 Key reference points on gender, women and power include J. L. Nelson, 'Gender and genre in women historians of the early middle ages', in J. P. Genet (ed.), *L'Historiographie médiévale en Europe* (Paris: Éditions du CNRS, 1991), pp. 150–63, reproduced in *eadem*, *The Frankish World, 750–900* (London: Hambledon, 1996), pp. 183–98; P. Stafford, *Queens, Concubines and Dowagers: The King's Wife in the Early Middle Ages* (London, 1983; repr. London: Leicester University Press, 1998); *eadem*, 'Women and the Norman conquest', *TRHS*, 6th ser., 4 (1994), 221–49; *eadem*, *Queen Emma and Queen Edith: Queenship and Women's Power in Eleventh-Century England* (Oxford: Blackwell, 1997); S. Mosher Stuard (ed.), *Women in Medieval Society* (Philadelphia: University of Pennsylvania Press, 1976); J. Carmi Parsons (ed.), *Medieval Queenship* (Stroud: Alan Sutton, 1994); Cordelia Beattie, 'Gender and femininity in medieval England', in Nancy Partner (ed.), *Writing Medieval History* (London: Hodder Arnold, 2005), pp. 153–70. For gender and religion in medieval studies, see Lisa Bitel, 'Introduction: convent ruins and Christian profession: towards a methodology for the history of religion and gender', in Lisa M. Bitel and Felice Lifshitz (eds), *Gender and Christianity in Medieval Europe: New Perspectives* (Philadelphia: University of Pennsylvania Press, 2008), pp. 1–15, at pp. 3–7; Leslie Brubaker and Julia M. H. Smith (eds), *Gender in the Early Medieval World: East and West, 300–900* (Cambridge and New York: Cambridge University Press, 2004). For recent approaches to ethnicity and gender, see Cordelia Beattie and Kirsten A. Fenton (eds), *Intersections of Gender, Religion and Ethnicity in the Middle Ages* (Basingstoke: Palgrave Macmillan, 2011).
3 E.g. R. R. Davies, *Domination and Conquest: The Experience of Ireland, Scotland and Wales, 1100–1300* (Cambridge: Cambridge University Press, 1990); *idem, The Matter of Britain and the Matter of England* (Oxford: Clarendon Press, 1996); *idem, The Age of Conquest: Wales 1063–1415* (Oxford: Oxford University Press, 1987; new edn, 2000);

M. T. Flanagan, *Irish Society, Anglo-Norman Settlers, Angevin Kingship: Interactions in Ireland in the Late Twelfth Century* (Oxford: Clarendon Press, 1989); R. Frame, *The Political Development of the British Isles, 1100–1400* (Oxford, 1990; revised edn, Oxford: Clarendon Press, 1995). For key articles on gender and ethnicity in the volume *Intersections of Gender, Religion and Ethnicity*, see Hannah Meyer, 'Gender, Jewish creditors and Christian debtors in thirteenth-century Exeter', pp. 104–24; Kirsten Fenton, 'Gendering the First Crusade in William of Malmesbury's *Gesta Regum Anglorum*', pp. 125–39; and Kim Phillips, 'Warriors, Amazons and Isles of Women: medieval travel writing and the construction of Asian femininities', pp. 183–207.

4 M. Griffiths, 'Native society on the Anglo-Norman frontier: the evidence of the Margam charters', *WHR*, 14 (1988–89), 179–216; Max Lieberman, *The March of Wales 1067–1300: A Borderland of Medieval Britain* (Cardiff: University of Wales Press, 2008); *idem*, *The Medieval March of Wales: The Creation and Perception of a Frontier, 1066–1283* (Cambridge: Cambridge University Press, 2010).

5 E.g. Michael Richter on Ireland: 'The interpretation of medieval Irish history', *Irish Historical Studies*, 24 (1985), 289–98. See also major literature from R. R. Davies especially on negotiation and integration – including the use of marriage.

6 W. R. Jones, 'England against the Celtic fringe: a study in cultural stereotypes', *Journal of World History*, 13 (1971), 155–71; J. Gillingham, 'The beginnings of English imperialism', *Journal of Historical Sociology*, 5 (1992), 392–409; *idem*, *The English in the Twelfth Century: Imperialism, National Identity and Political Values* (Woodbridge: Boydell, 2000); *idem*, 'The English invasion of Ireland', in B. Bradshaw *et al.* (eds), *Representing Ireland: Literature and the Origins of Conflict, 1534–1660* (Cambridge: Cambridge University Press, 1993), pp. 24–42.

7 Louise J. Wilkinson, 'Joan, wife of Llywelyn the Great', in M. Prestwich *et al.* (eds), *Thirteenth Century England X* (Woodbridge: Boydell and Brewer, 2005), pp. 81–93; Robin C. Stacey, 'King, queen and *edling* in the laws of the court', in T. E. Charles-Edwards, M. E. Owen and P. Russell (eds), *The Welsh King and his Court* (Cardiff: University of Wales Press, 2000), pp. 29–62.

8 Roger Turvey, *The Welsh Princes: The Native Rulers of Wales, 1063–1283* (Harlow: Longman, 2002), pp. 199–200.

9 David Cannadine, 'British History as a "new subject": politics, perspectives and prospects', in Alexander Grant and Keith J. Stringer (eds), *Uniting the Kingdom? The Making of British History* (London and New York: Routledge, 1995), pp. 12–28, at p. 26.

10 Gwyn A. Williams, *When was Wales? A History of the Welsh* (Harmondsworth: Penguin, 1985), p. 86.

11 J. Beverley Smith, *Llywelyn ap Gruffudd: Prince of Wales* (Cardiff: University of Wales Press, 1998), p. 605.

12 Williams, *When was Wales?*, p. 67.

13 Williams, *When was Wales?*, pp. 67–73.

14 R. R. Davies, 'The peoples of Britain and Ireland, 1100–1400, I: Identities', *TRHS*, 6th ser., 4 (1994), 1–20, at p. 17.

15 R. R. Davies, 'The peoples of Britain and Ireland 1100–1400, IV: Language and historical mythology', *TRHS*, 6th ser., 7 (1997), 1–24, at pp. 21–2.

16 Davies, *Age of Conquest*, p. 125.

17 Davies, 'The peoples of Britain and Ireland, 1100–1400, IV: Language and historical mythology', pp. 21–2.

18 Williams, *When Was Wales?*, p. 69.

19 Smith, *Llywelyn ap Gruffudd*, pp. 37–41.

20 Hugh Kearney, *The British Isles: A History of Four Nations* (Cambridge: Cambridge University Press, 1989; 2nd edn 2006), p. 65.

21 William of Malmesbury, *Willelmi Malmesbiriensis monachi De gestis regum Anglorum Libri Quinque: Historiæ novellæ libri tres*, ed. William Stubbs (2 vols, Rolls Series, 90; London: HMSO, 1887, 1889), ii. 305; Antonia Gransden, *Historical Writing in England c. 550 to c. 1307* (London: Routledge and Kegan Paul, 1974), p. 173; Pauline Stafford, *Unification and Conquest: A Political and Social History of England in the Tenth and Eleventh Centuries* (London and New York: Edward Arnold, 1989), p. 23; M. Chibnall, *The Debate on the Norman Conquest* (Manchester: Manchester University Press, 1999).

22 Kearney, *British Isles*, p. 70.

23 John Gillingham, 'Foundations of a disunited kingdom', in Alexander Grant and Keith J. Stringer (eds), *Uniting the Kingdom? The Making of British History* (London and New York: Routledge, 1995), pp. 48–64, at p. 64.

24 Gillingham, 'The beginnings of English imperialism'.

25 Wilkinson, 'Joan, wife of Llywelyn the Great', pp. 81–93.

26 Christopher McAll, 'The normal paradigms of a woman's life in the Irish and Welsh law texts', in Dafydd Jenkins and Morffydd E. Owen (eds), *The Welsh Law of Women: Studies Presented to Professor Daniel A. Binchy on his Eightieth Birthday, 3 June 1980* (Cardiff: University of Wales Press, 1980), pp. 7–22.

27 Stacey, 'King, queen and *edling* in the laws of the court'.

28 L. Beverley Smith, 'Towards a history of women in late medieval Wales', in Michael Roberts and Simone Clarke (eds), *Women and Gender in Early Modern Wales* (Cardiff: University of Wales Press, 2000), pp. 14–49.

29 Gwenyth Richards, *Welsh Noblewomen in the Thirteenth Century: An Historical Study of Medieval Welsh Law and Gender Roles* (Lewiston, NY: Edwin Mellen Press, 2009).

30 Ceridwen Lloyd-Morgan, 'Women and their poetry in medieval Wales', in Carol M. Meale (ed.), *Women and Literature in Britain 1150–1500* (1993; 2nd edn, Cambridge: Cambridge University Press, 1996), pp. 183–203.

31 Angela John, 'Lifers: modern Welsh history and the writing of biography', *WHR*, 25 (2010), 251–70, at p. 269.

32 K. L. Maund, *Princess Nest of Wales: Seductress of the English* (Stroud: Tempus, 2007); *Brut y Tywysogion* is a generic name for several related chronicles; these are addressed in detail in chapter 1.

33 Jane Cartwright, 'Virginity and chastity in medieval Welsh prose', in Anke Bernau, Ruth Evans and Sarah Salih (eds), *Medieval Virginities* (Cardiff: University of Wales Press, 2003), pp. 56–79; Juliette Wood, 'The calumniated wife in medieval Welsh literature', *Cambridge Medieval Celtic Studies*, 10 (1985), 25–38; Fiona Winward, 'Some aspects of women in *The Four Branches*', *Cambridge Medieval Celtic Studies*, 34 (1997), 77–106.

34 Wendy Davies, 'Looking backwards to the early medieval past: Wales and England, a contrast in approaches', *WHR*, 22 (2004), 210.

35 A. J. Roderick, 'Marriage and politics in Wales 1066–1282', *WHR*, 4 (1968–69), 3–20. Three essays in Jenkins and Owen (eds), *Welsh Law of Women*, address aspects of marriage in medieval Welsh law: Dafydd Jenkins, 'Property interests in the classical Welsh law of women', pp. 69–92; R. R. Davies, 'The status of women and the practice

of marriage in late mediaeval Wales', pp. 93–114; D. B. Walters, 'The European legal context of the Welsh law of matrimonial property', pp. 115–31.

36 Ceridwen Lloyd-Morgan, 'More written about than writing? Welsh women and the written word', in Huw Pryce (ed.), *Literacy in Medieval Celtic Societies* (Cambridge: Cambridge University Press, 1998), pp. 149–65.

37 Michael Hechter, *Internal Colonialism: The Celtic Fringe in British National Development* (2nd edn, New Brunswick, NJ and London: Transaction, 1999), pp. xxxviii, 4–5, 68; Chris Williams, 'Problematizing Wales: an exploration in historiography and post-coloniality', in Jane Aaron and Chris Williams (eds), *Postcolonial Wales* (Cardiff: University of Wales Press, 2005), pp. 3–22, at p. 8; J. Beverley Smith and Llinos Beverley Smith, 'Wales: politics, government and law', in S. H. Rigby (ed.), *A Companion to Britain in the Later Middle Age*s (Malden, MA and Oxford: Blackwell, 2003), pp. 309–34.

38 Benedict Anderson, *Imagined Communities: Reflections on the Origin and Spread of Nationalism* (rev. edn, London and New York: Verso, 2006), pp. 16, 36.

39 Anderson, *Imagined Communities*, p. 149.

40 M. Richter, 'The political and institutional background to national consciousness in medieval Wales', in T. W. Moody (ed.), *Nationality and the Pursuit of National Independence (Historical Studies*, 11 Belfast: Appletree Press, for the Irish Committee of Historical Sciences, 1978), pp. 37–55.

41 Williams, 'Problematizing Wales', pp. 12–17.

42 Huw Pryce, 'British or Welsh? National identity in twelfth-century Wales', *English Historical Review*, 116 (2001), 775–801.

43 Max Lieberman, 'Striving for Marcher liberties: the Corbets of Caus in the thirteenth century', in Michael Prestwich (ed.), *Liberties and Identities in the Medieval British Isles* (Woodbridge: Boydell, 2008), pp. 141–54; see also *idem, March of Wales*. For aristocratic women in the Shropshire March, see Emma Cavell, 'Aristocratic widows and the medieval Welsh frontier: the Shropshire evidence', *TRHS*, 6th ser., 17 (2007), 57–82.

44 Brock W. Holden, *Lords of the Central Marches: English Aristocracy and Frontier Society, 1087–1265* (Oxford: Oxford University Press, 2008); *idem*, 'The making of the middle March of Wales, 1066–1250', *WHR*, 20 (2000), 207–26; R. R. Davies, 'Kings, lords and liberties in the March of Wales, 1066–1272', *TRHS*, 5th ser., 29 (1979), 41–61.

45 R. R. Davies, 'The identity of "Wales" in the thirteenth century', in R. R. Davies and Geraint H. Jenkins (eds), *From Medieval to Modern Wales: Historical Essays in Honour of Kenneth O. Morgan and Ralph Griffiths* (Cardiff: University of Wales Press, 2004), pp. 45–63, at p. 50.

46 Susan Reynolds, 'Medieval *Origines Gentium* and the community of the realm', *History*, 68 (1983), 375–90; see also *eadem, Kingdoms and Communities in Western Europe 900–1300* (Oxford: Clarendon Press, 1984); *eadem*, 'The historiography of the medieval state', in M. Bentley (ed.), *A Companion to Historiography* (London and New York: Routledge, 1997; paperback edn 2002), pp. 117–38; *eadem*, 'There were states in medieval Europe: a response to Rees Davies', *Journal of Historical Sociology*, 16 (2003), 550–5. R. R. Davies, 'The medieval state, the tyranny of a concept?', *Journal of Historical Sociology*, 16 (2003), 280–300, which was a a response to Reynolds's 'The historiography'; see also his 'The peoples of Britain and Ireland, 1100–1400, 1: Identities' (which acknowledged the importance of Reynolds), p. 4 n. 5; see also *idem, Lordship and Society in the March of Wales, 1282–1400* (Oxford: Clarendon Press, 1978).

47 Robert Bartlett, 'Medieval and modern concepts of race and ethnicity', *Journal of Medieval and Early Modern Studies*, 31 (2001), 39–56, at pp. 39–42; for a more recent view see Cordelia Beattie, 'Introduction', in Beattie and Fenton (eds), *Intersections of Gender, Religion and Ethnicity*, pp. 1–11, at pp. 1–2. For women as representatives of the nation, see M. Sinha, 'Gender and nation', in Bonnie Smith (ed.), *Women and Gender History in Global Perspective* (Washington, DC: American Historical Association, 2006), pp. 1–40.

48 Francis James West, 'The colonial history of the Norman conquest?', *History*, 84 (1999), 219–36, which argues that colonialism was predicated on difference: difference has been seen as key in Beattie's work, see below.

49 *Giraldus Cambrensis Opera*, vol. 6: *Itinerarium Kambriæ et Descriptio Kambriæ*, ed. James F. Dimock (Rolls Series, 21(6); London: Longmans, Green, Reader, and Dyer, 1868), p. 91 (Gerald of Wales, *The Journey through Wales: and, The Description of Wales*, ed. Lewis Thorpe (Harmondsworth: Penguin, 1978), p. 189).

50 J. E. Lloyd, *A History of Carmarthenshire* (2 vols, Cardiff: W. Lewis Ltd for the London Carmarthenshire Society, 1935), i. 178; *idem*, *A History of Wales from the Earliest Times to the Edwardian Conquest* (2 vols, London, 1911; 3rd edn, London: Longmans, Green, 1939), ii. 417–18.

51 Huw Pryce, *J. E. Lloyd and the Creation of Welsh History: Renewing a Nation's Past* (Cardiff: University of Wales Press, 2011), p. 176, and further in chapter 5.

52 See, for example, Huw Pryce, 'The Normans in Wales', part of the BBC Radio Wales Millennium History series, *The People of Wales* (1999); *idem*, 'Medieval experiences: Wales 1000–1415', in Gareth Elwyn Jones and Dai Smith (eds), *The People of Wales* (Llandysul: Gwasg Gomer, 2000).

1

Abduction, conquest and gender

Du
URING the late eleventh and early twelfth centuries, Norman
expansionism had led to a fundamental reconfiguration of
political control in south-west Wales. This in turn caused ongoing social, economic and cultural changes in the wake of a process of
piecemeal conquest. The Norman incursions into Wales followed the
Norman conquest of England in 1066, although the Normans had not
initially turned their attention to the Welsh kingdoms after the conquest
of England. While William Rufus was king of England, the intervention
in Wales of Anglo-Normans which had already had an impact in the
1070s became more intense. Rhys ap Tewdwr had succeeded his second
cousin Rhys ab Owain as king of Deheubarth in 1079 in conditions of
some turmoil resulting from the rivalries of northern and southern rulers.
From 1072 to 1075, Bleddyn ap Cynfyn of north Wales had controlled
Deheubarth, before being killed by Rhys ab Owain (brother of the former
ruler Maredudd), only for Rhys ab Owain himself to be killed by
Trahaearn ap Caradog of north Wales in 1078. Rhys ap Tewdwr had allied
with Gruffudd ap Cynan (d. 1137) to destroy both northern and eastern
rivals at the battle of 'Mynydd Carn' in 1081. Rhys thereby secured
Deheubarth, and Gruffudd secured Gwynedd. Rhys was only to fall when,
in 1093, he clashed with the Norman settlers of Brycheiniog led by Bernard
of Neufmarché.

This ushered in a period of Norman and Flemish advance. Arnulf
de Montgomery, brother of Roger, earl of Shrewsbury, was established
in Pembroke. One of Rhys's sons, Hywel, was imprisoned by him, and
though he escaped he was maimed for life. Rhys's daughter, Nest, the
subject of this study, married Gerald of Windsor, Arnulf's steward at
Pembroke, probably soon after his arrival there in 1097. The spectrum
of the fate of the children of Rhys is completed by Gruffudd, who fled
to exile in Ireland. In 1108 or 1109, in the dramatic events which ensured

her prominence in Welsh history, Nest was taken from Gerald by her cousin, Owain ap Cadwgan of Powys, and although he was soon challenged, and driven into exile in Ireland twice, she had two sons with him. Owain returned to power in much of Powys, broadly tolerated by the Normans, from 1111, but his actions continued to be disruptive. The Norman influence grew stronger – King Henry I himself campaigned in Wales in 1114, partly to bring Owain to heel; probably during this time a liaison between Nest and the king resulted in the birth of a son, Henry. Gruffudd, meanwhile, was able to return to Wales, spending time in c. 1113–15 in Dyfed, some of it with his brother-in-law Gerald. Then he fled, seeking refuge in the north before returning to conduct a guerrilla campaign against the Normans. Owain, now in Henry's service, died in 1116, at the vengeful hands of Gerald, when sent by the king against Gruffudd.

Gruffudd was permitted a small estate, just one commote, Caeo in Cantref Mawr; eventually, in 1127, he was expelled even from this, but found his opportunity in the weak rule of Stephen to seize power again, in 1136, in alliance with Gruffudd ap Cynan, whose eldest daughter Gwenllian he had married. Nest was probably dead by this stage, and Gwenllian famously died fighting Maurice of London, lord of Kidwelly, near that lordship, while Gruffudd was in the north seeking the aid which, finally, enabled a convincing victory at Crug Mawr near Cardigan.

The abduction of Nest, the wife of Gerald of Windsor, constable of Pembroke castle, in 1109 by her cousin Owain ap Cadwgan of Powys is recorded in the *Chronicle of the Princes* or *Brut y Tywysogion*. The abduction led to a campaign by Owain's cousins, Madog and Ithel, who acted in concert with Llywarch ap Trahaearn and Uchdryd ab Edwin, who drove out Owain and his father. Owain fled to Ireland, while his father went to his lands held by right of his Norman wife to negotiate with royal officials.[1] T. Jones Pierce in the *Dictionary of Welsh Biography* argued that it was this episode which saw Nest become the Welsh Helen of Troy.[2] The abduction caused serious repercussions in south-west Wales and provided an opportunity for the king's official at Shrewsbury, Richard de Belmais/Beaumais, bishop of London, to take advantage of traditional Welsh rivalries and hostilities. As a result of the abduction, Cadwgan ap Bleddyn, Owain's father, was deprived of his lands for a time by Henry I. The raid has been seen as symptomatic of the inherent political instability of Powys in the early twelfth century,[3] and it is certainly the case that the abduction served to heighten political tensions and caused severe retribution. The abduction is a significant episode within the history of south-west Wales because it, in microcosm, reflects the fluidities and tensions within Welsh contemporary politics. Beginning with a close study of the portrayal of the abduction, the following analysis will consider the way that the abduction is presented in the *Brut*. The discussion will take account of the nature of the *Brut* and place it in the context of a discussion of the view of women offered within it more generally. Then, in order to contextualise the discussion, to consider the significance of abduction more generally, comparative material from the Welsh laws will be considered.

Nest was the daughter of Rhys ap Tewdwr, king of Deheubarth, and through him was therefore a descendant of Hywel Dda. Rhys had become the pre-eminent ruler in Deheubarth, having established himself as king in 1079 after the death of his second cousin. Rhys had secured his rulership after the defeat of the combined forces of Caradog ap Gruffudd of Gwent and Morgannwg in south Wales, Trahaearn ap Caradog the ruler of Gwynedd, and Meilyr ap Rhiwallon whose father had co-ruled Powys, at the battle of Mynydd Carn in 1081. Rhys had allied with Gruffudd ap Cynan who was Trahaearn ap Caradog's main rival for power in north Wales. Mynydd Carn was a key turning point for the political context of south Wales because it secured Deheubarth for Rhys and his descendants and eliminated key opponents. Further, as well as determining the destiny of Deheubarth, Mynydd Carn secured Gwynedd for the descendants of Gruffudd.[4] Contemporary Wales was a land of independent kingdoms which were each ruled by fiercely competitive dynasties. These dynasties were linked by marriage, made and broke political treaties, and engaged in war and trade with each other. The balance of power within each kingdom could change due to dynastic insecurities which were exacerbated by the Welsh system of partible inheritance, applied to inheritance of land, and the way it may have rubbed off on to notions of royal succession.[5] This then explains how Rhys was able to establish himself in the kingdom of Deheubarth after the death of a second cousin. Each kingdom waxed and waned in importance depending on the abilities of its rulers, and would-be rulers, in countering internal and external rivals. By 1079 when Rhys established himself as ruler of Deheubarth, the four main kingdoms of Wales were Deheubarth in the south-west, Morgannwg in the south-east, Powys in north-east Wales and Gwynedd in the north-west. Thus Welsh politics could be turbulent and was complicated by collateral succession, but was also affected by relationships with European and continental neighbours such as Scandinavia, Ireland, the Isle of Man and of course with England. The Norman conquest of England in 1066 had had little immediate effect upon Wales, but Mynydd Carn had fundamentally changed the balance of power in Wales and this resulted in a visit by William I to St David's in 1081.[6] The Norman assault on Wales began in earnest only after the accession of William Rufus in 1087, and several Welsh kingdoms disappeared as the Normans began a process of settlement and annexation of Welsh territory.[7] Nest's father was killed in 1093 in Brycheiniog in a skirmish with the Normans. Her brother fled to Ireland, and Nest was married, possibly in 1097, to a Norman, Gerald of Windsor, castellan of Pembroke castle and steward of the lordship of Pembroke.[8] Thus Nest was the daughter of a Welsh ruler whose kingdom had been taken over by Norman invaders, but the ruling dynasty of the kingdom of her mother, Powys, still retained control over its lands despite owing fealty to the Anglo-Norman kings. Nest's mother was Gwladus, daughter of Rhiwallon ap Cynfyn of Powys. The fluidities of the political realities in Wales were a key determinant of the socio-political context of the abduction. Norman power was becoming slowly entrenched in the south-east and borderlands of Wales, whilst parts of Wales remained independent and relatively unaffected by Norman colonisation and influence.[9]

Nest may have been born before 1092 and possibly died in about 1130.[10] Her husband, Gerald, was the son of a Norman constable of Windsor castle and had distinguished himself in the service of Arnulf de Montgomery. Prior to 1109, by Gerald, Nest had two sons, William fitz Gerald of Carew and Maurice fitz Gerald of Llansteffan, and a daughter, Angharad, who married William of Barry, by whom she had a son, Gerald of Wales. A further son of Nest and Gerald of Windsor, David, became bishop of St David's. Nest had a relationship with Henry I, possibly during 1114 when Henry I campaigned against Powys.[11] By Henry I, Nest had an illegitimate son, Henry fitz Henry, who was brought up in Nest and Gerald's household, eventually became lord of Narberth, and died fighting in the service of his uncle, Henry II, in Anglesey in 1157. There was also a son, William, by Gerald's successor in Pembroke, the sheriff Hait, a Fleming; that son later became lord of St Clears. Nest also had a relationship with Stephen the constable of Cardigan, and their son Robert fitz Stephen eventually held Cardigan and part of Cemais. Nest had a further three children by father(s) unknown: a daughter Gwladus and two sons, Hywel and Walter. Crouch notes that it is possible that Hywel was another son by Stephen the constable since Hywel had a later claim to Lampeter, lands which Stephen had acquired prior to 1136. Thus Nest was the mother of eight sons and two daughters.[12]

The key source for the abduction of Nest is *Brut y Tywysogion*.[13] Three versions of the chronicle survive. Those in Peniarth MS 20 (the most complete) and the *Red Book of Hergest* are based on separate copies of a Latin original, now lost, which was itself based on lost annals of the Cistercian house of Strata Florida. The third version of the lost Latin annals *Brenhinedd y Saesson* (*The Kings of the Saxons*) includes English annals as well as a version of the *Brut*, and one version ends 1197, whilst the *Black Book of Basingwerk* continues until 1461.[14] These texts are rich in evocative detail concerning the raid and abduction of Nest. Although the abduction of Nest has sometimes been seen as a romantic episode, a close analysis of the text and a contextualisation of the meanings of abduction within contemporary society utilising the evidence of Welsh law suggests otherwise: the inscription of Nest as a romantic heroine within a narrative of Welsh resistance to Norman incursions into Wales has more to do with national myth-making which fosters gendered ideas about women than with the brutal *realpolitik* of high medieval Wales.

The chronicle locates the origins of the abduction at a symbolic noble gathering of the political elite when it begins its portrayal with a depiction of the Christmas feast at the court of Cadwgan ap Bleddyn. According to Peniarth MS 20,

> Cadwgan ap Bleddyn prepared a royal feast for the leading men of his land. And he invited Owain, his son, from Powys to the feast. And he held that feast at Christmas in honour of Jesus Christ. And when the feast was ended, Owain heard that Nest, daughter of the lord Rhys ap Tewdwr, wife of Gerald the officer, was in the said castle [of Cenarth Bychan]. And when he heard, he went, and with him a small force, to visit her as though she were a kinswoman – and so she was, for Cadwgan ap Bleddyn and Gwladus, daughter of Rhiwallon, who was mother to Nest, were first cousins: for Bleddyn and Rhiwallon were brothers, sons of Cynfyn by Angharad, daughter of king Maredudd. And after that, at the instigation of the Devil, he was moved by passion and love for the woman, and with a small company with him – about fourteen men – he made for the castle by night. And unknown to the watchers, he came into the castle over the wall and the ditch, and surrounded the building where Gerald and Nest, his wife, were sleeping.

Owain set fire to the buildings and 'raised a shout'. The narrative continues:

> And Gerald awoke from his slumber and was afraid when he heard the shout, and knew not what he should do. And his wife said to him, 'Go not to the door, for there are thine enemies around it, but come with me.' And thus he did. And she led him to the privies which adjoined the building. And through the pit of the privies he escaped. And when Nest knew for certain that he had escaped, she shouted from within and said, 'Why do you shout in vain? He whom you were seeking has escaped.' And then they came inside and searched for him everywhere. And when they did not find him, they seized Nest and her two sons

and a third son, whom Gerald had by a concubine, and a daughter. And they utterly pillaged the castle and burned it. And he violated Nest and lay with her and then returned home.

(Y neb yd oedoch yny geiffyaw. ac wynteu yna adoethant ymewn ac ay keiffafant ymhob lle. agwedy nas kawffant daly nest awnaethant ay deuvab ar trydyd mad aoed ygerald o o[z] amerch ac yspeilyaw ykastell yn gwbyl awnaethant ay lofgi ath[z]eissyaw nest a wnaeth ef abod genthi ac odyna ymchwelud ad[z]ef.)[15]

Peniarth MS 20 relates that when Owain's father, Cadwgan, 'heard that story, he was grieved and was frightened for two reasons: because of the violation of the lady, and because of fear of king Henry on account of the injury to his officer'.[16]

This portrayal is complex and is confined by genre and context, but it reveals much about contemporary attitudes to gender, nation and conquest. By carefully analysing the portrayal it is possible to discern ideas about morality, codes of conduct, noble expectations, siege tactics, gender, sexuality and cultural mores. Fundamentally, male action which takes the form of sexual conquest and thus passion, in the forms of Owain's lust and love for Nest, are the given reasons for the abduction. There are differences between the versions of the tale. the *Red Book of Hergest* version elaborates that Owain had secretly 'made a hole under the threshold' to gain entry to the castle and that the attackers 'kindled tapers and set fire to the buildings to burn them'. Gerald escaped 'as is said, . . . by way of the privy hole'. Such details, which vary only slightly, suggest that the original tale had been transmitted with little deviation, perhaps through oral tradition.[17] Yet different versions of the *Brut* do also in important ways reveal a difference in emphasis. In the Peniarth MS 20 version of the *Brut*, Owain's actions, we are told, were the work of the Devil; the *Red Book of Hergest* states that it was at the instigation of God ('o annoc Duw').[18] According to Peniarth MS 20, Nest was raped ('a threissyaw nest a wnaeth ef'); by contrast the *Red Book of Hergest* version simply indicates that Owain had intercourse with her ('chytyaw'), without the more direct implications of force and violence.[19] This difference in the interpretation of the incident suggests that the author of the *Red Book of Hergest* version was sympathetic to Owain. The author of Peniarth MS 20 may well have expressed a typical clerical distrust of female sexuality, yet even this image is multi-layered. By contrast, *Brenhinedd y Saesson* simply says that Nest was seized, without any specific language relating to rape or any sexual act.[20]

There is still the possibility that the events were perceived as rape: both Peniarth MS 20 and *Red Book of Hergest* versions of the *Brut* suggest that Owain's father was frightened of retribution because of it. the *Red Book of Hergest* is explicit: 'A phann gigleu Gadwgawn y gweithret hwnnw, kymryt ynn drwc arnaw gann sorr a orucef hynny o achaws y treis gyt a wnathoedit a Nest uerch [ferch] Rys' ('And when Cadwgan heard of that deed, he was indignantly grieved thereat because of the rape that had been committed upon Nest, daughter of Rhys').[21] By contrast, again, *Brenhinedd y Saesson* does not mention this aspect of Owain's father's reaction, merely referring to an unlawful act committed against Gerald.[22]

Thus a Christmas feast at the royal court is the setting for Owain's decision to meet his cousin Nest and is therefore the catalyst for the events which follow. The Whitsun, Easter and Christmas feasts of the elite were important political and cultural events where social bonds were maintained at important gatherings of the noble elite in Wales.[23] Feasts and feast-halls were important for reinforcing social and political bonds: part of the fabric of medieval Welsh society, they had an important psychological role in the construction of identity.[24] More than this, Llinos Beverley Smith suggested that feasts themselves were functionally part of the Welsh identity and may well have been an element in the national psyche.[25] Yet we are shown that this celebration had the potential to disrupt social bonds as well as to reinforce them. Scholars have noted that late-medieval festivals of Corpus Christi could 'subvert the social body'.[26] Cadwgan's Christmas feast led to the process by which the Anglo-Norman political norm was disrupted through the actions of Owain. Thus the Christmas feast at Cadwgan's court is symbolically important. During the raid the reactions of Nest and Gerald to the surprise attack are portrayed to stress the effectiveness of Nest and the indecision of her husband. The Peniarth MS 20 version tells us that Gerald is afraid and 'knew not what he should do'. Nest on the other hand offers counsel, orchestrates his escape and gives him time to make his escape good. Having given Gerald time to get safely away, Nest calls out to the attackers and thus gives herself, and her children, up.[27] Captured in a burning building with two of her sons, a daughter and a son by Gerald's concubine, Nest was in a very precarious situation.

Commentators have been unsure over the nature of the alleged sexual union which apparently occurred at the castle of Cenarth Bychan: was the 'violation' therefore an act of rape and/or a violation of lordship? The *Brut* suggests that Owain raped Nest before the abduction. Indeed there is little agreement whether Nest left Cenarth Bychan willingly. Lloyd suggested that Nest was a 'willing victim', and this has been accepted by Davies and other commentators.[28] The attack has become romanticised as part of a mythology: the *Dictionary of Welsh Biography* calls the abduction romantic,[29] and it has been termed 'daring and disastrous'.[30] Andrew Breeze has considered the tale in terms of its literary merits. He suggests that the tale of Nest's abduction has the feel of an 'adventure story' and that the details owe more to constrictions of genre than a reliable and accurate record of events. His suggestion rests on similarities in the way that the story of Nest is similar in structure and content to the story of Pwyll in the *Four Branches of the Mabinogi*. More intriguingly Breeze argues that Gwenllian, Nest's sister-in-law, was possibly the author of the *Four Branches of the Mabinogi*, and drew on elements of the story of Nest to inform her own narrative. The key elements of this interpretation rest with the way that the structures of the stories in both the *Brut* and the *Mabinogion* as 'chronicle and legend' depict an 'enemy knee-deep in dirt and humiliated by sexual loss'.[31] This analysis is problematical. First, the transmission and reception of the Nest story, as Breeze admits, are hard to trace. The significance surely lies in the transmission of the detail, or the fictionalising and sensational details were recorded in the *Brut* to suit the purposes of the redactor. It may suggest a tradition which transmitted the memory of Nest as a decisive actor who took charge of events where she could, and her inscription as a symbol of Welsh resistance to the Norman invasion of Wales is effected by the creation of a romantic abduction tale, as Bollard and Austin suggest. However, the romantic gloss is not so 'romantic' on a close examination of the detail and the description of 'violation'. It is also complex because although the portrayal of Gerald as a cuckolded husband covered in dirt who leaves the narrative fits with a tale of heroic Welsh resistance by the Welsh against the Normans, it is inter-Welsh politics which also matters here. Nest is abducted by her kinsman, and manipulates him, for the good of her husband's children: her inscription as a heroine of Welsh resistance suggests that fluidities in her loyalties to her kinsman conflicted with those of her husband. She is a Marcher: her pragmatism reflects that dual allegiance, Welsh by birth, but married to a Norman. And here we see that perhaps the authors of the *Brut* are commenting indirectly on the conflicted allegiance that such marriages could bring to the women in such alliances.

Breeze is here attempting to trace the difficult process by which history and literature interact and inform each other. If we argue that the context of creation is significant, that narrative forms are the product of human imagination and that they therefore are products of a society capable of imagining such events, then whether or not Nest was abducted in the way that the *Brut* records, what we have is a resonant image of what was imagined to be possible within a specific context and genre. It is the image of politics, driven by sexual passion, in a period of flux and change. It is a Christian, judgemental image too – the passion of Owain was the work of the Devil; the setting for the start of the episode, a Christmas court, here reflective of developing Arthurian traditions. The *Brut* does not claim to be an eyewitness account and the transmission of the story is unknown. It may have been an oral tradition passed down by the *gogynfeirdd* or *cyfarwyddiaid*, which at some point became transmitted to written forms, perhaps in the late twelfth and early thirteenth centuries. This would certainly parallel the transmission and recording of contemporary vernacular poetry.[32] Thus the extent to which the original tale is embroidered is likewise unknown. There are tensions within the narrative, and in our lack of knowledge concerning the handing down of the memory of these events concerning Nest in the *Brut*, which are not easy to solve.[33]

Second, Breeze argues for a conflation of the *Brut* with 'history' and the *Four Branches* with 'legend',[34] which tends to suggest a distinction in purpose, based on ideas about genre, which may not have been so clear-cut to the respective authors. Breeze suggests that the portrayal of the abduction of Nest may well owe more to literary licence than to an accurate record of the way that events unfolded. Indeed he suggests that the story of Pwyll's attack on the court of Hefeydd the Old in the *Mabinogi* is not dissimilar to the way that the Nest story unravels in the *Brut*. He argues that when Pwyll attacked, Rhiannon persuaded 'her hated suitor' to place his foot in Pwyll's bag to press down on the food collected there, so that he can be trapped: Breeze suggests that Nest's intervention to help Gerald escape has a similar structure, since Gerald is forced to escape 'knee-deep in dirt', which resembles 'the cuckold of a fabliau'. Further, he suggests that the *Four Branches of the Mabinogi* are shaped by the political circumstances of Dyfed. Breeze suggests a 'sexual free and easy' in the *Four Branches* which is figured in the *Mabinogi* with Blodeuedd, who falls in love with Gronw when she welcomes him into the castle. In the absence of her husband, she acts. Breeze suggests that if Gwenllian was the author of the *Four Branches*, this morality might be affected by her relationship with Nest. He notes that, like Helen of Troy, the seductions of Nest and Blodeuedd started a war.[35] Although there are some parallels between the *Four Branches* and the portrayal of Nest in the *Brut*, unlike Blodeuedd, Nest's husband was present immediately prior to the assault of Cenarth Bychan. Breeze's approach is anachronistic: he mistakes the complicated norms surrounding sexual mores with a modernistic assumption of 'sexual free and easy'. Indeed there is the possibility that Nest's 'seduction' was not the romantic union implicit in his assumption. Further, Breeze follows a traditional approach which implicitly utilises double standards to make a judgement about Nest: Breeze focuses on female, that is Nest's, sexuality, and ignores Gerald's, for there is after all evidence of the existence of the daughter of Gerald's concubine. The location of the narrative within a construct of resistance in contemporary Dyfed is of course very obvious within the *Brut*, but the location of the *Four Branches* as a commentary on contemporary Dyfed – and by extension the assumption that the author was Gwenllian and from Dyfed – fails to take account of the portrayal of Owain ap Cadwgan and therefore that the abduction of Nest is a commentary also about his political strategies. Further, this may in fact represent an ideological watershed within the *Brut* if we see the events as a charged episode which utilises contemporary notions of methods of political usurpation of power through the abduction of a female who conveyed the power of sovereignty, or rights to lordship, in the sense of the transmission of title to rule. Finally, Breeze conflates the literary women in the *Mabinogi* with a historical personage and elides the two as if they were one and the same. Of course the distinctions between literature and history are not as clear-cut as they might seem, but nevertheless Nest's story was set into recent, real past, while the *Mabinogi* is located in a complex imagined, mythical and magical past.

Still, the meaning and messages of the raid within our sources are significant and suggest that it was functioning as a rich mix of metaphors. The power of the images as literary constructions has prompted the interpretation of the abduction within an Arthurian context. Bollard and Austin go so far as to suggest that Owain played the role of a flawed 'Arthurian idealist and headlong hero', while Gerald of Windsor was the 'dark pragmatic knight' and Nest the 'fair maiden'. Further, they go on to suggest that such portrayals have a political intention and the escape of Gerald is a 'potent metaphor' which subverts the narrative of Norman conquest into a story of 'constant resistance'. This is thematically linked to the view of Welsh history presented in the *Brut*. This then is a 'more subtle, more ambiguous and Welsh' view of the episode.[36] Although it is possible that the episode conveys a sense of proto-Arthurian values, it is hard to see this as the key interpretation within the writers of the *Brut*. So much of what the *Brut* conveys in the early twelfth century is representative of a society fractured by the experience of conquest. It is constructed in complex ways, and it suggests that the creation of a tableau of Arthurian prototypes serves as a complex method to convey resistance to foreign invasion. This is possibly an ongoing working out of the impact of conquest upon south Wales and its impact further afield in Wales in the eleventh and twelfth centuries. It is much more striking that the abduction of Nest forms part of a passage which is effectively a 'self-contained narrative' whose composition may well be independent of the *Brut* and which may even pre-date it.[37] Maund has suggested that care needs to be taken with the portrayal of events in the *Brut* since the unusually detailed entry and use of direct speech give the episode the characteristics of a prose tale, and that the section which includes these events in the Welsh vernacular chronicles was written at a later date and constructed to portray the house of Powys in a positive way.[38] Yet the portrayal is complex, and the way that Nest is situated in the text is ambiguous. Whether or not the episode is the fruit of an earlier com-position than the *Brut*, and whether or not the abduction narrative is part of a narrative which is pro-Powysian in essence, it is the transmis-sion of the memory of the abduction tale which gives it resonance. Its power lies in the sense of adventure certainly, and its narrative of resis-tance is significant, but it also has much to tell us about the role of gendered ideals in socio-political contexts of the early twelfth century, as well as the interpretation of these events later.

A key to understanding the significance of the abduction tale lies in the propagandistic purposes of the authors of the *Brut*. Yet we can go further and consider the importance of the meanings of Nest within the story to appreciate more fully the multi-layered nature of the episode. For example, when we consider the abduction tale within a paradigm which takes account of legal interpretations of rape and abduction a deeper analysis is possible which takes account of other subtleties pre-sent within the portrayal. There is an undercurrent of gender stereo-typing in the way that the dramatic story is told. This is evident in the fact that most of the action, for example the attack on the castle and the escape by Gerald, is precipitated by male action and initiative, but nevertheless there are opportunities for Nest to direct events. Having taken decisive action to ensure Gerald's escape, Nest calls to her would-be captors. Her sons and Gerald's daughters as minors are portrayed as passive victims. Despite her action to save Gerald through her quick thinking, Nest is almost portrayed as 'spoil'.

Nest's action prior to her capture draws on female stereotypes within contemporary literature: she uses her guile to persuade Gerald to escape, and then speaks to reveal her hiding place. This use of speech to convey female guile is clarified when the chronicler reports that Nest persuaded Owain to release her and Gerald's children: 'And Owain, because the woman was for ever saying unto him, "If thou wilt have me true and keep me for thyself, release my sons to their father," – and in his infatuation for the woman, he released the two sons and the daughter.'[39] There are slight variations between the different versions. For example, in the *Red Book of Hergest* Nest asks to have 'my children escorted to their father'. Owain does so 'in his infatuation and love for the woman' and releases them 'for the steward'.[40] Nevertheless it is Nest's implied ability, or, indeed, her subtle threat of sexual infidelity, that triggers his release of the children since the text is explicit: she will only stay with him and remain faithful to him if he does so. It suggests that Nest was able to exert more choice in the situation than would at first appear, and she effectively manipulated Owain to ensure the safety of the children.

An alternative contemporary view of abduction and rape is provided by the Welsh lawbooks. They date from the twelfth and thirteenth centuries, and the principal vernacular versions are the Cyfnerth, Blegywryd and Iorwerth redactions; there are also five Latin redactions. This sequence, with Cyfnerth first and Iorwerth last, has been termed a 'rising order of sophistication'; from the point of view of this study, it is also important to note that those with the strongest connection to south-west Wales are Cyfnerth and Latin D, which is the precursor of Blegywryd.[41] There are of course inherent difficulties when using a thirteenth-century lawbook to reflect on twelfth-century social realities. There has been considerable debate about the historicity and age of the assumptions inherent within the lawbooks and the date at which a tradition of legal writing emerged in Wales. Yet it is generally agreed that the lawbooks contain authentic elements of ancient oral tradition; the debate hinges on the emergence of written traditions. Similarly scholars have considered the lawbooks in the context of emerging ideas about Welsh national identity in an analysis which considers the political interpretative weight which may be assigned to them. This takes account of the idea that the laws as written down reflect a view which may be projected back to expose legal forms. By the time the Welsh laws were written down law was a complex mixture of continuing evolution and conservative or even obsolete material. That they could be inherently slow to adjust to changing realities is certainly possible, and indeed that they promulgate an ideological view is also significant.[42] The ownership of this ideology has been succinctly addressed by Huw Pryce, who argued that the Welsh lawbooks were primarily tools for 'conserving and transmitting native law and for promoting the authority of legal experts'. Further, he suggests that for the *uchelwyr* the prologues of the lawbooks were important in defending the integrity of the law against challenges by princes and others.[43] The importance of the lawbooks for the history of the political elite has been particularly well served. The 1980 volume on *The Welsh Law of Women* in which the contributors explored various aspects of the laws to reflect on women in Welsh society has suggested the richness of the Welsh laws as sources for the history of women in medieval Wales.[44] The Welsh laws are thus complex and rich sources which offer the historian a view of contemporary ideologies and societal attitudes within which the abduction of Nest was written. They offer a view of the social context in which the meaning and punishment of abduction and rape can be explored.

It has been suggested that rape within Welsh law carried both 'public and private' as well as property implications. The violence done to a woman was an insult to the victim, and thus *sarhaed*, *dilystod* and *agweddi* should be paid to her, whilst her *amobr* and *dirwy* should be paid to her lord.[45] It is worthwhile considering briefly the meanings of these terms in order to contextualise the legal framework of abduction and sexual unions. *Agweddi* is a complex term which refers to property that a woman was entitled to on the occasion of a justified separation from her husband. Before the marriage had lasted seven years, according to her natal, or rather her patrilineal, status, she was entitled to a specific sum, the *agweddi*, from the pool of matrimonial property. After seven years, she was entitled straightforwardly to half of that marital property.[46] *Amobr* was the fee payable to the lord of a woman for a sexual relationship, originally perhaps payable for the loss of virginity; it was also sometimes taken in respect of a 'second' sexual activity. It became a lordly income.[47] *Dirwy* was a payment for one of the more serious offences, and *dirwy trais*, the payment for rape, was made to the king by an offender for rape because it had caused the king injury, since he was deprived of payment of *amobr*,[48] applying to unmarried women since married women were under the protection of their husband.

Sarhaed was a term which might mean both an insult offered to an individual and the compensation to be paid to the victim.[49] It was also directly related to *galanas*, that is, it was heavily associated with status and compensation values measured by *life price* (Anglo-Saxon *wergild*). This is striking because *galanas* also contained associations through its root *gal* with 'heat, valour, steam' and might also mean both an accepted reason for feud and 'kin enmity' itself. The feud might originally have been settled by a payment made between kin groups, but it eventually became a fixed sum varied according to status and linked to *sarhaed*.[50] It may not have been applied as strictly as the Welsh legal texts suggest,[51] but nevertheless this legal context of *sarhaed* and its associations with *galanas* are important contexts for our understanding of Owain's father's reaction to the news of the abduction. The different versions of the texts of the Welsh laws have different implications for the consequences of rape. The Cyfnerth, Blegywryd and Latin A texts refer to the concept of *sarhaed* or its Latin equivalent *iniuria*. The Iorwerth text gives the victim rather her *wynebwerth* (honour-price, a term frequently used for compensation paid for offences within marriage) while allocating *sarhaed* to the husband of the victim.[52] This definition of the implications of rape is identified by Morfydd Owen, who clarified the law on Welsh women's property: rape is significant because of its implications for the values of payments which might be drawn from property. Indeed, the rape of a married woman has also been considered to be of 'no concern to the king, for he owes her no special protection. The married woman is under the lordship of her husband.' The *sarhaed* payable was 'particularly high', to be rendered in three instalments because it could cause 'kin enmity'.[53] Thus the law enshrined a view that rape of a married woman was a personal insult to her, and to her husband, and was an offence which might have political and social ramifications within the kin since it could cause feud.

The law code is graphic and specific in detailing how an allegation of rape is to be made:

> let her take the man's penis in her left hand and put her right hand upon the relics, and let her swear to those relics that he penetrated her with that penis by rape upon her, and that he caused shame and insult to her, and to her kindred and to her lord.[54]

It is hard to know whether the above was ever enacted, and it is equally difficult to assess the historicity of the details, and indeed the contemporary meanings of this description are hard to evaluate. Conventional approaches to the lawbooks which interpret them as mnemonic aids or legalistic tools are less useful as analytic devices. It may well be more fruitful to consider this description within a context which takes account of Nerys Patterson's work on the legal burlesque. Patterson suggests that social control of malefactors or would-be offenders was achieved through community sanctions of ostracism and compensation by public shaming and through the offender's participation in a burlesque of the offence. As such, burlesques reveal ideas about the social order and conceptions of justice in which men participate in burlesques where their offence was dereliction of duty, and women participate for sexual transgressions.[55] Can we really consider the above description a burlesque? Certainly the offence that action described seeks to remedy is sexual transgression but this is against the woman, not by her. The idea that burlesques represent social status and that they involve the subordinate's shame for having transgressed their social superior's honour is at the heart of Patterson's analysis. However, this application of considerations of social status at the heart of the burlesque cannot apply here since women were not as a social category seen as superior to men. Yet shame is integral to the offence of rape: the shame experienced is that of the victim. It is possible that the above accusation procedure thus shames the perpetrator and gives this power of public shame to the victim, who has herself been shamed through sexual violation. Alternatively Robin Chapman Stacey noted that the Welsh laws, in the case of divorce, were gendered, charged with sexual imagery and were an object lesson in the cost of divorce. Stacey argues that the laws served to discourage divorce since the division of joint possessions, such as household goods for example, forced the couple to enact in public a gendered performance which stressed the social costs of divorce.[56] In the above ritual concerning the accusation of rape, the 'couple' who had been united through an act of sexual aggression were here reunited through a symbolic hand-holding ritual which could only serve to shame the woman in public, and the man likewise would presumably have been publicly humiliated, indeed, the procedure was an object lesson in the shame and dishonour caused by rape.

The laws in the above act must have served to deter false accusations. It emphasised the public nature of the offence and the crime was seen to have personal and social, and thus communal, implications. The unspoken assumption here is thus that it could have a political impact as well, since an offence against a lord was an offence against an individual who held political power. This then explains the *Brut*'s clarification of Cadwgan's reaction. His response was a reasonable reaction given the gravity of the offence and reflects the rape as a personal and political affront. The attack and rape of Nest was an offence against Gerald of Windsor since he was supposed to protect his wife. The fear of Henry I's retribution as the lord of Gerald of Windsor shows that a response within lordship to a rape was to be expected, especially within the political climate of twelfth-century Wales. The retribution visited upon Owain culminating in his exile to Ireland can be interpreted thus as a community response, supported by royal lordship, to the abduction and rape of Nest, given that later Welsh law clarified that rape could cause kin enmity. It is also explicable in terms of the personal insult to Gerald of Windsor.

Abduction as a way to obtain a wife was, however, recognised within the Welsh laws. It was seen as an offence and its recognition suggests that abduction occurred often enough that a formal legal mechanism for dealing with it evolved. The ecclesiastical view of marriage implied that the usual way for the legitimisation of sexual union was through marriage. Yet Welsh custom and law allowed for nine categories of sexual union.[57] Abduction was abnormal, could be associated with consent, and was thus akin to an elopement. The Welsh laws clarified categories of women within these two scenarios, and in the case of elopement the laws 'distinguished between a maiden (*morwyn*, Latin *puella*, i.e. *merch*, a girl, who is a virgin) whom her kindred can compel to return home, and a woman (*gwraig*, Latin *mulier*) who may decide her own fate'.[58] In the mid-thirteenth-century redaction of Welsh law, the 'Iorwerth text',[59] the laws suggest that marriage by abduction caused the woman to lose her status: 'If it happens that a man abducts a woman, let her be until the end of seven years upon [that is, with a contingent entitlement to] three bullocks whose horns are as long as their ears ... And since she herself has lost her status, let her remain with that status.'[60] In the earliest redaction of the Welsh laws, the 'Cyfnerth' version, whose earliest surviving manuscripts date from the early fourteenth century but which seems to have been originally compiled towards the end of the twelfth century (to judge by the prologue at least), compensation was allowed for a mature woman who has eloped with a man and who is then 'released'.[61] In English law, rape and abduction came to be seen as indistinguishable, and were seen as in a similar way to the ravishment of heirs, associated with rights to wardship and property.[62] Further, the abduction of women as a way of seizing both her and her property was redefined as a felony in the late middle ages, although this redefinition related to women who were subsequently married and was aimed at abduction for profit.[63] It is arguable that the 'profit' that Owain gained, by contrast, was political 'profit': his physical appropriation of Nest's body was a dramatic symbol of his own potency.

The link between abduction of women and profit in later medieval thought is pertinent in the Welsh context since there is the remaining question of the (albeit subtle) portrayal of Nest as 'spoil' or property to be carried off by Owain. This is suggested by the presentation of ideas concerning sexual intercourse within the text where the physical act is recorded in the clause which follows the description of the collecting of booty. Nest's consent is suggested in the *Red Book of Hergest* version. The first portrayal of sexual interaction between them appears as a reference to Owain's 'burning the castle and collecting spoil, and having intercourse with her'. The specific word used to describe sexual intercourse, *chytyaw*, lacks any connotation of force or violence.[64] The allegation of rape occurs, significantly, only in the entry which relates to Owain's father's reaction to 'the rape' (*treis*), a word which indicates violence.[65] The translator of Peniarth MS 20 unambiguously implies rape through the use of the term 'violation'.

This clarifies some of the reasons why Cadwgan was disturbed by Owain's abduction of Nest. It was an offence which carried a range of recognised personal and, potentially, wider lordship- and kinship-based ramifications. If there was a rape of Nest, it was a personal act which carried serious consequences in terms of social and political community responses. The risk that Owain took in his attack on Cenarth Bychan castle was thus explained by the *Brut* in terms of untamed sexual passion. Thus the whole episode is charged with multiple and complex meanings within a larger narrative of Welsh resistance and action to maintain territories and to explain the complexities of shifting Welsh political allegiances. It is interlaid with gender stereotypes: here Owain represents the active, war-like male aggressor, while Nest is the passive female who is acted upon, but who nevertheless takes action to protect her husband and children. Indeed it is the dynamic intermixture of political and cultural meaning that is so striking, and those cultural influences include Irish elements.

Thus if we look beyond the story and consider it within a broader cultural perspective which takes account of Irish influences the nuances of the story for contemporaries can be explored. This is important because the proximity to Ireland directly affected the trajectory of Welsh history, and similarly the Welsh, and especially the descendants of Nest, affected the course of Irish history. Ireland provided a place of refuge for Owain after he was driven out of Deheubarth in retribution for his abduction of Nest. Nest's brother Gruffudd took refuge there after the death and defeat of his father in 1093. In early medieval Ireland it is possible that the abduction of women was a mechanism for seizing political power. Links between Ireland and Wales in literature prior to the story of Branwen in the *Mabinogi* are well known to scholars of early Irish and Welsh literature. They have disputed the extent of these links, but not that such links existed. That Welsh literature was subject to Irish influence is intriguing since it suggests a common intellectual environment, but more interesting still is the question of the significances of these borrowings and how far literary traditions were revisited in later Welsh literature. In particular, it is apparent that the idea of abduction as an integral part of a political narrative has its roots in the first half of the eighth century in Ireland.[66] The idea of female abduction that figures in the *Brut* is therefore possibly a motif of ancient origin.

In the early middle ages the idea of women as 'bearers of sovereignty' in both literal and figurative senses was reflected in naming patterns in Ireland. The abduction of queens was a way for rivals to establish a claim to political power, and for James Doan it is this context within which the abduction of Nest should be seen. Thus this approach sees the abduction of women in early Irish medieval society as frequent and as indicative of the view that women were important politically.[67] It is deeply significant that Nest was abducted by her husband's rival, given that her marriage was clearly an attempt by the Normans to establish control of Pembrokeshire through Nest's marriage to Gerald of Windsor. Following the abduction, Nest stayed with her cousin having ensured that her children were sent back to their father, and it is the details concerning the abduction within the *Brut* which makes the episode significant. The uniqueness of the portrayal of the abduction suggests that it was charged with symbolic meanings. There are few sources which portray abductions in medieval Wales: this may suggest that high-level political abduction was rare and may hint that the nature of politics was changing. This raises the question of whether we are perhaps here able to get a partial view of an example of a different way of conducting politics which was eclipsed as society changed, or an example of cross-cultural borrowing. Although the abduction of Nest is unique within the *Brut* there is evidence in the *Book of Llandaff* which gives a brief view of abduction which was followed by resolution and compensation.[68]

In Ireland it was the abduction of a high-status married woman, a queen, which ultimately caused the Anglo-Norman conquest of Ireland in the twelfth century. Gerald of Wales suggested in his portrayal of the Norman conquest of Ireland that Derbforgaill, the wife of Tigernán Ua Ruairc, prince of Meath, was abducted, not unwillingly, by her husband's rival Diarmait mac Murchada.[69] The abduction of Helen of Troy features as a subtext in Gerald's account, and Gerald uses the episode to launch an invective against the fickleness of women. Although the story has similarities to the abduction of Nest, Gerald is silent – there and elsewhere in his writings – on the abduction of his maternal grandmother. In brief, the train of events that Gerald relates suggests that Diarmait mac Murchada swore an oath of fealty in 1172 in Aquitaine to Henry II in return for aid. As part of his attempt to get support for a campaign to reclaim his lands in Ireland he promised his daughter Aífe (Eva) in marriage to Richard 'Strongbow', Richard fitz Gilbert de Clare, earl of Striguil, in return for his support.[70]

We can see similarities to the portrayal of Nest's abduction in the *Brut*. The role of the 'wounded husband', that is a husband who has been insulted, is played by Gerald 'the officer' in the *Brut*, 'Helen' by Nest, the 'high king' is Henry I and Owain is thus 'Paris'. The *Brut* thus sees the train of events as of seismic importance. It is indicative of a retrospective view of events: Henry I as 'high king' confirms the acceptance of the early success of the Norman incursions into Wales as permanent, when such permanency may not have seemed so apparent to contemporaries. Henry I's thoroughly well-planned invasion of 1114 after all did little other than to confirm his position as overlord.[71] Yet it is the totemic symbolisms and message of resistance that are emphasised by the account.

Finally, whatever the truth of the reports of the attack on Cenarth Bychan castle, scholars are unable to agree its location. It is possible that Cenarth Bychan was either Carew castle or Cilgerran. The latter is the more conventionally accepted identification, having appeared as early as the MS C version of the *Annales Cambriae*.[72] Place-name evidence is inconclusive, while pointing to a location in the vicinity of Cilgerran.[73] Archaeological evidence is, however, also of some use here. According to David Austin, Carew castle might well have been known by another name prior to the building of the twelfth-century stone keep and fortifications. Austin argues that the name Carew only appears in documentary evidence in the twelfth century. Carew is a toponym of Old Welsh origin, and the archaeological evidence based on multiple defence ditches suggests that the Old Welsh name 'the fortifications' might well be the reason for the name. This evidence is the basis for a tentative suggestion that Carew might well have been the location for the infamous raid, although ultimately both the place-name and archaeological evidence for Carew as the site of the abduction are inconclusive.[74] It is of course possible that it was at another location and was possibly a motte and bailey wooden structure which has since disappeared. It is worth considering at this point that Carew castle was important to Nest's dynasty and the significance was symbolised by the Carew cross. The cross dates from the early eleventh century and the inscription is to Maredudd ap Edwin, king of Deheubarth 1033–35.[75] It thus bears the name of one of Nest's ancestors, and immortalised through memorialisation the name of a king of the Deheubarth royal dynasty. The site of the Carew cross is suggestive that as a royal site it was of importance to the dynasty. It is possible that Nest held the lordship in her own right.[76] It has been suggested that the allocation of this land as dowry was 'highly appropriate' if the site had been a 'royal centre (*maerdref*) containing the ancient hall of her royal dynasty'.[77] Thus although Carew may have been deeply symbolically important, it is nevertheless impossible to know whether it was the site of the abduction.

The *Brut* records that the retribution visited upon Owain and Cadwgan was severe. It was enacted by Richard, bishop of London, 'who was then officer to the king at Shrewsbury' and who 'thought to avenge upon Owain the injury done to Gerald'. His tools were Owain's cousins Madog and Ithel ap Rhirid ap Bleddyn, who forced Owain into exile in Ireland. They ravaged Owain's people and lands, and burnt crops and buildings, yet obtained little spoil, which was, no doubt, the object of their depredations, having obtained 'nothing save Cadwgan's stud'.[78] Indeed Owain appears in an almost heroic mould. The portrayal of Owain in the *Brut* is one of constant resistance to Henry I until 1114, and then accommodation and reconciliation with the king. Indeed Owain paid tribute to Henry I and was rewarded; he was even knighted by Henry and went to Normandy with him for a year.[79] The *Brut* records that Owain was killed in 1116 by Gerald of Windsor in retribution for the abduction of Nest, his earlier burning of Cenarth Bychan castle and his taking of spoil.[80] The *Brut* shows that Owain found support where he could such as from the 'hotheads from Ceredigion'. His depredations in Dyfed suggest that his supporters raided, killing cattle, burning houses and selling captives into slavery. Owain is shown to have had principles: he went to Ireland after his father was dispossessed of his territory by Henry I in retaliation for the murder of William of Brabant by Owain,[81] and is shown as a brave fighter and respected leader of his men. He avenged the murder of his father on Madog ap Rhirid his cousin, by 'gouging out his eyes'. His portrayal in the *Brut* is very much a model of a dynamic political leader who could command and retain loyalty, who was principled and brave, loyal to his father, if headstrong and driven by passion.

This contrasts with the way that Gerald of Windsor is portrayed. He is described as Gerald 'the officer' in the *Brut*.[82] If we take into account the context of the *Brut*'s portrayal of Welsh resistance to conquest, then this statement of identity implies that it was office-holding that gave Gerald status. This reinforces the idea that Gerald was the king's, that is, Henry I's, man in a larger narrative of resistance. He is not mentioned in the *Brut* after his role in the death of Owain ap Cadwgan. Within the *Brut*, Nest's pedigree is carefully depicted because although she was married to a Norman 'officer' she represented a crucial link to Welsh royal lineages. This role as a link between Norman and Welsh Deheubarth is evident in the passages which discuss her brother, Gruffudd ap Rhys. It is worth noting that Nest appears later in the *Brut* in a narrative which concerns Gruffudd following his return to Wales in 1113 after his exile in Ireland. Gruffudd was forced into exile when their father was killed by the Normans in 1093. The *Brut* condemns the duplicity of Henry I and suggests that Gruffudd ap Rhys was the victim of a deception 'as it was the custom of the French to deceive men with promises'. It states that Gruffudd ap Rhys returned from Ireland and stayed 'for about two years with his kinsmen, a part thereof with Gerald the officer of Pembroke castle . . . – for the latter's wife was Nest, daughter of Rhys, a sister of the said young man called Gruffudd – at other times with friends of his, sometimes in hiding, sometimes openly proclaimed'. He fled to the court of Gruffudd ap Cynan because of allegations made at the court of Henry I that he intended to rebel and assume the lordship of Deheubarth. However, because of the deception of Henry I, Gruffudd ap Cynan agreed to capture Gruffudd ap Rhys, and the *Brut* continues that on the return of Gruffudd ap Cynan to Gwynedd he searched for Gruffudd ap Rhys. However, 'some of those who loved Gruffudd ap Rhys said to him, "Shun the prescence of Gruffudd ap Cynan until thou know how the world may turn."' The dramatic episodes which follow are part of a wider narrative which concerns the struggle of Gruffudd ap Rhys to take control of parts of the kingdom of Deheubarth.[83] The *Brut* portrays Gruffudd ap Cynan as deceived by Henry I and willing to collaborate with him to the detriment of other Welsh kingdoms; it also presents an image of generational conflict, since Rhys was joined by 'young hotheads'.[84] Yet the image is more complex, presenting a multi-layered view of events: in some ways Gruffudd ap Rhys resembles a hero who has been exiled, returns, faces great difficulties establishing his claim with some measure of popular support, and who is therefore obliquely referenced as a wanderer who returns to his kingdom. He is inscripted as a Welsh leader who could rekindle the hopes of the Welsh in a dramatic interlude in which he only just managed to escape to the sanctuary of Aberdaron church.[85] Nest is named as his sister and her marriage to Gerald is included as a justification for the hospitality extended to Gruffudd. She provided a link with the Anglo-Normans and therefore indirectly a position from which he could build support, although this is not directly stated in the *Brut*.

In order to put the portrayal of Nest into context, it is worth considering the portrayal of women in the *Brut* more generally. Although the portrayal of Nest may well draw on a well-known literary convention of women as the cause of war with its reference to Helen of Troy, such a portrayal is unique in the *Brut*. Women appear in the narrative most frequently within genealogical excursions.[86] Davies argues that native writers, such as the authors of the *Brut*, loved to unravel genealogical tracts that are evidence of the Welsh 'pride in descent' and in their respect 'of the obligations of kinship'.[87] The genealogical details were central to the purpose of explaining the history of the *Brut* in which kinship links were crucial in the definition of social status. Kinship was at the hub of political life. Writers portrayed kinship links as central to political processes. Thus the marriage of Gerald and Nest, for example, and their descendants mattered because of what that family achieved, what they represented, but also because events were predicated and explicable only when family and dynastic links were clarified. In this sense the writers of the *Brut* imposed an order on events which necessitated the insertion of genealogical detail into the narrative. Intense kindred and family relationships, which bound the elite to each other throughout the narrative, underpinned the way that the writers made sense of history. Women were part of those dynasties, and it may well be that their names were recorded in the *Brut* as a way of memorialising them. In other words, they were included by the writers where they could be: conventions of genre dictated their inclusion. For example, the death of Angharad the wife of Gruffudd ap Cynan is noted, as is the date and place of death of Gwladus, daughter of Llywelyn ap Iorwerth, in 1251, and a list of partners of Owain's father Cadwgan ap Bleddyn is provided, all the Welsh women being named and their fathers given, while his wife is simply 'a Frenchwoman, daughter of Picot of Sai', indicative of *Brut*'s focus on native dynasties rather than incomers.[88] Most notably the death and place of burial of Joan, illegitimate daughter of King John and wife of Llywelyn ap Iorwerth, are recorded. The detail concerning Joan is striking. The *Brut* records in the year 1237 the 'Lady of Wales, wife of Llywelyn ap Iorwerth and daughter to the king of England – her name was Joan – died in Llywelyn's court at Aber in the month of February; and her body was buried in a consecrated enclosure which was on the shore-bank. And there after that bishop Hywel consecrated a monastery for the Barefooted Friars to the Honour of the Blessed Mary. And the Prince built it all at his cost for the soul of his Lady.'[89] Given the paucity of detail concerning most entries concerning women, apart from genealogical detail, the length of this entry is striking. It suggests not only that Llywelyn and Joan were reconciled after her alleged affair, but that Joan was an important figure within the Gwynedd dynasty. Llanfaes, the monastery in question, must have been an important religious house for the north Welsh political elite.[90] The *Brut* also furnishes detail concerning Eleanor de Montfort, sister of Simon de Montfort, who had married 'the Lord Llywelyn' ap Gruffudd, grandson of Llywelyn the Great, and who died in childbirth and was also buried at Llanfaes. Her daughter Gwenllian was seized and 'taken into captivity in London' after Llywelyn's death and 'was made a nun against her will'.[91] These events were recorded because the political landscape of Wales had changed with the death and defeat of Llywelyn. Gwenllian was the link to the dynasty, and her incarceration in a convent effectively ensured that her potential role in the continuation of the dynasty was prevented. It suggests the recognition by the English king of her importance to the Welsh sense of historical dynamism that was tied to dynasty.

While there are references to husbands and their wives in the *Brut*, few dates of marriages recorded there form the explicit focus for entries; those that are noted concern significant marriages which are politically significant.[92] For example, Henry I's marriage to Adeliza of Louvain, 'a daughter of a prince of Germany', is noted, as is that of Emma, sister of Henry II (an illegitimate daughter of Geoffrey of Anjou), to Dafydd ap Owain of Gwynedd. The marriage was a political union concluded 'because he [Dafydd] thought he could hold his territory in peace thereby'.[93] In sum, the inclusion of women in the narrative afforded by the *Brut* is in specific spheres, namely marriage and genealogy, and rarely political chronology. Given this, the inclusion of Nest in the narrative in such a distinctive and detailed way suggests that the episode had important meanings within the narrative, and thus within the trajectory of Welsh history as perceived by the authors of the *Brut*. The normative method of portraying the political chronology almost serves to exclude women from a narrative focused on political turbulence within 'Welsh' Wales, and is suggestive of the tensions generated in south-west Wales by the Norman conquest of Deheubarth.

The role of Nest in this narrative was portrayed within conventions of genre which had multiple and interconnecting dynamics. Thus she is the representative of the ancient royal house of Deheubarth, but as a woman she was subject to male stereotypical distrust of female power; and thus although it is her cousin Owain who initiates the sequence of events, Nest is proactive in the unravelling of the uneasy peace within Deheubarth achieved through her marriage to Gerald. Although the construction of events may well owe more to a classical stereotype of woman as a cause of war and may be an oblique reference to an alleged Trojan descent of the Welsh elite from Brutus, it is nevertheless instructive that the episode portrays all these elements. It also drew on contemporary legal ideas, and cultural norms concerning marriage and legitimacy, and is thus reflective of different intellectual traditions. That such a variety of ideas was current in the late twelfth to early thirteenth centuries reflects the richness of the Welsh intellectual tradition, its adaptability as well as its conservatism, as much as the reality of events as they unfolded. The image of Nest abducted by a heroic Welshman, from the grip of a Norman invader, was totemic, and it may well be Powysian sympathies which effect this portrayal:[94] yet fundamentally it shows the importance of Nest as a woman of action, fundamentally a Welsh princess, who was central to the political processes of south-west Wales, and yet the narrative is ambiguous. At the heart of the portrayal of the abduction are concerns about lordship, abduction and rape which inextricably link the series of events of 1109 with ideas about Nest's sexuality. Yet scholars have persisted in seeing the events as a romantically inspired affair. It is not going too far to suggest that Nest's sexual conquest by Owain was romanticised since the portrayal of Owain in the *Brut* generally is positive, and his reconciliation with Henry I and his knighthood later in the narrative certainly present a positive image. However, centrally, later commentators may have glossed over his part in the rape and abduction of Nest in an ongoing male-centred narrative in which Nest's rape was part of a narrative of heroic Welsh resistance to the Anglo-Normans. As such the abuse of a Welsh princess by the prince of another Welsh dynasty draws attention to the importance of personal actions and responsibility. Thus the sexual relationship, her capture and subsequent actions for her children were interpreted to suggest compliance if not outright willingness to cuckold her husband. While commentators have noted the violence meted out on male members of ruling Welsh dynasties, violence against women is rare. It may well be that an acknowledgement that Nest's abduction may have been forced, and could have included rape, did not suit the purposes of later, eighteenth- and nineteenth-century, commentators who wanted to inculcate a romantic view of medieval Wales. In such a world women, and especially high-status Welsh women, were treated honourably by their fellow Welsh men. The *Brut* suggests that Nest's resistance to the destruction of her life was channelled to ensure her children's safety. Nest's infamous abduction in 1109 by her cousin Owain ap Cadwgan was constructed within the *Brut y Tywysogion* in a way which subverted normative forms of narrative of male action and resourcefulness to create a dynamic image of active participation that was predicated on contemporary ideas about the role of Welsh resistance to invasion which interacted with gender and Norman lordship.

Notes

1 K. L. Maund, *Princess Nest of Wales: Seductress of the English* (Stroud: Tempus, 2007), pp. 135–41.

2 J. E. Lloyd and R. T. Jenkins (eds), *The Dictionary of Welsh Biography down to 1940* (London: Honourable Society of Cymmrodorion, 1959; based on first Welsh edition, as *Bywgraffiadur Cymreig hyd 1940*, London: Anrhydeddus Gymdeithas y Cymmrodorion, 1953), p. 683.

3 R. R. Davies, *The Age of Conquest: Wales 1063–1415* (Oxford: Oxford University Press, 1987; new edn 2000), p. 43.

4 J. E. Lloyd, rev. David E. Thornton, 'Rhys ap Tewdwr (d. 1093), ruler in Wales', *ODNB*. For more on Rhys, see Robert S. Babcock, 'Rhys ap Tewdwr, king of Deheubarth', *ANS*, 16 (1993), 21–35; see also Huw Pryce, 'In search of a medieval society: Deheubarth in the writings of Gerald of Wales', *WHR*, 13 (1987), 265–81.

5 The extent to which this applied is controversial, especially following J. Beverley Smith's reappraisal, 'Dynastic succession in medieval Wales', *BBCS*, 33 (1986), 199–232.

6 J. Wyn Evans, 'St David and St David's and the coming of the Normans', *Transactions of the Honourable Society of Cymmrodorion*, new ser., 11 (2004), 5–18.

7 For the impact of the Normans upon Gwent, for example, see David B. Crouch, 'The transformation of medieval Gwent', in Ralph A. Griffiths, Tony Hopkins and R. C. Howell (eds), *Gwent County History*, vol. 2: *The Age of the Marcher Lords, c.1070–1536* (Cardiff: University of Wales Press on behalf of the Gwent County History Association, 2008), pp. 1–45; see also Paul Courtney, 'The Norman invasion of Gwent: a reassessment', *JMH*, 12 (1986), 297–313; and for Glamorgan, David B. Crouch, 'The slow death of kingship in Glamorgan', *Morgannwg*, 29 (1985), 20–41.

8 David Crouch, 'Nest (b. before 1092, d. c.1130), royal mistress', *ODNB*, explores the difficulties of establishing Nest's dates. He probably rightly places the marriage soon after Gerald's arrival as steward.

9 See the works of R. R. Davies, especially his *Age of Conquest*, and his series of articles in the *TRHS*, including 'The peoples of Britain and Ireland, 1100–1400, I: Identities', *TRHS*, 6th ser., 4 (1994), 1–20; Brian Golding, *Conquest and Colonisation: The Normans in Britain, 1066–1100* (revised edn, Basingstoke and New York: Palgrave, 2001).

10 Crouch, 'Nest'.

11 Judith A. Green, *Henry I: King of England and Duke of Normandy* (Cambridge: Cambridge University Press, 2009), p. 132. Crouch, 'Nest'.

12 Robert Bartlett, 'Gerald of Wales [Giraldus Cambrensis, Gerald de Barry] (c.1146–1220x23), author and ecclesiastic', *ODNB*.

13 The incident appears briefly, without a mention of Nest, in *Annales Cambriæ*, ed. John Williams ab Ithel (Rolls Series, 20; London: Longman, Green, Longman, and Roberts, 1860), p. 34.

14 *Brut y Tywysogion, Peniarth MS. 20 Version*, ed. T. Jones (Cardiff: University of Wales Press, 1941); *Brut y Tywysogion, or, The Chronicle of the Princes, Peniarth MS. 20 Version*, trans. T. Jones (Cardiff: University of Wales Press, 1952), especially his comments on origins, at pp. xxxv–lxiii (which follow J. E. Lloyd, 'The Welsh chronicles', *Proceedings of the British Academy*, 14 (1928), 369–91); *Brut y Tywysogion, or, The Chronicle of the Princes, Red Book of Hergest Version*, ed. and trans. T. Jones (1955; 2nd edn, Cardiff: University of Wales Press, 1973); *Brenhinedd y Saesson, or, The Kings of the Saxons*, ed. T. Jones (Cardiff: University of Wales Press, 1971). David Stephenson, in 'Welsh chronicles' accounts of the mid-twelfth century', *Cambrian Medieval Celtic Studies*, 56 (2008), 45–57, has challenged J. Beverley Smith's note, in 'Castell Gwyddgrug', *BBCS*, 26 (1974), 74–7, which argued that parts of the *Brut* were expanded in the late

thirteenth century. For *Brenhinedd y Saesson*, see J. Beverley Smith, 'Historical writing in medieval Wales: the composition of *Brenhinedd y Saesson*', *Studia Celtica*, 42 (2008), 55–86. For commentary on texts produced in the twelfth and thirteenth centuries, see Huw Pryce, 'The origins and the medieval period', in Philip Henry Jones and Eiluned Rees (eds), *A Nation and its Books: A History of the Book in Wales* (Aberystwyth: National Library of Wales in association with Aberystwyth Centre for the Book, 1998), pp. 1–23, at pp. 7–12; I. Jack, *Medieval Wales* (London: Hodder and Stoughton for the Sources of History Ltd, 1972), pp. 30–1. For the Latin chronicles, see K. W. Hughes, 'The Welsh Latin chronicles: *Annales Cambriae* and related texts', *Proceedings of the British Academy*, 59 (1973), 233–58, at p. 233.

15 *Brut, Peniarth MS. 20* (1941), p. 41; *Brut, Peniarth MS. 20* (1952), pp. 28–9.

16 *Brut, Peniarth MS. 20* (1952), p. 29 ('aphan gigleu gadwgawn ychwedyl hwnw d[z]wc vv ganthaw a brawhau awnaeth ef o dwyfo[z]d o achaws treis yr ar glwydes ac oachaws ofyn henri v[z]enhin am sarhaed y swydwr': *Brut, Peniarth MS. 20* (1941), pp. 42–3).

17 *Brut, Red Book of Hergest*, pp. 54–7.

18 *Brut, Red Book of Hergest*, pp. 54–5; *Brut, Peniarth MS. 20* (1952), p. 28.

19 *Brut, Peniarth MS. 20* (1941), p. 42; *Brut, Peniarth MS. 20* (1952), p. 28; *Brut, Red Book of Hergest*, pp. 56–7.

20 *Brenhinned y Saesson*, pp. 104–7 ('Ac yna y daliassant Nest').

21 *Brut, Red Book of Hergest*, pp. 56–7. Jones's translation of the Peniarth MS 20 version says that Cadwgan was afraid because the actions amounted to a 'violation', a term which might well suggest the delicacies of a 1950s translator responding to the original 'treis yr arglwydes': *Brut, Peniarth MS. 20* (1952), p. 28.

22 *Brenhinned y Saesson*, pp. 106–7 ('A gwedy klywet o Cadwgon yr anghyfreith a wnathoed Oweyn y Gerald').

23 L. Beverley Smith, 'On the hospitality of the Welsh: a comparative view', in Huw Pryce and John Watts (eds), *Power and Identity in the Middle Ages: Essays in Memory of Rees Davies* (Oxford: Oxford University Press, 2007), pp. 181–94, at p. 184. On Whitsun as a campaign season see the poem by Llywarch ap Llewelyn, which states 'it is Whitsun, campaign time for warriors', in *Medieval Welsh Poems*, ed. J. P. Clancy (Dublin: Four Courts Press, 2003), 'A love poem for Gwenlliant', at p. 156.

24 Marjorie A. Brown, 'The feast hall in Anglo-Saxon society', in Martha Carlin and Joel Thomas Rosenthal (eds), *Food and Eating in Medieval Europe* (London and Rio Grande: Hambledon Press, 1999), pp. 1–28, at p. 1. John Meddings, 'Friendship among the aristocracy of Anglo-Norman England', *ANS*, 22 (2000 for 1999), 187–204, at p. 201.

25 Smith, 'On the hospitality of the Welsh', p. 94.

26 Katie Normington, *Gender and Medieval Drama* (Woodbridge: D. S. Brewer, 2004), p. 83.

27 *Brut, Peniarth MS. 20* (1952), p. 28.

28 J. E. Lloyd, *A History of Wales from the Earliest Times to the Edwardian Conquest* (2 vols, London, 1911; 3rd edn, London: Longmans, Green, 1939), ii. 417; Davies, *Age of Conquest*, p. 86; Andrew Breeze, *Medieval Welsh Literature* (Dublin: Four Courts Press, 1997), p. 97.

29 Lloyd and Jenkins (eds), *Dictionary of Welsh Biography*, p. 683.

30 Davies, *Age of Conquest*, p. 43.

31 Breeze, *Medieval Welsh Literature*, pp. 97–9.

32 Pryce, 'Origins and the medieval period', p. 8. See also Brynley Roberts, 'Oral tradition and Welsh literature: a description and survey', *Oral Tradition*, 3 (1988), 61–87, and Daniel Huws, *Medieval Welsh Manuscripts* (Cardiff: University of Wales Press, 2000).

33 See note 14 above for the debate between J. B. Smith and D. Stephenson on the contemporaneity of the *Brut* account of the twelfth century. See also K. L. Maund, 'Owain ap Cadwgan: a rebel revisited', *Haskins Society Journal*, 13 (2004 for 1999), 65–74.

34 Breeze, *Medieval Welsh Literature*, p. 99.

35 Breeze, *Medieval Welsh Literature*, pp. 98–9.

36 John K. Bollard and David Austin, 'Carew castle: the earliest documentary evidence', in D. Austin (ed.), *Carew Castle Archaeological Project: 1994 Season Interim Report* (Lampeter: Department of Archaeology, University of Wales, 1995), pp. 6–7.

37 Bollard and Austin, 'Carew castle: the earliest documentary evidence', p. 6.

38 Maund, *Princess Nest*, p. 136; J. Beverley Smith, *Yr Ymwybod â Hanes yng Nghymru yn yr Oesoedd Canol: The Sense of History in Medieval Wales* (Aberystwyth: Coleg Prifysgol Cymru, 1991), comments on the role of dialogue in *Brut* and in the prose tales.

39 *Brut, Peniarth MS. 20* (1952), p. 29

40 *Brut, Red Book of Hergest*, pp. 56–7.

41 Dafydd Jenkins and Morfydd E. Owen (eds), *The Welsh Law of Women: Studies Presented to Professor Daniel A. Binchy on his Eightieth Birthday, 3 June 1980* (Cardiff: University of Wales Press, 1980), p. 132. See also T. M. Charles-Edwards, *The Welsh Laws* (Cardiff: University of Wales Press on behalf of the Welsh Arts Council, 1989). Latin B, C and E are clearly northern; in respect of the laws of women, A has material from both Cyfnerth and Iorwerth.

42 Davies, 'Peoples of Britain and Ireland, 1100–1400, Identities', pp. 9–10; J. L. Nelson, 'Family, gender and sexuality', in M. Bentley (ed.), *Companion to Historiography* (London and New York: Routledge, 1997; paperback edn 2002), p. 155. For new genres of legal writing, e.g. *Llyfr y Damweiniau* and *Llyfr Cynghawsedd*, see Charles-Edwards, *Welsh Laws*. On material that was not intended to be taken as 'law' in a modern sense, Robin C. Stacey, 'Law and literature in medieval Wales', in Helen Fulton (ed.), *Medieval Celtic Literature and Society* (Dublin: Four Courts Press, 2005), pp. 65–82.

43 Huw Pryce, 'Lawbooks and literacy in medieval Wales', *Speculum*, 75 (2000), 29–67, at p. 67; *idem*, 'The prologues to the Welsh lawbooks', *BBCS*, 33 (1986), 151–87; *idem*, 'The context and purpose of the earliest Welsh lawbooks', *Cambrian Medieval Celtic Studies*, 39 (2000), 39–63. See also J. G. Edwards, 'The historical study of the Welsh lawbooks', *TRHS*, 5th ser., 7 (1962), 141–55, at p. 142, who stresses the longevity of the Welsh laws following the Norman and Edwardian conquests. For further discussion of lawbooks, see chapter 3.

44 Jenkins and Owen (eds), *Welsh Law of Women*.

45 'The "Cyfnerth" text', in *Welsh Law of Women*, pp. 138–9.

46 Jenkins and Owen (eds), *Welsh Law of Women*, p. 188: clarification that there were variations within the texts concerning the status of different unions predicated on the consent of the kin.

47 Jenkins and Owen (eds), *Welsh Law of Women*, p. 190.

48 Jenkins and Owen (eds), *Welsh Law of Women*, p. 200.

49 Jenkins and Owen (eds), *Welsh Law of Women*, p. 216.

50 Jenkins and Owen (eds), *Welsh Law of Women*, pp. 202–3.
51 Davies, *Age of Conquest*, pp. 124–5. Davies emphasises the involvement of the kin in dispute resolution in homicide. My interpretation of the laws on rape suggests similar paradigms applied.
52 Dafydd Jenkins, 'Property interests in the classical Welsh law of women', in Jenkins and Owen (eds), *Welsh Law of Women*, pp. 69–92, at p. 87–8.
53 Morfydd E. Owen, 'Shame and reparation: woman's place in the kin', in Jenkins and Owen (eds), *Welsh Law of Women*, pp. 40–68, at p. 50.
54 'The Iorwerth Text' is that of Peniarth MS 35 (Aneurin Owen's G, in his *Ancient Laws and Institutes of Wales* (London, 1841)): Jenkins and Owen (eds), *Welsh Law of Women*, p. 161; for text see pp. 170–1 (Iorwerth # 50). The *Welsh Law of Women* contains a selection of excerpts from Latin Redaction A, from Peniarth MS 28, dating from the mid-thirteenth century. The Peniarth MS 28 suggests the ways that rape was categorised and dealt with: 'Latin Redaction A', in *Welsh Law of Women*, pp. 154–5 (# 35–40).
55 Nerys Patterson, 'Honour and shame in medieval Welsh society', *Studia Celtica*, 16–17 (1981–82), 73–103, at pp. 73–7.
56 Robin C. Stacey, 'Divorce, medieval Welsh style', *Speculum*, 77 (2002), 1107–27.
57 Huw Pryce, *Native Law and the Church in Medieval Wales* (Oxford: Clarendon Press, 1993), p. 109. There is some doubt as to how far the list in 'Naw Cyniweddi Deithïog' was customary by the twelfth century: T. M. Charles-Edwards, 'Nau Kynywedi Teithiauc', in Jenkins and Owen (eds), *Welsh Law of Women*, pp. 23–39.
58 D. B. Walters, 'The European legal context of the Welsh law of matrimonial property', in Jenkins and Owen (eds), *Welsh Law of Women*, pp. 115–31, at p. 117.
59 Pryce, 'Lawbooks and literacy', p. 39.
60 'The "Iorwerth Text"', in Jenkins and Owen (eds), *Welsh Law of Women*, pp. 168–9 (# 3).
61 'The "Cyfnerth Text"', in Jenkins and Owen (eds), *Welsh Law of Women*, p. 141. Dating of text: Pryce, 'Lawbooks and literacy', p. 39.
62 Corinne Saunders, *Rape and Ravishment in the Literature of Medieval England* (Cambridge: D. S. Brewer, 2001), pp. 58–9. For ravishment of heirs see Sue Sheridan Walker, 'Common law juries and feudal marriage customs in medieval England: the pleas of ravishment', *Illinois Law Review*, 3 (1984), 705–18.
63 E. W. Ives, '"Agaynst taking awaye of women": the inception and operation of the Abduction Act of 1487', in E. W. Ives, R. J. Knecht and J. J. Scarisbrick (eds), *Wealth and Power in Tudor England: Essays Presented to S. T. Bindoff* (London: Athlone Press, 1978), pp. 21–45.
64 *Brut, Red Book of Hergest*, pp. 56–7: 'A gwedy llosci y castell a chunullaw anreith a chytyaw a hitheu ymhoelt a orauc dracheneuen y'w wlat' ('And after burning the castle and collecting spoil, and having intercourse with her, he returned to his land.')
65 *Brut, Red Book of Hergest*, pp. 56–7: 'A phann gigleu Gawwgan y gweithret hwnnw, kymryt ynn drwc arnaw gann sorr a oruc hynny o achaws y treis gyt a wnathoedit a Nest uerch Rys' ('And when Cadwgan heard of that deed, he was indignantly grieved thereat because of the rape that had been committed.')
66 Proinsias Mac Cana, *Branwen Daughter of Llŷr* (Cardiff: University of Wales Press, 1958), p. 48, citing R. Thurneysen, 'Die Sage von CuRoi', *Zeitschrift für celtische Philologie*, IX (1913), 189–234.
67 James Doan, 'Sovereignty aspects in the role of women in medieval Irish and Welsh society', *Proceedings of the Harvard Celtic Colloquium*, 5 (1985), 94–5.

68 See chapter 3, pp. 85–8.

69 Gerald of Wales, *Expugnatio Hibernica: The Conquest of Ireland*, ed. A. B. Scott and F. X. Martin (Dublin: Royal Irish Academy, 1978), p. 25, and see discussion in chapter 2.

70 Gerald of Wales, *Expugnatio Hibernica*, p. 25; Doan, 'Sovereignty aspects in the roles of women', pp. 96–7. For the significance of Aífe's marriage to Strongbow, see M. T. Flanagan, *Irish Society, Anglo-Norman Settlers, Angevin Kingship: Interactions in Ireland in the Late Twelfth Century* (Oxford: Clarendon Press, 1989), pp. 118–20.

71 Davies, *Age of Conquest*, p. 42.

72 *Annales Cambriæ*, p. 34. The *Annales Cambriæ* are discussed in greater detail below, pp. 70–1.

73 Iwan Wmffre, *The Place-Names of Cardiganshire* (3 vols, Oxford: Archaeopress, 2004), i. 65, 77. J. E. Lloyd noted the name Cenarth Bychan was 'long forgotten' and suggested that it may well refer to a castle near Cenarth Mawr in the cantref of Emlyn: *The Story of Ceredigion (400–1277)* (Cardiff: University of Wales Press Board, 1937), p. 41.

74 David Austin, 'The context and the research design', in D. Austin (ed.), *Carew Castle Archaeological Project: 1992 Season Interim Report* (Lampeter: Department of Archaeology, University of Wales, 1993), pp. 6–7. There is an unexplained statement here that Gerald of Windsor was Anglo-Saxon in origin rather than a 'true Anglo-Norman'. This must be based upon the assumption that Gerald's mother was Anglo-Saxon since his father was a Norman constable of Windsor castle. For Gerald, see David Walker, Windsor, Gerald of (d. 1116×36), soldier and dynast, *ODNB*. Carew castle had a stone curtain wall and the old tower dates to *c.* 1100: Thomas Lloyd, Julian Orbach and Robert Scourfield, *Pembrokeshire* (The Buildings of Wales; New Haven and London: Yale University Press, 1994), p. 152.

75 Nancy Edwards, with contributions by Heather Jackson, Helen McKee and Patrick Sims-Williams, *A Corpus of Medieval Inscribed Stones and Stone Sculpture in Wales*, vol. 2: *South-West Wales* (Cardiff: University of Wales Press, 2007), pp. 303–10.

76 Lloyd, *History of Wales*, ii. 422

77 Austin, 'Context and the research design', p. 7.

78 *Brut, Peniarth MS. 20* (1952), pp. 29–30.

79 *Brut, Peniarth MS. 20* (1952), p. 38.

80 *Brut, Peniarth MS. 20* (1952), p. 45.

81 *Brut, Peniarth MS. 20* (1952), pp. 33–4.

82 *Brut, Peniarth MS. 20* (1952), p. 28.

83 *Brut, Peniarth MS. 20* (1952), p. 39.

84 Cf. Robert S. Babcock, 'Imbeciles and Normans: the ynfydion of Gruffudd ap Rhys reconsidered', *Haskins Society Journal*, 4 (1993 for 1992), 1–9.

85 T. F. Tout, rev. Huw Pryce, 'Gruffudd ap Rhys (d. 1137), ruler in south Wales', *ODNB*. See also the story in Gerald's *Itinerarium* of birds singing for Gruffudd on Llangorse Lake: *Itinerarium*, pp. 34–5. This could possibly be oral tradition passed down by Gerald's family, although it could also just be local tradition in Brycheiniog.

86 See, for example, the detail concerning Cadwallon ap Gruffudd ap Cynan who killed his three uncles in 1125: 'And a little after that, Cadwallon ap Gruffudd ap Cynan, the man who was mentioned above, slew his three uncles, namely Goronwy and Rhirhid and Melilyr, sons of Owain ab Edwin: for Angharad, daughter of Owain, as wife to

Gruffudd ap Cynan and mother of Cadwallon and Owain and Cadwaladyr and many daughters.' *Brut, Peniarth MS. 20* (1952), p. 49. NB the impact on the mother Angharad of her husband's kin being thereby drawn into a feud: see discussion by T. M. Charles-Edwards in *idem* and Paul Russell (eds), *Tair Colofn Cyfraith: The Three Columns of the Law in Medieval Wales: Homicide, Theft and Fire* (Bangor: Welsh Legal History Society, 2007). Other examples, *ibid.*, p. 28 (detail on Nest's mother Gwladus, and Angharad wife of Cynfyn ap Gwerstyn, mother of her uncles Bleddyn and Rhiwallon. Other examples, see pp. 41, 45, 66).

87 Davies, *Age of Conquest*, p. 122.

88 Angharad wife of Gruffudd ap Cynan: *Brut, Peniarth MS. 20* (1952), p. 62; Gwladus daughter of Llywelyn ap Iorwerth, *ibid.*, p. 109; partners of Cadwgan ap Bleddyn, *ibid.*, p. 31. Others: the death of Angharad, wife of Gruffudd ap Cynan, daughter of Owain ap Edwin: *ibid.*, p. 49. Death of Matilda de Braose, wife of William de Braose at Windsor castle in 1210, starved to death with her son at the hands of King John: *ibid.*, p. 84.

89 *Brut, Peniarth MS. 20* (1952), p. 104.

90 Huw Pryce pointed out to me that male members of the dynasty, including Llywelyn himself, were buried at Cistercian Aberconwy, so it could be that founding Llanfaes and having Joan buried there showed both her special status and a certain distancing of her from symbolic centres of dynastic power.

91 *Brut, Peniarth MS. 20* (1952), p. 117.

92 An exception would be the mentions of Cadwgan ap Bleddyn noted above, n. 88.

93 *Brut, Peniarth MS. 20* (1952), p. 47 (Henry I to Adeliza of Louvain), p. 70 (Emma, daughter of Henry II and Dafydd ap Owain); political alliance of 'earl Richard, son of Gilbert Strongbow with king Diarmaid' secured through the marriage to his daughter (1165), p. 65; marriage of Rhys Grug to the 'daughter of the earl de Clare' (unnamed) and John de Braose to 'Margaret, the daughter of Lord Llewelyn for his wedded wife' (1219), p. 97; marriage of Llywelyn ap Gruffudd with Eleanor the sister of Simon de Montfort (1275), p. 117.

94 As would make sense if the *Brut* was being composed at Llanbadarn Fawr by 1109 onwards (as Lloyd argued, and Stephenson recently rehabilitated after this was challenged by Hughes and Dumville – see above, n. 14).

2

Gerald of Wales, Nest, gender and power

'ALMOST all the world's most notable catastrophes have been caused by women, witness Mark Antony and Troy,' wrote Gerald of Wales in his *Conquest of Ireland* completed in 1189.[1] This invective had been provoked by the story of the downfall of Diarmait Mac Murchada, prince of Leinster, who in 1152, according to Gerald, in revenge for some earlier insults, abducted the wife of his rival, for whom he had 'long been burning with love'.[2] Gerald tells us that the woman colluded in this and that circumstances favoured them: Diarmait had taken 'advantage of her husband's absence. No doubt,' stated Gerald, 'she was abducted because she wanted to be'. He continued, 'woman is always a fickle and inconstant creature', and further, 'she herself arranged that she should become the kidnapper's prize'.[3] According to Robert Bartlett, Gerald's hostility to women is apparent in his other writings, and his prejudice against women was founded on a 'purient or fascinated obsession with the vexatiousness of marriage and women's irrationality'.[4] Huw Pryce too noted Gerald's general hostility to women and argues that women appear in Gerald's works as sources of 'temptation and expense for men'.[5] Yet Gerald's view of women, although founded in a fierce hostility to women in general, nevertheless sees women as central to the political process of conquest and settlement. Beginning with an analysis of the presentation of Nest in his works, Gerald's portrayal of Nest will be considered in more detail in order to consider the specific contexts in which she appears in Gerald's narrative. This will take account of Gerald's view of women more generally as well as focusing on specific portrayals of women in order to consider how his views about gender, conquest and war were shaped by his attitude to women.

Gerald was a prolific writer and he wrote about Ireland and Wales because he felt they had been neglected by contemporary writers.[6] His *Topographica Hibernica* (*Topography of Ireland*) and *Expugnatio Hibernica*

(*Conquest of Ireland*) were both published in the period 1188–89. His *Itinerarium Cambriae* (*Journey through Wales*) was completed in *c.* 1191, his *Descriptio Cambriae* (*Description of Wales*) in *c.* 1194, and it is these works which mention Nest. Gerald wrote local history as well as the *De Principis Instructione* (*On the Instruction of a Prince*). He has been characterised as 'sharp, critical, and occasionally savage, yet also precise, vivid and credible'.[7] His writings on Wales and Ireland demonstrate this keenness of observation, and his vibrant style is informed by a revival of classical modes of writing. His reference to Helen of Troy to condemn women in general demonstrates not only his antipathy to women but also his familiarity with antiquity. His ethnographic writings on the Welsh and Irish in general were sharply observed and were a form of social anthropology.[8] His writings are acutely observant of the social customs and economic, military and political contexts of contemporary society. Scholars are agreed that the contribution of his family to the conquest of Ireland is a key component in his narratives on Ireland and Wales, and Gerald was proud of his lineage. Scholars have long been aware of the value of Gerald's writings yet they still have much to tell us about the importance of contemporary conceptions of gender, nation and conquest.

The importance of nation and conquest to the trajectory of Welsh history in the high middle ages is beyond dispute and they are the key dynamics shaping contemporary Wales. Yet ideas about gender and the role of women were interwoven into such narratives: they assume symbolic roles within texts and they therefore have a didactic purpose. Nest appears in Gerald's writings in the contexts of family and lordship in, for example, his discussion of the marriage of Gerald of Windsor to Nest. He states that Gerald of Windsor, in order 'to make himself and his dependents more secure', married 'Nest the sister of Gruffydd, Prince of South Wales, by whom he had an illustrious progeny of both sexes' and 'by whose means both the parts of South Wales were retained by the English, and the walls of Ireland stormed'.[9] Gerald thus argued that the marriage thus secured Gerald *and* his dependents, that is, his followers whom he had knighted during the siege after fifteen soldiers had deserted. His role as lord was thus strengthened through marriage, and indeed it is well accepted that during this period marriage was used as a strategy for ensuring the permanence of conquest; intermarriage between conquerors and natives had occurred in England following the Norman conquest of England,[10] and it was a strategy deployed in Wales. The statement concerning the marriage appears in the narrative after a description of the clever stratagems used by Gerald of Windsor to wage a propaganda war to hold on to Pembroke castle during a siege. These included the use of vivid visual propaganda when, despite great hardship and lack of provisions, he had four pigs slaughtered and thrown over the castle walls to give the impression that the besieged had plenty of food. To reinforce this impression of strength to confuse the Welsh was the fabrication of sealed letters to Gerald's lord, Earl Arnulf of Montgomery, stating there was no need for him to come to the assistance of the besieged. These letters were left conveniently outside the house of Wilfrid, bishop of St David's, for the opposing forces to find, as if they had been 'dropped accidentally by one of Gerald's messengers'. The Welsh abandoned their siege and the Normans thus held on to Pembroke castle.[11] Gerald of course included these vignettes to portray Gerald of Windsor in a positive way, and his marriage to Nest and the reference to their illustrious progeny who then went on to conquer Ireland are key to Gerald of Wales's interpretation of his family. Gerald implies that Nest and Gerald of Windsor were married shortly after the siege of Pembroke castle. Gerald of Wales is unequivocal: the marriage occurred soon after the siege of Pembroke castle which had been a challenging and difficult period. Nest thus has a specific dynastic and political function within Gerald's narrative in which political struggles and the links between family and lordship were the great forces shaping contemporary life in Wales and Ireland. The narrative of his grandfather's success in holding Pembroke castle inscribes his maternal grandfather as a cunning soldier who maintained Norman control through a mixture of military ingenuity and political connections gained through his marriage. It does not suggest a narrative of the Norman conquest in Pembrokeshire as one of overwhelming force, but rather one of smart strategies and integration into existing political networks through the connections to the previous dynasty embodied through Nest. Thus the role of his family in Wales, and the conquest and domination of Ireland through war and lordship, is a significant strand within Gerald of Wales's writings. This interpretation qualifies the views of historians such as R. R. Davies and G. Duby that marriage was a strategy within a theatre dominated by male power and politics. Male actors are central and violence is important, yet the use of force was not overwhelming, and other strategies were deployed. The portrayal of Nest has more to tell us than merely to confirm modern interpretations. Nest's role within the medieval sources was more than as a pawn in a marriage strategy as part of a process of conquest. In Gerald of Wales's writings she is the key to understanding the connections between the dominant political families in south-west Wales and Ireland and even the English royal family. For example, Gerald, in his *Journey through Wales*, states that '[t]wo great noblemen were sent to the island [Ireland] by the King. They were my own uncles: Henry, son of King Henry I and uncle of King Henry II, the child of Nest, the nobly born daughter of Rhys ap Tewdwr, Prince of Dyved in South Wales; and Robert FitzStephen, Henry's brother, but by a different father,' but of course they have the same mother, Nest.[12] It is noteworthy that Gerald uses specific epithets to describe Nest: she is called 'nobly born' in his *Expugnatio Hibernica*, when he is discussing the lineage of his uncle Robert fitz Stephen, whose mother was '*matre namque nobili scilicet Nesta, Resi magni filia*'.[13] It is also significant that there are no comments regarding the legitimacy of the births of his uncles. The context here informs the nature of Gerald's description since it is part of his portrayal of Robert fitz Stephen, whose parentage and thus dynastic links to the Welsh and the Normans could have potentially caused him to have split loyalties. Gerald explains his allegiance to the English crown in terms of loyalty, and his desire for honour and reputation in posterity. Gerald explains how his relatives could become conflicted due to divided loyalties due to their mixed heritage. Robert fitz Stephen had been imprisoned at Cardigan castle of which he was castellan. He was released on condition that he allied himself with Rhys ap Gruffudd his cousin and his half-brothers against the king of England. Robert, however, chose to go to Ireland, and Gerald goes on to narrate his conquests.[14] Gerald repeats the details concerning Robert's mixed parentage in the context of providing an explanation of a statement of 'the old prophecy of Merlin the Wild' that a 'knight sprung of two races, will be the first to break bonds with Ireland'. Gerald explains this was a reference to Robert's parents: 'on the father's side he was bound by natural ties of loyalty to his lord the king – for since his mother was the noble Nest, daughter of the great Rhys, he was Rhys ap Gruffydd's Cousin'.[15] The use of the word 'noble' is not accidental: it confirms Nest's social status, and the importance of noble lineage is a significant strand within Gerald's writings, reflecting contemporary perceptions. As R. R. Davies has pointed out, in contemporary Welsh lawbooks there were three grades within the descending categorisation of social hierarchy: king, noble (Welsh *breyr*) and villein (Welsh *bilian*), although of course this is a simplification, it nevertheless indicates the importance of status in contemporary Wales.[16] The inclusion of a reference to Merlin is also an allusion to legendary history, and thus confirms the antiquity of the noble lineage. The matter of Britain was at the heart of this passage: it referred to the origins of Britain and was a reflection of the division of Britain at the foundation of the kingdom. This specific reference to Merlin invokes a prophetic link to the past which is obliquely therefore Gerald's own ancestry, and Gerald here stresses the ties of ancestry and lordship which framed his Anglo-Norman and Welsh connections and which were fundamental to his conception of the place of his lineage. These references bolstered the status of Gerald's ancestors and relatives within his version of Welsh history. Mixed-race parentage therefore gave strength to Robert fitz Stephen, and of course Gerald had the same mixed heritage. The linkage made to the ancient race of Britain serves as a subtle reminder that Anglo-Normans were relatively recent settlers in Wales. Gerald therefore reflects the fact that writers in and about Wales had a legitimate and different view of the trajectory of the history of Wales.[17] More than this, however, it suggests the influence of the writings of Geoffrey of Monmouth upon Gerald.[18] The history of Wales as portrayed by Gerald is ancient, dynamic and legitimate, and the reference to Troy, with its underlying message of a civilisation ultimately doomed to defeat due to a war caused by a woman, is associated with a message of hope for deliverance. Gerald suggests the possibility of delivery of the Welsh from their subjugation, and their doom, by reference to prophecy and the association made with the idea of deliverance for the Britons, by which he means the Welsh, the descendants of the ancient Britons. It is a mixed-race knight who would prove decisive. Davies pointed out that contemporary texts defined that the 'innate freeman' was a man of 'untainted noble Welsh stock on both his father's and mother's side'. Gerald's message is thus that a mixed-race family, or his family in particular, were fundamental to the working out of Merlin's prophecy: it thus legitimated the position of his mixed parentage because his twin ancestral links were key to the destiny of Ireland. Within his history Nest was portrayed as the key binding link between significant related families in Wales and Ireland in the 1170s and 1180s. This of course confirms the importance that lineage had for Gerald and in contemporary Welsh and Anglo-Norman society.[19] It also suggests, as Robert Bartlett has pointed out, that although biological descent was one element used by writers to construct race, this in turn was one component of a national consciousness.[20] Given this, Gerald carefully deploys his family connections within the text and in so doing presents an image of the strain that the dual lineage presents for Robert fitz Stephen, who leaves Wales to avoid tarnishing his reputation, shaming his people through 'accusations of disloyalty'. Yet Gerald presents links between his family and legendary history and related it to the fulfilment of an ancient prophecy, and Nest was at the centre of the ancestral web which facilitated the trajectory of that history. Nest was important as a binding link, and the connection through prophecy to the breaking of bonds with Ireland is a way of linking the Geraldines with the potent force of prophecy. Gerald genders his view of the dynamic processes of conquest and change with the implicit suggestion that bonds were made and broken by a *knight* through interactions in Ireland.

The reference to prophecy conveys the legitimacy of his relatives' actions in Ireland. Their role was foreordained. Yet legitimacy is a key theme within his writings on Ireland and Wales. For example, Gerald reminds his readers that he was legitimately born and descended lawfully from great families. In his discussion of himself in his *Autobiography* he states that he 'was the youngest of four brothers, lawfully born of the same womb'.[21] This comment serves to emphasise his lawful birth from his mother Angharad. It confirms that by the early thirteenth century there was still a fluidity in the way that families understood their links with the past. It suggests that male patrilineal primogeniture had yet to predominate over broader kinship alliances in late-twelfth- and early thirteenth-century Wales.[22] For Gerald, matrilineal connections were the most obvious way of making sense of the network of family relationships: a kin network which had Nest at its core. This confirms the importance of R. R. Davies's view that, in contemporary Wales, status was determined by noble ancestry not personal wealth or income.[23]

Although without doubt noble ancestry was pivotal in determining social status, land and its acquisition through conquest were also significant. It was the acquisition of land in Ireland which gave Gerald's relatives prestige beyond their traditional territories in south-west Wales. In this connection Nest becomes even more important in defining identity for Gerald. Nest was the lynchpin of his family's, and thus Gerald's, status. She forms the central figure in a rebuttal by Gerald of the claims of his uncle, Rhys ap Gruffudd, 'prince' of south Wales, that the Geraldines were significant 'only in a corner of Wales'. Gerald's long rebuttal focuses on his family's achievements in Ireland, through an explanation of the lordships which Nest's children and grandchildren held. His detailed explanation suggests that the accusations that his family merely had local significance clearly stung Gerald. The acquisition of territory is key to his argument and in describing this he listed the lands held by Nest's male descendants, thereby demonstrating the extent of landholdings and influence of the family. This of course shows that the acquisition of land was important and gave prestige and that success in war and conquest was key. He also details the marriages made by his aunt and his mother, Gwladus and Angharad. Yet the dominant theme is the connection with Nest: 'Since then the offspring of Nest have held some seven cantrefs of Wales . . . it cannot be said that the offspring of Nest are not to be found save in a corner of Pembroke. But it can be most truly said that the sons of Gruffudd seem not to be found anywhere outside a small portion of South Wales.'[24] Gerald had great pride in the achievements of the 'Geraldines', as his male relatives who conquered Ireland came to be known. In an eloquent appraisal he asks, 'Who are the men who penetrate the enemy's innermost strongholds? The FitzGeralds. Who are the men who protect their native land? The FitzGeralds. Who are the men the enemy fear? The FitzGeralds. Who are the men whom envy denigrates? The FitzGeralds.'[25] This latter reference serves to remind the reader of the difficulties faced by his kinsmen in their military campaigns. The important tie which binds the family is descent through Nest, and this is linked with the acquisition and conquest of land which is key to their contemporary significance. Gerald thus stresses the antiquity of his family's lineage but also their contemporary political significance. Gerald's use of the term 'Geraldines' to explain the network of kin-association shows that as a group they worked together to effect group advantage. In this they are representative of the contemporary ideal of what Crouch termed 'cosinage' or 'parage', or the mutual benefits of lineage-based group cohesion.[26] Yet here it is female descent (and often illegitimate descent) which constructs and legitimises that group cohesion.

Scholars are agreed that kinship was pivotal in twelfth-century Wales, and Gerald's writings on Nest and his kinship networks confirm the importance of kin in the maintenance of identity and family memory. Such a view has been called 'clannish',[27] yet what is significant here is the construction of such an identity through a maternal ancestor. Thus Gerald was proud of the achievements of his kin, and it is female descent through kindred to Nest that is the key focal point for this construction of family identity. This is important because Gerald, writing at the end of the twelfth century, had a perception that female descent was significant to the creation of family memory. As David Crouch suggests, families were not dominated by the idea of patrilineal primogeniture: indeed, inheritance structures were more fluid, families continued to make provision for sons and daughters, and primogeniture was only dominant by the thirteenth century.[28]

This example of the Geraldines serves to suggest that, in Wales at least, kin networks which recognised female descent were still significant in the construction of family memory. The kindred links were used to form patterns of association which were lived political realities. Gerald's view of the familial nature of the Geraldines' conquest of Ireland stems from this web of political interaction which sprang from a kin network that had practical and real political consequences. Even more interestingly, it is possible that the fitz Geralds of Wales were related to the fitz Geralds of Essex. Both families had a tradition of royal service as constables, and indeed high-status women, including Adeliza the widow of Henry I, may well have assisted the family's rise in political fortunes.[29] David Crouch noted the way that prominent families, such as the Clare family and the Giffard family, worked within the socio-political networks of the twelfth century for mutual protection and advancement. He suggests that the idea of parage, that is, of horizontal ideas of family ties based on the present, could have a 'cash value in that families would work to secure advantage for other family members in, for example, preferments or positions of power, such as ecclesiastical office'.[30] Gerald's portrayal of the Geraldines suggests that family identity took account of broader perceptions of kinship which were not solely based upon patrilineal primogeniture. If anything he seems to have deliberately downplayed the legitimate descent represented by the de Barris, who remain consequently obscure.[31] Gerald's construction of his family identity with its awareness of mixed racial heritage, and thus ethnicity, added a further, integral element in the construction of family memory. Gerald's roots lay in Deheubarth, and his portrayal of his homeland reveals an image of a dynamic, frontier society which was multiracial and multicultural.[32] Yet his Welsh heritage was used by his enemies to attack him and he was denied the bishopric of St David's on account of his Welsh ancestry.[33]

In order to put the portrayal of Nest into a sharper analytical context for what it can reveal about Gerald's attitude towards her, it is worthwhile considering his view of women more generally. Gerald draws on contemporary anti-female stereotypes.[34] Yet the depictions are more complex and are carefully deployed within his writings. Gerald portrays noblewomen in his writings in an array of contexts and situations as the wives, mothers and sisters of powerful political men whose marriages create and maintain political alliances. Gerald therefore deploys stock portrayals of women and marriage: marriages feature in Gerald as an integral part of the political and military processes by which the Anglo-Normans imposed control over Ireland. Although women as a social category are condemned, social status nevertheless impacts on the way that women are portrayed and this presents a dichotomy in those portrayals. However, it is significant that the marriage of Raymond le Gros to Basilia, the sister of Earl Richard Strongbow, is portrayed as a love match, a match which nevertheless neatly fulfilled the expectations of reward that a knight might require in service to a lord. Gerald, in this case, links military adventures with romance. Gerald tells us that Raymond was urged by letter to go to Ireland by Strongbow because Strongbow was 'in dire straits' as a result of the siege of Waterford. In his letter to Raymond the earl promised that he would give him his sister in marriage on his immediate arrival in Waterford. Gerald continues that when Raymond received the letter he was 'fired with a passionate desire to enjoy the embrace of a woman so noble and so desired by him, and was eager to test his powers and assist his lord at a time when he was in dire need'. This subtle reference to lordship is written in chivalric terms by the deployment of motifs such as the inspiration of love, the stress on the nobility of Strongbow's daughter and Raymond's aid given to his lord. Raymond armed his men, took fifteen ships to Waterford and defeated the rebellious townspeople. After this, Raymond would not leave Wexford until the marriage was secured: he ensured that messengers were sent to Dublin in great haste to fetch Basilia. The marriage was 'duly solemnized, and as is usual with weddings, a whole day had been spent in feasting and a night in enjoying the delights of the bridal bed, when news came that Ruadri [Roderic] of Connaught, having completely devastated Meath' and had taken Dublin. Raymond 'not in the least slowed down by the effects of either wine or love' mustered troops and marched to defeat his enemy.[35] Later Basilia, in a fraught political context, acted quickly to support her husband. Gerald states that she sent a coded letter to Raymond to warn him of the death of her brother, Earl Richard Strongbow, who had perhaps been a thorn in her side. Gerald tells us that a messenger arrived for Raymond 'with all haste' from Dublin with a letter from his wife Basilia. 'He did not however know its contents. The letter was read to Raymond in secret by a cleric of his own retinue.' '"His wife Basilia desires for her most loving lord and husband Raymond the same health and happiness as for herself. Dearest, be it known to you, my true and loving husband, that that large molar tooth, which caused me so much pain, has now fallen out. So I beg of you, if you have any thought for your own future safety or mine, return quickly and without delay."' Raymond left Limerick having evacuated and handed over the city to Domnall (Duvenald) prince of Thumond. He told only a few of his most trusted retainers about the death of Strongbow and went to Dublin. Strongbow was buried only after Raymond arrived.[36] The secrecy and urgency of this letter is apparent, and it is clear that Basilia acted quickly to inform Raymond of the potential political crisis and Gerald indicates that the situation was grave since the earl had died earlier but that the news of his death had been kept secret until Raymond had returned with his garrison. She wrote in code, suggestive of pre-designed methods devised to communicate, and she was clearly relied upon by Raymond who responded immediately to her news. Her actions suggest political acumen, and the description shows that Gerald of Wales was aware that powerful women could take decisive action in the political sphere. Gerald's portrayal of high-status women is, therefore, complex and dependant on context. The coded letter tells us that the situation in Limerick was precarious: the death of Strongbow was enough for Raymond to evacuate. It also suggests that Basilia was an important source of information and her careful arrangements concerning the 'secret' intelligence suggest the care she took and the difficult context in which she worked since she ensured that the letter would not fall into the wrong hands. Gerald's portrayal of the marriage as a love match may well be genuine.

This is, of course, Gerald's interpretation, but nevertheless indicative that Gerald here portrays a positive view of marriage: in this case, the marriage works as a successful partnership. These themes will be addressed more fully later; it is the significance of the political marriage which matters here. Gerald describes the political nature of marriages in a short chapter which demonstrates that marriage and territorial acquisition made political alliances within lordship.[37] The marriage between Basilia and Raymond is portrayed as a political alliance but is given the gloss of a long-desired love match. Gerald devotes a short chapter to the subject of political marriage and his chosen title, 'Intermarriages among the families from Wales and territorial grants', makes explicit the links between marriage and the land transfer within the high political elite. For Gerald the significance of these alliances lies in the way that marriage serves as a mechanism through which rivalries for patronage and power were linked. For example, Raymond's rival for power, Hervey, is portrayed as seeking a marital alliance in order to increase his power through the family connections of his potential spouse. Intermarriage between the high-elites as a political alliance is common in contemporary society, and Gerald explains the political context of the marriage of Aife (Eva), daughter of Diarmait 'prince of Leinster', following the capture of Waterford, since the marriage was 'solemnized, according to, and in confirmation of, the treaty made'.[38]

The marriage agreement was part of a political process, and historians have long accepted the political role of marriage. Yet Gerald genders the role of women in his portrayal of the conquest of Ireland and this interacts with his ideas about ethnicity and his justification of the conquest. This can be seen in his portrayal of the abduction of a high-status woman, and for Gerald the complicity of the woman was key to understanding her role as a cause of war between nations. His vehicle for these views concerns the abduction of the wife of a king. The narrative offers an insight into Gerald's view of abduction, and its consequences, but of course this is complicated by the Irish setting and therefore any analysis must take account of Gerald's broader ethnic biases and misogyny in general.[39] Gerald does not, by contrast, mention the abduction of his maternal grandmother. His invective had been provoked by the story of the downfall of Diarmait Mac Murchada, prince of Leinster, who in 1152 abducted Derbforgaill, the wife of his rival, Tigernán Ua Ruairc. He did this, says Gerald, in revenge for some earlier insults and because he had 'long been burning with love for' her. After the abduction he took her to his castle at Ferns. Gerald tells us that the woman colluded in this and that circumstances favoured them: Diarmait had taken 'advantage of her husband's absence. No doubt', says Gerald, 'she was abducted because she wanted to be.' Gerald adds, 'woman is always a fickle and inconstant creature': she arranged that 'she should become the kidnapper's prize'.[40] Derbforgaill was the daughter of Murchad Ua Máelsechlainn, king of Meath, and it is likely that the abduction was an attempt by Diarmait to gain an influence in this territory; certainly after 1169 when he was in a position to challenge for the high-kingship of Ireland Diarmait made significant incursions into Meath.[41]

The abduction precipitated cataclysmic political reconfigurations in the long term: the retribution and war in Ireland resulted in the conquest of Irish territory by the Normans with long-lasting results. As a result of the disgrace that the abduction of his wife caused him, the husband, King Tigernán Ua Ruairc of Meath, gathered his forces and in revenge caused Diarmait to flee Ireland when his men turned on him. In exile Diarmait sought the help of Henry II. Henry promised to help but the aid promised failed to materialize. Diarmait then met with Richard fitz Gilbert de Clare, known as Strongbow, and offered him his daughter in marriage in return for his help in restoring Diarmait to his kingdom. Thus in 1170 Richard fitz Gilbert left Wales for Ireland as the ally of Diarmait. Strongbow and his forces thus began the Norman assault on Ireland which historians have long argued has proved to be of fundamental importance for the trajectory of Irish history. Revisionists such as Michael Richter have sought to place the political changes in Ireland in a broader context which stresses the continued importance of Hiberno-Scandinavian connections, and a European perspective of conquest and change.[42] As such this offers us an interesting perspective and raises the intriguing question of whether the *Song of Dermot and the Earl*, recently re-edited under the name *The Deeds of the Normans in Ireland*, and Gerald's *Expugnatio Hibernica* were written to stress the importance of the Anglo-Norman and Welsh connections. Both authors were aware that the Scandinavian involvement in Ireland was still significant. Certainly, as Seán Duffy has shown, the Anglo-Norman incursion into Ireland should be seen in the context of ongoing and long-standing connections between Wales and Ireland.[43] Gerald, of course, wrote to stress the importance of his family in the conquest of Ireland and, in order to justify the conquest, Gerald resorts to racial stereotyping and suggests that the conquest was needed because the conquerors would reform the corrupt Irish Church.[44]

Strongbow's story is best known from Gerald of Wales's *Expugnatio Hibernica*. Yet the *Song of Dermot* has much to tell us about the process by which the 'Welsh' Normans penetrated and settled parts of Ireland.[45] Both sources are late twelfth-century and neither claim to be eyewitness accounts of the events that they describe. The author of the *Song of Dermot* tells us that he has written his work in accordance with what people say, or what older people say, yet it is likely that the *Song* was written shortly after the events. Historians have contrasted the way that the two works present the story of the conquest of Ireland, for example casting reflections upon the way that ideologies of conquest were constructed by the Normans to justify their actions. Evelyn Mullally, for example, the editor of the most recent version of the *Song*, draws attention to differences between the texts, including genre. Gerald wrote in prose whilst the *Song* is in verse; Gerald used rhetorical and learned devices to inform his prose, but, for Mullally, his skill 'renders him suspect' since he wrote to 'promote the prestige of his Geraldine connections in Ireland'. The author of the *Song*, by contrast, employs no literary devices and thus there is little literary distortion in the text. The text is designed for oral delivery, with, as Mullally argues, 'unsophisticated syntax and meagre vocabulary'. Both Gerald and the *Song* favour the newcomers; the Irish are viewed from the outside. Yet Mullally has suggested that the biggest difference between Gerald and the author of the *Song* 'is the absence of all cultural reference'. She suggests that there are no 'stock measures of comparison such as the wisdom of Solomon' nor any interest whatsoever in the Church: as such the *Song* is 'consistently secular'.[46] We are therefore presented with a secular view of the origins of the Norman conquest of Ireland and thus given a different perspective from that offered by Gerald.

The *Song* states that Diarmait was deceitful, he only pretended to be in love with the woman: 'he made a fair show of loving her but he did not really love her at all ... but only wanted to avenge the great shame which the men of Leth Cuinn had previously inflicted' on him. The *Song* portrays the abduction as a consensual event, Diarmait wooing his object with letters and messengers, Derbforgaill collaborating with him to ensure the success of the abduction, a willing partner. The *Song* is emphatic, 'She would let King Diarmait know from what place he might take her where she would be in private ... where he could take her away without challenge.'[47]

Yet a real point of confluence between the two sources lies in their fundamental agreement that a woman was the cause of all the trouble in Ireland which precipitated Anglo-Norman involvement in Irish affairs. Historians have long been aware that Gerald makes allusions to the wheel of fortune as a literary device, yet he also alludes to the problems caused by women throughout history. As such Gerald genders the trajectory of history itself since the course of history has been fundamentally altered by men's reactions to women. Anti-female Christian bias also infiltrates the *Song*. Mullally suggests that the author of the *Song* 'is unaware of such literary commonplaces', yet the *Song* is uninterested in offering a view of the victim of the abduction beyond emphasising her collusion and the lack of genuine attachment on the part of her abductor. We are told that at one point during Diarmait's flight he stayed at 'the house of Robert Harding according to what people say, the queen his wife was there as well'.[48] The *Song* tells us that Ua Ruairc 'lamented bitterly' the loss of his wife and his fierce resentment fuelled his actions which led to the exile of Diarmait.[49] Gerald tells us that Ua Ruairc was 'stirred to extreme anger' because of the 'disgrace, rather than the loss of his wife'.[50] Interestingly both Gerald and the *Song* utilise the motif of the 'exile and return of the king', a motif which, it has been pointed out, was commonly used in insular romance in the late twelfth century.[51] The motif has been given space to grow in the context of 'exile' from the homeland since the adventurers who shape Ireland's fortunes did so on foreign soil. Yet the 'exile and return of the king' motif is here not fully utilised since when Diarmait returns with an invading force to help him reclaim his inheritance, he is not met by a traditional welcoming party, but by the 'rich and poor, humble and great' who have 'journeyed night and day' to join him to fight for his restitution. The perspective of the authors of both of these texts then is one of the deeds of one's identity-group as makers of the destiny of their own and other nations. Both texts place women at the heart of the cause of the conflicts.

That the abduction of Derbforgaill inaugurated a series of actions which inexorably led to war suggests that Gerald was aware of the function of abduction as a symbol of political disorder as well as, ultimately, social dislocation. As Saunders found through an analysis of the classical examples of Lucretia and Helen of Troy, the abduction of a queen was politically charged: it struck at the heart of a nation.[52] This view of course assumes that a nation had been formed, or at the least assumes an imagined community of nation. The symbolic function of abduction within texts is key to understanding the abduction of Derbforgaill and also the abduction of Nest as portrayed in the *Brut*. Gerald's portrayal of the abduction of Derbforgaill is in marked contrast to his silence on his maternal grandmother. It suggests that Gerald suppressed the narrative in his writings on Wales due to shame or embarrassment, rather than that it was unknown to him, or even that it is a fabrication in the *Brut*. Gerald, in his discussion of Basilia, the wife of Strongbow, and of Derbforgaill portrays the importance of women to the political processes at work in contemporary politics. As Brendan Smith has pointed out, the involvement of women in the conquest of Ireland was more than as chattels to be handed from one man to another in political marriages; women were involved in the political and military processes by which the Anglo-Normans imposed control over Ireland.[53] Gerald's stress on the role of his kin in the conquest of Ireland is rooted in a kin network which centres on Nest. His silence on the abduction of Nest is perhaps indicative of his reluctance to discuss an episode which was politically charged and which cast his grandmother in a less positive role. His view of the principal actors in the abduction episode in Ireland is not positive, which contrasts with his portrayal of Basilia and Strongbow. These examples suggest that his view of women was more complex and nuanced than a simple misogynistic parody.

This complexity was rooted in his distinction between women as a category and women as individuals. His view of his great-aunt, Nest's sister-in-law Gwenllian, the wife of Gruffudd ap Rhys, confirms the link between family and politics, gender and lordship which informs Gerald's writings. Gerald is the only source to note the role of Gwenllian, who led an army to war against the lordship of Kidwelly in 1136 and was killed on the battlefield.[54] The site of the battle at Kidwelly has been known locally as 'Maes Gwenllian' even until relatively recently, which is suggestive of the longevity of her significance in local memory.[55] The political context of the battle is significant since there was a more general threat to the English domination of south Wales as a result of a resurgence of Welsh confidence after the death of Henry I in 1135.[56] The years 1135–36 were critical in the politics of south-west Wales and the March. Norman control of these areas was seriously threatened through an upsurge in rebellion by Welsh and disgruntled Normans.[57] The threats to Norman dominance of south-west Wales in 1136 were significant given the context of the revolts in Gower, Gwent, Brecon and Ceredigion following the death of Henry I. Both Davies and Turvey have argued that J. E. Lloyd's view that there was a 'national revival' in a self-conscious form is an exaggeration of the political hegemony of the revolts.[58] These views suggest that period was critical not only because of the resurgence in native power in Wales but also because the revived political hopes were founded on a vision of the Welsh past and potential future. As such the role of Gwenllian in carrying forward that vision in Gerald's text is symbolically potent.

Gerald of Wales discusses the episode in his *Journey through Wales*, and he pinpoints the precise timing of the attack on Kidwelly: it occurred at a moment when 'her husband, Gruffydd ap Rhys, Prince of South Wales, had gone to North Wales for reinforcements,... the Princess Gwenllian rode forward at the head of an army, like some second Penthesilea, Queen of the Amazons'. Her defeat by Maurice of London, lord of Kidwelly, and Geoffrey the constable of Roger, bishop of Salisbury led to her decapitation: 'Gwenllian herself had her head cut off, and so did many of her followers.' Gerald tells us that she was 'so sure of victory' that she 'had brought her two sons with her'. One was captured, the other killed.[59] The image of a woman leading men to battle is a familiar topos in medieval literature, including that of the twelfth century.[60] Such women were described in texts as having unusual characteristics, and the portrayal of Gwenllian as amazonian and exceptional fits this pattern. The image of Gwenllian in Gerald of Wales is similar in tone to that of Orderic Vitalis who, earlier in the twelfth century, had called Juliana, an illegitimate daughter of Henry I who attacked her father, an 'unlucky amazon'.[61] Gerald thus portrayed Gwenllian within accepted conventions. His account of the violent nature of her death is, however, a portrayal of an exceptional event, although powerful women who took political action are usually portrayed as meeting an ignominious end.[62] Gwenllian's beheading on the battlefield is a uniquely violent portrayal of female leadership in war. In medieval texts wives are often portrayed as supporting their husbands, thus, in this aspect, Gwenllian's actions as wife and mother supporting her husband and sons were a legitimate avenue for the exercise of female power and Gerald drew on this model in his text. It is the *nature* of her action which is unusual, even if the context is explicable. Gwenllian fought against the Anglo-Normans in a proactive campaign. Although therefore the depiction of Gwenllian as a female leader of a war-band is written within an accepted literary convention it may well have inculcated a gendered view of the acceptability of her actions through her catastrophic defeat by the English. Does this portrayal of brutality on the battlefield against a woman within Wales confirm that the conduct of war was less civilised there and that, as Gillingham argued, the Welsh were 'beyond the pale' because they were less civilised than the English?[63] The idea that Wales was not as civilised as England was key in Gerald's writings and was an idea which was articulated in earlier twelfth-century sources.[64] Gerald therefore gives a view which is close to the current English imperialistic views of the barbarity of the Celtic peoples and this serves to provide a justification for the brutal treatment of the Welsh at Kidwelly. He also indirectly commented upon the horror and dangers of war, and his view of the death of Gwenllian is complex, since she was his maternal aunt and died at the hands of Anglo-Normans. Further, whether or not chivalric codes of war were developing or had developed, it is clear in Gerald's view that if women rode to war in early to mid-twelfth-century Wales it was dangerous. Her defeat and the death of her sons function as a symbol of loss and defeat in the text. Gerald states that Gwenllian's husband had travelled to north Wales to seek help, and the context of the joining together of the forces of Powys with those of Gwynedd must have seemed potentially catastrophic for the Normans who had traditionally exploited animosities between different Welsh kingdoms. Gwenllian's actions were disastrous and her example here serves as a warning against female leadership in war.[65]

It is noteworthy that the above story is followed immediately by an anecdote concerning Maurice of London and his wife. A cursory reading could suggest that this was one of Gerald's fanciful 'digressions' which were, according to Gransden, recorded to amuse readers.[66] Gerald begins his account with a fine distinction between the English and Welsh: 'During the reign of Henry I, King of the English, Wales enjoyed a period of peace.'[67] He tells us that Maurice of London possessed an area of forest that was well stocked with game and especially deer and that Maurice was very protective of his animals. 'As always happens, his wife was only too well aware of her husband's foibles.' Gerald relates how the wife tricked her husband through a clever ruse by which she suggested that the deer had been attacking and eating their sheep, and had had 'two stags cut open and then padded their intestines with wool'. Convinced of the guilt of the deer Maurice unleashed his hunting dogs. Gerald characterises Maurice as a 'simple sort of man, but very jealous of his possessions'. In the direct speech reported by Gerald it is noteworthy that Maurice's wife focused on the fact that Maurice had lost control of his deer: 'Your deer do exactly as they wish. Instead of taking their orders from you, they seem to be telling you what to do! They run completely wild.'[68] It is possible to view this as nothing more than a fantastic story designed to amuse, but given the position of this anecdote next to the story concerning Gwenllian, the tale surely has multiple and ambivalent messages. It undermines Maurice of London's credibility, is critical of his possessiveness, and utilises gendered stereotypical images to portray the wife. First, she gives counsel, an accepted wifely role in the middle ages and one often portrayed in medieval literature, yet here her counsel is foolish and wickedly destructive, which results in the savaging of the deer. What does the wife gain from this? The deer after all were valuable creatures both economically and symbolically. Hunting deer was an aristocratic pursuit and thus symbolised exclusivity and social prestige. It is possible, however, that this image relates to the previous tale of Gwenllian in a more subtle, coded way. Deer were related to Diana, the goddess of nature, the huntress in Roman classical mythology, and were associated with innocence. Dogs symbolised loyalty. Are the deer the Welsh, the natural people of Wales who are falsely accused of having attacked the Anglo-Normans, in the form of the sheep, and who were defeated by their supporters the English, Maurice's dogs? Was Gwenllian this innocent with a literary allusion to Diana's role as a huntress? Alternatively this story is laced with epic-tragic meanings. Maurice here has the seeds of his own destruction within himself since his possessiveness of his deer and sheep leads him to destroy the very thing he holds dear, his own possessions. It is also a critique of Maurice of London since, although he was able to defeat a woman on the field of battle, he is portrayed as here unable to outwit his scheming wife. Here the portrayal of the internal dynamic of the marriage is one of conflict and confrontation, deception and foolishness and is indicative of Gerald's generally pejorative view of women.

The story is thus a moralistic lesson. It is well accepted that the medieval intellectual tradition of understanding the Bible, or exegesis, assumed at least four levels of meaning within biblical texts: literal, allegorical, tropological (or moral) and anagogical (or spiritual). This intellectual tradition dominated when Gerald of Wales wrote his *Journey through Wales* and it is possible that any or all of these meanings could be intended in his humorous 'digressions'. In this analysis the above story does merely reflect Gerald's credulity, as Gransden suggests. However, it is also accepted that Gerald wrote to instruct and to moralise: for example, Gransden argues that Gerald wrote to instruct rulers on how Wales and Ireland could be administered.[69] The portrayal could have a deeper didactic purpose, although the messages in this example are ambiguous. The wife is portrayed in a gendered female stereotypical role as a cunning deceiver, a view which is of course reflective of a misogynistic Church view of women generally in medieval society and which stemmed from Eve's role in original sin. Although Maurice of London had participated in the defeat of Gwenllian the 'amazon' he is then portrayed as simplistic and gullible with heavily resonant imagery which worked in multiple ways to evoke ambiguity.

Gerald had a penchant for writing character sketches of powerful men such as Henry II, his sons and other significant secular rulers such as Diarmait, prince of Leinster, or Richard Strongbow.[70] Gerald's descriptions suggest personal knowledge and are remarkable because they convey a real sense of personality as well as physical description: Henry II, he says, had grey bloodshot eyes that flashed in anger, for example.[71] It is noteworthy, however, that there are no character sketches of any women. Indeed, pen portraits of women are rare in contemporary literature.[72] Women feature briefly only in relation to male kin. As such the gender-specific descriptions give us a very real sense of the ideal man and lord. Gerald's relative Robert fitz Stephen is described as courteous, and his pen portraits of Henry II and his sons are laced with Gerald's biases.[73] Indeed, Gerald is sensitive to nuances of gender constructions and sought in his autobiography to confirm his masculinity as a cleric. He describes himself as 'tall and handsome' endowed with 'warlike characteristics of the warlike stock from which he was sprung'.[74] His pen portrait of Baldwin, archbishop of Canterbury, is laced with anti-female rhetoric where his description reveals Baldwin to have an 'honest, venerable face, . . . inclined to be thin rather than corpulent' yet Baldwin's real deficiencies lay with his inability to rule effectively: 'He sustained his people with his staff, instead of castigating them with his stick, acting more like a mother offering her breasts than a father wielding his rod, and he was publicly criticized for his laxness'.[75] Gerald's description uses highly charged evocative language where the image of breast-feeding, or the act of nurturing his flock, is seen as a feminised weakness which made Baldwin unfit for high office: he was better as a monk than an archbishop. By deploying an image of motherliness Gerald undermines Baldwin's masculinity and suggests that this meant Baldwin did not have the masculine ability to impose discipline. The complexities of Gerald's view of masculinity contrast with his references to women as a group, which are usually derogatory, and he draws on quotations from Ecclesiastes and Cicero to support his view. Thus he states, 'It is not to be wondered at if a woman bears malice, for this comes to her naturally,' and citing Cicero he states, 'Women will not hesitate to commit every crime in the calendar simply to satisfy a passing whim'.[76]

Gerald's anti-female biases are more obvious in two *vitae* that he wrote in the 1190s, writings that are therefore contemporaneous with this *Description of Wales* and his *Journey through Wales*. His *History of the Conquest of Ireland* of 1188 expressed similar anti-female views. Indeed his most extreme anti-female opinions surface in his rewritings of hagiographical *vitae*. In the 1190s Gerald reworked the *Life of David*, from the original composed by Rhygyfarch of Llanbadarn, and the *Life of Ethelbert* written by Osbert of Clare. The language used in Gerald's versions of these *vitae* has been termed 'fiercely misogynistic' and full of 'antisexual rhetoric'.[77] Gerald's rewritings in these instances certainly reinforced views of women which were hostile and laced with gendered ideals of women as sexual temptresses, but were also related to complex issues of genre. His more extreme views were articulated in the above saints' lives which he had composed at the express wishes of the monks of the canons of Hereford and St David's. His intended audience was thus male clerics who one could suppose would be sympathetic to his more rabid views. It is intriguing then, and possible, that Gerald wrote an image of women which suited the biases of his patrons within the hagiographic genre, a genre which had a certain fixed and unchanging form and function, yet which could also be reworked to suit contemporary norms, literary styles and political contexts.[78]

His misogynistic views on women as a social group are less extreme in his *Journey through Wales* and his *Description of Wales*. The second edition of his *Description of Wales*, which presented a less harsh view of women, was dedicated to Hugh of Lincoln. In the *vita* written as part of a campaign to have Hugh canonised, the portrayal of women is complex, sympathetic almost, but of course within a didactic framework dictated by the conventions of genre. For example, St Hugh is shown to be at ease with women in the charged ritualistic images of sharing meals with them.[79]

By contrast Gerald's portrayals of sexual double standards appear in his writings on Ireland: the first edition of *Topographica Hibernica*, which was dedicated to Henry II, and the *Expugnatio Hibernica*, the first edition of which was dedicated to Richard, whilst the second edition was dedicated to John.[80] They are intriguing because there are descriptions of sexual deviancy, particularly bestiality, in Ireland. For example, Gerald describes the offspring of a bestial sexual union but saves his worst invective for a woman accused of having sex with a goat, rather than the men of an Irish tribe who are alleged to be addicted to the practice of having sex with cows.[81] His portrayal of a woman who is alleged to have had regular intercourse with a goat is followed by the same allegation of a woman seducing a lion. Both are fantastical, indeed voyeuristic and laced with anti-female bias, and employ the motif of woman as sexual temptress. According to Gerald, citing Old Testament justification, the latter woman and the lion were justly killed for their abominations.[82] He has pity for offspring of these alleged bestial sexual unions and, for example, relates that the killing of a half-man half-ox was done in secret because of the mockery made of the Irish by the Anglo-Normans, not because the creature deserved it.[83] Such notions of ethnic superiority in the sphere of sexual relations were a potent site for the expression of bigotry. John Gillingham has argued that 'right-thinking' English clerics in the twelfth century regarded Irish marriage customs as both 'polygamous and incestuous'.[84] This suggests ignorance or disdain for Irish secular law which strictly regulated marriage.[85] It may also suggest unease with differing marriage customs and perhaps a lack of sympathy for Gaelic traditions which tolerated concubinage and trial marriage and gave women some rights to control property they brought to the marriage.[86] In early modern England, it has been suggested that stories of sexual deviancy denote a society in discord, and that such deviancy reveals ideas about those at the margins of society, and the meanings of such stories to contemporaries remain elusive.[87] Such stories may also represent Gerald's unease with the material world,[88] or perhaps his own anxiety at his ancestral hybridity given his Anglo-Norman and Welsh origins.[89] It is significant that many of Gerald's descriptions of bestial sexual activity are located in Ireland and thus Gerald's views of the Irish stem from his entrenched anti-female bias which interacted with ideas about the sexual degeneracy of the Irish, the race considered to be at the margins of civilisation. These views stemmed from his anti-Irish sentiment and they were thus also reflective of more widely held contemporary biases against the Irish. This served to portray the Irish as an ethnic group who were sexually degenerate and is of course related to a justification of their defeat at the hands of his kinsmen. It is this which should be read here rather than a general judgement against all women, and yet it is women who are portrayed in a worse light than Irish men, since gender-bias underpinned his writings and this interacted with his anti-Irish stance. His writings on Ireland were dedicated to male secular rulers in whose reigns the conquest of Ireland was begun and continued. Thus distorted fantastical stories occur in works which in part served to treat the Irish with contempt and thereby to justify the ongoing process of conquest and colonisation. Gendered ideas about sexuality and barbarity were therefore part of this justification.

Such views should be contrasted with his portrayal of the young daughters of an ancient Briton, Brychan, who were all dedicated to a life of sanctity and ended their lives happily. This positive image of girls, that is, girls who are as yet non-sexual, appears in a description of a custom of a church where both men and women join in a ritual in which they seem to be involved in a dance which leads to a trance-like state. This ritualistic behaviour is conducted under the auspices of a Christian ceremony. Here Gerald makes no distinctions between the behaviour of men and women.[90] This different image of women is explicable in terms of religion and ethnicity. The story is of course didactic, the rite is Christian, the girls are dedicated to God, and they are ancient Britons, the ancestors of the Welsh.

Gerald's view of women is rooted in complex views of women which drew on some contemporary stereotypes. Yet his anti-feminist views were tailored for his readership. It is apparent that in his writings on Wales his views on social class, ethnicity and gender interacted to produce less rabidly anti-feminine views than those expressed in his hagiographic works, and less monstrous than the works on Ireland which depicted species cross-breeding. It might be argued that this reflected tensions in Gerald's identity as a member of a Marcher family who was also a reforming ecclesiastic. Genre here interacted with gender to produce a more savage view of women than those in which Nest appears. Such a context matters because, although the mentions of Nest are sparse, they appear in those works where a less extreme misogynistic view of women is portrayed. The balance must surely be prompted by the personal connection to his grandmother Nest, and therefore Gerald's writings on Wales reflect a complex set of views where social status and family connection overrode his clerical distrust of women to produce a less destructive view of women as a social category subject to gendered views grounded in preconceived biases based on sexual proclivity. Social status and kin networks were vital elements in the definition of personal identity. Such complexities created tangible webs of relationships, and thus Gerald made sense of these within terms that reflect his understanding of society and its rhythms of power. These complex views are important because the numerous offspring of Nest who conquered Ireland and took active roles in the political life of twelfth-century Wales were Gerald's kin. Thus, his ethno-centric portrayals of sexual deviancy served to justify the actions of his kin. The interests of his kin, even with women at the centre of the kin network, are a more powerful influence on Gerald than the negative clerical gender-stereotyping prevalent in his work.

The interest of kin was of central importance to Gerald and his pride in his kin is a well-established trait of his works. For example, in his *Journey through Wales* he states that 'Two great noblemen were sent to the island by the King, Henry son of king Henry I and uncle of Henry II, the child of Nest, the nobly born daughter of Rhys ap Tewdwr, Prince of Dyfed in South Wales.' This was a powerful statement of his connection as kin to both Anglo-Norman and Welsh royalty since Gerald by reference to 'Henry, son of king Henry', his half-uncle, therefore made a kin-connection to Henry I through Nest. Most scholars are agreed that Nest had a son by Henry I although the date of the relationship is a matter of dispute and it is difficult to be sure when the relationship with Henry occurred. It is possible that it happened after her abduction by her cousin in 1109, and possibly before the death of her husband Gerald of Windsor. Judith Green and David Crouch suggest that it is possible that the relationship began during Henry I's campaign against Wales in 1114, whilst Kari Maund argues that it probably occurred before her marriage to Gerald of Windsor and the accession of Henry I in 1100.[91] As Green points out, Henry had many mistresses and children, and although Green argues that there is no particular social status or nationality which predominates, it appears that most of those we know about were drawn from prominent Anglo-Norman landholding families. As Green acknowledges, there may have been more liaisons with women of lower status who do not appear in the historical record.[92] Kathleen Thompson however suggests that Nest may not have had a relationship with Henry I and therefore that the Henry fitz Henry, mentioned above, may not have been Henry I's illegitimate son. Her main evidence for this assertion comes from the *Annales Cambriae* and a reading of the entry relating to Nest's son which states, 'Henry the son of Gerald, as others would wish (*velut alii volunt*) the son of King Henry'.[93] This is enough evidence, Thompson argues, to suggest that a brief liaison may have occurred between Nest and Henry I which was in no sense a relationship which would place Nest in the position of alternative consort and that there is sufficient doubt as to the paternity of Nest's son. David Crouch, however, who has considered the evidence for the *Oxford Dictionary of National Biography* is satisfied with Gerald's interpretation and states that Henry was Henry I's son.

It is worth considering the entry in the *Annales Cambriae* in more detail in order to assess the validity of its critique of the paternity of Nest's son Henry. The *Annales Cambriae* are a group of manuscripts which pre-date the *Brut y Tywysogion* (which is derived from them) and survive in three extant versions known as A, B and C that seem to have a common source which was composed at St David's. The earliest, A, dating from the third quarter of the tenth century, was a source for B, composed at or for the Cistercian Neath Abbey and continued there until the late thirteenth century.[94] The third copy, C, was also produced at St David's.[95] It is the B version which has the interpolation concerning the paternity of Henry fitz Henry, Nest's son.[96] This is more intriguing given that there are few differences between the B and C copies. There is no mention of Henry Nest's son in C, the St David's version; but there is, with this odd qualification, in the Neath version. Thus the interesting question which arises is the question of why, rather than passing over Henry fitz Henry in these events in silence, as the St David's version does, in the Neath version the author goes out of his way to mention Henry fitz Gerald and say some would wish he was the son of Henry I?

Yet the evidence of the *Brut* tradition is that there was unequivocal belief in Henry's paternity.[97] Also, to suggest that Gerald of Wales was either mistaken about the paternity of Henry or that Gerald fabricated a royal connection with the Anglo-Norman royal dynasty would be at odds with Gerald's background. He was proud of his family and kindred connections and their role in conquering Ireland. He also obliquely recognised the place of illegitimacy in his kin networks in his casual stress on his legitimacy. As discussed above, Gerald wrote that he was one of four brothers 'born of the same womb'.[98] The phrase is a clear statement of full brotherhood, and of course Gerald's uncles, Nest's sons by different fathers, may or may not have been legitimate. It also suggests a tacit recognition that sexual liaisons could produce brothers of the same womb by different fathers, or by different mothers of the same father. It is a loaded phrase given the ancestry of the Geraldines and one which implicitly suggests an acknowledgement of illegitimacy and kinship, and therefore suggests that they were powerful forces which shaped the way that Gerald constructed a view about political relationships in the late twelfth and early thirteenth centuries.

The comment in B may be a conscious rebuttal of Gerald of Wales and is best analysed in the context of Gerald's failed bid to become bishop of St David's as his uncle had before him. St David's was important politically to the Anglo-Norman kings and Gerald's family. Three bishops were descended from Nest.[99] His uncle, David, son of Gerald of Windsor and Nest, became bishop of St David's on 14 December 1148 and he was consecrated on 19 December at Canterbury.[100] He assumed a role in the coronation of the young king Henry on 14 June 1170,[101] and thus the political significance of the role can be seen in the fact that David allied himself with the future of the English crown. This is a significant date since it is at the turning point in Henry II's relations with the Welsh and Norman Marcher barons after the conclusion of a six-year period of struggle against the native Welsh.[102] Thus Gerald, who had been associated with his uncle David, sought election to the bishopric: this was unacceptable to Henry II given the conquest of

Ireland by Gerald's relatives, an initiative which had discomfited the king, but Gerald's later bid was a still more serious challenge.

Gerald's second bid for the bishopric, in the face of at least four other candidates, may well have foundered due to the contemporary secular political situation. St David's had long claimed metropolitan and archiepiscopal status. Gerald's attempt finally failed in 1203, leaving victory to Canterbury. Davies argues that it was the political nature of the issue which decided the case against St David's since the English king could not have an alternative ecclesiastical authority because the Church was used as an arm of the English king's domination of Wales. Davies further argues that Gerald of Wales had been 'shrewd enough' to point this out, and the outcome was 'despite Gerald of Wales's torrent of words on this issue'.[103] King John refused to give his assent to the election of Gerald and the pope quashed both elections. This resulted in the election of Geoffrey of Henlow, the prior of Llanthony by Gloucester, who was consecrated on 7 December 1203. Gerald alleged that Geoffrey was the father of Osbert archdeacon of Carmarthen, against whom Gerald claimed the prebendary of Llanrhian.[104] Llanthony by Gloucester is close to the heartland of the lordship of the earl of Gloucester. Mabel fitz Haimon was married to Robert fitz Roy, the first earl of Gloucester, Henry I's eldest illegitimate son. Mabel had inherited her lands from her father in Glamorgan and the West Country and also in Normandy.[105] Earl Robert had built up his lands in Glamorgan, which dispossessed the local Welsh dynasty. This secular domination was confirmed with the foundation of the castle, and ecclesiastical influence was extended through the establishment of the abbey of Neath. There was thus a direct family connection to the abbey. It is possible that the comment concerning the legitimacy of Nest's son Henry originated either at Neath Abbey because of Gloucester's antipathy to half-blood brothers with links to the Welsh dynasty who might compete for royal favour; or at St David's in the context of Gerald's failed bid to become a bishop. Either way, there are good reasons for both versions to be judged to have grounds for bias against Gerald. The derisive comment about Henry, son of Nest, is indicative of the recognition of the importance of links between kin within contemporary society and also of the antagonism that Gerald of Wales, whose two books on Wales had been completed in the early 1190s, could arouse. The tone of the comment tells us more about the snobbery of the insecure author who penned his remark, than guiding us to any overlooked insights into Nest or indeed Gerald.

Gerald is silent on the abduction of his grandmother, which suggests either that he suppressed the story possibly either because of shame given the close kin relationship between Owain and Nest, or that he did not know about it, which hardly seems credible if the abduction had occurred. Ultimately it is hard to see why Gerald does not discuss the abduction. Despite his hostility and general misogyny, Gerald was proud, first and foremost, of his family, and that family connection had Nest at its core. There are few instances of abduction in twelfth-century sources, which is suggestive of the unusual nature of such events. We do, however, have evidence of an abduction in the writings of Gerald's friend Walter Map – a case of abduction and sexual union which was legitimised by marriage and involved a royal response.

Walter Map had a similar career to Gerald: both he and Gerald forged careers for themselves in royal service, and through connections made at court both became clerics and archdeacons. Like Gerald, Map was unsuccessful as a candidate for the bishopric of St David's. Map may well have been part-English, part-Welsh, from a border family living in Hereford-shire. Like Gerald of Wales he may have studied at St Peter's Abbey, Gloucester and he certainly studied at Paris. He eventually entered royal service in the court of Henry II and became an itinerant royal justice. His work is significant because, although it is not principally historical in focus, it allows the historian a view of contemporary attitudes and developments in historical and literary techniques. For our purposes Map is a useful source for a rare insight into contemporary attitudes to abduction.

Walter Map wrote *De nugis curialium* (Courtiers' Trifles) in *c.* 1181–82, but it was added to incrementally thereafter.[106] C. N. L Brooke considered *De nugis* to be hard to categorise in terms of both genre and subject, designed to entertain, satirical in part, but also a 'jumble of stories' and thus it should be considered within a context which allows that it 'is a kind of mental furniture or florilegium of a learned and witty twelfth-century clerk'.[107] A. G. Rigg suggested that *De nugis* should be understood as a satirical and anecdotal work and considered on its literary merits. Rigg argues that Map was particularly concerned to satirise the court, marriage and those in holy orders. Rigg suggests that the tract against marriage was apparently popular with Map's contemporaries and is par-ticularly acerbic concerning women, yet 'should not be taken seriously as antifeminism'.[108] Although the tract against marriage may itself be considered for its literary merits, *De nugis*, like Gerald's work, neverthe-less deploys the full range of misogynistic stereotypes within the text as a whole. Gransden agrees with Rigg on the satirical nature of the work and stresses that it was written episodically, heavily influenced by clas-sical literature, and concerned with the 'folly and frailty and the cor-ruption' of the age. Map was also interested in preserving the history of great men, and for Map these are Cnut, Earl Godwin, Henry I and Henry II.[109] Robert Edwards has deconstructed Map's texts within a context which takes account of satire as a genre that was popular in the late twelfth century, and which was deployed in different modes by authors. Thus satire could be utilised in letters and in instructional texts such as those written by John of Salisbury and Gerald of Wales, but according to Edwards, Map was primarily concerned with authorship rather than moral correction. Edwards also suggests that although satirical in part, Map's writings have a broad range. It is this broad range which has led scholars to have conflicting views concerning Map's intention and the significance of his work: as Edwards suggests, Map has been interpreted variously as a modernist writer by Rigg, and yet for other scholars who have deconstructed Map's auto-commentary (the purpose of his writing), Map is interpreted as a postmodernist.[110] In essence the debate concerning Map's significance is a result of the complexity and range of Map's interests, which is made more problematic due to the difficulties of determining his purpose. Taking account of these complexities the following discussion will consider the way that Map portrays a narrative which details an instance of marriage by abduction that occurred in Lydbury, an area near the Welsh March. He tells us that:

> We know that in the time of William the Bastard, a man of distinguished quality who owned Lydbury North, carried off the most beautiful lady from among a company of women who were dancing by night, wedded her and begot a son by her. The king hearing of the wonder of her beauty and of her abduction, was amazed, and had her brought before him at the council in London, and when she had acknowledged the truth of the story, sent her home again.[111]

This late-twelfth-century narrative of an abduction tale reveals an insight into late-twelfth-century attitudes to such events and also conceptions of how this was viewed in the past. This is important because Map is here giving an account of an abduction which is relatively close to that of Nest in 1109. Map, given his noted satirical and bitter responses to marriage noted above, is surprisingly non-judgemental here. He merely notes that the woman was beautiful, married her abductor and subsequently had a child. These are all tropes which appear in the Nest tale. Further, Map suggests that the Lydbury abduction triggered a royal response since William I was 'amazed' by the story, and conducted some form of enquiry into the events. This involved the appearance of the woman at a royal court. After the woman's testimony confirmed 'the truth' the king 'sent her home'. Map does not specify the location of her 'home' and thus it is unclear whether she was returned to the place from which she was abducted or the place where she had had her son. The narrative shows that the abduction provoked a royal response and the investigation occurred at the royal council in London. It therefore suggests the gravity of the offence since the woman was brought to court to account for the veracity of the story. We are thus pointedly shown that abduction was taken very seriously by the royal court and led to royal intervention. Less explicable and more intriguing is the reference to the site of abduction as a night raid on a company of women who were dancing by night. Map does not elaborate further. Thus it is arguable that abduction was viewed as a serious offence, which here invited royal scrutiny, but Map makes no more of the episode, and it serves as a diversionary tale in his work. It is a unique portrayal and suggests the unusual nature of the events. It suggests that the events were of interest to public order and provoked a royal response. This latter aspect in some ways is similar to the Nest abduction and places an emphasis on lordship as a key element in ensuring social harmony. There is no sense within Map's portrayal of censure; it is rather an anecdote which intrigues Map and is historical in focus. Overall, like Gerald, Map utilised misogynistic stereotypes within a broader narrative privileging male action and events.

Similarly, the portrayal of women within the writings of Gerald of Wales is therefore rooted in contemporary stereotypes and drew upon literary conventions which fundamentally inform the organisation and content of his writings. It is his maternal grandmother Nest who is central in his construction of a family identity, portrayed as rooted in military success and its ancestry. Gerald's general anti-female biases are obvious within his writings and as such draw on identities which are about women as a category of analysis, rather than as individuals who are observed. This is in direct contrast to his portrayals of his male relatives, evidenced in the rich, complex pen portraits which give us models of masculinity and contemporary ideals of male nobility. This of course suggests a gendered concept of political society. Yet his silence on Nest's pivotal role in the abduction of 1109 stifled any debate about the legitimacy of the Geraldines as a cohesive force and their loyalties since Nest's abduction is a narrative which demonstrated that Nest had conflicted loyalties. His cogent attacks on the morality of the Welsh, discussed elsewhere,[112] by contrast, reveal inherent contradictions in his views. He is at once both proud of his noble Welsh heritage, but condemns 'Welsh' customs such as incestuous marriage. It may well be it is this that explains his silence on the abduction tale. He records his kin network, but where the *Brut* acknowledges Owain's cousinship to Nest,

Gerald suppresses this because of his strongly held views on incest. His views are complex and as such reflect the complexity of contemporary society, yet also the mutability of his views which could, in the case of women, be informed by his views on ethnicity and social status. It is thus possible that he viewed the abduction of his maternal grandmother with a deep and reserved ambivalence, and thus on the matter he remained, for the historian, frustratingly silent. This may be related to his knowledge that his grandmother is an example of the conflicted nature of family loyalties. Her abduction from her Anglo-Norman marriage into a relationship with Owain ap Cadwgan of Powys was symbolic of fluctuating political loyalties, and perhaps this element of flexibility in relationships was best suppressed by Gerald who wrote to inform posterity about the importance of his family as a way of confirming his own status and social position. Nest's position as the daughter of the last native ruler of Deheubarth and her role as an ancestral figure was key in his view of his family. The elements of romance in the abduction tale portrayed in the *Brut y Tywysogion*, such as the passion of Owain for Nest and the departure of Gerald of Windsor leaving the scene of attack through the privy, generate an ambiguous portrayal since the 'romance' elements mitigate against the threat of, or actual, rape which occurred. This discourse of power in south-west Wales in the *Brutiau* thus turns on the political and symbolic aspects of Nest's marriage, whereas for Gerald it is Nest's role in procreation and thus lineage which is significant. The abduction narrative in the *Brut* serves to confirm the importance of women not just as pawns to be used by powerful men, but their centrality and ability to participate in subversion of the political order by their choices. It genders such portrayals by recourse to stereotypical and romance motifs which are obliquely deployed: thus Nest is the passive female who, enclosed in a castle, waits for her 'rescuer', a young Welsh hothead,[113] and uses her voice to persuade her husband to leave, whilst passively thereby accepting her fate. The theme of political subversion of women is evident in the writings of Gerald on Ireland and central to the *Song of Dermot and the Earl*. Such texts are concerned with the centrality of individual choice to the conflict between the Anglo-Normans and native dynasties and placed sexual politics and gender norms as central causative elements in narratives of conquest.

Notes

1 Gerald of Wales, 'Expugnatio Hibernica', in *Giraldi Cambrensis Opera*, vol. 5: *Topographia Hibernica, et Expugnatio Hibernica*, ed. James F. Dimock (Rolls Series,

21(5); London: Longman, Green, Reader, and Dyer, 1867), Book I, ch. I, pp. 225–6 (Gerald of Wales, *Expugnatio Hibernica: The Conquest of Ireland*, ed. A. B. Scott and F. X. Martin (Dublin: Royal Irish Academy, 1978), pp. 24–5).

2 Derbforgaill, daughter of Muchand Ua Máelechlainn, king of Meath. It took place in 1152. See Gerald of Wales, *Expugnatio Hibernica*, ed. Scott and Martin, p. 286, note 5.

3 Gerald of Wales, 'Expugnatio Hibernica', Book I, ch. I, pp. 225–6 (Gerald of Wales, *Expugnatio Hibernica*, ed. Scott and Martin, pp. 24–5).

4 Robert Bartlett, 'Rewriting saints' lives: the case of Gerald of Wales', *Speculum*, 58 (1983), 598–613, at pp. 602–3.

5 Huw Pryce, 'In search of a medieval society: Deheubarth in the writings of Gerald of Wales', *WHR*, 13 (1987), 265–81, at p. 280.

6 Antonia Gransden, *Historical Writing in England c. 550 to c. 1307* (London: Routledge and Kegan Paul, 1974), p. 245.

7 Robert Bartlett, 'Gerald of Wales [Giraldus Cambrensis, Gerald de Barry] (c.1146–1220x23), author and ecclesiastic', *ODNB*. For Gerald more generally, see *idem, Gerald of Wales, 1146–1223* (Oxford: Clarendon Press, 1982); Brynley Roberts, *Gerald of Wales* (Cardiff: University of Wales Press on behalf of the Welsh Arts Council, 1982); M. Richter, 'Gerald of Wales: a reassessment on the 750th anniversary of his death', *Traditio*, 29 (1973), 379–90; D. Walker, 'Gerald of Wales', *Brycheiniog*, 18 (1978–9), 60–70; M. Richter, *Giraldus Cambrensis: The Growth of the Welsh Nation* (rev. edn, Aberystwyth: National Library of Wales, 1976).

8 Gransden, *Historical Writing*, p. 245; Bartlett, 'Gerald of Wales'; see also Bartlett, *Gerald of Wales*, p. 6.

9 'Itinerarium Kambriæ', in *Giraldi Cambrensis Opera*, vol. 6: *Itinerarium Kambriæ et Descriptio Kambriæ*, ed. James F. Dimock (Rolls Series, 21(6); London: Longmans, Green, Reader, and Dyer, 1868), Book I, ch. XII, pp. 90–1: *Nec mora. Giraldus ille, ut altiores in finibus illis sibi suisque radices figeret, Griphini principis Sudwalliæ sororem, cui nomen Nesta, sibi lege maritali copulavit* (Gerald of Wales, *The Journey through Wales: and, The Description of Wales*, ed. Lewis Thorpe (Harmondsworth: Penguin, 1978), p. 149).

10 E. Searle, 'Women and the legitimisation of succession at the Norman conquest', *ANS*, 3 (1981 for 1980), 159–70.

11 'Itinerarium Kambriæ', Book II, ch. I, p. 90 (*Journey through Wales*, ed. Thorpe, pp. 148–9).

12 'Itinerarium Kambriæ', Book II, ch. VII, p. 130 (*Journey through Wales*, ed. Thorpe, p. 189).

13 Gerald of Wales, 'Expugnatio Hibernica', Book I, ch. II, p. 229 (Gerald of Wales, *Expugnatio Hibernica*, ed. Scott and Martin, pp. 28–31).

14 Gerald of Wales, 'Expugnatio Hibernica', Book I, chs II–IV, pp. 228–36 (Gerald of Wales, *Expugnatio Hibernica*, ed. Scott and Martin, pp. 28–39).

15 Gerald of Wales, 'Expugnatio Hibernica', Book I, chs II–III, pp. 229–30 (Gerald of Wales, *Expugnatio Hibernica*, ed. Scott and Martin, pp. 28–31).

16 R. R. Davies, *The Age of Conquest: Wales 1063–1415* (Oxford: Oxford University Press, 1987; new edn 2000), p. 115.

17 Gerald of Wales, 'Expugnatio Hibernica', Book I, ch. III, p. 230 (Gerald of Wales, *Expugnatio Hibernica*, ed. Scott and Martin, pp. 30–1); 'Itinerarium Kambriæ', Book II, ch. VII, p. 130 (*Journey through Wales*, ed. Thorpe, p. 189).

18 Yoko Wada, 'Gerald on Gerald: self-presentation by Giraldus Cambrensis', *ANS*, 20 (1998 for 1997), 223–47, at p. 243; J. C. Crick, 'The British past and the Welsh future: Gerald of Wales, Geoffrey of Monmouth and Arthur of Britain', *Celtica*, 23 (1999), 60–75.

19 Davies, *Age of Conquest*, pp. 115–16.

20 Robert Bartlett, 'Medieval and modern concepts of race and ethnicity', *Journal of Medieval and Early Modern Studies*, 31 (2001), 39–56, at p. 54.

21 Gerald of Wales, *The Autobiography of Giraldus Cambrensis*, ed. H. E. Butler (London: Jonathan Cape, 1937), pp. 35, 79.

22 J. Beverley Smith, 'Dynastic succession in medieval Wales', *BBCS*, 33 (1986), 199–232, at p. 208; D. Simon Evans, *A Mediaeval Prince: The Life of Gruffudd ap Cynan* (Felinfach: Llanerch, 1990), p. 5, note 36.

23 Davies, *Age of Conquest*, p. 115; T. M. Charles-Edwards, *Early Irish and Welsh Kinship* (Oxford: Clarendon Press, 1993), emphasises the importance of matrilineal descent in establishing royal status in relation to Gruffudd ap Cynan. Roger Turvey, *The Welsh Princes: The Native Rulers of Wales, 1063–1283* (Harlow: Longman, 2002), p. 24, argues that kinship determined political allegiance.

24 Wada, 'Gerald on Gerald', p. 236.

25 Gerald of Wales, 'Expugnatio Hibernica', Book II, ch. XV, pp. 334–7 (Gerald of Wales, *Expugnatio Hibernica*, ed. Scott and Martin, pp. 166–73).

26 David Crouch, *The Birth of Nobility: Constructing Aristocracy in England and France 900–1300* (Harlow: Pearson/Longman, 2005), pp. 145–6.

27 N. Vincent, 'Warin and Henry Fitz Gerald, the king's chamberlains: the origins of the FitzGeralds Revisited', *ANS*, 21 (1998), 248–9, 251–2.

28 Crouch, *Birth of Nobility*, pp. 114–15.

29 Vincent, 'Warin and Henry Fitz Gerald', pp. 251–2.

30 Crouch, *Birth of Nobility*, pp. 136, 146.

31 The de Barris seem to have Devon links, for whom see Huw Pryce, 'A cross-border career: Giraldus Cambrensis between Wales and England', in Reinhard Schneider (ed.), *Grenzgänger* (Veröffentlichungen der Kommission für Saarländischen Landesgeschichte und Volksforschung, 33) (Saarbrücken: Kommissionsverlag SDV, 1998), pp. 45–60.

32 Pryce, 'In search of a medieval society', p. 268.

33 Bartlett, *Gerald of Wales*, pp. 3, 15–17.

34 Cf. the views of Pryce and Bartlett noted above at notes 4 and 5.

35 Gerald of Wales, 'Expugnatio Hibernica', Book II, ch. III, pp. 311–13 (Gerald of Wales, *Expugnatio Hibernica*, ed. Scott and Martin, pp. 138–41).

36 Gerald of Wales, 'Expugnatio Hibernica', Book II, ch. XIV, pp. 332–4 (Gerald of Wales, *Expugnatio Hibernica*, ed. Scott and Martin, pp. 164–7).

37 Gerald of Wales, 'Expugnatio Hibernica', Book II, ch. IV, p. 314 (Gerald of Wales, *Expugnatio Hibernica*, ed. Scott and Martin, pp. 142–3).

38 Gerald of Wales, 'Expugnatio Hibernica', Book I, ch. XVI, p. 255 (Gerald of Wales, *Expugnatio Hibernica*, ed. Scott and Martin, pp. 64–7); see also M. T. Flanagan, *Irish Society, Anglo-Norman Settlers, Angevin Kingship: Interactions in Ireland in the Late Twelfth Century* (Oxford: Clarendon Press, 1989), pp. 91–105.

39 Gerald of Wales, 'Expugnatio Hibernica', Book I, ch. I, pp. 225–6 (Gerald of Wales, *Expugnatio Hibernica*, ed. Scott and Martin, pp. 24–5).

40 Gerald of Wales, 'Expugnatio Hiberncia', Book I, ch. I, pp. 225–6 (Gerald of Wales, *Expugnatio Hibernica*, ed. Scott and Martin, pp. 24–5).

41 M. T. Flanagan, 'Mac Murchada, Diarmait (*c.*1110–1171)', *ODNB*; Flanagan, *Irish Society*, pp. 94–5.

42 M. Richter, 'The interpretation of medieval Irish history', *Irish Historical Studies*, 24 (1985), 289–98.

43 Seán Duffy, 'The 1169 invasion as a turning-point in Irish–Welsh relations', in Brendan Smith (ed.), *Britain and Ireland, 900–1300: Insular Responses to Medieval European Change* (Cambridge: Cambridge University Press, 1999), pp. 98–113.

44 Laura Ashe, *Fiction and History in England 1066–1200* (Cambridge: Cambridge University Press, 2007).

45 *The Deeds of the Normans in Ireland: La Geste des Engleis en Yrlande: A New Edition of the Chronicle Formerly Known as The Song of Dermot and the Earl*, ed. Evelyn Mullally (Dublin: Four Courts Press, 2002); see also Bartlett, *Gerald of Wales*, p. 2.

46 *Song*, pp. 32–3.

47 *Song*, p. 54, lines 64–71.

48 *Song*, p. 59, lines 232–8.

49 *Song*, p. 95, lines 100ff.

50 Gerald of Wales, 'Expugnatio Hibernica', Book I, ch. I, pp. 225–6 (Gerald of Wales, *Expugnatio Hibernica*, ed. Scott and Martin, pp. 24–5).

51 Ashe, *Fiction and History*, p. 110; see also Rosalind Field, 'The king over the water: exile and return revisited', in Corinne Saunders (ed.), *Cultural Encounters in the Romance of Medieval England* (Woodbridge and Rochester, NY: D. S. Brewer, 2005), pp. 41–53.

52 Corinne Saunders, *Rape and Ravishment in the Literature of Medieval England* (Cambridge: D. S. Brewer, 2001), p. 183.

53 Brendan Smith, '"I have nothing but through her": women and the conquest of Ireland, 1170–1240', in Christine Meek and Catherine Lawless (eds), *Studies on Medieval and Early Modern Women: Pawns or Players?* (Dublin: Four Courts Press, 2007), pp. 49–55.

54 'Itinerarium Kambriæ', Book I, ch. IX, pp. 78–9 (*Journey through Wales*, ed. Thorpe, pp. 136–7). It has been suggested by Andrew Breeze that Gwenllian was the author of one of the *Four Branches of the Mabinogi*, although this is unlikely: *Medieval Welsh Literature* (Dublin: Four Courts Press, 1997), pp. 75–9. See pp. 26–8 above and below 195.

55 A. G. Prys-Jones, *The Story of Carmarthenshire* (2 vols, Llandybie: Christopher Davies, 1959–72), vol. I: *From Prehistoric Times to the Beginning of the Sixteenth Century*, p. 97.

56 Flanagan, *Irish Society*, p. 140.

57 Davies, *Age of Conquest*, pp. 45–7.

58 Davies, *Age of Conquest*, p. 47; Turvey, *Welsh Princes*, p. 75.

59 'Itinerarium Kambriæ', Book I, ch. IX, p. 79 (*Journey through Wales*, ed. Thorpe, pp. 136–7).

60 J. L. Nelson, 'Gender and genre in women historians of the early middle ages', in J. P. Genet (ed.), *L'Historiographie médiévale en Europe* (Paris: Éditions du CNRS, 1991), p. 150.

61 Susan M. Johns, *Noblewomen, Aristocracy and Power in the Twelfth-Century Anglo-Norman Realm* (Manchester: Manchester University Press, 2003), p. 18.

62 For discussion of the above and other examples, see Johns, *Noblewomen, Aristocracy and Power*.

63 J. Gillingham, *The English in the Twelfth Century: Imperialism, National Identity and Political Values* (Woodbridge: Boydell, 2000), p. xviii.

64 J. Gillingham, 'Civilising the English: the English histories of William of Malmesbury and David Hume', *Historical Research*, 74 (2001), 17–43, at p. 19; see also his 'The travels of Roger of Howden and his views of the Irish, Scots and Welsh', *ANS*, 20 (1998 for 1997), 151–69.

65 For a discussion of the distinctions between women as commanders and as combatants, see Kim Phillips, 'Warriors, Amazons and Isles of Women: medieval travel writing and the construction of Asian femininities', in Cordelia Beattie and Kirsten A. Fenton (eds), *Intersections of Gender, Religion and Ethnicity in the Middle Ages* (Basingstoke: Palgrave Macmillan, 2011), pp. 183–207, at pp. 184–5, who notes that medieval writers became 'increasingly uneasy with the figure of the female warrior'.

66 Gransden, *Historical Writing*, p. 246.

67 'Itinerarium Kambriæ', Book I, ch. IX, p. 79 (*Journey through Wales*, ed. Thorpe, p. 137).

68 'Itinerarium Kambriæ', Book I, ch. IX, pp. 79–80 (*Journey through Wales*, ed. Thorpe, pp. 137–8).

69 Gransden, *Historical Writing*, pp. 245–6.

70 Gerald of Wales, 'Expugnatio Hibernica', Book I, ch. VI, pp. 237–8 (Dermot), ch. XXVII, p. 272 (Richard) (Gerald of Wales, *Expugnatio Hibernica*, ed. Scott and Martin, pp. 40–3, 86–9).

71 Gerald of Wales, 'Expugnatio Hibernica', Book I, ch. XLVI, pp. 301–6 (Gerald of Wales, *Expugnatio Hibernica*, ed. Scott and Martin, pp. 124–33).

72 See Crouch, *Birth of Nobility*, p. 318, for a translated example of a pen-portrait of a woman, that of Agnes, countess of Meulan, who died in 1181.

73 'Topographica Hibernica', in *Giraldi Cambrensis Opera*, vol. 5: *Topographia Hibernica, et Expugnatio Hibernica*, ed. James F. Dimock (Rolls Series, 21(5); London: Longman, Green, Reader, and Dyer, 1867), pp. 193–5 (distinctio iii, cap. xlix).

74 Gerald of Wales, *Autobiography of Giraldus Cambrensis*, p. 104.

75 'Itinerarium Kambriæ', Book II, ch. XIV, pp. 148–9 (*Journey through Wales*, ed. Thorpe, pp. 205–6).

76 'Itinerarium Kambriæ', Book I, ch. II, p. 30 (*Journey through Wales*, ed. Thorpe, p. 90).

77 Bartlett, 'Rewriting saints' lives', pp. 599, 602.

78 See Gransden, *Historical Writing*, pp. 105–7, 310–11; Michael E. Goodich, *Lives and Miracles of the Saints: Studies in Medieval Latin Hagiography* (Aldershot and Burlington: Ashgate/Variorum, 2004); *idem*, 'Biography, 1000–1350', in D. M. Deliyannis (ed.), *Historiography in the Middle Ages* (Leiden: Brill, 2003), pp. 353–85.

79 Susan M. Johns, 'Poetry and prayer: women and the politics of spiritual relationships in the early twelfth century', *European Review of History – Revue européenne d'Histoire*, 8 (2001), 12–14.

80 Gransden, *Historical Writing*, p. 244, notes 211–13.

81 Gerald of Wales, 'Topographica Hibernica', dist. II, ch. XXI, p. 108.

82 Gerald of Wales, 'Topographica Hibernica', dist. II, ch. XXIII, p. 110 (goat); ch. XXIV, p. 111 (lion).

83 Gerald of Wales, 'Topographica Hibernica', dist. II, ch. XXI, pp. 108–9.

84 Gillingham, 'Travels of Roger of Howden', p. 164.

85 Bartlett, *Gerald of Wales*, p. 44.

86 Such different practices continued through the late middle ages; Gillian Kenny asserts that the models of marriage were fundamentally opposed, and this caused conflict throughout the middle ages: Gillian Kenny, 'Anglo-Irish and Gaelic marriage laws and traditions in late medieval Ireland', *JMH*, 32 (2006), 27–42, at pp. 29, 32.

87 David Cressy, *Travesties and Transgressions in Tudor and Stuart England* (Oxford: Oxford University Press, 2000), pp. 4, 26–7.

88 Caroline Walker Bynum, 'Metamorphosis, or Gerald and the werewolf', *Speculum*, 73 (1998), 987–1013, at p. 1000.

89 Bartlett notes the 'hybrid nature' of south-west Wales, *Gerald of Wales*, p. 3; Asa Simon Mittman suggests anxiety in 'The other close at hand: Gerald of Wales and the "Marvels of the West"', in Bettina Bildhauer and Robert Mills (eds), *The Monstrous Middle Ages* (Cardiff: University of Wales Press, 2003), pp. 97–112, at p. 104.

90 'Itinerarium Kambriæ', Book I, ch. II, pp. 31–2 (*Journey through Wales*, ed. Thorpe, pp. 91–2).

91 David B. Crouch, 'Nest (b. before 1092, d. c. 1130), royal mistress', *ODNB*, xl. 441–2; Green, *Henry I*, p. 132; K. L. Maund, *Princess Nest of Wales: Seductress of the English* (Stroud: Tempus, 2007), pp. 8, 115.

92 Green, *Henry I*, p. 27; for other comments concerning Nest, see p. 308.

93 K. Thompson, 'Affairs of state: the illegitimate children of Henry I', *JMH*, 29 (2003), 129–51, at pp. 131–2.

94 B was written on the flyleaves of a Breviate Domesday (National Archives, E 164/1), copied in 1286–1304. K. W. Hughes, 'The Welsh Latin chronicles: *Annales Cambriae* and related texts', *Proceedings of the British Academy*, 59 (1973), 233–58, at p. 253.

95 London, British Library, Cotton Dom. A. 1.

96 *Annales Cambriae*, p. 47.

97 *Brut, Peniarth MS. 20* (1952), p. 60.

98 See above, note 18.

99 Gwyn A. Williams, *When was Wales? A History of the Welsh* (Harmondsworth: Penguin, 1985), p. 69.

100 See M. Richter, 'A new edition of the so-called *Vita Davidis Secundi*', *BBCS*, 22 (1966–68), 245–9, esp. p. 248, for the charge that the election was uncanonical.

101 John Le Neve, *Fasti Ecclesiae Anglicanae IX, 1066–1300: The Welsh Cathedrals*, compiled by M. J. Pearson (London: University of London, School of Advanced Study, Institute of Historical Research, 2003), p. 46.

102 P. Latimer, 'Henry II's campaign against the Welsh in 1165', *WHR*, 14 (1988–89), 523–52, at p. 543.

103 Davies, *Age of Conquest*, p. 191. A later 1210 decision merely confirmed Canterbury's dominance.

104 Le Neve, *Welsh Cathedrals*, pp. 46, 55.

105 Robert was involved in military action in south Wales when his lands in Glamorgan were subject to depredations made by Morgan ab Owain from the east and the sons of Iestyn ap Gwrgant from the west. David Crouch, 'Robert, first earl of Gloucester (b. before 1100, d. 1147), magnate', *ODNB*; see also *idem*, 'Robert, earl of Gloucester, and the daughter of Zelophehad', *JMH*, 11 (1985), 227–43.

106 Walter Map, *De nugis curialium: Courtiers' Trifles*, ed. and trans. M. R. James, rev. C. N. L. Brooke and R. A. B. Mynors (Oxford, 1983); repr. with corrections (Oxford: Clarendon Press, 1994). His work survives in a fourteenth-century copy, and was first published in 1850.

107 C. N. L. Brooke, 'Map, Walter (d. 1209/10), royal clerk, raconteur, and satirist', *ODNB*.

108 A. G. Rigg, *A History of Anglo-Latin Literature 1042–1422* (Cambridge: Cambridge University Press, 1992), pp. 88, 90; see also Juliette Wood, 'Walter Map: the contents and context of *De nugis curialium*', *Transactions of the Honourable Society of Cymmrodorion* (1985), 91–103.

109 Gransden, *Historical Writing*, p. 243.

110 Robert R. Edwards, 'Walter Map: authorship and the space of writing', *New Literary History*, 38 (2007), 273–92, at p. 274.

111 Map, *De nugis curialium*, pp. 348–51.

112 Pryce, 'In search of a medieval society', p. 265, esp. note 3, notes that the debate about Gerald's writings can move beyond a focus on his views of Wales and the Welsh.

113 See Robert S. Babcock, 'Imbeciles and Normans: the ynfydion of Gruffudd ap Rhys reconsidered', *Haskins Society Journal*, 4 (1993 for 1992), 1–9.

3

Charters and contexts: gender, women and power

THIS CHAPTER will consider charter evidence as a guide to women's power in twelfth-century Wales, in order to place the analysis of Nest in a broader analytical framework. Much evidence and scholarship now ascribes considerable influence to royal and aristocratic women in England and other parts of western Europe in the eleventh and twelfth centuries – yet little has been done to date on Wales in this respect. Building on the previous chapter's observations about the portrayal of women within chronicles and the significance of kin structures within the political elite of Wales, this chapter will argue that powerful women of the high elite were involved in Welsh politics during this period, and that internal and external factors were promoting this even further. This was seen in war, domestic policy, and the formation and dissolution of political alliances. The misogynist assumptions of chroniclers and those who recorded legal and administrative forms screen some of this from us, but a close and contextualised reading of this evidence, sensitive to nuances of gender constructions, allows a very detailed picture to be built up. This will be achieved through a close analysis of particular case studies of not only particular documents, but also of specific women, such as Joan, the wife of Llywelyn ap Iorwerth, and will place them in a broader analytic framework. This chapter will begin with a discussion of charter evidence, and will then go on to broaden the discussion of the interactions of high-status women of the elite with the dominant power structures. Such dominant power structures include economic, kindred, political, cultural and legal elements. Charters have much to tell us about the roles of noblewomen in medieval Wales, the ways that they participated in the affairs of their kin, and in political, religious, social, cultural and economic spheres of interest typical of the European aristocratic elite.

Although the evidence is skewed to those Marcher lordships that are relatively well documented and the north Welsh kingdoms, especially Gwynedd, charters nevertheless suggest patterns of activity which could be indicative of patterns of activity in other, less well-recorded parts of Wales, and show that business was recorded in ways similar to charters produced in England and Normandy. Our surviving documentary base is meagre and as such allows only a partial view of political life in medieval Wales. Nevertheless it is worth investigating the roles of powerful women in Wales and the Marches through what charters we have since it facilitates a broader view of the participation of noblewomen in the exercise of power in medieval Wales. Power of course takes many forms: coercive, judicial, moral, economic, social, cultural, ideological, administrative, religious and political. Many of these forms of power were expressed in medieval society through the institution of lordship, which was itself a gendered construct. Charters give a view of the operation of lordship, and even such a partial view given by them of medieval Wales provides evidence of the milieu in which Nest and her contemporaries moved. Charters are of course concerned with the disposition of economic wealth, usually land but also moveable goods, especially money. There is less charter evidence for twelfth-century Wales compared to surviving evidence for *acta* from Scotland and England. The Welsh charters are a relatively neglected source.[1] The understanding of charters has been advanced by scholars working on evidence from St David's and Margam Abbey.[2] Further, the work by Wendy Davies on the Llandaff charters and the publication of *The Acts of Welsh Rulers* by Huw Pryce and his work on their value as a guide to the culture and power of Welsh rulers stand out as seminal contributions.[3] Historians have long been aware of the importance of charters as a source for the history of Wales.[4] There are studies which explore patterns of land tenure, for example,[5] and scholars have considered both the political relationships in the Anglo-Norman frontier and the significance of titles within charters and their political significance.[6] Ceridwen Lloyd-Morgan, exploring the relationship of Welsh women and literacy in the middle ages, utilised charter evidence and focused on Welsh-speaking indigenous women, considering language as a guide to nationality and as a boundary for historical interpretation.[7] Otherwise, however, very little has been done to explore the ways in which charters can be utilised as a source for the history of gender relations or the power of women in Wales.

Further, a view of Wales which only considers 'Welsh-speaking Wales' echoes the partition of Wales into 'Welsh Wales' and 'Marcher Wales' and thus emphasizes difference between them rather than commonalities and interactions. Although the cultural interface between *pura Wallia* and *Marchia Wallie* serves to help clarify and explain commonalities and differences, the analysis of the documentary evidence provides the framework for discussion. This chapter will consider how reading charters with an awareness of gender can illuminate questions about the way that the actions of men and women were constructed.

A charter in the *Book of Llandaff* records that in *c.* 1040 'King Meurig violated Llandaff's sanctuary by seizing Seisyll's wife and wounding one of Bishop Joseph's *familia*; eventually he was pardoned, returned the woman, and returned *Uilla Tref Gulich* . . . to the saints of Llandaff.'[8] A further charter records more detail: 'Caradog ap Rhiwallon, a *comes* of king Meurig, violated sanctuary by seizing Seisyll's wife at the church door while in Meurig's retinue; he sought pardon at Llandaff' and in order to atone for his act made a grant of land 'with king Cadwgan's guarantee'.[9]

These charters are interesting because they provide evidence of the abduction of the wife of a king, and the process whereby the wrongdoing was resolved. Davies suggests that the 'essence' of the charter was probably recorded at or near the time of the transaction.[10] The charter was written into the *Book of Llandaff* in the period 1120–29.[11] Thus the redaction is a near-contemporary document to the abduction of Nest, although it is preserving the memory of much earlier events. However, although the documents are geographically and temporally removed from early twelfth-century Deheubarth, given that they record events in eleventh-century Gwent and Glamorgan, they are nonetheless significant because they provide evidence of the abduction of the wife of a member of the military elite in Wales. The memory of the resolution of the dispute was preserved in the 1120s, a by-product of the purposes of the copyist who recopied and rewrote the charter material that became the *Liber Landavensis*. As such it presents an ecclesiastical view of the events, and the primary focus of the copyist was Llandaff's episcopal rights and privileges.

These rights and privileges were defended in a seven-stage process during which the charters were copied and rewritten into the *Book of Llandaff*. These represent various stages of collection and editing before a final stage of copying and embellishment. Davies calls the *Liber Landavensis* 'a clever work of forgery'.[12] Nevertheless Davies has elegantly shown how vitally important the charters are for the evidence they contain relating to the disputes concerning the episcopal powers and privileges claimed by the bishops of Llandaff in the twelfth century. The context of production is significant since the *Liber Landavensis* was produced in the period when there were disputes between Hereford and

Llandaff, and Llandaff and St David's, during the years 1119 to 1134. This context of production within a framework of conflict and dispute has parallels with the evidence of the abbeys of Westminster and St Albans which, Crick suggests, were rewritten and produced in a context of recurrent crisis.[13] Such a sense of crisis may well explain the context of the production of *Liber Landavensis*. The charters, despite the elements of 'forgery', are significant for the way they present the construction of the memory of the past. The process of selection and redaction points to continuing contemporary relevance of that past in the minds of the scribes who compiled the *Liber Landavensis*. As Bates has pointed out, the term forgery is a difficult one since a charter may do 'no more than couch long-held rights and possessions in language acceptable to contemporaries'.[14] It is such contemporary resonances which render forgeries significant for the historian. Nonetheless, Davies demonstrates that the Llandaff charters contain the kernel of authenticity. Thus the compilers of *Liber Landavensis* made additions to documents where the original documents were inadequate in some measure. This makes the body of material problematic since there are a virtually unknowable number of opportunities for the corruption of the original texts which underlie the final versions as presented in the *Book of Llandaff*. Nevertheless Davies's analysis of the diplomatic suggests that earlier, authentic charters lie behind the charters as presented. Further, this analysis of the diplomatic, especially the Notification and Disposition clauses, and the uniformity of structure with the charters of other Celtic monasteries, leads Davies to suggest that the charters are evidence of a 'Celtic' form of charter.[15] Dauvit Broun however doubted the existence of 'Celtic charters' since there are too many variations in the Narrations and considered the way that the information was transcribed into monastic records is problematic.[16] The Narrations are an interesting feature of these charters because their content is specifically linked to the events they describe. Davies argues that the precise detail within the Narrations, the standard formulae used and the lack of syntactic interpolations suggest that the use of a Narration in a charter became standard in the eleventh century.[17] The Narrations were likely to have been based on earlier versions. All the above suggests that the *Book of Llandaff* contains the memory of events and that the preservation of that memory and its context was significant to the copyists in the twelfth century. Given this, it is likely that the abduction of Seisyll's wife by a *comes* of King Meurig, and the process of resolution of the dispute, are evidence of an authentic sequence of events. The resolution had a three-stage process: first the seeking of pardon, second the return 'of the woman' and return of the land, and finally, a grant of land 'with king Cadwgan's guarantee'. It is this charter by which Caradog ap Rhiwallon made reparation for his violation of sanctuary 'while in Meurig's retinue' which clarifies further details.[18] The inclusion of and stress upon the guarantee made by Cadwgan suggest the importance of bonds of affinity, and the abduction by a member of Cadwgan's retinue caused his involvement in the reparations and surety given when the episode was resolved.

The memory of the abduction of the wife of King Seisyll by Meurig was preserved since the action of abduction was carried out with violence and involved seizure of territory and the wounding of one of the bishop's *familia*. For Llandaff the episode was a violation of the right of sanctuary and therefore an offence against Llandaff. Violation of sanctuary is evidenced in three other charters.[19] Davies points out that violations of Llandaff's privileges were 'usually followed by excommunication, a request for pardon, the summoning of a synod by the bishop, and then the enjoining of penance, often in the form of a grant of land'.[20] Certainly the charter shows that Caradog ap Rhiwallon was pardoned and reparation was made by which the land seized was returned to Llandaff, and as part of this resolution the 'woman' was returned to Seisyll. The abduction of the person and the seizure of the land were thus memorialised as intrinsically linked in a sequence of events which was articulated as a violation of sanctuary. It suggests that the possession of the land and the seizure of the woman were enacted as the same event and constructed as such in the abbey's memory concerning its land. The resolution of the offence occurred when the land was returned to the abbey and the 'woman' to her husband. The narrations of these charters provide a brief view of an abduction and transfer of rights to land in the early eleventh century. Yet this evidence was produced in the context of the construction of memory concerning ecclesiastical right and privilege in charters with a view to contemporary resonance. As such it is the rights and privileges of Llandaff which are the key object of interest for the redactors of the charter; the abduction of the woman, who is not even named, is part of the memory but, since she is not the property of Llandaff, of no interest. Nevertheless the return of her to her husband as part of the resolution process was significant, and the guarantee given by King Cadwgan suggests that that process was enacted in the context of secular lordship, against which the *comes* in his abduction of a wife had certainly offended. In this Llandaff example, the resolution of political dispute required the agreement of all parties concerned. The charters offer a valuable insight into the process of conflict resolution concerning abduction and violation of sanctuary, and show the woman involved as a passive victim of male aggression, an image which conflicts with the rich textual detail concerning Nest offered in the *Brut*. Yet there are similarities in the presentation of events. The anonymised woman in the Llandaff evidence functions as a key to the memory of events and to the offence which was committed against Llandaff's privileges and secular lordship. The parallels to the construction of Nest's abduction and role in the memory of events are striking. She is memorable for her direct action and response, but both events are tied in to political contexts, and both offer a view of abduction as an offence against ideas of lordship, although obviously the political ramifications of Nest's abduction took much longer to resolve. Thus the similarities concern the abuse, or protection, of lordly rights and privileges, which is of course exactly the dynamic behind much charter material. Further, for the historian, the problems of our sources militate against a clear understanding of these abductions, and offer a clerical perspective.

If we turn our attention to what charters can tell us about other aspects of the role and status of women in high medieval Wales, we find the actions of high-status noblewomen in religious benefaction recorded in *acta*. There is, for example, evidence of the participation of a high-status English aristocratic woman who had married into the dynasty of Gwynedd in the transfer of land to an ecclesiastical institution. Emma of Anjou was the illegitimate half-sister of Henry II, the natural daughter of Geoffrey of Anjou. In 1186–94, as the wife of Dafydd ab Owain, prince of north Wales (d. 1203), she acted with her husband together with their son Owain, and consented to the grant by which Stockett (in Ellesmere) was conveyed to Haughmond Abbey.[21] Emma's charter which confirmed this grant was from the same period. The lands relate to her marriage portion.[22] The sealing clause in the cartulary copy suggests that she may have had a personal seal. She also granted further lands to Haughmond in the period 1194–1203, possibly in 1197–98.[23] These charters are significant because they indicate that Emma jointly participated in religious benefaction with her husband and thus performed a public and significant aristocratic role. Husband and wife jointly granted further lands to Haughmond Abbey in 1194–97 or 1198–1203.[24] Yet if we look more closely at the periods in which the above grants were made it becomes clear that the contemporary political context is significant in determining how we should view these charters. Dafydd and 'Dame Emma', as she is called in the *Brut*, had been married in 1174.[25] As has been pointed out, this was an important dynastic marriage.[26] It may well have been a result of Dafydd's loyalty to Henry II in 1173–74 when Henry II faced an uprising from his sons.[27] The address clauses of the charters were statements of identity and of political power. They can be read to analyse how an individual's power was framed, through analysis of the ways that they varied. In turn the fluctuations in the power of individuals and thus the reality of the transient nature of that power in twelfth-century Gwynedd can be explored. In the charter of 1186–94 Dafydd son of (ap) Owain *'princeps Norwallie'* makes the grant *'assensu Emme uxoris mee et Owini heredis mei'* (with the assent of Emma my wife and Owain my heir). In an earlier charter of 1177–87 to Haughmond he is *'David rex'*.[28] Dafydd retained the kingship despite the partition of Gwynedd with his brothers, and his charters show a plurality of titles which were used to express his authority.[29] In Emma's charter confirming Dafydd's 1186–94 grant, which has a sealing clause, the address clause is a clear statement of her status framed in terms of her title first, her kinship by birth second and finally her marriage connections: *'Domina Emma soror Henrici regis, uxor David filii Owini principis'*.[30] She is thus, pre-eminently, identified as 'Lady', and this was the first indication of her status, her relationship as sister to the king of England preceded her identity and position as wife to the prince of north Wales. It is of note that *Brut y Tywysogion* MS 20 states that Joan, wife of Llewelyn ab Iorwerth, was 'lady of Wales' and Llewelyn built a priory for the soul of 'his lady'.[31] After Dafydd lost control of his Welsh lands to Llywelyn ap Iorwerth in 1197, and his brief imprisonment and then ejection from Wales, the charters reflect the loss of status which affected both him and Emma. In the address clause of his charter of 1194–97 or 1198–1203 the charter is given by *'David filius Owini et Emma uxor mea'*. In earlier charters he was called *'David rex filius Owini'*, *'David rex Norwallie'* and *'David filius Owini princeps Norwallie'*.[32] In her later confirmation charter Emma is *'Emma sponsa David filii Owini'*.[33] Both charters have a less strident tone since each opens with a conventional greeting of *'Sciant omnes tam presentes quam futuri'*, whereas in their earlier charters their name and status were given before the greeting clause. Emma and Dafydd's demotion in status to 'distressed gentlefolk'[34] after 1197 explains the change in tone in the charters and reflects the harsh political realities and their loss of office. This confirms that charters have much to tell us about contemporary perceptions of power and its relationship to social and political contexts. The charters were probably drafted by the beneficiary and were sensitive to the social and political realities. It has been noted that there was a certain concordance in the way that charters were framed by Haughmond, which is suggestive of diplomatic practice framed in similar ways to, and hence familiarity with, current Anglo-Norman or Angevin diplomatic practice.[35] The bureaucratic process involved in the creation of the charter articulates broader social and cultural differences. That is, the recorded involvement of Emma in the documentary evidence was related to the documentary provenance and form as well as the cultural expectations of the scribe who constructed the text within a framework which took account of her appropriate role in religious benefaction enacted according to Anglo-Norman/Angevin custom. It was becoming customary for the *acta* of high-status noblewomen to be sealed with their personal seal, and in this respect Emma's charter is reflective of such conventions regarding the security of the document since the cartulary copy includes a sealing clause. This reference to the seal of a high-status woman from the Plantagenet family married into the Welsh political elite is one of the earliest references to female sealing practice by the wife of a Welsh ruler. Certainly in twelfth-century England and northern France the spread of sealing practice among the aristocratic and noble elite would suggest that a woman of such high status would have had a personal seal. Isabella, countess of Gloucester and Mortain, the wife of King John, sealed charters, and counter-sealed *acta* in the period 1187–1214 in favour of Margam Abbey.[36] It was by no means unusual for high-status noblewomen to participate in religious patronage, Margam charters show that within Marcher Wales the processes whereby the transfer of lands to a religious house was recorded utilised routine conventions. There is other evidence to show that a Welsh woman, Gwenllian ferch Morgan ap Caradog, gave lands to Margam Abbey *c.* 1208–*c.* 1217 and she too sealed the charter. Her charter was given in the same period as that of her brothers Lleision and Owain.[37] These charters demonstrate the cultural interactions between Welsh women and a religious house that was founded by Anglo-Normans. In the late 1190s *Thatherch* daughter of *Katherech* sealed a charter by which she quit-claimed land in *Peyteuin* to Margam Abbey. She made an affidavit on the altar of the church of Margam.[38] Her seal was a conventional vesica shape, in brown wax, and depicted a fish with the simple legend + *SIGILLUM. TADERECH.* Noblewomen increasingly used vesica-shaped seals in England, Normandy and France in the mid- to late twelfth century. This is an early example of a woman using a seal in Wales to authenticate a charter. It is evidence of the process of cultural diffusion of sealing practice within Wales. The iconography of the seal is unusual since the seals of women generally depict tall standing figures holding objects such as a bird of prey or a stylised fleur-de-lys. Although it is unusual it is not unique, as there is an extant example from *c.* 1170 of a fish utilised on the seal of a woman in England.[39] Both seals are reflective of increasing variety in iconography as the use of seals became more common. As such this suggests that seal usage by women in Wales may have been more usual than surviving evidence might imply since it is usual for seals to have fairly limited iconographic motifs when they are used by the high nobility. It is as their use spreads to lower ranking individuals that the iconography shows variety. Another document, a *conventionem* or agreement, concerning the same land was drawn up in *c.* 1197 by which Thaderech as '*filia Ketherici Du*' confirmed land which she held '*in feudo Peiteuin*'. The grant stipulated that she gave the land for her lifetime for half a marc rendered annually at the feast of St Michael for all services. The monks would give 'for the agreement' the 'render of six years, that is three silver marcs' at the purification of St Mary next after the capture of '*Griffini filii Resi*'.[40] These charters are typical of *acta* of landholders in favour of religious houses in the late twelfth and early thirteenth centuries, but the clause which states that the render would be paid after the capture of Gruffudd ap Rhys is an unusual clause which linked the agreement to political upheaval. Thaderech sealed this charter with a round seal depicting an eight-petalled flower. That Thaderech used two seals in the late twelfth century is unusual, but not unprecedented. It is likely that she was the heiress to the lands in question because the scribe who drew up the charter used the *filia* designation in the charter. In late-twelfth-century England the *filia* designation was not status- or gender-specific but was used to suggest inheritance rights in the land that the charter ratified.[41] These charters are the earliest evidence for the descendants of John Ddu who gave 'lands of the Poitevin' to Margam in the late twelfth and early thirteenth centuries. Given the context of Anglo-Norman settlement and dominance in the lowlands of south Wales,[42] these charters suggest the engagement of female Welsh landholders in the religious benefaction of an Anglo-Norman institution.

There is also charter evidence that Welsh noblewomen were recipients of grants of land. For example, in 1273 Owain ap Maredudd granted his wife Angharad ferch Owain the whole of the commote of Anhuniog in Ceredigion in free marriage.[43] This document is significant because, as Beverley Smith suggests, within Wales, partitioned as it was between *pura Wallia* and *marchia Wallie*, both Welsh and English customs were observed by the ruling elite to create a hybrid agreement that had elements of both traditions. The particular customs in question here relate to the provision of dower. It is clear that the key distinction for the nomination of dower was in the nature of the land tenure: whether they were held by English or Welsh tenure and thus under which seigneurial jurisdiction the land fell. As Beverley Smith argues, the contrast lay in 'those areas where the statute of Wales took effect, and those where it did not'. Under Welsh law, women's property rights related to moveable wealth, *cowyll* and *agweddi*; the Statute of Wales stated that, previously, Welsh women had not been dowered with land, but had received dowry in the form of such moveable wealth.[44] Beverley Smith argues that this 1273 agreement took the form of dower as described by Glanvill in the twelfth century, that is, land that was given to the wife by the husband at the church door, which was normally associated with *maritagium*, and this is in contrast to usual custom since this usually took the form of moveable wealth. We have evidence from Edeirnion that Maredudd ab Owain, Owain ap Maredudd's father, had made a similar provision in 1246, a grant ratified by Henry III and enrolled on the English patent roll but possibly not put into written form elsewhere.[45] Intermarriage and the allocation of resources to support widows was thus a spur for diplomatic innovation. Indeed the political impact of Marcher practice for allocation of economic resources to women was monitored at the Prince's court, and the confirmation of the 1273 agreement at the Prince's court suggests that innovation was used to protect against conflicts of interest between Welsh custom and Marcher custom, caused potentially through intermarriage.[46]

However, if we accept the differing systems of settlement of resources on women at their marriage, then we can clarify see how an earlier agreement of 1222 should be viewed. By this settlement made between Llywelyn ab Iorwerth, and Ranulf, earl of Chester, Helen, the daughter of Llywelyn ab Iorwerth, prince of north Wales ('*dominum Lewelinum principem Norwallie*') married John the Scot, the nephew and heir of Ranulf, earl of Chester and Lincoln '*dominum Rannulphum comitem Cestrie et Lincolnie*'.[47] John the Scot was a minor in the custody of his uncle. He was the son of Ranulf's sister Mabel and David, earl of Huntingdon, who had died in 1219. The chirograph was drawn up some months before the marriage occurred and was witnessed by Reiner, bishop of St Asaph, and the abbot of Chester, as well as highly placed individuals in the households of both Ranulf and Llywelyn, including, for Ranulf, Hugh de Lacy and Philip de Orreby, Ranulf's justiciar,[48] and for Llywelyn, his leading and trusted adviser/seneschal Ednyfed Fychan. The presence of the high political elite at the ratification of the ceremony suggests the political resonance and importance of the event. The marriage was to seal the peace between Ranulf and Llywelyn, and the marriage portion included the manors of Bidford (Warwick) and Suckley (Worcestershire). Llywelyn also gave 1,000 marks. The manors had been given to him in frank marriage when he had married Joan, the daughter of King John. There is no doubt the ceremony which this chirograph records was conducted in a public arena with the participation of Helen and John the Scot: it is recorded that the couple made their affidavit in the hands of Reiner, bishop of St Asaph. Thus this document illustrates clearly that Helen was provided with a settlement in the form of a landed endowment as well as moveable wealth at the time of her marriage. The lands were held by English land tenure and the charter confirms that the nature of the land tenure was the crucial relationship governing its deposition, but also shows that the intermingling of traditions noted in the 1240s by Beverley Smith was happening at least as early as the 1220s. This can be seen in the evidence relating to the lands given to Gwenllian de Lacy, the sister of Gruffudd ap Llywelyn, by Tangwystl and Llywelyn ap Iorwerth. Gwenllian had received lands at the time of her marriage to William de Lacy in *c.* 1222–23. It is likely the lands were granted in free marriage. The marriage occurred at a time of political crisis when Llywelyn ap Iorwerth, her father, was in alliance with Hugh de Lacy, the half-brother of William. She was given the lands at a politically sensitive period and this was later to cause tension within her kin. As a widow she had trouble maintaining control over them and she was involved in a dispute to recover the lands against her half-brother, Dafydd ap Llywelyn. It is yet more evidence of the rift between Llywelyn ap Iorwerth's sons, since Gwenllian was the daughter of Llywelyn by Tangwystl, the mother of Llywelyn's eldest son, Gruffudd.[49] It is possible that Gwenllian (d. 1236), the wife of Rhys ap Gruffudd, had held lands given as *maritagium* by 1236–44.[50] The stress on the descent of the lands through Gwenllian is evidence of the transmission of claims to land through female kin. There is also evidence to suggest that Gwenllian, the wife of Rhys ap Gruffudd of Deheubarth held Welsh land and granted it to a religious institution. The foundation charter of Strata Florida Abbey includes details of gifts to the abbey by Rhys and his sons Gruffudd, Rhys and Maredudd 'in the hand of the abbot, ordering firmly before many of the army'. Gwenllian gave lands to Strata Florida 'with the counsel of Rhys and his sons'.[51] On 22 January 1198, when Maelgwyn ap Rhys confirmed the foundation of the abbey, by contrast Gwenllian was recorded as having given her consent for the gift by her husband of the land on the boundary between Marchdy and a township. The charters therefore differ in the way that they present the role of Gwenllian: the original charter stresses her action at the advice of her husband and sons, yet her son's confirmation charter merely records that she gave her consent to an action by her husband.[52]

Another example of the transmission of the claims to land through female kin may be seen in a grant of 1207 to Strata Marcella Abbey by

Gruffudd Goch ap Gruffudd Carno, whose mother was Lleucu daughter of Cadwallon. As Huw Pryce notes, Lleucu is named in the text of the charter and this may well reflect that Gruffudd's claims to the lands named in the charter were based on his mother's.[53]

The document relating to Helen and John of Scotland of 1222 must be put into the political context of Llywelyn's territorial ambition to pass on to his son a strong, cohesive territorial kingdom of Gwynedd. It is noteworthy that the lands given to Helen were those that Llywelyn had acquired through marriage to Joan and were transmitted through marriage to the daughter: in other words the patrimony, or hegemony, of the Welsh kingdom of Gwynedd remained intact and the lands gained through entitlement via marriage and thus lands which were given as *maritagium* to the mother were used in turn to endow a daughter.[54] The marriage was obviously an important political alliance and as such the ceremony surrounding the agreement was witnessed by the political elite of Cheshire and north Wales. Matthew Paris alleges that Helen poisoned her husband.[55] It is hard to know whether the allegation has any substance, but it possibly reflects an anti-Welsh prejudice combined with a distrust of women since the stereotype of the female poisoner was a well-utilised device in medieval literature. It may well reflect therefore the distrust of the purpose of the marriage, which sealed a peace between Ranulf and Llywelyn, and the distrust was articulated as hostility to Helen.

The marriage has been seen by Richard Eales as an attempt by Ranulf to buttress his position by strengthening an alliance with Llywelyn that had been negotiated in 1218.[56] The political context for both sides is significant. Ranulf was increasingly ambivalent in his loyalty to the English crown and he only gave 'grudging support' to Hubert de Burgh's campaign against the Welsh in 1221 and 1223. For Llywelyn on the other hand, the marriage alliance meant that his eastern borders were more secure, especially given Ranulf's increasing disaffection with the English crown. It is also significant that Ranulf's new castles on the March, for example that at Beeston begun 1225, were built to reinforce his control. The date of the marriage is also significant because it occurred in the same year that Dafydd was recognised as Llywelyn's heir. Dafydd's half-brother Gruffudd, the son of Tangwystl, Llywelyn's mistress/wife, had been placed in captivity by King John as surety for Llywelyn's compliance following John's defeat of Llywelyn in 1211. The legitimisation of Dafydd was an attempt by Llywelyn to avoid the dissipation of his hard-won territories by escheat into the hands of the English crown should Llywelyn die without legitimate heirs by his marriage to Joan, daughter of John. The ordinance clearly set out the principle, according to Smith, that

Dafydd was chosen as an *edling* over Gruffudd because of the latter's illegitimacy in order to secure Gwynedd's security.[57]

The fact that Llywelyn went to such great lengths to legitimise his son Dafydd and the later papal decree legitimising Joan in 1226 suggest that the question of legitimacy was significant in the politics of late-twelfth-/early thirteenth-century Gwynedd. Dafydd had been recognised as Llywelyn's heir in 1220 by Henry III's minority government.[58] In 1222 this was confirmed by the pope. The words used by the papacy to record this decision throw light on contemporary notions of legitimacy and illegitimacy. The language is striking. It is recorded that Llywelyn had petitioned for the decision, and that this petition had indicated that there was a 'detestable custom' in his country, that 'the son of the hand-maid should be heir with the son of the free woman', putting legitimate and illegitimate sons on the same footing. The ordinance to legitimise Dafydd was made with the consent of King Henry, Stephen, cardinal archbishop of Canterbury, and the papal legate the bishop elect of Norwich, Pandulf.[59] Thus Tangwystl was a 'hand-maid' and Princess Joan 'the free'. The choice of language is striking, since the opposition of the terms suggests that the relationship between Llywelyn and Tangwystl in some way made her unfree. The evidence for the papal view of the legitimisation of Dafydd is contained in a papal letter, so obviously this reflects the Church view of the union. Yet it is the choice of language which is interesting: the use of the term 'hand-maid' is possibly an allusion to the *Magnificat* and would have had an immediate resonance to contemporaries, especially the clerically trained clerks who composed and read Llywelyn's correspondence. The Vulgate version of Luke states, 'And Mary said, Behold the handmaid of the Lord; be it unto me according to thy word. And the angel departed from her.'[60] The response therefore conveys an ambivalent papal attitude to Tangwystl; the allusion to Mary suggests that the union with Tangwystl places her in the role of servant (*ancilla*/hand-maid) who had produced a son in the service of her 'lord'. This role as procreator made her less than Joan, 'the free woman', and although the harshest tone is reserved for the 'detestable custom that the son of the hand-maid should be heir with the son of the free', it is not Tangwystl who is condemned, but the custom. The nature of her role as a servant is one of procreation and the papacy was finding a way to express this which was ambivalent. Such ambivalence is reflective of the Church view of marriage and sexual union and played into the hands of lay society. Beverley Smith considered the allusion to be a biblical reference to Galatians, and that in effect Llywelyn stressed not that dynastic inheritance was non-partible and a guiding principle of dynastic policy, but that the choice of heir was to be the son of a legitimate marriage. The land used as *maritagium* was a recent acquisition through Llywelyn's own marriage, and thus the patrimony remained intact.[61] Huw Pryce agreed with Beverley Smith that the reference to Tangwystl as a hand-maid has close parallels with Galatians 4:30.[62] Whilst the exact biblical reference may be debateable, what is beyond dispute is that we are see-ing here the way that different sexual unions were viewed, and it is clear that Llywelyn in pursuit of political hegemony was utilising both secular and clerical routes to secure his long-term strategic goal of a united, cohesive territorial principality which dominated Wales: and in part this developed the papal view of his previous relationship to secure his aims.[63]

The choice of Dafydd as heir to Llywelyn was not uncontentious: custom in Wales was such that legitimate and illegitimate sons could share in the inheritance.[64] Beverley Smith argues that in 1220 the Welsh drew distinctions between a legitimate and an illegitimate son becoming heir designate, that is, the *edling*, and in fact indivisible inheritance was already well established. Further, Llywelyn had intended that Dafydd should inherit the supremacy over neighbouring kingdoms that Llywelyn had established. Llywelyn made provision for Gruffudd but the core of the territorial lordship of Gwynedd and the overlordship of south Wales were to pass intact to Dafydd.[65] The later legitimisation of his mother Joan served to reinforce Dafydd's position. The papal decree legitimising Joan stated that Pope Honorius III did so 'so that the defect of her birth should not detract from the honour of her husband Llywelyn' because of his devotion to the Roman Church and his faith.[66] It is intriguing that Llywelyn went to such lengths and departed from the Welsh custom which accepted legitimate and illegitimate heirs equally, and the process raises the important question of whether this illustrates that the north Welsh elite were becoming more assimilated to English customs. Certainly, as Smith has shown, Rhys ap Gruffudd intended that Deheubarth should descend to one heir.[67] It is possibly also a determined attempt to out-manoeuvre the English crown by leaving no possible avenues for conten-tion open. Thus he moderated Welsh inheritance custom to ensure that his son's succession would be safe.

Joan provides a model of queenship in thirteenth-century Gwynedd. It has been suggested that the role of the queen may have become more expansive and prominent in contemporary Gwynedd and this was reflected in changes in the way that the Iorwerth version of the Welsh lawbooks treated the queen's household and officers, when that version was redacted.[68] It is just possible that such ideas may have affected the way that Nest was portrayed in *Brut y Tywysogion*. There is a general acceptance amongst scholars that Joan played important political roles when she acted as an intermediary between her husband and the royal court, and it is worthwhile considering these in more detail since charters have a role in shedding light on her activities, while other sources reveal more details. The political context of her actions ensures her visibility in our sources. Louise Wilkinson argued that Joan's position in 1212 was difficult given the context of deteriorating political relations between England and Gwynedd, and the humiliating defeat of Llywelyn by John. Joan wrote to her father King John warning him of possible treachery by his magnates.[69] Prior to December 1212 she intervened to request the release of Llywelyn's hostages.[70] These two documents do not survive in their original forms. The letter warning John of possible treachery is mentioned by Roger Wendover and Matthew Paris. As Pryce points out, Matthew Paris's second version, in the *Chronica Majora*, contradicts both Wendover and his own *Historica Anglorum* by suggesting that John ignored the information contained in Joan's letter, continued to Chester and only on receiving further warnings then abandoned his campaign.[71] Huw Pryce has argued that the balance of the evidence is against this second version. The interpolation is, however, interesting for two reasons. First, Paris suggests that Joan's advice was considered untrustworthy and was thus ignored, which could simply be explained away by the male clerical distrust of women, which in turn draws on a common literary stereotype of women as untrustworthy and giving poor advice. Yet Paris was highly critical of John and developed a critique of royal power which grew from the intellectual influence of Roger Wendover upon Paris.[72] Thus the portrayal is less a critique of Joan than of John, and must be viewed in the broader context of Paris's distrust of centralising royal authority and his belief in the community of the realm, as well as his distrust of women. He also wrote with the benefit of hindsight and thus knew that John's reign was a litmus test of tensions concerning ideas about the community of the realm. Second, it is suggestive of the importance of political links between Cheshire and north Wales that Chester remained loyal to John. The immediate political context of this letter is significant: twenty-eight Welsh hostages had been massacred in 1211 at the order of John. Joan's role at this juncture was critical. Louise Wilkinson argued that Joan was the key intermediary in the peacemaking between John and Llywelyn.[73] Joan intervened on behalf of a hostage held by John in 1215, when it is likely that she petitioned John by letter, since John released Gwyn ap Iorwerth to the clerk sent by Joan.[74]

In 1230–31 Joan wrote to Henry III, her half-brother, seeking to allay suspicions concerning her husband and her clerk Instructus. The language used in the letter has much to tell us about the way that Joan's identity was constructed. The letter is addressed to her half-brother as 'King of England, Lord of Ireland, Duke of Normandy and Aquitaine and Count of Anjou', whilst Joan is identified as 'J[oan] Lady of Wales'. Huw Pryce notes that the royal chancery addressed Joan as 'Lady of North Wales' in April 1230, and recognized her as 'Lady of Wales' on 8 November 1235.[75] There were earlier antecedents to such titles, however: Emma of Anjou, the wife of Dafydd ab Owain in the late twelfth century, was styled *Domina* in her charter of 1186.[76] Dafydd was supplanted in Gwynedd by Llywelyn in 1197. Building on these precedents, Joan's title as Lady of Wales was an attempt to articulate the changed political landscape in north Wales. It is also significant that neither Emma's nor Joan's title was a direct correlation of their husbands': neither is 'Princess of North Wales'. They were both half-sisters of the English king, and therefore half-nieces to the Empress Matilda who had, in the period after 1141, become known as 'Lady of the English' during her struggle for the throne of England. The use of the word 'Lady' was conjured by scribes in England to articulate Matilda's position with regard to the political elite of England.[77] It is arguable that in Wales, therefore, it may well have served the same purpose. The scribes who composed the charters attempted to find a word which would define the position of Emma and Joan, and 'Lady' with its connotations of lordship and pre-eminence was chosen. Lordship was certainly stressed in Dafydd ap Owain's charter in which he was 'Prince of Wales'. The title 'Lady of Wales' articulated the position and social status of the wife of the prince of Gwynedd, but the status of both Joan and Emma was buttressed by their kinship with the king of England, and the title of 'Lady of Wales' related their status to a territorial political kingdom, in much the same way that their aunt had used a title to lay claim to a people's loyalty, and further to a concept of pre-eminence within Wales as a whole.

Thus Joan's status as daughter of King John and wife of Llywelyn ap Iorwerth facilitated her participation in the political affairs of Gwynedd and acted as an important link between the kingdom of Gwynedd and the English royal court. Her filial status combined with her marriage to give her political legitimacy within the political community of Gwynedd, and, by extension, her title claimed 'Wales'. Further, the concept of queenship was developing in twelfth-century Wales, to a point where Gerald of Wales in *c.* 1202 could receive a letter from the 'Queen of North Wales'. It is unclear who the 'Queen' could be, since the letter itself has disappeared. It cannot be Joan, who married Llywelyn in 1205, and, although it is possible that it refers to Tangwystl, daughter of Llywarch Goch and the mother of Llywelyn's son Gruffudd, scholars doubt that Tangwystl and Llywelyn were married. Huw Pryce has suggested that the sender was possibly a sister of Ranulf III, earl of Chester, whom Llywelyn seems to have married in 1192.[78] This letter to Gerald of Wales with its suggestion of queenship is intriguing, not only because it is impossible to know who the sender was, but also for the use of the title 'Queen'. The concept appears already in the Latin *life* of Gruffudd ap Cynan, which Russell dates to 1137x48.[79] The Welsh lawbooks provide evidence that the idea of queenship in north Wales was conceived of as an office with attendant household officers.[80] The date that the lawbooks were redacted is critical here, and the nature of these sources must also be considered in a context which takes account of their purpose. Huw Pryce suggests that the Cyfnerth text, the earliest redaction of the Welsh lawbooks, contains details from a twelfth-century lawbook, and that the Iorwerth version was produced during the reign of Llywelyn ap Iorwerth, while the Blegywryd version was produced at the end of the thirteenth or in the early fourteenth century. He further suggests that their primary purpose was as instructive texts for lawyers, who fought to control the nature of the native legal tradition.[81] Robin Chapman Stacey argues that the Iorwerth redaction was a direct commentary on the politics of the reign of Llywelyn ap Iorwerth. This is based upon a reading of the texts which takes account of the language used, for example, to discuss divorce, and the reference to the splitting of household goods by couples which rendered implements such as quern stones useless has been interpreted as a method by which the costliness of divorce was enacted within communities. Further, Stacey analysed the clauses relating to the division of foods within the lawbooks and suggested that Iorwerth changed the way that this was expressed. The language used in Iorwerth to suggest that the husband received the 'hung meat' is, Stacey argues, a reference to the hanging of William de Braose by Llywelyn after his alleged affair with Joan.[82] This perspective offers a different interpretation of the contemporary relevance of the lawbooks in early thirteenth-century Wales given that the traditional focus on the date of composition and the purpose of the lawbooks, and whether the lawbooks had any contemporary relevance, or whether they present an ossified redaction of antiquated custom, is crucial to an assessment of their value as a source.

Hitherto historians have tended to interpret the prologues to the Welsh law, given their overtly political nature, within a framework which takes account of the political nature of the texts, and their role in the consolidation of princely power in Gwynedd under the Lord Rhys of Deheubarth and Llywelyn ap Iorwerth. The importance of the lawbooks as evidence of the political ideals of the elite has been interpreted by Huw Pryce as evidence of the interests of the *uchelwyr* rather than of the princes who were the intended readership.[83] R. R. Davies argues that the Welsh laws may not have been a tool for forging an ideology even though they ultimately became a 'potent symbol of Welsh national identity' in the struggles between Edward I and Llywelyn ap Gruffudd.[84] Thus the political nature of the lawbooks has been at the forefront of scholars' interpretations of them. If the lawbooks were crafted to symbolise Welsh national identity and were an exercise in the construction of a political vision for Wales, then the way that the royal household was portrayed, and within this the role of the queen, is part of that identity. There has been some analysis of the lawbooks in terms of understanding the role of the queen: it has been suggested that the Iorwerth redaction with its descriptions of the queenly household, its officers and their duties, provides a direct commentary on the queenly household of Joan.[85] Yet the texts discuss the officers of the queenly household rather than the functions of the queen herself, and there is even 'indifference' to the activities of the queen.[86] Such 'indifference' contrasts with the charter evidence and as such may well be a reflection of male antipathy to powerful women, even queens. Such antipathy had deep historical roots. Yet the lawbooks retain the memory of the office of queenship, although there are differences in the different versions: for example, the earlier Cyfnerth redaction has fewer details concerning the queen than Iorwerth. It has been argued that Cyfnerth may be a commentary on Deheubarth;[87] if so, it is likely that Cyfnerth offers a view of queenship which can be related to the significance of Nest for the royal dynasty within Deheubarth, and this tradition of recognition continued. Thus in effect there is recognition in one of the most important sources for the period, that the royal house of Gwynedd was one which was headed by a king and queen. The *Life of Gruffudd ap Cynan* in its portrayal of Gruffudd emphasises his royal status and prestige. It does so by stating, for example, that lesser kings, '*reguli minori*', would attend his court for advice and support. This is augmented by the evocation of royal grandeur and largesse in its portrayal of Gruffudd's preparations for his death, which depicts that as Gruffudd lay dying he received the last rites, where he was attended by high-status clerics and the queen '*regina Angharad*'. The image is a carefully constructed portrayal of royal magnificence, and the use of such regnal language allows an intriguing insight into contemporary language and conception of the role and status of the ruling dynasties.[88]

The lawbooks were intended for consumption within Wales; they served as mnemonic aids, preserving the idea of Welsh kingship and queenship – and the models, if they are a statement about Gwynedd in the 1230s, are Joan and Llywelyn. The rhetoric of queenship may well have been developing in the late twelfth and early thirteenth centuries, and the complexities of the rhetoric of queenship suggest the multifaceted nature of queenly position and power and its central role in the production of texts.[89] The political discourse within the lawbooks served to legitimate Joan as sovereign and as queen. The pragmatic title 'Lady' in a charter contrasts with the allusions to queenship in the (more conservatively framed) lawbooks but nevertheless puts her pre-eminent within the community of the realm. There was thus a limited range of terms to describe the consorts of Welsh rulers. Welsh male rulers were described in a variety of ways through the twelfth century.[90] The subtle layers of power represented by the fine distinctions in Welsh are suggestive of the importance of kin, and Smith notes that the poetry of the other twelfth-century poets Meilyr Brydydd and Gwalchmai ap Meilyr portrays an image of kingship that is centred on men whose tenure of their territories was related to their royal status. Further, he notes that kingship was an integral part of the ideological battle which was waged during the thirteenth century.[91]

Thus if the lawbooks represent an ossified antiquated system at odds with current social custom they represent an image of queenship which no longer had contemporary relevance. In this respect they serve as the guardian of political memory of past sovereignty within Wales. If, however, they are a pertinent commentary on contemporary Gwynedd then the allusions to queenship are evidence of the ideological possibilities of female participation in sovereignty. Collections of laws were works of 'political theology' and were central in the creation of a political ideology and helped to define a people.[92] The rhetoric of queenship in confluence with that of kingship was constructed in the lawbooks, which thus presented an image of a royal court and preserved its memory. At the heart of the lawbooks is an abiding sense of legitimacy, order and justice, which was predicated on political ideals as well as ideas about social status and gender, and such ideals include conceptions about the role of the king and of the queen. Ideas about political legitimacy and the community of the realm were becoming linked in the early thirteenth century and explain in part the upheavals associated with Magna Carta.

If the political dialogue which underpinned the actions of the political elite was that of ideas about regnal solidarity and could express ideas about ethnic identity within that concept,[93] then such ideas were capable of inculcating a view on gender, as is evident from the discourse concerning legitimacy in contemporary records. For example, ideas about legitimacy, and his concomitant distrust of royal and papal power, affected Paris's portrayal of Senana the wife of Gruffudd ap Llywelyn and of Helen, wife of John the Scot, earl of Chester. Our sources articulate a complex view of an emerging political discourse that is gender-specific and predicated on genre and context. Such contexts affected the portrayal of Nest in the *Brutiau*. For our purposes, therefore, it is important to consider the portrayal of Senana's participation in negotiations with the English royal court and her role in the formation of political alliances. On 12 August 1241 Senana met Henry III at Shrewsbury to make an agreement concerning the release of Gruffudd who was held in captivity by his brother Dafydd. The text of the agreement was enrolled in the English charter rolls and also survives in the *Chronica Majora* of Matthew Paris.[94] It is likely that Paris's version of the text was written soon after the events of 1241: he began compiling his *Chronica* in 1240 or soon after, and wrote the entry for each year within a year of the events that he describes.[95] According to Paris, the end of the convention was sealed with the seal of Gruffudd 'by the hand of Senana', with the seal of Senana and with that of King Henry. The names of the men who stood pledge for her are listed and include many great Welsh and Marcher lords such as Gruffudd ap Madog of Bromfield (and his brothers Hywel and Maredudd), Ralph Mortimer, Walter Clifford, Roger of Mold, seneschal of Chester, and Maelgwn ap Maelgwn. They all proffered their 'written instruments' to support their pledge. It is noteworthy that those who stood pledge reflect diverse and complex political relationships in Marcher Wales. This was not political division along ethnic identities: the Welsh were willing to pledge to the English with Marcher support to undermine the position of Dafydd ap Llywelyn, Gruffudd's younger half-brother. This agreement is also important because it is evidence of the range of economic resources available to Senana. She pledged to pay for Gruffudd's release through a combination of cattle, money and horses. The details of this agreement have been interpreted by Turvey as evidence of political and economic change within Wales during the twelfth and early thirteenth centuries: earlier rulers would have demanded tribute in the form of cattle, but by the 1240s the Welsh economy had developed to be able to support large payments in coin.[96] J. Beverley Smith saw the documents in a broader context which had implications for the political hegemony of Gwynedd since the agreement meant in practice that the 'custom and law of Wales' would be judged in the English king's court by the king's decision and applied to a major lordship. Thus Smith rightly identifies the intention of the English king to partition Gwynedd into two parts, and the justification for treating Dafydd and Gruffudd as tenants-in-chief equally was thus Welsh inheritance custom. The agreement with Senana at Shrewsbury has been characterised as 'a diplomatic feat for which would be difficult to find as fiendish a parallel in the whole history of Anglo-Welsh relations'.[97] Ostensibly Henry III was doing justice to Gruffudd who was in captivity, but he was invoking 'the custom of Wales' to the advantage of the English crown. Central to this, however, was Senana's position. Thus the 1241 agreement at Shrewsbury reveals the complex politico-economic context of Gwynedd and its relationship with the English monarchy and it demonstrates that Senana was a key element in the diplomatic process.[98]

The agreement describes in detail the arrangements made to ratify and thus consolidate the agreement made with Henry III. Senana agreed to pay 600 marks to free Gruffudd and their son Owain; she undertook to pay 300 marks annually to the king at Shrewsbury, in two biannual payments. Senana agreed that her two sons Dafydd and Rhodri would be handed over as hostages to ensure the terms of the agreement were kept. She swore on the Gospels 'on behalf of herself and her husband', and undertook to ensure that Gruffudd would do the same on his release. Senana submitted herself to the jurisdiction of the bishops of Hereford and Coventry and agreed to ensure that Gruffudd made written confirmation of all the above details and would give this to the king. In order to ratify the agreement this document was sealed with three seals, that of Gruffudd, that of Senana and that of Henry III. It is worth considering in more detail the significance of Paris's statement concerning the sealing of the agreement. The document is obviously remarkable because it is clear evidence that as a woman of the high political Welsh elite, Senana could take decisive action in the political negotiations with the English king. Her authority was rooted in her position as wife. This is indicated in the use by Senana of Gruffudd's seal to ratify the document and she thus acted with authority in his name. It is, however, also significant that Senana had her own seal which was appended alongside that of Henry III. Senana thus acted with the full authority of Gruffudd, used his seal, and yet also had her own and that this was significant is acknowledged because her seal was placed on the document. In a broader context, given the poor rate of seal survivals from medieval Wales, this evidence suggests that female Welsh nobility had personal seals by the thirteenth century and could also utilise their husband's seal to ratify documents of political and economic importance. It suggests that the clerks who drew up the document, and Matthew Paris who transcribed the above details, knew that the use of a personal seal by a high-status woman such as Senana was symbolic of her authority and that the use of her husband's seal encapsulated ideas about joint authority in lord-ship. Gruffudd ap Llywelyn granted lands to Strata Marcella and con-firmed a grant by Dafydd *Gohwe* Fychan 'by the arbitration of six trust worthy men of Cyfeiliog' (Powys) in *c.* 1226 since they had no seal of their own; this suggests the high status of his seal and that of Senana.[99] Paris may have assumed that such joint authority was the norm in Anglo-Norman politics and therefore that such protocols were the norm in Welsh practice. There is, however, evidence relating to the later thir-teenth century in the form of a document written as a notification of surety given for the good conduct of a Welsh landholder at a critical juncture in the internal politics of the kingdom of Gwynedd. The letter patent concerns an agreement whereby a group of Welsh nobles stood surety to Llywelyn ap Gruffudd for Gruffudd ap Budr ei hosan. The sureties bound themselves to pay £120 and sealed the document; the sealing clause indicates the seal confirmed the surety since those that did not have a seal were 'bound to perform their suretyship with their own hands before the prince's attorney'.[100] Thus by the latter half of the thir-teenth century seals stood as evidence of surety and replaced the need for the physical act of surety given in the hand of a lord.

In order to fully appreciate the significance of the 1241 Shrewsbury agreement as recorded by Matthew Paris it is important to place it into context, first within the writings of Paris and second within the broader political context of Anglo-Welsh–Marcher relations of the thirteenth century. It is worthwhile considering why Paris should have included the details of the agreement in his *Chronica Majora*. According to Gransden, Paris was implacably opposed to centralised authority in both Church and state. Paris's core beliefs lay in the liberties and customs of the commun-ity of the realm. Indeed, Gransden argues that Paris depicts Henry III as politically naive, weak and unable to withstand pressure from an overbearing pope.[101] Seen in this light, Paris's portrayal of the agreement with Senana and the support given to her by powerful Marcher barons assumes a greater significance. Paris has painted a picture of the female representative of the political community of the supporters of the heir to part of the Welsh kingdom of Gwynedd acting together with the Marcher political elite to ratify an agreement with the English king to partition Gwynedd to both parties' advantage and thus the disadvantage of Dafydd. However, according to Beverley Smith, this policy was a direct threat to the hegemony of Gwynedd since it undermined the long-term strategy of the Welsh princes to forge a united, independent kingdom.[102] It seems the real issue here was the tradition of partible inheritance: of course, as Beverley Smith argues, Henry III acted to ensure the best possible advantage to the English crown, whereas Senana acted to utilise the English crown to achieve her own objectives – the freedom of Gruffudd and his accession to his hereditary possessions according to Welsh custom. It is where the balance of power lies that makes this so interesting. Beverley Smith suggests that Gruffudd sought help from a strong English king who aggressively sought to divide Gwynedd in order to weaken it. Welsh custom is the issue here, and the innovations sought by Llywelyn ap Iorwerth suggest that he knew full well that his attempts to legitimise Joan, his marriage strategies and his decision to give Dafydd the whole share of Gwynedd were an attempt to buttress a difficult position and to mediate the impact of divisible inheritance. The agreement of Senana with Henry III must therefore be placed into the political context of the relationships of Gwynedd with the English crown, but nevertheless she and Joan serve to show that women were at the heart of these political relationships and could participate in contemporary politics effectively and decisively. The inclusion of the sealing clause by Paris is indicative of this executive power and confirms that Paris knew the significance of the use and ownership of a seal.

Such seals were symbolically powerful and the seal matrices themselves as tangible objects resonated with symbolic associations. Just over thirty years later the obliteration of the royal power and inheritance of Gwynedd by Edward I after the defeat of Llywelyn ap Gruffudd involved measures to counter the potential transmission of claims to sovereignty through women. Llywelyn's daughter Gwenllian was incarcerated in the Lincolnshire nunnery of Sempringham, and while the sons of his brother Dafydd were incarcerated at Bristol castle, his daughters too were placed in nunneries in Lincolnshire. The destruction of royal power was also, however, symbolically enacted and represented through the destruction of symbolic objects of his son and daughter-in-law. The coronet of Llywelyn ap Gruffudd and the matrix of his seal, and that of his wife, Princess Eleanor, as well as that of his son, Dafydd ap Gruffudd, were taken by Edward I. Beverley Smith states that the coronet was presented to the shrine of St Edward at Westminster Abbey, while the seal matrices were 'melted down'. Beverley Smith comments that this occurred 'unceremoniously',[103] yet the jewels roll of 1284 makes it clear that they were made into a silver chalice that was to be given to Vale Royal Abbey, in Cheshire, as a gift.[104] If we consider the symbolic importance of Vale Royal to Edward I in more detail, the significance of the action taken by the English king to destroy the seal matrices can be clarified. It could be argued that the seal matrices, far from being 'unceremoniously' reused, were in fact recast in a way that was highly charged with symbolic meanings related to the destruction of executive power and authority in Gwynedd. Their crafting into a religious artefact was an act of cultural reconstruction deeply imbued with ceremonial significance. The choice of the religious house to receive the chalice was itself, without doubt, of great symbolic importance. Vale Royal was founded by Edward I following a vow made when caught in a storm at sea as he was returning from the Holy Land. An earlier foundation was replaced by another at Darnhall, which was renamed Vale Royal by Edward in order to stress its pre-eminence among all religious houses in his kingdom. On 13 August 1277, Edward laid the foundation stone of the altar at a crucial period during the preparations to invade Wales. Queen Eleanor and Edward's companions also laid stones, and at the foundation Edward gave a portion of the Holy Cross and other relics.[105] This portion of the Cross was one of Edward's most precious relics, that 'in every battle [was] worn around his bare neck' and was 'the most sacred ensign of Christ'. Queen Eleanor was also a significant benefactress of the abbey.[106] Thus the intention which underlay the foundation of Vale Royal was to create a superlative religious house that more than any other symbolised the magnificence of Edward's reign and his success: the ceremony of the laying of the foundation stone of its chief altar was thus inextricably linked with the conquest of Wales. Seen in this light, the reuse of the royal seal matrices from the princely dynasty in Gwynedd assumes a far greater symbolic resonance. It emphasised Edward's view that the defeat of Gwynedd was God-given; the seals which symbolised temporal power and authority were destroyed and then transformed into religious symbols commended to the care of God forever. And the seals that were so treated were not just those of the prince and his heir, but that of his wife.

We can go one step further and see this perhaps as an act of national significance. Edward saw himself as having acted as the hand of God in Wales through military power and having recast Gwynedd into a new form. The man-made objects, the seals and coronets, were recast into other man-made objects, which suggests the essence of the seal, the silver, retained a Christological charge despite the change in form. The seal matrices of Llywelyn and of his wife which served a range of interpretative functions as objects of secular power were transmuted by the act of conquest into a functional, powerful and religious object contained in the abbey. Brigitte Bedos-Rezak has argued that seals had, among other uses, Christological functions. They symbolised presence and were tools of social control and identity, and were stereotypic, that is, they assigned socio-cultural functions.[107] The appropriation of the seal of the princely dynasty of Gwynedd by the English king and its reuse symbolically showed that Edward took control of the seals' functions and they were physically recast to continue to have new Christological functions. This was accomplished through the secular power of the king, whose power was sanctioned by God. The seals, once destroyed, could no longer symbolise the presence of the temporal power of the dynasty of Gwynedd. A gender-based analysis is relevant here since it leads us to consider the implications of the fact that it was not only the men's seals which were recast, but also the woman's. The objects were treated as equally significant, and it was their functional symbolic roles of social status, political value and representational purposes which were transformed into a religious artefact. Bedos-Rezak has shown how the seal matrices of the Scottish king were taken and destroyed after his defeat by Edward, and how the seals of the bishops of Durham were recast into chalices after their death in order to maintain a sense of presence. The example of the seal matrices of Gwynedd confirms the importance of the control of their essence by Edward and crucially confirms their potent symbolic force, but even more importantly emphasises the gender parity with which their power was viewed.

Matthew Paris recognised the importance of the symbolic function of seals in conveying ideas about the ideological and temporal power and imagery of Gruffudd's princely dynasty and he thus recorded Senana's use of them. It confirms the importance of the executive authority and power of Senana, as the wife of Gruffudd. If we consider gender roles it is possible to move beyond an appreciation of the 1241 agreement as a litmus test of English/Welsh relationships, and consider the significance of Senana's role. Although we may consider Senana as another important example of high-status noblewomen actively pursuing political objectives in the high middle ages, it is also important to consider the reasons why Paris included such rich detail concerning the 1241 agreement. Senana's role is structured within lordship, and her role is thus explicable within accepted conventions concerning the community of the realm. The political community of the realm could and did include powerful women such as Senana and Princess Joan, whose roles were legitimate because of the ideas constructed around the twin poles of family and lordship. Senana's pledges were underpinned by statements of support from important Welsh and Marcher lords, and she laid herself under the jurisdiction of the Church. She acted as the representative of her husband and son, and the agreement was made as solid as such an agreement could be through recourse to hostages, pledges and ecclesiastical jurisdiction. Thus her role was constructed through recourse to gender norms since her role as a wife stemmed directly from ideas about appropriate female roles as supportive to their husbands and sons. Her involvement was legitimate because she acted as a wife, because the political context in which she acted was one in which there was a transfer of power to Senana due to Gruffudd's imprisonment.

Marriage as a political partnership was a difficult concept for medieval chroniclers steeped as they were in anti-female biases. This chapter began with a review of charter evidence relating to women of the elite in Wales to evaluate how it can facilitate a reading of women's power and thus provide a context for understanding twelfth-century Wales. This context was further clarified by a reading of Matthew Paris and Gerald of Wales. The evidence suggests that for powerful women in Wales in the high middle ages interaction in high politics was driven from many perspectives. Further political developments in Wales did not necessarily result in the dominance and subordination of the Welsh or of the female high political elite. The evidence above suggests that opportunities to exert power and influence were seized upon by the wives of powerful men and thus gender roles played a role in the way that these were carried out. Princess Joan's roles were those of powerful wife and supplicant daughter and she acted in the political interests of Gwynedd. Senana, as a wife, conducted high-level political negotiations and this involved her in making commitments formalised through binding written agreements. The approach here suggests an interpretation of Wales in the late eleventh and twelfth centuries which is about more than domination and conquest, though these are without doubt pivotal forces. By exploring the role of women in negotiation and integration strategies realised through, for example, marriage, it is possible to put women such as Princess Joan and Senana back into the sort of exchanges described by Davies. An analysis of the lawbooks and charters provides evidence of the way that ideas about the appropriate roles for women were articulated in the later sources. The effect is to allow a fuller appreciation of the dynamics of political power in Wales in the high middle ages in which women were central to the political processes.

Notes

1 Huw Pryce, 'Culture, power and the charters of Welsh rulers', in Marie Therese Flanagan and Judith A. Green (eds), *Charters and Charter Scholarship in Britain and Ireland* (Basingstoke: Palgrave Macmillan, 2005), pp. 184–202, at p. 185.

2 *St. Davids Episcopal Acta 1085–1280*, ed. Julia Barrow (South Wales Record Society, 13; Cardiff, 1998); Julia Barrow, 'Editing St Davids episcopal acta 1085–1280', *The Carmarthenshire Antiquary*, 34 (1998), 5–10. For Margam: Robert B. Patterson, *The Scriptorium of Margam Abbey and the Scribes of Early Angevin Glamorgan: Secretarial*

Administration in a Welsh Marcher Barony, c. 1150–c. 1225 (Woodbridge: Boydell Press, 2002); F. G. Cowley, 'Margam Abbey, 1147–1349', *Morgannwg*, 42 (1998), 8–22; Robert B. Patterson, 'The author of the "Margam annals": early thirteenth-century Margam Abbey's compleat scribe', *ANS*, 14 (1991), 197–210; Marvin L. Colker, 'The "Margam Chronicle" in a Dublin manuscript', *Haskins Society Journal*, 4 (1993 for 1992), 123–48; W. Greenway, 'The annals of Margam', *Transactions of the Port Talbot Historical Society*, 1 (1963), 19–31; M. Griffiths, 'Native society on the Anglo-Norman frontier: the evidence of the Margam charters', *WHR*, 14 (1988–89), 179–216.

3 David B. Crouch, *Llandaff Episcopal Acta 1140–1287* (Cardiff: South Wales Record Society, 5, 1989); *The Llandaff Charters*, ed. Wendy Davies (Aberystwyth: National Library of Wales, 1979); see also Wendy Davies, 'Charter-writing and its uses in early medieval Celtic societies', in Huw Pryce (ed.), *Literacy in Medieval Celtic Societies* (Cambridge: Cambridge University Press, 1998), pp. 99–112; *The Charters of the Abbey of Ystrad Marchell*, ed. G. C. G. Thomas (Aberystwyth: National Library of Wales, 1997); *The Acts of Welsh Rulers 1120–1283*, ed. Huw Pryce (Cardiff: University of Wales Press, 2005).

4 For a comprehensive bibliography concerning charters and charter studies see *Acts of Welsh Rulers*, ed. Pryce, pp. xxiii–xlv, 1–2, and notes to individual documents.

5 Griffiths, 'Native society'; D. H. Williams, *The Welsh Cistercians* (2 vols, Caldey Island, Tenby: Cyhoeddiadau Sistersiaidd, 1984); *Llandaff Charters*; J. Beverley Smith, 'Land endowments of the period of Llywelyn ap Gruffudd', *BBCS*, 24 (1970–72), 77–93.

6 David B. Crouch, 'The slow death of kingship in Glamorgan', *Morgannwg*, 29 (1985), 20–41; *idem*, 'The March and the Welsh kings', in Edmund King (ed.), *The Anarchy of King Stephen's Reign* (Oxford: Clarendon Press, 1994), pp. 255–89; *idem*, 'The earliest original charter of a Welsh king', *BBCS*, 36 (1989), 125–31; *idem*, 'The last adventure of Richard Siward', *Morgannwg*, 35 (1991), 7–30. J. Beverley Smith, 'Magna Carta and the charters of the Welsh princes', *English Historical Review*, 99 (1984), 344–62; Charles Insley, 'From *Rex Wallie* to *Princeps Wallie*: charters and state formation in thirteenth-century Wales', in J. R. Maddicott and D. M. Palliser (eds), *The Medieval State: Essays Presented to James Campbell* (London: Hambledon, 2000), pp. 179–96; *idem*, 'Fact and fiction in thirteenth-century Gwynedd: the Aberconwy charters', *Studia Celtica*, 33 (1999), 235–50; Emma Cavell, 'Aristocratic widows and the medieval Welsh frontier: the Shropshire evidence', *TRHS*, 6th ser., 17 (2007), 57–82; Roger Turvey, 'King, prince or lord? Rhys ap Gruffydd and the nomenclature of authority in twelfth-century Wales', *The Carmarthenshire Antiquary*, 30 (1994), 5–18.

7 Ceridwen Lloyd-Morgan, 'More written about than writing? Welsh women and the written word', in Pryce (ed.), *Literacy in Medieval Celtic Societies*, pp. 149–65.

8 J. Gwenogfryn Evans, with the cooperation of John Rhys, *The Text of the Book of Llan Dâv Reproduced from the Gwysaney Manuscript* (Oxford: J. G. Evans, 1893; facsimile edition, Aberystwyth: National Library of Wales, 1979), pp. 259–60; *Llandaff Charters*, no. 259, p. 127.

9 *Text of the Book of Llan Dâv*, pp. 261–2; *Llandaff Charters*, no. 261.

10 *Llandaff Charters*, no. 261, pp. 127–8.

11 *Llandaff Charters*, p. 2. It should be noted, however, that Kari Maund challenged Davies's dating of charter 259 to *c.* 1040. She also, based on an analysis of the narrations of this charter and five others, suggested that the narrations of the charters were 'conventionalised explanations' which were 'designed to strengthen Llandaff's twelfth-century claims'. Further, Maund doubts, in her analysis of charter 261, the

historical authenticity of the detail concerning Seisyll. K. L. Maund, *Ireland, Wales and England in the Eleventh Century* (Woodbridge: Boydell, 1991), pp. 193–5. John Reuben Davies agrees that there is authentic earlier material in the charters: *The Book of Llandaf and the Norman Church in Wales* (Woodbridge: Boydell, 2003), p. 5; for analysis of the diplomatic, pp. 98–108.

12 *Llandaff Charters*, p. 2. See Richard Mortimer, 'Anglo-Norman lay charters, 1066– c. 1100: a diplomatic approach', *ANS*, 25 (2003), 153–75, at p. 173, for a discussion of forgeries with a 'grain of truth'.

13 J. C. Crick, 'St Albans, Westminster and some twelfth-century views of the Anglo-Saxon past', *ANS*, 25 (2003), 65–83.

14 David Bates, 'Charters and historians of Britain and Ireland: problems and possibilities', in Marie Therese Flanagan and Judith A. Green (eds), *Charters and Charter Scholarship in Britain and Ireland* (Basingstoke: Palgrave Macmillan, 2005), pp. 1–14, at p. 3.

15 *Llandaff Charters*, p. 26.

16 Dauvit Broun, *The Charters of Gaelic Scotland and Ireland in the Early and Central Middle Ages* (Cambridge: Department of Anglo-Saxon, Norse and Celtic, University of Cambridge, 1995), pp. 38–40.

17 *Llandaff Charters*, p. 22.

18 *Llandaff Charters*, no. 261.

19 *Llandaff Charters*, nos. 218, 239, 261.

20 *Llandaff Charters*, p. 22.

21 *Acts of Welsh Rulers*, no. 200; *Handlist of the Acts of Native Welsh Rulers, 1132–1283*, ed. K. L. Maund (Cardiff: University of Wales Press, 1996), no. 116, citing Shrewsbury Public Library 1, fo. 209v, s.xv ex.

22 *Acts of Welsh Rulers*, no. 202; *Handlist of the Acts of Native Welsh Rulers*, no. 117.

23 *Acts of Welsh Rulers*, no. 203; *Handlist of the Acts of Native Welsh Rulers*, no. 121.

24 *Acts of Welsh Rulers*, no. 201; *Handlist of the Acts of Native Welsh Rulers*, no. 119.

25 *Brut y Tywysogion, or, the Chronicle of the Princes: Red Book of Hergest Version*, ed. and trans. T. Jones (1955; 2nd edn, Cardiff: University of Wales Press, 1973), p. 165.

26 A. D. Carr, 'Hywel ab Owain Gwynedd (d. 1170), prince of Gwynedd and poet', *ODNB*; see also R. R. Davies, *The Age of Conquest: Wales 1063–1415* (Oxford: Oxford University Press, 1987; new edn 2000), p. 239.

27 Carr, 'Hywel ab Owain Gwynedd' also including 'Dafydd ab Owain Gwynedd (d. 1203)', *ODNB*.

28 *Acts of Welsh Rulers*, no. 198.

29 Carr, 'Hywel ab Owain Gwynedd' and 'Dafydd ab Owain Gwynedd'.

30 *Acts of Welsh Rulers*, no. 202.

31 *Brut, Peniarth MS. 20*, p. 104.

32 *Acts of Welsh Rulers*, nos. 201, 198, 199, 200.

33 *Acts of Welsh Rulers*, no. 203.

34 Davies, *Age of Conquest*, p. 239.

35 Pryce, 'Culture, power and the charters of Welsh rulers', p. 188; Crouch, 'Earliest original charter', p. 128.

36 NLW, Penrice and Margam Ch. 113, 117; for her charters, see *Earldom of Gloucester Charters: The Charters and Scribes of the Earls and Countesses of Gloucester to*

A.D. 1217, ed. R. B. Patterson (Oxford: Clarendon Press, 1973), no. 137 as countess of Mortain and Gloucester; nos. 140–5, 149, 150 as widow *c.* 1217.

37 NLW, Penrice and Margam Ch. 123; printed, *Acts of Welsh Rulers*, no. 169; NLW, Penrice and Margam, Ch. 2032, this charter was also sealed.

38 NLW, Penrice and Margam, Ch. 69; *Cartae et alia munimenta quæ ad domininum de Glamorgancia pertinent*, vol. II: *MCXCVI – circ. MCCLXX*, ed. G. T. Clark (2nd edn, Cardiff: William Lewis, 1910), no. 239.

39 Susan M. Johns, *Noblewomen, Aristocracy and Power in the Twelfth-Century Anglo-Norman Realm* (Manchester: Manchester University Press, 2003), pp. 122–51, fish seal in context p. 128. For the seal of Petronella, daughter of Adam *Haranc, ibid.*, p. 215. See also Brigitte Bedos-Rezak, 'Women, seals and power in medieval France, 1150–1350', in M. Erler and M. Kowaleski (eds), *Women and Power in the Middle Ages* (Athens, GA and London: University of Georgia Press, 1998), pp. 61–82, and *eadem*; 'Medieval women in French sigillographic sources', in J. T. Rosenthal (ed.), *Medieval Women and the Sources of Medieval History* (Athens, GA and London: University of Georgia Press, 1990), pp. 1–36.

40 NLW, Penrice and Margam Ch. 206; *Cartae et munimenta*, II, no. 226.

41 Johns, *Noblewomen, Aristocracy and Power*, pp. 72–3.

42 Griffiths, 'Native society', pp. 193–4.

43 *Acts of Welsh Rulers*, no. 71; *Handlist of the Acts of Native Welsh Rulers*, no. 15.

44 J. Beverley Smith, 'Dower in thirteenth-century Wales: a grant of the commote of Anhuniog, 1273', *BBCS*, 30 (1982–83), 348–55, at p. 348.

45 Smith, 'Dower in thirteenth-century Wales', p. 352; *Acts of Welsh Rulers*, no. 69; *Handlist of the Acts of Native Welsh Rulers*, no. 46.

46 J. Beverley Smith, *Llywelyn ap Gruffudd: Prince of Wales* (Cardiff: University of Wales Press, 1998), pp. 304–5.

47 *The Charters of the Anglo-Norman earls of Chester, c. 1071–1237*, ed. G. Barraclough (Record Society of Lancashire and Cheshire, 126, 1988), no. 411; *Acts of Welsh Rulers*, no. 252.

48 Philip de Orreby was justiciar of Chester 1202/3–29: B. E. Harris, A. T. Thacker and C. P. Lewis (eds), *A History of the County of Chester* (Victoria History of the Counties of England; Oxford: Oxford University Press for the University of London Institute of Historical Research, 1979–2005), II, p. 3.

49 *Curia Regis Rolls* (20 vols, London: HMSO, 1922–2006), 16, no. 1596; for comment and dating, *Acts of Welsh Rulers*, p. 412, no. 251.

50 *Acts of Welsh Rulers*, p. 224, no. 84.

51 *Acts of Welsh Rulers*, no. 28; *Handlist of the Acts of Native Welsh Rulers*, no. 19.

52 *Acts of Welsh Rulers*, no. 35; *Handlist of the Acts of Native Welsh Rulers*, no. 22.

53 *Acts of Welsh Rulers*, no. 10.

54 Cf. J. Beverley Smith, 'Dynastic succession in medieval Wales', *BBCS*, 33 (1986), 199–232, for discussion of emphasis on the distinction between core patrimonial lands and outlying lands granted as apanages.

55 Matthew Paris, *Chronica Majora*, ed. H. R. Luard (7 vols, Rolls Series, 57; London: Longman and Co., 1872–84), iii. 394.

56 Richard Eales, 'Ranulf (III), sixth earl of Chester and first earl of Lincoln (1170–1232)' (first published 2004), online edn, *ODNB* (2008).

57 *Acts of Welsh Rulers*, p. 28; Roger Turvey, *The Welsh Princes: The Native Rulers of Wales, 1063–1283* (Harlow: Longman, 2002), p. 89; Smith, *Llywelyn ap Gruffudd*, pp. 12–14; for discussion of *edling* 'the one who shall rule after the king and be most honoured at the court after the king and queen' see *idem*, 'Dynastic succession', p. 201.

58 Davies, *Age of Conquest*, p. 249.

59 *Calendar of Entries in the Papal Registers Relating to Great Britain and Ireland: Papal Letters*, i: *A.D. 1198–1304*, ed. W. H. Bliss (London: HMSO, 1893), p. 87. *Handlist of the Acts of Native Welsh Rulers*, no. 466; *Acts of Welsh Rulers*, no. 253.

60 Luke 1:38: 'dixit autem Maria ecce ancilla Domini fiat mihi secundum verbum tuum et discessit ab illa angelus'; see also Luke 1:48 'quia respexit humilitatem ancillae suae ecce enim ex hoc beatam me dicent omnes generationes'.

61 Smith, *Llywelyn ap Gruffudd*, pp. 12–15.

62 *Acts of Welsh Rulers*, no. 253 notes.

63 Cf. Llywelyn's exploitation of canon law to get out of his proposed marriage to the daughter of Reginald, king of Man and the Isles, so he could marry Joan; A. D. Carr, 'Llywelyn ab Iorwerth (*c.* 1173–1240)', *ODNB*.

64 Davies, *Age of Conquest*, p. 124.

65 Davies, *Age of Conquest*, p. 249.

66 *Acts of Welsh Rulers*, no. 279.

67 Smith, 'Dynastic succession', pp. 212–13, who suggests Rhys ap Gruffudd may have designated his eldest legitimate son, Gruffudd, as successor over and above his eldest, but illegitimate, son Maelgwn.

68 Robin C. Stacey, 'King, queen and *edling* in the laws of the court', in T. M. Charles-Edwards, M. E. Owen and P. Russell (eds.), *The Welsh King and his Court* (Cardiff: University of Wales Press, 2000), pp. 29–62, at p. 55; cf. David Stephenson, 'The laws of court: past reality or present ideal?', in Charles-Edwards *et al.* (eds), *Welsh King and his Court*, pp. 400–9, at pp. 401–2.

69 *Acts of Welsh Rulers*, no. 276; *Handlist of the Acts of Native Welsh Rulers*, no. 464.

70 *Acts of Welsh Rulers*, no. 277; *Handlist of the Acts of Native Welsh Rulers*, no. 465.

71 *Acts of Welsh Rulers*, no. 276, p. 445.

72 Gransden, *Historical Writing*, p. 368.

73 Louise J. Wilkinson, 'Joan, wife of Llywelyn the Great', in M. Prestwich *et al.* (eds), *Thirteenth Century England X* (Woodbridge: Boydell and Brewer, 2005), pp. 81–93, at p. 85.

74 *Acts of Welsh Rulers*, no. 278.

75 *Acts of Welsh Rulers*, no. 280; *Handlist of the Acts of Native Welsh Rulers*, no. 340. *Acts of Welsh Rulers*, no. 281, in a letter patent of Henry III; Pryce suggests she may have been given a new title as early as May 1230, when Llywelyn may well have adopted his new title 'Prince of Aberffraw and Lord of Snowdon' (but since she was imprisoned until 1231, perhaps 1231 is more likely).

76 *Acts of Welsh Rulers*, no. 202.

77 M. Chibnall, *The Empress Matilda: Queen Consort, Queen Mother and Lady of the English* (Oxford: Blackwell, 1991), pp. 102ff, stresses that this title was always ambiguous, accepted in unprecedented circumstances.

78 *Acts of Welsh Rulers*, no. 275.

79 *Vita Griffini Filii Conani: The Medieval Life of Gruffudd ap Cynan*, ed. and trans. Paul Russell (Cardiff: University of Wales Press, 2005), pp. 88–9; David Moore, 'Gruffudd

ap Cynan and the medieval Welsh polity', in K. L. Maund (ed.), *Gruffudd ap Cynan: A Collaborative Biography* (Woodbridge and Rochester: Boydell and Brewer, 1996), pp. 1–60, at p. 5 notes that the *Vita* was a twelfth-century source.

80 Stacey, 'King, queen and *edling*', pp. 54–8.

81 Pryce, 'Lawbooks and literacy', pp. 39, 50–3, 57, 63.

82 Robin C. Stacey, 'Divorce, medieval Welsh style', *Speculum*, 77 (2002), 1107–27, at p. 1127.

83 See Stacey, 'Divorce, medieval Welsh style', p. 1109; R. R. Davies, 'Law and national identity in thirteenth-century Wales', in R. R. Davies, Ralph Griffiths, Ieuan Gwynedd Jones and Kenneth Morgan (eds), *Welsh Society and Nationhood: Historical Essays Presented to Glanmor Williams* (Cardiff: University of Wales Press, 1984), pp. 51–64.

84 Davies, *Age of Conquest*, p. 18.

85 Stacey, 'King, queen and *edling*', p. 55.

86 Stacey, 'King, queen and *edling*', p. 53. See p. 54 and note 96, where Stacey notes the differences in interpretation between his approach and that of Dafydd Jenkins. The former argues that the lawyers attempted to confine the queen in the domestic sphere, whereas Dafydd Jenkins suggests that the Iorwerth redaction gave the queen a higher status by doubling the number of her officers by comparison with the other redactions: Dafydd Jenkins, 'Prolegomena to the law of court', in Charles-Edwards, Owen and Russell (eds), *Welsh King and his Court*, pp. 15–28, see table 1.1 p. 19 and table 1.2 p. 27 for the lists of officers of the king and queen.

87 Huw Pryce, 'The prologues to the Welsh lawbooks', *BBCS*, 33 (1986), 151–87, at pp. 153, 165; Stacey, 'King, queen and *edling*', p. 34.

88 *Life of Gruffudd ap Cynan*, pp. 88–9.

89 Liz Oakley-Brown and Louise J. Wilkinson, 'Introduction', in Liz Oakley-Brown and Louise J. Wilkinson (eds), *The Rituals and Rhetoric of Queenship: Medieval to Early Modern* (Dublin: Four Courts Press, 2009), pp. 11–19, at p. 19.

90 For the great variety of ruler terms in Welsh, see Dafydd Jenkins, 'Kings, lords and princes: the nomenclature of authority in thirteenth-century Wales', *BBCS*, 26 (1974–76), 451–62, at p. 452, who notes that *princeps* was translated as *twysog* in Welsh. Welsh male rulers were still called 'king' *brenin/rex* in the thirteenth century, yet from the late twelfth century the title was no longer used in Latin narrative sources and documents. David Stephenson noted that the increasing use of *arglwydd* (lord) replaced king in many contexts in lesser dynasties: *The Governance of Gwynedd* (Cardiff: University of Wales Press, 1984), p. 164; see also T. M. Charles-Edwards and Nerys Ann Jones, 'Breintiau Gwŷr Powys: the liberties of the men of Powys', in Charles-Edwards, Owen and Russell (eds), *Welsh King and his Court*, pp. 191–223, which argues that there was a variety in the number of terms used to designate royal status in the late twelfth century where five types of royal lord are distinguished. The uncertain political realities in Powys after the period 1160 explain the attitudes to power recorded in the poem *Breintiau Gwŷr Powys*, 'The Privileges (or Liberties) of the Men of Powys', by the *pencerdd* poet of Powys Cynddelw Brydydd Mawr; see a major analysis of poets' terminology by Rhian M. Andrews, 'The nomenclature of kingship in Welsh court poetry 1100–1300, part I: the terms', *Studia Celtica*, 44 (2010), 79–110, and *eadem*, 'The nomenclature of kingship in Welsh court poetry 1100–1300, part II: the rulers', *Studia Celtica*, 45 (2011), 53–82.

91 Smith, *Llywelyn ap Gruffudd*, pp. 5–6.

92 R. R. Davies, 'The peoples of Britain and Ireland, 1100–1400, III: Laws and customs', *TRHS*, 6th ser., 6 (1996), 1–23, at p. 6; Alan Harding, '*Regiam Majestatem* amongst medieval law books', *The Juridical Review*, 29 (1984), 97–111; Robin C. Stacey, 'Law and order in the very old West: England and Ireland in the early middle ages', in Benjamin Hudson and Vickie Ziegler (eds), *Crossed Paths: Methodological Approaches to the Celtic Aspect of the European Middle Ages* (Lanham: University Press of America, 1991), pp. 39–61; for women and sovereignty, James Doan, 'Sovereignty aspects in the role of women in medieval Irish and Welsh society', *Proceedings of the Harvard Celtic Colloquium*, 5 (1985), 87–102; Louise Olga Fradenburg (ed.), *Women and Sovereignty* (Edinburgh: Edinburgh University Press, 1992); Oakley-Brown and Wilkinson (eds), *Rituals and Rhetoric of Queenship*, pp. 15–19.

93 Susan Reynolds, *Fiefs and Vassals: The Medieval Evidence Reinterpreted* (Oxford: Oxford University Press, 1994), p. 476; see J. Gillingham, ' "Slaves of the Normans"? Gerald de Barri and regnal solidarity in early-thirteenth-century England', in Pauline Stafford, Janet L. Nelson and Jane Martindale (eds), *Law, Laity and Solidarities: Essays in Honour of Susan Reynolds* (Manchester: Manchester University Press, 2001), pp. 160–71, at p. 162.

94 Paris, *Chronica Majora*, IV, 316–18; *Acts of Welsh Rulers*, no. 284.

95 Gransden, *Historical Writing*, pp. 356, 360.

96 See *The Merioneth Lay Subsidy Roll, 1292–3*, ed. Keith Williams-Jones (Cardiff: University of Wales Press, 1976), p. xvii, who noted that there was a 'dramatic leap' in the volume of coin in circulation, which came to replace payments made by head of cattle by the early thirteenth century.

97 Smith, *Llywelyn ap Gruffudd*, pp. 32–3, 37–9; for discussion of Senana, see G. A. Williams, 'The succession to Gwynedd, 1238–47', *BBCS*, 20 (1962–64), 393–413; Gwenyth Richards, *Welsh Noblewomen in the Thirteenth Century: An Historical Study of Medieval Welsh Law and Gender Roles* (Lewiston, NY: Edwin Mellen Press, 2009), pp. 23–42.

98 Compare the way Gwenllian who deputed for absent husband Gruffudd ap Rhys in 1136; for discussion see chapter 1, p. 20, and chapter 2, pp. 62–4.

99 *Acts of Welsh Rulers*, no. 283, pp. 450–1

100 *Acts of Welsh Rulers*, no. 612, at pp. 809–10.

101 Gransden, *Historical Writing*, p. 369.

102 Smith, *Llywelyn ap Gruffudd*, p. 33.

103 Smith, *Llywelyn ap Gruffudd*, p. 34.

104 Smith, *Llywelyn ap Gruffudd*, p. 332.

105 Harris *et al.* (eds), *History of the County of Chester*, III, pp. 156–7. The abbey received further gifts, including books, after the initial foundation.

106 *The Ledger Book of Vale Royal Abbey*, ed. John Brownbill (Record Society of Lancashire and Cheshire, 68, 1914), ch. 8, p. 9.

107 Brigitte Bedos-Rezak, 'In search of a semiotic paradigm: the matter of sealing in medieval thought and praxis, 1050–1400', in Noel Adams, John Cherry and James Robinson (eds), *Good Impressions: Image and Authority in Medieval Seals* (London: British Museum, 2007), pp. 1–7.

4

Rediscovering Nest in the early modern period

T HE WAY THAT Nest was remembered in the early modern period has much to tell us about the way that Welsh writers conceptualised the past, and this chapter will therefore explore a relatively little examined set of themes in the historiography. It will consider how the critical early years of Norman incursions into Wales were portrayed by later writers and thus discuss the way that later writers conceptualised the Norman past. It will cast reflections on the role of ideas about women, gender and conquest and the place of Nest in a narrative of Wales from the early modern period. This will be achieved through a discussion of the writings of two gentlemen with antiquarian interests, George Owen of Henllys and Rice Merrick, respectively from Pembrokeshire and Glamorganshire. Owen and Merrick are representative of a number of Welsh gentlemen who turned their attention to collecting, preserving and fostering Welsh culture and history. Other men such as Edward Stradling, Humphrey Llwyd, David Powel and Sir John Price also appropriated and nurtured the history of Wales within a British context. Protestant humanists welcomed the Tudors and turned their attention to the Welsh past as part of a project to generate propaganda for nascent Welsh protestant patriotism.[1] Historians of the early modern period have drawn attention to the imagined communities that such antiquarians created and have considered how this affected conceptions of Britain through the creation of enduring ethnic stereotypes. Thus, influenced by Michael Hechter's approach to the period, there has been considerable debate on the way that elites created identities both to foster a sense of nationalism and to subordinate communities.[2] The interrelationship of Wales with the Tudor state has been much debated. In particular, the involvement of the gentlemen who played a key part in county politics and administration has generally provoked historians such as John Gwynfor Jones to consider the cultural role of the elite and to relate this to a broader project, here the understanding of the creation of a Welsh identity in a British context. Thus historians have tended to view the activities of seventeenth-century Welsh antiquarians in the context of an intellectual revival in Welsh culture led by Welsh gentlemen who saw the Tudor period as a positive period for the rehabilitation of Welsh culture as part of a British whole.[3] Within this rehabilitation of Welsh culture, ideas about women, gender and conquest played an integral part in creating approaches to a Welsh past to serve the needs of a Welsh present, as indeed did the demands of local, or county, political interests.

Such an approach represents a striking departure from the situation which had pertained through most of the middle ages. Not all English commentary had been negative, but most late-medieval writers paid little attention to Wales and the Welsh. It was by the fourteenth century possible for a major English authority such as Ranulph Higden, located as he was in Chester in close proximity to Wales, to express considerable sympathy for the lot of the Welsh. He described their mythological kinship with Priam, being of the blood of Jupiter, and the progeny of Dardanus. He provided a significantly female-gendered explanation for the name of 'Wales', as derived from Queen Gwalaes, daughter of Ebrank, although with an alternative derivation from Gwalio, a gentleman.[4] Again using a female-gendered metaphor, Wales, he said, though smaller than England, was as fertile – '*In matre et in filia*'. And for Higden the Welsh might be, in Gildas's word, '*fragiles*', but he saw it as no wonder they were unsettled because they themselves had been put out of their land.[5] It is only with the rebellion of Dafydd ap Gruffudd in 1282 that the Welsh become the 'false Welsh', and a tone of condemnation appears.[6] But his account of the Welsh in the early fourteenth century is one of a people who had, after the failure of the rebellion of Madog ap Llywelyn in 1294, started to live as Englishmen, gather treasure, and fear the loss of their goods. This was in spite of the fact that his main source was Gerald's itinerary and description.[7] One sign of this is, in his description of Ireland, a reference to the idea that both Irish and Welsh old women transform themselves into hares to suck the milk of their neighbours.[8]

Later historians borrowed heavily from Higden, but often differ from his emphases. Henry Knighton was more negative, although in a particularly sparsely expressed way. He took from Higden brief details of Aethelstan's conquests, and of the activities of Godwin and of Harold in Wales.[9] He offered an account of Henry, Robert of Bellême and the Welsh, but for 1219 he recorded simply '*Wallenses rebellarunt*'.[10] In 1386, in his own time, the Welsh are among a group of local inhabitants from the north and west of Britain who are accused of having committed plunder when, having been summoned to help defend against a French threat, they were disbanded without pay.[11] For Capgrave, in the middle of the fifteenth century, Wales has become a subject of very limited interest, given by Brute to Camber, conquered by Edward the Elder, then not mentioned again until the time of Edward I, and subsequently only referred to occasionally in connection with military action, and finally providing a setting for the futile ventures of Henry IV. None of this is gendered other than straightforwardly male.[12]

In all this writing the descriptions of the Welsh refer barely at all to women, and the narratives of conquest and control and of rebellion are gendered male.[13] The one exception in Higden is the role of Joan, referred to as marrying Llywelyn and then with William de Braose referred to as blamed for adultery with her, imprisoned and hanged by Llywelyn, this being the cause for great discord between king and prince.[14]

This therefore provides the context for the developments of the sixteenth century – the inheritance was of an English historiography which paid little attention to Wales and saw the conquest in limited terms as the result of the actions of kings and the caricatured actions of rebels.

It was Welsh writing about Wales which developed an alternative approach. In a work complete by 1559, Humphrey Llwyd included details of Nest's abduction in his *Cronica Walliae a Rege Cadwalader ad annum 1294*. The version of the abduction narrative has similarities to the version presented by the *Brutiau*, although it has been demonstrated that it is difficult to identify Llwyd's sources, which he does not himself specify. His *Cronica Walliae* includes details drawn from a diverse range of sources, some of which are clearly not the known versions of the *Brutiau*, and which Llwyd identifies as a Welsh chronicler, a version of the *Brut* which is no longer extant.[15] The view of the abduction presented in the *Cronica Walliae* replicated many details of the history presented in all versions of the *Brut y Tywysogion*, and this is despite the diversity of versions presented within the *Brutiau*. That Llwyd ignored any possible variations in the abduction tale presented by different versions of the *Brut* should not be considered exceptional. Llwyd rarely discussed discrepancies within the different versions of the same events given in his sources.[16] Given that Llwyd may have used sources for his view of the abduction other than the version we are familiar with presented by Peniarth MS 20, the *Red Book of Hergest* and *Brenhinedd y Saesson*, it is of note that many of the essential features of the narrative of abduction portrayed by them were retained by Llwyd. It suggests that the traditions were part of an identified and accepted narrative of the turmoil in the early twelfth century in south-west Wales. Thus, the abduction is portrayed, as in the *Brutiau*, as part of the wider story of the broader political disputes of the kingdom of Deheubarth and its resistance to and accommodation with the English monarchy. Llwyd's narrative of the abduction, as in the *Brutiau*, follows a passage in which he mistakenly relates that Gerald of Windsor had rebuilt the 'castell of Penbroke in a place called Kengarth Vechan, and brought thither all his househoulde stuffe, and other goodes with his wief and his children'. The abduction narrative begins with the Christmas feast of 'Cadwgan ap Blethyn' in Dyfed. Owain 'hearde the beautie of Nest . . . praysed above all women in the lande'. This provoked his desire to see her. Under the guise of friendship he visited Nest and 'findinge trueth to surmmont the rumour' he returned 'enflammed with love of the woman'. That night he attacked the castle with a 'sorte of wilde companions' and set fire to the house. Llwyd then relates how Nest prevented Gerald from confronting Owain and counselled him to escape by pulling up the boards of the privy. Nest calls to her attackers and is then abducted by Owain and his companions: 'when they colde not finde him they toke her, and her twoe sonnes and a sonne and a daughter borne by a concubyne to Geralde, and caryed them awaye to Powys'.[17] Thus, although the narrative describes Nest in a model which is very close to those presented by extant versions of the *Brutiau*, Llwyd romanticises the abduction with his choice of language. Nest is, for example, key to the escape from the castle by Gerald. Llwyd does not, however, mention the possible rape of Nest at the point of abduction, unlike the extant versions of the *Brutiau*. Llwyd includes the details of Nest's intervention to have her children sent to their father and states that Cadwgan, Owain's father, was 'very sorye, and feared the Kinges displeasure'. This indicates that Cadwgan was afraid of the damage done to the Anglo-Norman–Welsh political relationship, damage wrought by his son's impetuosity and violence. There is no indication that, in the words of Peniarth MS 20, the 'violation' to Nest was of any concern. The view of royal lordship is expressed in the language deployed to describe the agreement made by Richard bishop of London and Ithel and Madoc, the sons of Rhirid ap Bleddyn, who were offered 'riche giftes, and great rewardes, besides the rule of the whole countrey, yf they colde take or kill Owen to revenge the dishonor he hade done to the Kinge'. Alongside the omission of the direct reference to sexual intercourse, there is a clearer emphasis on Owain as a heroic figure, whose death while fighting 'manfully' and 'couragiousely' is more typical of his life as a whole.[18]

As a result of Llwyd's approach, the abduction narrative became more firmly rooted in Welsh tradition. It represented a rich mix of traditions which demonstrated the complexity of the political context of south-west Wales in the early twelfth century. Llwyd's work, through its adaptation and publication by David Powel to whom we will turn shortly, was a key influence on Welsh historiography until the early twentieth century.[19] Llwyd therefore helped develop the abduction narrative as a tale of eroticised conquest inspired by female beauty, in a presentation which had lost the clearer connotations of rape or violation. The portrayal of Nest as an object of conquest and her retrieval from the castle of Cenarth Bychan was constructed in Llwyd without specific reference to sexual union, whether consensual or not. It was a tale which featured female passive resistance where sexual politics and sexual conquest were obliquely referenced but nevertheless were fundamental in shaping perceptions of a defiant Welsh past rooted in tradition. Such traditions were thus essentially portrayed in different versions of the *Brut*, and, despite small variations in the traditions associated with the abduction,[20] at the heart of the narrative was the perception of Welsh impetuosity, royal response and retaliation conducted through Welsh and Anglo-Norman forces, and devastation in Ceredigion within a tale which emphasised the eventual reconciliation of Owain with Henry I. Llwyd's interest in these events in south Wales was not a local patriotism: Llwyd's description of Denbigh, his home town, occupied more space than was devoted to the whole of the history of the kingdom of Brycheiniog, and Williams has noted that Llwyd made mistakes concerning some topographical description of south Wales and provided a preponderance of northern material, two-thirds of the descriptions being of north Wales compared with a third concerning the south.[21] Rather it was a sign of the increasing significance of gender in his complex response to his sources for the conquest of Wales, representing his underlying sympathy for the Welsh position in their relationship with the English.[22]

The writings a few years later of another gentleman with antiquarian interests, Sir Edward Stradling of St Donat's, were influential in the sudden rise to prominence of a tradition which similarly drew on the Norman conquest as a pivotal period, in this case in his own county of Glamorgan, and which again, in one important version, involved a woman and her contested fate. Stradling had wide interests in history, language and the arts. He was prominent in local affairs, serving as a sheriff for the county in 1573–74, 1582–83 and 1595–96, as well as deputy lieutenant in the 1590s. He had links with prominent intellectuals including Rice Merrick and William Camden. During the reign of Elizabeth, at some point between 1561 and 1566, Stradling sent a copy of his family tree and an account of 'The winning of the lordship of Glamorgan out of the

Welshmen's hands' to William Cecil, the queen's principal secretary. This story about twelve knights of Glamorgan, which had already appeared in the 1550s in Llwyd's *Cronica Walliae* and in general terms can be traced back into the fifteenth century,[23] spuriously claimed that many of the local families then prominent had ancient roots in the county at the time of the Norman settlement of Wales. Ralph Griffiths convincingly argued that there are both elements of historical accuracy and downright inventions within the narrative.[24] Sir Edward wrote his 'Winning of the lordship of Glamorgan' without doubt to give his family a more ancient and respectable pedigree than it merited, but it is striking that the defeat of the native Welsh through association with the Norman conquest is the method by which he chose to do so. The association with William Cecil brought the symbolisms of conquest and domination in Glamorgan to the very heart of the Elizabethan court. Cecil himself required a family pedigree of illustrious descent, and it is possible, as Griffiths suggested, that his request for Stradling's genealogy was intended to provide a model for his own pedigree. The influence of Stradling's 'Winning of the lordship of Glamorgan' was long-lasting and helped to bind the story of a key dynasty at the Tudor and Stuart court, the Cecils, to the accounts of Welsh history in David Powel's *The Historie of Cambria now called Wales*, published in 1584, for which it was a key source. Powel added a postscript to Stradling's 'Winning of the lordship of Glamorgan' from records held by William Cecil and his kinsman William Sitsyllt from Herefordshire. The Cecil addition to Stradling's essay included details of how his ancestors had become established in Gloucestershire and Herefordshire when Robert Sitsyllt made a fortuitous marriage as a result of his role in this episode, following Einion ap Cedifor.[25]

As Griffiths has argued, Powel's *Historie*, dependent on Stradling's account as well as that of Llwyd, remained the most influential account of Norman arrival in Wales for over three hundred years.[26] According to Humphrey Llwyd's account, Einion ap Cedifor, son of the lord of Dyfed, and Iestyn ap Gwrgant rebelled against Rhys ap Tewdwr's overlordship and became allies who sought Norman assistance from Robert fitzHamo, earl of Gloucester, and then advanced and killed Rhys. Iestyn then refused to allow Einion to marry his daughter, as previously agreed, and 'laughed him to scorne': at which point Einion called back the Normans, who defeated Iestyn, divided up Glamorgan, and were thenceforward dominant.[27]

The *Cronica* was used by David Powel, and informed his approach, although some of the material was misrepresented and uncritically accepted.[28]

Stradling's account varies slightly: Einion is not linked to Dyfed but rather is a servant of Iestyn. Einion calls back Robert fitzHamo after the defeat of Rhys ap Tewdwr not because of Iestyn's daughter but because Iestyn refused to pay to fitzHamo the amount originally agreed. As Griffiths points out, however, the variations are around the same theme: the Welsh invite the Normans, which is a fatal error.[29] As Griffiths has shown, the account of the twelve knights was 'overlaid with fable and partially shot through with error' because Edward Stradling attempted to write a history which would demonstrate his own family's roots in Wales which hinged on their role in the conquest.[30] What this demonstrates is that the Norman conquest was seen as a key point of legitimacy for the Glamorganshire gentlemen such as Stradling for the establishment of their genealogies. The important point for us is that the narratives show that the Welsh were responsible for their own conquest because they were unable to co-operate, and at the heart of this, in Llwyd's account, lay a dispute about a marriage agreement. As such, marriage negotiations and their failure lie as a causative factor at the heart of this later interpretation of the Norman conquest of Glamorgan. A marriage contract is thus a destabilising force in contemporary political culture.

It is probable that Stradling's version reflects the political sensitivities of the writer finely attuned to the current political climate at Elizabeth's court. Blanche Parry, as Welsh lady-in-waiting to Elizabeth, drew Powel's attention to the story of the twelve knights.[31] Parry was a kinswoman of Sir Edward Stradling, and the tale emphasised her family's importance in Glamorgan. It is a story in which the political importance of marriage was stressed, and it may reflect contemporary political rivalries – rivalries which in a few years were to be played out in stark fashion. In July 1588 Sir John Perrot, a prominent Pembrokeshire gentleman, returned from Ireland where he had served as lord deputy. Perrot, through court patronage, was pre-eminent in Pembrokeshire politics, and George Owen of Henllys and other county gentlemen had been his target in land suits as Perrot sought to build his power by any means possible. Yet Owen had allied himself to Perrot through marriage, and the two must have formed a working relationship when they both had served under the earl of Pembroke as deputy lieutenants. In 1591 Perrot dramatically fell from favour and in 1592 was found guilty of treason and condemned to death for allegedly secretly negotiating with Philip II of Spain.[32] After this disgrace it was four gentlemen from Glamorgan who, at the suggestion of the queen to the earl of Pembroke, were sent to Pembrokeshire to assume the duties of Owen and Perrot as deputy lieutenants in charge of military affairs. The queen felt she could not rely on Pembrokeshire gentlemen to organise an army against the potential threat of a Spanish armada since there were 'no others', meaning no other Pembrokeshire gentlemen, to take over from Perrot and Owen. The four appointed were Sir William Herbert of Swansea, Richard Basset and Thomas Mansell esquires, and Sir Edward Stradling.[33] Stradling, of course, had stressed the importance of Glamorgan within Wales; Powel's work, building on his, was first published just four years before the disgrace of Perrot. It is significant that the defeat of the princely house of Deheubarth, which had its heart in Pembrokeshire, by his native Glamorgan, was central to Stradling's narrative. Regional divisions and rivalries historically were stressed at a period of great uncertainty in Pembrokeshire, and in England more generally, due to the threat of a Spanish armada. Thus Sir Edward Stradling assumed a public role in the county which had been defeated by his forbears. His view of the Norman conquest of south Wales was linked to the inner workings of Elizabeth's court through the connections with Sir William Cecil and his relative Blanche Parry, her lady-in-waiting.

Powel in his *Historie of Cambria* also developed and extended the narrative of the abduction of Nest, using what he found in Llwyd's *Cronica Walliae*. He states that Owain was roused to action on 'hearing the beautie of Nest wife to *Gerald* steward of *Penbrooke* praised aboue all the women in the land' and on seeing her '& finding the truth to surmount the fame, he came home all inflamed with hir loue'.[34] The abduction narrative then very closely follows the version taken up by Llwyd: in particular, as with Llwyd there is no specific reference to sexual intercourse, consensual or not ('they tooke hir and hir two sons').[35] Following Llwyd, Powel perpetuated ideas about Wales and the Welsh which were derived from, or close to those of, the *Brut*, and both authors wrote in the context of political change and religious and cultural transformations of the sixteenth century. We have already noted the direct influence of William Cecil on the account provided by Powel of the conquest of Glamorgan; his influence on the work in general is suggested by his provision of privileged access to manuscript material. Powel's work on Llwyd's manuscript, in the custody of his patron Sir Henry Sydney, a project inherited from John Dee, was an integral part of a career that included the vigorous promotion of Protestantism in the vicinity of his livings in the diocese of St Asaph and assistance in the project for the translation of the Bible into Welsh.

Contemporaries and later commentators in the early modern period drew on the *Historie* and adapted elements of the Nest tale in the context of local identity. Such localism can be seen in the works of other early modern gentlemen such as Rice Merrick and George Owen, who both wrote county histories in the late sixteenth century. The *Morganiae Archaiographia* by Rice Merrick has been described as an important link in Welsh historiography,[36] and it was concerned with, among other topics, the Norman settlement of Glamorgan. William Herbert and Henry Herbert, first and second earls of Pembroke, were the patrons of Rice Merrick. His son married into the Herbert family. He himself was married to Mary Fleming, who was a descendent of one of the families who could trace their descent to the Normans who first entered Glamorgan. Merrick's sources included Welsh and oral sources; he borrowed manuscripts from Sir Edward Stradling of St Donat's. He drew on Stradling's story of the conquest of Glamorgan by twelve knights under the Norman fitzHamo and incorporated the details into his *Morganiae Archaiographia*. As a historian Merrick drew on a variety of written and oral sources and his view of the defeat of Rhys ap Tewdwr and conquest of Glamorgan is drawn in part from Stradling's account. It was, however, the oral tradition which took precedence as a source for the reasons for the internecine disputes in south Wales.[37]

Merrick explains the collapse of native princely houses in south-west Wales within a context which takes account of, and eroticises, the rivalries between the ruling dynasties. His view is that their defeat brought 'lamentable disherison'.[38] There are no original manuscripts of Merrick's work now extant, but it is thought that Merrick wrote his *Morganiae* in the period 1578–84, but it was never completed.[39] Both Merrick and Owen were figures of note in their respective counties and present a view of their county within a broader conceptual framework underpinned by Welsh identity but very much conceived of in local terms. Both sought a narrative to explain their family origins; both take their narratives back to the twelfth century. Indeed the twelfth century is pivotal to their narratives, and the arrival of the Normans is seen as the origination of family legitimacy.

Merrick divides the history of Glamorgan into three phases ruled by three 'governments'. First, he argues that Glamorgan was ruled by the Britons or Welshmen, who were 'the most ancient inhabitants' and who were defeated by 'strangers', by which he means the Normans. This defeat led to the second stage in its history when Glamorgan was ruled 'by the lord thereof' until the Acts of Union. This ushered in the third phase when Glamorgan was ruled by 'the kings and queens of England'. He is careful to distinguish that Glamorgan was only a part of the ancient kingdom of Morgannwg. The territories and extent of the kingdom are discussed in some detail.[40] Merrick does so, he argues, because 'later writers' have confused the two kingdoms. Merrick states that he has used ancient sources to clarify and inform his discussion of the kingdoms. This then forms the context for his discussion of the pivotal event in the history of Glamorgan – the defeat of its native rulers by Norman invaders, which moves the narrative into its second phase. Merrick explains that during the reign of William Rufus, Iestyn ap Gwrgant was lord of Glamorgan and Morgannwg and that Rhys ap Tewdwr was lord of Deheubarth, which included the shires of Carmarthen, Pembroke and Cardigan. Merrick states that enmity arose between these 'two great lords' and that he will explain it derived from information from 'continual fame and memory from antiquity . . . preserved in both their seigniories'.[41] Relying on these oral sources, he argues that Rhys and Iestyn argued not from a desire merely to exert power over each other, but because Rhys had an infatuation with the wife of Iestyn. Merrick states that Rhys ap Tewdwr was inflamed with desire for the wife of his rival through the stories he heard from the *beirdd* (bards) who sang at his court. In response to a question from Rhys as to what entertainment they had witnessed in Morgannwg, they had

> answered Nothing else but that Deheubarth and Morgannwg want both one thing, viz a meet match; which might have been well remedied if Iestyn had been married to his wife and he to Iestyn's wife, whom they with high praises extolled as well for her beauty as for her good qualities, in whom nature and fortune contended who could show greater force and power.

As a result of this 'the ruin and decay of both families' was brought by 'this lusty prince' who was 'in the flower of his youth and voluptuousness' and was 'kindled with Venus's dart and fervent desire to see her'. Rhys 'closed up his eyes to reason' and thought of a ruse to meet her. He arranged for a meeting 'near the borders of his kingdom' at Neath on the pretext that they should 'treat matters which concerned their seignories, as well as to solace themselves' and also to renew friendships 'and confirm amity between them'. Iestyn and his wife travelled with a 'great train of gentlemen and gentlewomen'. After greetings, and

> familiar entertainment, they feasted each other. But Rhys ap Tewdwr, after he had viewed Iestyn's wife, thought she surmounted the praises of her unto him reported, which so inflamed his heart with fire that he determined, either by secret entreaty or by enforcement, to possess his desired prey.

The use of the word 'prey' is here suggestive that Iestyn's wife was a passive victim of Rhys's duplicitous and scheming behaviour: it was his passion that was the cause of the dispute. Rhys, under the pretext of other causes, used covert talk to tell her 'his secret suit and determinate purpose'. Iestyn's wife then told her husband about Rhys's plan 'and lest violence be offered to her, which she mistrusted' persuaded her husband to leave secretly in the night. Rhys was furious that he was 'disappointed of his hoped prey' and returned to Deheubarth in a rage 'complaining of Iestyn's discourtesy and ingratitude, affirming it to be in contempt of him and spite of him' and threatened revenge. Merrick in an aside states that Rhys did not make public the reason for Iestyn's sudden departure. Iestyn was also 'kindled with displeasure'. Rhys refused to be reconciled to Iestyn: 'they must needs seek the other's destruction'. Rhys was 'overcome with frenzy' and was so 'marred to his wife's affection' that nothing could 'assuage his fury'. Thus he was 'determined to end their quarrel by fortune of battle; for the predestinate ruin to both their families'.[42]

At this point in his narrative Merrick states that he has never seen any 'title of subjection of Morgannwg to Deheubarth', a deliberate refutation of the views of Humphrey Llwyd's *Breviary of Britain*, which alleged that Glamorgan was always 'rebellious against its lawful Prince'.[43] Thus Merrick argues that Iestyn was forced to send 'a gentleman of his Einion' (ap Cedifor) to Robert fitzHamo, who agreed to help 'for a certain salary'. Thus fitzHamo and twelve of his knights joined forces with Iestyn to defeat Rhys ap Tewdwr in a pitched battle. Merrick here takes pains to refute the views of Robert Fabyan, who suggests that the cause of the war was that Rhys had attacked Englishmen 'upon the border'. Thus Merrick suggests that the native Welsh had not attacked the English and further gives different reasons for Iestyn's death at the hands of the Normans. First, he states that in one tradition Iestyn dismissed his men and then entertained the Normans. FitzHamo and his men then attacked and killed Iestyn because he refused to honour the bargain struck by Einion with fitzHamo. Second, Merrick reports a tradition that Iestyn had treated fitzHamo honourably but that Einion, who was disappointed not to have married Iestyn's daughter, then caught up with fitzHamo near Pwll Meurig near Chepstow, complained of Iestyn's treatment of him, and offered them the country in return for their support in defeating Iestyn. The third scenario suggested stresses Norman duplicity. Merrick argues that Robert fitzHamo had, once retained by Einion, hoped to secure some lands in Glamorgan once he and his companions had seen for themselves how attractive the region was. Merrick argues that 'the greediness of sovereignty and dominion allured fitzHamo', who took advantage of the fractured nature of Welsh local politics. He illustrates this with an anecdote which relates that 'the Breconians' were too busy with internecine disputes to attack and kill Iestyn. Merrick also argues that such a conquest would be favourably viewed by Rufus.[44] Merrick further reports a tradition that Einion had caught up with fitzHamo at Penarth, when he was about to board a ship. Again the point of contention was Einion's failure to have the hand of Iestyn's daughter Nest in marriage, so Iestyn had refused to honour the bargain struck with Einion.

Merrick expends considerable energy on these different traditions, and the plurality of traditions concerning Iestyn's defeat at the hands of the Normans is indicative that different traditions were then current. The essential cause of the dispute, however, he attributes to Rhys's underhand and duplicitous behaviour. Merrick argues that 'estates' and inferiors should 'look upon and remember the fruit of sensuality; the success of discussion and malice; and what a dangerous matter it is to incite strangers in to a prosperous country'.[45] He writes that 'others' have interpreted events wrongly, a reference to Stradling who does not mention Rhys's rage at his inability to consummate his desires as the cause of the war. So although a woman was the cause of the dispute between Morgannwg and Deheubarth, the real problem for the native Welsh was their use of the Normans to support their military campaigns and their inability to control their passions.

There are several interconnected complex themes which suggest that political, and national, success were linked to good conduct. The relationship with the Welsh was an unwitting trust in them as allies who were then taken advantage of. Thus it is the inability of some among them to control themselves, which is the fateful flaw. Thus there is an underlying message, which is that the Welsh are not hostile to the English, that they are not rebellious as such, but that they cannot control themselves – and now, through Protestantism, they have a code to live by which will allow them to be full members of Britain. Thus Merrick utilises oral sources to confect a view of the rivalry and dispute between Iestyn and Rhys of Deheubarth in which the topos of woman as the cause of destructive war is utilised. This war harmed the native Welsh kingdoms and allowed the foreign invaders an advantage, and this theme, which is so prevalent in the Nest story, is also seen in the conquest of Glamorgan by the Normans. Thus the Norman conquest is linked here with ideas about an attempted sexual conquest, although in Merrick it is the attempted sexual conquest of the wife of a political rival which is the cause of dispute, whereas in the Nest story we see in Owen's sexual conquest of Nest a metaphor for the conquest of the kingdom, and the dispute over her body is nothing less than a dispute for legitimacy of political rule. It is possible that Merrick is here suggesting that the twin themes of sexual conquest and foreign military advantage are somehow tied to untamed sexual passion and that such deep emotions were played out, catastrophically in the long term, in Glamorgan first. This in some way relates to the Nest story since it concerns the sexual passion of Nest's father whose inappropriate personal emotions and lust lead to his downfall, and this prefigures Nest's infamous abduction and the disputes which followed. So it is possible that Merrick deliberately constructed a version of the events in which the dynasty of Deheubarth was destroyed due to illicit, untamed but unconsummated passion. The actions of Rhys were reprehensible because of the way that he schemed to entrap the wife of his rival for power. It differs in this respect from the narrative of Nest because, although woman as a cause of war is at the core of both disputes, the Glamorgan version of the trope stresses that the honour of the wife of Iestyn was not compromised. On the contrary it was Rhys who was dishonoured. Glamorgan's history at the time of the Norman conquest is therefore a history that was more honourable, and was a complicated narrative which demonstrated the importance of marital fidelity. In Merrick's version, the wife stayed loyal to her husband and made good her escape from her would-be 'attacker'. Merrick therefore argues that Glamorgan had its own beauty with wars fought over her person, and there are interesting parallels here with the way that women are seen as a cause of war, and as objects of male desire; it is the inability of Rhys of Deheubarth to control his desire which is at the root of the conquest. Such ideas were articulated in the *Brutiau* in the narrative of Nest. Further, a key interpretation of the abduction of Nest as presented in the *Brut*, that of youthful, rash actions which had catastrophic consequences, was deployed by later writers.[46] This tradition survived in some form in the bardic culture, which is possibly how the Nest story was given to the authors of the *Brut*. Bardic tradition, in a different context although of course related to the same family, was then taken up by Merrick in his tale of Rhys. George Owen relied on the *Brut* for his view of Nest in the late sixteenth century. It is just possible that Merrick utilised the abduction and romance elements of the Nest story which were modelled in the *Brut* so that the Nest model of abduction politics was taken up and remodelled by Merrick with contemporary values intermingled through his incorporation of local traditions.

The parallels between the Nest story in the *Brut* and the story told by Merrick have much to tell us about the way that such early modern gentlemen conceptualised past conquest and were influenced by motifs or themes within earlier texts. In Merrick's narrative Rhys is moved by stories about the beauty of Iestyn's wife so that he was filled with desire to see her, just as Owain was allegedly moved by descriptions of Nest's beauty. Both relate that the fatal meeting is engineered by the aggressor, yet there are differences in location. In the *Brut* Owain visits Nest at the castle of Cenarth Bychan. This perhaps is symbolic: the meeting occurred at the centre of lordship, at the very seat of Gerald of Windsor's power. Rhys, by contrast, invites Iestyn to meet on the 'borderlands' of Glamorgan at Neath. It is possible that this is a literary metaphor in which the borderlands function as a metaphor for borders, in the sense of borders of behaviour/appropriate conduct. Merrick suggests that Rhys offended the honour of Iestyn by his predatory behaviour. Nevertheless the parallels between the two traditions have other dimensions. In particular both traditions suggest that the bards were significant in setting up the events which then unfold. The bards, we are told by Merrick, sang to Rhys about the beauty of Iestyn's wife and this kindles his desire. On seeing Iestyn's wife, Rhys finds that her beauty surpasses the bardic descriptions and plots her sexual conquest. This is very close to the scenario recorded in the *Brut* in which Owain is similarly determined to visit Nest as a consequence of hearing about her from the bards. Thus in both tales the importance of the bards in shaping the mental landscape of Rhys and Iestyn is apparent and this sets in train a sequence of events which have political and symbolic consequences. Thus both tales serve to disclose the belief of later authors in the importance of bards as causative elements, or important formers of contemporary opinion. The bards set in train a series of events which spiral out of control in both stories.

Yet both narratives have their own trajectories. For example, Rhys discloses his intent to his object, Iestyn's wife, who informs her husband and persuades him to leave Rhys's hospitality. Thus Iestyn's wife saves herself and her honour and this shows the ironic situation that she was in. By leaving the feast her husband lost honour, and the loss of honour by both men causes war. Nest of course too saves her husband, who also leaves the theatre of events (the castle) in disgrace; but she cannot (or does not) save herself and stays behind with her children. Whether or not Merrick was influenced by the Nest story in the *Brut*, it is obvious that a view of women as the cause of war is used by Merrick to explain the internecine disputes between rival Welsh leaders in the period of the Norman arrival in Wales. Thus in both stories beautiful women, who are wives, cause disputes and thus both are the cause of their husbands' humiliation, and severe political consequences follow from this. That the topos is used by the authors of the story suggests that ideas about gender roles were used to underpin the portrayal of what were, ultimately,

events which caused lasting political consequences. The women are portrayed as victims of male desire, but who nevertheless take action to
avert the worst consequences of the passion they have inspired in their
admirers. In the case of Nest she saves her husband's life at the cost of
her reputation if she consented to the abduction, and possibly rape if
she did not. The wife of Iestyn saves her honour, and thus ironically that
of her husband, even though they are both dishonoured by their hasty
departure from Neath in order to prevent her rape. It could be argued
then that the bardic tradition influences Merrick's depiction of Iestyn's
wife as the cause of the defeat of Iestyn. This of course ultimately led to
the defeat of Morgannwg by the Normans. The Nest story, however, is
a tale of resistance to the Normans, although both suggest sexual politics
as pivotal to the fate of Deheubarth – but of course the tradition of her
abduction may have been preserved within bardic lore before it was
redacted in the early thirteenth century. Thus both tales may well preserve
elements of bardic tradition. This then raises the possibility that the
bards had an interest in perpetuating stories which stressed their importance in society: since bards lived by patronage they necessarily needed
to write and create works which patrons would value. They may have
perpetuated ideas about their role within the Welsh past to stress their
importance to it.

According to Gwynfor Jones, the importance of bards was declining
in the fifteenth and sixteenth centuries, but they inculcated an image of
the male gentry, the *uchelwyr*, as Renaissance men: their central concern
was to promote an image of the Welsh Renaissance gentleman who lived
a life of courtesy.[47] We can certainly sense these values in Merrick where
he tells us that the gathering of Iestyn and Rhys's retinues were both
'accompanied by a great train of gentlemen and gentlewomen . . . where
after gentle salutations and familiar entertainment, they feasted each
other',[48] and in a passage where Merrick reflects on the frailty of man
and worldly honour.[49] The decline in the importance of the bards, Jones
suggests, may have been linked to an awareness by the gentry that their
praise poetry, written to classical models, was irrelevant framed as it was
by excessive eulogy.[50] Merrick may well have shared in the culture of
support for the poets who visited Glamorgan, and as such his portrayal
of the centrality of the bards as maintaining tradition and as important
in the framing of the political context may reflect this. Yet it also suggests
that the idea that the beauty of the wife of Iestyn, which surpassed the
bardic eulogy, may demonstrate an awareness that in some cases such
eulogising was apposite, and indeed in the case of Nest and Iestyn's wife
did not go far enough. It also suggests an awareness that in the past the

bards did have influence upon the ideas and attitudes of their patrons: they could create the dynamic which caused events of seismic importance to occur. In the sixteenth century bardic tradition emphasised the stability of the *uchelwyr* in changing social conditions in which the bonds of obligation served as the social glue which held society together.[51] Thus Merrick's interpretation of Iestyn's behaviour when he secretly fled the company of Rhys as dishonourable is reflective of a set of ideas from contemporary Tudor Wales grafted onto twelfth-century politics. It is also almost an inverted sense of order: Iestyn's behaviour in leaving the gathering was dishonourable, but if he had not left it is clear that the seduction of his wife was likely. J. Gwynfor Jones argues that the *uchelwyr* lived in an age which was forsaking medieval concepts of chivalry and where status was derived from a 'combination of virtues including self-esteem and self-assertiveness' and that 'defence of honour and reputation' was pivotal in gentry culture and to political survival.[52] The portrayal by Merrick therefore conforms to contemporary ideas: the Iestyn story shows that Iestyn's behaviour was discourteous and his political survival was jeopardised by his behaviour even though it was Rhys who was the cause of the dispute. Merrick therefore suggests that the inability of husbands to defend the honour of their wives is a critical failure, and, further, failure in the heart of the marital union leads to failure in the kingdom.

That Merrick should have chosen to discuss these events in such terms suggests that he was attuned to the symbolism of sexual conduct and predatory behaviour as morally degenerate and also politically destructive. It has been suggested that Merrick was eulogised by the poets as a descendant of Caradog, whose descendant Cynfyn ap Cynfyn had been displaced by the Normans in Ystrad Yw in Dyfed. Further, according to this tradition, his grandson had opposed the introduction of Norman custom into Wales by Gilbert de Clare. The poets also told of his ancestry through the female line and this connected him to Iestyn ap Gwrgant. Merrick lived at Bonvilston near Miskin where his ancestors had held power for over eight generations.[53] Merrick's approach to the narrative of the conquest may well have been inspired, therefore, by the oral traditions of the poets and informed by a knowledge of his connection to key figures of the Norman phase of settlement in Glamorgan.

There is also, however, an instructive contrast to be drawn with Llwyd. We have already seen that Llwyd privileges north Wales in his writings, and this perhaps in part explains the relative brevity of his writings on the south and his portrayal of Deheubarth. Llwyd's description of the defeat of Rhys ap Tewdwr and the conquest of Glamorgan makes no mention of the alleged infatuation of Rhys with the wife of Iestyn ap Gwrgant, and it is possible that the lack of interest of a northerner in the affairs of the south lies behind this. More likely, however, this sprung from the way that Llwyd viewed the resistance to the Normans within a framework which suggested that the Welsh were God's chosen people.[54] He states that the resistance to William Rufus who campaigned 'with great pomp and pride' was effected by the 'Britons [who] put their hope onely in the almightie Lorde, turned to him in fasting and prayer, and repentaunce of their sinnes, and he, that never forsaketh the penitent and contrite heart, herde their prayer, so that the English and the Normans durst never to enter the lande'.[55] This was derived from the *Brut*, which stated that the ferocity of the Britons was such that 'the French, not daring to invade the woods or wilderness against the Britons ... returned home dejected and empty-handed'.[56] Llwyd thus extended the *Brut*'s careful note that it was 'woods or wilderness' to evoke a sense of the Britons' 'lande'. Rufus was thus driven out of Wales by a pious people who had unjustly been deprived of their 'countreyes'. Llwyd discusses the Norman advance into Wales and describes the successes of Gruffudd ap Cynan and Cadwgan ap Bleddyn in 1093 against the Normans in Cardigan where they 'killed a great number of the Normaines' since they were 'not being able any longer to suffer their great pride and crueltie'. Llwyd justifies further Welsh resurgence against the Normans in 1094 when the 'inhabitants of Gwyr, Brechynog, Gwent and Gwentllwg cast of their necks the burthen of the Normaines that had wonne their countreyes and held them in subjection'. Llwyd tells us that the 'countrey men ... abhored their pride and cruell rule' and that in their resistance they had fought 'manfully'.[57] This is an early example of the concept of the 'Norman Yoke' applied to the history of Wales. The idea of the Norman Yoke had its origins in the early post-conquest period in England. It was a concept which was linked by writers and historians to the Norman conquest and it encapsulated ideas about the oppression of the Anglo-Saxons by the Normans after 1066, and a concomitant loss of liberty. The idea of the 'Norman Yoke' was given a new impetus by the political developments of the seventeenth century.[58] Llwyd's use of the concept of oppression is therefore a use of the concept which obliquely referenced the trajectory of English history and he links this to the Welsh experience of conquest. Hence there is no mention of the passion of Iestyn in Llwyd, probably because of his sense that conflict with the Normans at this point is about divinely approved resistance to tyranny, not about the weakness of the Welsh when they fall victim to ungodly passions.

Yet the story of Wales in Welsh historiography became the story of north Wales as the heart of Wales retaining Welsh tradition. The tradition of Nest's father as a passionate man whose lust caused the downfall of Deheubarth may well reflect the oral nature of this tradition which was particular to south Wales and accessible to Merrick, not Llwyd writing as he was in the north. By contrast, the story of Nest which was central to recorded south Wales traditions was not minimised or lost to the sense of national narrative since it was recorded in the *Brut* and carried forward from this key source by Llwyd. Llwyd looked at the medieval past as a history of the Welsh and their struggle against the English: his history stopped after the failure of a Welsh rebellion in 1295 and he wrote in English for an English-language readership. His narrative was intended to be a history of the Welsh, and his concern with the abduction narrative was drawn from a version of the *Brutiau*, and therefore the tale of Welsh resistance in south Wales became an eroticised part of their resistance in a national narrative.

Such national narratives were important in later writings in Wales in which antiquarian scholars wrote local history. The Nest abduction narrative features in the *Description of Penbrokeshire* written by George Owen of Henllys in *c.* 1610. The passages occur in the chapter 'A catalogue of the Earles of Pembroke' and thus the context is that of a description of the creation of the earldom of Pembroke, which Owen traces from the 'rulers' of Pembroke through to the conquest of south-west Wales. The description focuses on the sequence of Normans who ruled Pembrokeshire. Gerald of Windsor appears succeeding to Pembroke castle after Saer de Quincy 'who enjoyed it not much a year'. Gerald 'had then married Nest the daughter of Rees ap Tewdwr being a goodly and beawetifull ladie, one whome a litle before the said King h [Henry] had begotten a sonne called Robert who was after Earle of *Gloucester* and *Bristow*'.[59] In essence, the details concerning the marriage and abduction of Nest follow a similar trajectory to that of the story as told in the *Brut*. There is no condemnation of Nest; she is merely a lady, beautiful, and daughter and cousin of powerful men. Owen states that it was Nest's beauty which caused her abduction and, like the *Brut*, states the kinship between Nest and Owain. His narrative is a close rendition of the *Brut*, including Gerald 'convayeinge himselfe awaye through a privie'. Yet although in most details the story is derivative of the *Brut*, Owen elaborates a view that the illegitimate son of Henry I by Nest became earl of Gloucester and Bristol. This is an intriguing addition. Robert earl of Gloucester was Henry I's favourite illegitimate son and one of the most powerful earls in England during the civil war of Stephen's reign when he was effectively the leader of the Angevin faction, half-brother as he was to the Empress Matilda. Owen thus makes a connection between the dynasty of Deheubarth and the royal court through Nest, emphasised by the birth of Nest's illegitimate son. Here the illegitimacy is without question no impediment, rather it serves to elevate Owen's connection to the twelfth-century elite of Pembrokeshire by making an explicit claim of kinship with Henry I. It is an interesting view from the pen of a protestant loyalist whose personal life was complicated by issues of illegitimacy and conflict with other powerful families in Pembrokeshire. Owen had an agenda, and it was more complex than merely elevating his ancestry or an antiquarian interest in local history. In order to put these views into context it is useful first to explore Owen's family connections and the allegedly 'British' intellectual context of his writings.

George Owen was the son of William Owen (*c.* 1488–1574), of Henllys, Nevern, near Newport (Pembrokeshire) and William's second wife Elizabeth, daughter of Sir George Herbert. Elizabeth's mother was the niece of William Herbert, first earl of Pembroke. George's father was a successful lawyer, and his grandparents, Rhys ab Owen (d. *c.* 1544) and Elizabeth, had a strong connection to the Perrots, another important Pembrokeshire family, through Elizabeth's mother Janet, the daughter of Sir Thomas Perrot of Eastington. William Owen had five children by Jane Lee and four more children by other mistresses. George married Elizabeth, the daughter and co-heir of William Philipps of Picton castle, and Janet, daughter of Thomas Perrot of Haroldston. Janet's brother was Sir John Perrot, Philipps' rival in the shire. Thus Owen had family connections to the most important families in Pembrokeshire, although there was bitter rivalry between Owen and the Perrots for prominence within the shire. Owen had seven illegitimate children by his mistress Anne (or Ankred), whom he married as his second wife following the death of his first wife Elizabeth in 1606.

Owen's interest in the history of Pembrokeshire has several influences. First, since he was related to the earls of Pembroke and his work may well be a reflection of the importance of this connection to him. Yet his ancestry also connected him to the Welsh elite, given that he was the grandson of Rhys ab Owen. Second, it seems, according to Dillwyn Miles, that Owen was concerned to enforce his seigneurial rights on his lands and he was deeply unpopular with the Pembrokeshire gentry.[60] Third, both he and his father fathered illegitimate children, which suggests an acceptance of it, indeed that it was normal in his family. In this context the discussion, and mistakes, concerning the identity of Nest's illegitimate son by Henry I and the consequent elevation of his status as the pre-eminent noble in the reign of Henry I places the offspring of the dynasty of Deheubarth through Nest into the highest political sphere in the twelfth century. Owen seems to have been no stranger to fabrication of fact. Owen had been charged with counterfeiting deeds and forgery although no evidence was found to support these claims; the charge of adultery levelled against him was, however, irrefutable. Owen spuriously claimed that his father had lived to be one hundred and five; he also has been accused of giving a misleading account of his coat of arms.[61] Owen falsely claimed that his ancestry reached back to the twelfth century, claiming that his ancestry linked him to one 'Rickart ap Lucas Hood of Tre Rickart, and Frenchman by birth' who had married a certain Ales, the alleged co-heir of 'Nichlas ap Syr William Martin. Lord of Kemes'.[62] Given this weight of evidence we can at least assume that Owen was no stranger to invented traditions: the question is why. Owen draws on the tradition of Nest's abduction, and it is attached to ideas of beauty and romantic love, and is thus an edited version of that supplied by the *Brut*. Owen's family had links with the lordship of Cemais, and Nest was linked with this lordship, so, perhaps, Owen claimed a link to her through a connection with lordship.

Owen had wide intellectual interests, including topographical, heraldic, literature, bardic, geographical and historical subjects. According to B. G. Charles, 'however insidious the Anglicising side-effects of the new antiquarian movement and fashionable English education may have been, George Owen and his family remained Welsh to the core'.[63] Yet it is a Welshness which is rooted in local particularism. Thus Owen is concerned with the 'praise and worthines of the people, and this Countey' (Pembrokeshire), which he is happy to term 'a second or little *England*', but he excuses himself through recourse to his 'love and affection of my Countrey'.[64] Drawing on Gerald of Wales he interprets the medieval Wales as a kingdom which kept its seas and coasts in 'obedience to the crown of *Englande* & overcome and conquered the Realme of *Irelande*'. Owen thus emphasises the ethnicity of the people of Pembrokeshire in terms of descent from Flemish settlers. Owen's views are derived from Gerald of Wales and he calls the people of Pembrokeshire a 'nacion (meaneinge the Englishmen of *Penbrokeshire*) [who] derive their discent from *Flanders*', who are a 'valiant and strong people, in contynuall conflictee of battle, a nacion most hateful to the Welshmen', and he goes on to stress the mercantile interests and industrious nature of the Flemish settlers who spare no pain and are fearless at sea or land, a 'nation both stoute and happye'.[65] He acknowledges that these are the views of Gerald of Wales and obliquely references Nest in his claims that '*Penbrokeshire*' people were the means of subduing Ireland and Wales to the kings of England, and as such it was a marvel that it was magnified 'above all the rest of Wales to be *Countye Palatyne*', so the king of England could be justified in calling it his '*litle England beyond Wales*'.[66] He ends his chapter with a comment on the unity of the 'Ile of Brittaignei' which was enjoying a unity not seen since the days of Brutus, 'first king of the whole'. Here his project is clear: Britain united again, its historical trajectory is a cause for 'joy in the hartes of the people', and for Owen, a Pembrokeshire patriot, that trajectory is complete by reference to the British whose history was founded by Brutus and relates back to the age of Troy. Owen, then, posits a view of history in which the unity of Britain has the legend of Troy as central. Further, he offers an interpretation in which Nest's offspring are central, even if it is equivocal at best about the Welsh in a way that other texts are not. Owen's view is a sign that Nest can serve very different agendas, since in Owen her ancestral role and the subtle linkage to the classical past and Helen of Troy is suggestive of his view of the centrality of Pembrokeshire to the narrative of Britain.

According to Roberts, Edward Stradling wrote to rehabilitate the history of the Welsh so that they would be accepted as honourable and equal members of the kingdom of Britain.[67] Owen has been called a student of Llwyd, but Owen did not write to rehabilitate the history of Pembrokeshire, he drew on the past to justify the Pembrokeshire of the present within a British context, and it is a united British present which was foreshadowed in the Welsh mythical past when Britain was united under Brutus during the age of Troy. Owen was a gentleman whose interests and political focus lay within the county, and as such he was not untypical and his attachment to locality is to be found in his near-geographical contemporary, Rice Merrick.

Thus a narrative of Wales was produced by gentlemen antiquarians in south Wales which maintained the abduction tale as part of a reliance on the *Brut*. The narrative was taken up by figures such as Llwyd and Powel and incorporated into county histories.

English writers were clearly aware of the ways in which Welsh scholars were deploying these narratives in their accounts of Wales. It is, however, important to note that from early in the sixteenth century their currency in England was evident. John Leland was an early example of exterior observers who were interested in Wales. His view of Wales is worth considering here as an example of how English writers constructed a view of Wales and his use of ideas about Welsh history. Leland travelled through Wales and described the topography of the country but rarely commented on the Welsh in terms of ethnic stereotypes. Yet, in a passing, but very revealing, comment, he stated 'Walschmen yn tymes past, as they do almost yet, did study more to pasturage then tylling as favorers of their consuete idilness'.[68] Leland's interest in the people of Wales rarely extended beyond brief notes concerning the gentry or aristocracy within each county. For example, he lists the gentlemen dwelling in the west 'Thawän betwyxt Thawän and Alein' which included, amongst others, Edward Stradling 'yongger brother to the heir'.[69] Few if any individuals stand out in his writings, although he mentions a witch called 'Malt Walbere' who lived in a forest near Llandovery, and who allegedly built a building out of stone and Brecon castle. He continues that some called her 'Matabrune, of whom so many fables be told'.[70] Such digressions into local lore and fable are rare in Leland. Leland was interested in topographical description; most of the individuals named are male gentry or aristocracy, and he mentions few women.[71] An exception to this is one Alice of London, the only noblewoman mentioned by name who is of interest because she repaired the castle of Carmarthen.[72] Leland was aware of the writings of Gerald of Wales since he references them in his *Itinerary*.[73] As Griffiths noted, Leland's source seems to have been similar to those available to David Powel.[74] One of these rare and significant digressions is that in which Leland incorporates a version of the 'twelve knights of Glamorgan'. The matter appears under a section that details the county's bridges. The material is written in a brief style and contains the essential features of the narrative of the twelve knights as later elaborated by Edward Stradling, in particular the centrality of the breach of promise in relation to marriage. Leland notes that, encountering 'great troble' with 'Theodore Prince of Wales [Rhys ap Tewdwr]', Iestyn 'desired help of one Inon [Einion] a Walsch man borderer onto hym, promising to hym his doughtter with greate landes'. Leland continues that Einion then utilised help from the Normans and, because 'Justine [Iestyn] kept no promise' with him, 'Inon and the xii. knightes drave Justine away and occupied his landes'.[75] Given the consistent focus upon geography and place, the incorporation of the twelve knights into his *Itinerary* suggests that Leland was aware of the fundamental importance of this story to the history of Glamorgan and the role of the Normans in shaping the identity of the prominent families, identifying in particular the Stradlings. Certainly he notes the importance of ancient lineage to one notable local family, '[t]he Lysans [who] say, that theire familie was there in fame afore the Conquest of the Normans'.[76] Further, it is surely symbolic that the 'twelve knights' material appears in a section which deals with bridges. It is possible that Leland, subconsciously or otherwise, here placed the historical material with a metaphorical or allegorical meaning. The material is rendered into a context in which structures, here bridges, represent a link between two places over an obstacle, here different geographies. The account is a long digression quite untypical of Leland. As such the material is distinctive and is suggestive that Leland considered the tale reliable and an important tradition worth incorporating into his *Itinerary*. Further, Leland's knowledge of the tale of the 'twelve knights' indicates that he may have had access to the written sources from which the tale later appeared, but may also have come into contact with oral sources which had knowledge of the tradition.

Such accounts, and the portrayal of Nest in particular, allow us to reflect on a possible gendered ordering of the 'imagined communities' of Hechter's internal colonialism thesis. Tim Thornton has suggested that Hechter's thesis presents only a limited view of the complexities of ethnic stereotyping, as applied to Wales in the works of scholars such as Mark Stoyle and Lloyd Bowen, who find the Welsh almost exclusively portrayed as godless buffoons. Thornton has suggested that the writings of John Taylor, the self-styled 'Water Poet' whose book described his tour of Wales in 1652, are indicative of a 'market of some kind for a text which celebrated the Welsh and their difference'.[77] Certainly, as Thornton suggests, John Taylor did not negatively ethnically stereotype the Welsh and wrote appreciatively of the towns and country houses of Wales. As Bernard Capp has pointed out, however, Taylor's welcome was less warm in the houses of parliamentarians although he was welcomed by royalists; he was a self-publicist who funded his travels through subscription – persuading patrons to fund his journeys and to buy the books which were the products of his adventures.[78] In this sense his journey through Wales was an adventure conducted at a critical point after the civil war. Taylor, who carefully avoided any political commentary in his writings, was affected by the reception and the hospitality received at the country houses of the gentry. For him this was a key measure of gentle behaviour and this, as well as his gender, affected his portrayal of his rejection by the servants of a Sir Thomas *Esquire* in Glamorgan. He relates that he arrived unexpectedly at the house of Sir Thomas and was rebuffed by the household staff 'like so many buzzards and woodcocks about an owl'. He describes one of the male servants as a 'shotten thin sculled shadow brained simpleton fellow'. He then relates his treatment at one 'Mrs Fumpkins' who 'looking scornfully askew over her shoulders' suggested that he might sleep in the field. He continues 'the said ungentle gentlewoman (with her posterior, or but end towards me) gave me a final answer'.[79] His ire was thus directed at those who refused him hospitality and in some measure his mockery of 'Mrs Fumpkins' has an acute observation, a comedic effect, which draws attention to the body and posture of the woman. His view of Wales and the Welsh thus turned on his perception of their hospitality and manners. His view was politicised, but ethnicity was not a key determinant in his view; it was, rather, informed by his reception.

Such views of Wales written by English observers present an interpretation of the country which was not fundamentally hostile, and although gender might play a role in stereotyping, it does seem that when it came to the story of Nest, some English observers saw her in a relatively positive light. Thomas Fuller's *The History of the Worthies of England*, published in 1662, has been called the 'first biographical English dictionary'. It describes the noteworthy features of the counties of England and Wales and also includes information on prominent individuals from those counties.[80] Under the entry for Pembrokeshire, Fuller states that the east of the county 'has the most pleasantest part of Wales' and notes that Nest was a daughter of 'Reese', prince of south Wales, in a short introductory paragraph to a section which discusses Gerald of Wales. Gerald's ancestry is given, his father is named as Gerald de Barry, and Nest is named as the mother of Angharad, Gerald's mother. Fuller has great sympathy for Gerald's thwarted ambitions and states that Gerald became bishop of St David's. He recounts Gerald's 'complaint' that 'the English did not love him because his mother was a Welshwoman and the Welsh did hate him because his father was an Englishman' and goes onto clarify Gerald's view that he was unable to get preferment because of his mixed parentage as due to 'the Antipathy of the English who thought that no good could come out of Wales'.[81] Fuller does not comment on the veracity of this view, but it is striking that he repeats the comment twice in his brief section on Gerald. These details about Gerald's family and career appear under a subsection 'Writers'.[82] Fuller argues that Gerald deserved better treatment because of the quality of his writings; perhaps Fuller felt that the same could be said of him. Fuller was a clergyman whose career fluctuated with the fortunes of the royalists, and his sympathies for Gerald's thwarted ambition may have stemmed from his experiences as someone who had lost various livings and preferments as a result of political upheavals and regime change. It has been suggested that Fuller's work should be appreciated in the context of a tradition of collective biographical writing which had an exemplary function. The authors of such works sought to create and understand their personal and national identity through them.[83] Whatever the merits of this view, it is clear that Nest's identity had become associated as an ancestral name in Fuller's work; her abduction narrative here lost, unknown or discounted. Nest was recorded in the context of her family connections and her name is thus memorialised in a traditional context of family and genealogy. This genealogical remembrance of Nest appears in other contemporary English writings. Robert Brady, writing a *Complete History of England* in 1685, included her as the 'daughter of Rheese ap Tewdur Prince of South Wales' at the head of a section on the 'natural children' of Henry I in which she appears as the mother of Earl Robert of Gloucester, Henry's favoured illegitimate son. He also notes that she was the mother of Henry, another son by Henry I.[84] Thus her importance was as a link between powerful men in her role as progenitor of a lineage. In Brady's case more than Fuller's she is related to an English narrative of Henry I's kingship and interaction with the Welsh. In the later seventeenth century the abduction story was not used in mainstream English texts. Thus, the abduction story had been important in Owen's local country history because Owen constructs and employs the Nest story within a work written from a Pembrokeshire perspective. By drawing on the *Brut* Owen reiterates a story of native resistance and resurgence, but also one of accommodation with the Normans, reflected in the episodes in which Owain ap Cadwgan was reconciled to Henry I and Nest's son was killed fighting for Henry II against the Welsh in Anglesey in 1157. Thus the story of Nest was taken up by antiquarian scholars in the early modern period and they perpetuated a story which had essentially originated in south Wales but was a narrative which was rooted in a national story.

As part of the narrative of the Norman conquest of Wales created by such men, the Nest story was an essential ingredient in a potent mix which therefore was deeply influenced by sources which originated in the twelfth and thirteenth centuries. As such the ideals about the role of women in war and the construction of gender were linked with a historical view which could be adapted to present ideals. Thus, for example, William Camden noted the role of Gwenllian the wife of Nest's brother Gruffudd ap Rhys of Deheubarth, who died in a battle at Kidwelly in 1136 in his *Britannia*, first published, in Latin, in 1586. The popularity of this text is beyond doubt; it went through several editions before being translated into English in 1610 by Philemon Holland, collaborating with Camden, and published as *Britain, or, A Chorographicall Description*.[85] Camden's account was reliant on Gerald of Wales yet he nevertheless commented on Gwenllian's character and reflected on the nature of her actions. Camden notes that Gwenllian was a 'stout and resolute woman in the highest degree, [who] to recover the losses and declining state of her husband, came with displaid banner into the field and fiercely assailed him [Maurice of London]'. He continues: 'but the successe, not answerable to her courage, she with her son *Morgan*, and other men of especiall note . . . was *slaine in battaile*'. A marginal note describes her in gendered terms as 'Guenliana, a woman of manly courage'.[86] Camden included details of the arrival of Gerald of Windsor in Pembrokeshire, his position as castellan of Pembroke castle, and the resistance of the Welsh to him. Camden states that Gerald fortified both town and castle, 'and at length, that as well his owne estate, as theirs that were his followers and dependants, might the better grow to greatnesse in these parts he tooke to wife *Nesta*, sister to *Gruffin* the Prince, of whom he begat a goodly faire Progeny, by the which . . . the *Englishmen both kept still the Sea-costs of South-wales, and wonne also the walles of Ireland*'.[87] Camden was reliant on Gerald of Wales, and thus presents a version of the role of the Geraldines in Ireland which is close to that presented by Gerald. He presents a positive view of Nest as an ancestral figure who conveyed strength to the Norman Gerald in Pembrokeshire, and the abduction is mentioned under his discussion of the county of Cardigan. The context for the narrative is a commentary on the loyalty shown by Cadwgan, Owain's father, to the English. Camden states that Cadwgan was 'a right wise prudent Britain: who was highly esteemed, and of great powre throughout all Wales'. Owain is portrayed as a 'furious and heady yong man' who rebelled against the English during the reign of Rufus and who therefore caused his father to lose his lands. Camden states that Cadwgan was subsequently restored to favour with the English crown, only to suffer again when Owain abducted Nest. Camden sees this as a return to Owain's previous behaviour, and the abduction narrative is briefly mentioned as the cause of Owain's death: 'But Oen returning to his old bias and rebelling afresh, was slaine by Girald the Castellan of *Penbrock*, whose wife *Nesta* he had carried away and ravished.'[88] The abduction is important as a motive for Gerald's retribution, and as a cause of political dispute; there is no mention of the destruction within Cardigan as a result of the royal reaction to the abduction, nor any sense of the way that the narrative of the Norman incursions into south Wales were seen as a pivotal moment in the history of the Welsh. Writing from the point of view of an English observer, Camden sees the event in the context of a long-term process of change and conquest of the Welsh.

Nest's tale of resistance and sexual politics was a narrative which was rediscovered in later writings, and in the early modern period perpetuated in Wales in the writing of local history by Owen and reported in Llwyd and Powel in their 'national' histories. These, it can be argued, therefore perpetuated and constructed an image of south Wales in which Norman activity was linked to a Welsh native nobility among whom politics could be destabilised by sexual passion. The tale of the twelve knights as presented by Stradling in his the 'Winning of the lordship of Glamorgan' represents a contested eroticised theme, which was utilised to explain the arrival of the Normans and their success against the Welsh rulers. At the heart of that tale lay a broken marriage agreement, and Rice Merrick even presents an image of Nest's father as a man driven to scheming politics guided by sexual desire for another man's wife. Thus commentators on the Welsh medieval past utilised themes of sexual conquest and gender in their writings which demonstrate the importance of these as definitive elements in the construction of a view of the Welsh medieval past.

Notes

1   Peter Roberts, 'Tudor Wales, national identity and the British inheritance', in Brendan Bradshaw and Peter Roberts (eds), *British Consciousness and Identity: The Making of Britain 1533–1707* (Cambridge: Cambridge University Press, 1998), pp. 8–42, at p. 23.

2   Michael Hechter, *Internal Colonialism: The Celtic Fringe in British National Development* (2nd edn, New Brunswick, NJ and London: Transaction, 1999); see Hugh Kearney, *The British Isles: A History of Four Nations* (Cambridge: Cambridge University Press, 1989, 2nd edn 2006); Keith Robbins, *Great Britain: Identities, Institutions and the Idea of Britishness* (Harlow: Longman, 1998).

3   John Gwynfor Jones, *The Welsh Gentry 1536–1640: Images of Status, Honour and Authority* (Cardiff: University of Wales Press, 1998); *idem*, 'The Welsh gentry and the image of the "Cambro-Briton", c. 1603–25', *WHR*, 20 (2001), 615–55; *idem*, *Concepts of Order and Gentility in Wales 1540–1640: Bardic Imagery and Interpretations* (Llandysul: Gomer, 1992); Felicity Heal and Clive Holmes (eds), *The Gentry in England and Wales, 1500–1700* (Basingstoke: Macmillan, 1994).

4   Ranulph Higden, *Polychronicon*, ed. Churchill Babington and Joseph Rawson Lumby (9 vols, Rolls Series, 41; London: Longman, Green, Longman, Roberts, and Green, 1865–86), i. 394, 396.

5   Higden, *Polychronicon*, i. 402–4.

6   Higden, *Polychronicon*, i. 264, 266, 268.

7   Higden, *Polychronicon*, i. pp. xxxvii–xxxix.

8   Higden, *Polychronicon*, i. 358.

9   Henry Knighton, *Chronicon Henrici Knighton, vel Cnitthon, monachi Leycestrensis*, ed. Joseph Rawson Lumby (London: HMSO, 1889–95), i. 20, 38, 47.

10   Knighton, *Chronicon Henrici Knighton*, i. 116, 207.

11   Henry Knighton, *Chronicle, 1337–1396*, ed. G. H. Martin (Oxford: Clarendon Press, 1995), pp. 348–51; see also the negative view of the contemporary Welsh in *Chronicon Angliae, ab anno Domini 1328 usque ad annum 1388, auctore monacho quodam Sancti Albani*, ed. Edward Maunde Thompson (Rolls Series, 64; London: Longman, 1874), pp. 7, 135, 185 (1370–90).

12 John Capgrave, *The Chronicle of England*, ed. Francis Charles Hingeston (Rolls Series, 1; London: Longman, Brown, Green, Longmans, and Roberts, 1858), pp. 37, 115, 164–6, 186, 231, 245, 283, 290, 291.

13 E.g. Higden, *Polychronicon*, v. 338, 348, vi. 242, vii. 188, 214, 354, 362, viii. 40, 158, 160, 186, 188, 262, 264, 266, 268, 280, 282.

14 Higden, *Polychronicon*, viii. 186, 206.

15 Humphrey Llwyd [sic], *Cronica Walliae*, ed. Ieuan M. Williams (Cardiff: University of Wales Press, 2002), pp. 18–25.

16 Llwyd, *Cronica Walliae*, ed. Williams, pp. 134–5.

17 Llwyd, *Cronica Walliae*, ed. Williams, p. 21.

18 Llwyd, *Cronica Walliae*, ed. Williams, p. 145.

19 Huw Pryce, 'The Normans in Welsh history', *ANS*, 30 (2008 for 2007), 1–18.

20 See chapter 1, above, pp. 20–30, 34–40.

21 Ieuan M. Williams, 'Introduction', in Llwyd, *Cronica Walliae*, ed. Williams, pp. 15, 23, where he notes that Llwyd made mistakes concerning Welsh place-names in south Wales.

22 Compare Williams's observations on Llwyd's presentation of Madog's alleged impact on the New World: Llwyd, *Cronica Walliae*, ed. Williams, pp. 25, 167–8.

23 Llwyd, *Cronica Walliae*, ed. Williams, pp. 125–6; it first appears in Ieuan Rudd's (*fl. c.* 1470) *cywydd* on the marriage of Sir Rhys ap Tomas and Sioned, daughter of Thomas Mathew of Radyr and widow of Thomas Stradling of St Donat's, who died in 1480: C. W. Lewis, 'The literary tradition of Morgannwg', in T. B. Pugh (ed.), *Glamorgan County History*, vol. 3: *The Middle Ages: The Marcher Lordships of Glamorgan and Morgannwg and Gower and Kilvey from the Norman Conquest to the Act of Union of England and Wales* (Cardiff: University of Wales Press for the Glamorgan County History Committee, 1971), pp. 449–554, at p. 457.

24 Ralph A. Griffiths, 'The Norman conquest and the twelve knights of Glamorgan', *Glamorgan Historian*, 3 (1966), 153–69, at pp. 152–4; see also *idem*, 'The rise of the Stradlings of St Donat's', *Morgannwg*, 7 (1963), 15–47. The MS of 1561–66 is Cardiff Central Library MS 4.943.

25 Griffiths, 'Norman conquest and the twelve knights', pp. 155, 157; Caradoc, of Llancarvan, *The Historie of Cambria, now called Wales: A Part of the Most Famous Yland of Brytaine, Written in the Brytish Language Aboue Two Hundreth Yeares Past: Translated into English by H. Lhoyd Gentleman: Corrected, Augmented, and Continued out of Records and Best Approoued Authors, by Dauid Powel Doctor in Diuinitie* (London: printed by Rafe Newberie and Henrie Denham, 1584) [hereafter Powel, *Historie of Cambria*], pp. 121–41 (Stradling's 'Winning of the lordship of Glamorgan'), 141–8 (Cecil additions).

26 Griffiths, 'Norman conquest and the twelve knights', p. 155; the Llwyd-derived material is Powel, *Historie of Cambria*, pp. 119–21.

27 Llwyd, *Cronica Walliae*, ed. Williams, pp. 125–6.

28 Williams, 'Introduction', in Llwyd, *Cronica Walliae*, ed. Williams, p. 3.

29 Griffiths, 'Norman conquest and the twelve knights', pp. 115–16.

30 Griffiths, 'Norman conquest and the twelve knights', p. 168.

31 Griffiths, 'Norman conquest and the twelve knights', p. 154; Powel, *Historie of Cambria*, p. 121.

32 Brian Howells (ed.), *Pembrokeshire County History*, vol. III: *Early Modern Pembrokeshire 1536–1815* (Haverfordwest: Pembrokeshire Historical Society, 1987), pp. 140–3.

33 B. G. Charles, *George Owen of Henllys: A Welsh Elizabethan* (Aberystwyth: National Library of Wales Press, 1973), p. 62.

34 Powel, *Historie of Cambria*, p. 163.

35 Powel, *Historie of Cambria*, p. 164.

36 C. W. Lewis, 'Merrick, Rice [Rhys Meurug] (*c.* 1520–1587), landowner and antiquary', *ODNB*.

37 Rice Merrick, *Morganiae Archaiographia: A Book of the Antiquities of Glamorganshire*, ed. Brian Ll. James (South Wales Record Society, vol. 1, 1983), p. xxii.

38 Merrick, *Morganiae Archaiographia*, p. 16.

39 Merrick, *Morganiae Archaiographia*, p. xvi.

40 Merrick, *Morganiae Archaiographia*, pp. 6–15.

41 Merrick, *Morganiae Archaiographia*, p. 17.

42 Merrick, *Morganiae Archaiographia*, p. 17.

43 Merrick, *Morganiae Archaiographia*, pp. 17–18.

44 Merrick, *Morganiae Archaiographia*, p. 21.

45 Merrick, *Morganiae Archaiographia*, p. 25.

46 The topic of Welsh masculinity and its interactions with ethnicity remains to be explored and would be a fruitful avenue of enquiry.

47 Jones, *Concepts of Order*, p. 6.

48 Merrick, *Morganiae Archaiographia*, p. 17.

49 Merrick, *Morganiae Archaiographia*, p. 25.

50 Jones, *Concepts of Order*, pp. 2, 17, 25.

51 Jones, *Concepts of Order*, p. 37.

52 Jones, *Welsh Gentry*, p. 108.

53 T. J. Hopkins, 'Rice Merrick (Rhys Meurig) of Cottrell', *Morgannwg*, 8 (1964), 5–13, at p. 8.

54 J. Beverley Smith, *Yr Ymwybod â Hanes yng Nghymru yn yr Oesoedd Canol: The Sense of History in Medieval Wales* (Aberystwyth: Coleg Prifysgol Cymru, 1991).

55 Llwyd, *Cronica Walliae*, ed. Williams, p. 129.

56 *Brut, Peniarth MS. 20*, p. 20.

57 Llwyd, *Cronica Walliae*, ed. Williams, pp. 127–8.

58 It thus achieved a new historiographical force within contemporary writings and into the Victorian period. This new focus was in part related to the intellectual ferment caused by the English civil war, and interpretations of Norman activity therefore saw liberty and freedom as key to the English present. The events of 1688/89, the 'Glorious Revolution', gave this a new force and the settlement with the monarchy was interpreted as a victory of the forces of liberty against autocratic monarchy in the later seventeenth century. For the classic statement on the Norman Yoke as a concept see Christopher Hill, *Intellectual Origins of the English Revolution Revisited* (Oxford: Clarendon Press, 1997; rev. edn of the text first pub. 1965); Hugh Jenkins, 'Shrugging off the Norman Yoke: Milton's History of Britain and the Levellers', *English Literary Renaissance*, 29 (1999), 306–25; R. B. Seaberg, 'The Norman conquest and the common law: the Levellers and the argument from continuity', *The Historical*

Journal, 24 (1981), 791–806; Rachel Foxley, 'John Lilburne and the citizenship of "Free-Born Englishmen"', *The Historical Journal*, 47 (2004), 849–74.

59 George Owen of Henllys, *The Description of Penbrokshire*, ed. H. Owen (4 vols, Honourable Society of Cymmrodorion, Cymmrodorion Record Series, 1, 1892–1936), i. 15–16.

60 Dillwyn Miles, 'George Owen (1552–1613), antiquary', *ODNB*.

61 Miles, 'George Owen'.

62 Charles, *George Owen*, pp. 3–4.

63 Charles, *George Owen*, p. 123.

64 Owen, *Description of Penbrokshire*, i. 256.

65 Owen, *Description of Penbrokshire*, i. 257.

66 Owen, *Description of Penbrokshire*, i. 260.

67 Roberts, 'Tudor Wales', p. 26.

68 John Leland, *The Itinerary in Wales of John Leland in or about the Years 1536–1539*, ed. Lucy Toulmin Smith (London: G. Bell and Sons, 1906), p. 104.

69 Leland, *Itinerary in Wales*, p. 32.

70 Leland, *Itinerary in Wales*, p. 112.

71 Leland, *Itinerary in Wales*, pp. 32 (gentlemen of Glamorgan), 70–2 (Denbighshire), 73 (Flintshire).

72 Leland, *Itinerary in Wales*, p. 59.

73 Leland, *Itinerary in Wales*, pp. 104, 123–4.

74 Griffiths, 'Norman conquest and the twelve knights', p. 153.

75 Leland, *Itinerary in Wales*, p. 38.

76 Leland, *Itinerary in Wales*, p. 30.

77 Tim Thornton, 'Nationhood at the margin: identity, regionality and the English crown in the seventeenth century', in Len Scales and Oliver Zimmer (eds), *Power and the Nation in European History* (Cambridge: Cambridge University Press, 2005), pp. 232–47, at p. 235; M. Stoyle, 'Caricaturing Cymru: images of the Welsh in the London press, 1642–6', in D. Dunn (ed.), *War and Society in Medieval and Early Modern Britain* (Liverpool: Liverpool University Press, 2000), pp. 162–79; Lloyd Bowen, 'Representations of Wales and the Welsh during the civil wars and interregnum', *Historical Research*, 77 (2004), 358–76.

78 Bernard Capp, 'Taylor, John (1578–1653)', *ODNB*.

79 J. Taylor, *A Short Relation of a Long Journey, made Round or Ovall by Encompassing the Principalitie of Wales, from London. . . . This painfull Circuit Began . . . the 13 of July . . . 1652, and was Ended . . . the 7 of September Following, being near 600 Miles. Whereunto is annexed an Epitome of the Famous History of Wales* (London, 1653); compare Powel, *Historie of Cambria*, pp. 19–20.

80 W. B. Patterson, 'Fuller, Thomas (1607/8–1661)', *ODNB*.

81 Thomas Fuller, *The History of the Worthies of England who for Parts and Learning have been Eminent in the Several Counties: Together with an Historical Narrative of the Native Commodities and Rarities in each County* (London: printed by J. G[rismond]., W. L[eybourne]., and W. G[odbid] for Thomas Williams, 1662), pp. 58–9.

82 Fuller, *History of the Worthies of England* (1684), p. 971.

83 'Introduction', in David Bates, Julia Crick and Sarah Hamilton (eds), *Writing Medieval Biography, 750–1250: Essays in Honour of Frank Barlow* (Woodbridge: Boydell Press, 2009), pp. 1–13, at p. 5.

84 Robert Brady, *A Complete History of England from the First Entrance of the Romans under the Conduct of Julius Caesar unto the End of the Reign of King Henry III . . . : Wherein is Shewed the Original of our English Laws, the Differences and Disagreements between the Secular and Ecclesiastic Powers . . . and Likewise an Account of our Foreign Wars with France, the Conquest of Ireland, and the Actions between the English, Scots and Welsh . . . : All Delivered in Plain Matter of Fact, without any Reflections or Remarques* (Savoy, London: printed by Tho. Newcomb for Samuel Lowndes . . . , 1685), p. 271.

85 Wyman H. Herendeen, 'William Camden (1551–1623), historian and herald', *ODNB*.

86 William Camden, *Britain, or, A Chorographicall Description of the Most Flourishing Kingdomes, England, Scotland, and Ireland, and the Islands Adjoyning, out of the Depth of Antiquitie . . .* trans. Philemon Holland (London: George Bishop and John Norton, 1610), p. 649.

87 Camden, *Britain*, trans. Holland, p. 652.

88 Camden, *Britain*, trans. Holland, p. 658.

5

Remaking Nest: eighteenth- and nineteenth-century views

THIS CHAPTER WILL consider the narratives of Nest, and other medieval women, during the late eighteenth and nineteenth centuries. Key sources include contemporary accounts of Welsh history and travel writing by authors such as Thomas Pennant and George Nicholson. This will include a discussion of the ways in which narratives of medieval women were replicated and how, and crucially if, they formed part of a narrative of Wales, in a number of texts that have been selected since they are useful for illustrating key themes. These writings about Wales will be examined to assess the thesis that particular factors lay behind the enduring appeal of medieval Welsh women. Cultural change forms a key context for discussion. Further, writers on Wales were influenced by the growth in nationalism, Celticism and industrialism. The following discussion will consider how writers from the eighteenth and nineteenth centuries revisited Welsh history and portrayed specific women such as Nest, or Gwenllian, the wife of Rhys ap Gruffudd, who was killed on the battlefield in 1136. It will discuss whether a gendered view of the Welsh medieval past was inculcated in writings on Wales before the birth of formal academic history in the country with the landmark publication of Lloyd's 1911 *History of Wales*. Eighteenth- and nineteenth-century views of Nest and other prominent women were therefore reconstructing the role of women in the history of Wales under the impetus of distinct cultural and ideological contexts. This chapter will consider the import-ance of identity within these texts and how far, if at all, gender was important in the construction of a Welsh identity. Attitudes to the medi-eval past expressed in later writings evidence that writers, by looking to the past, resolved issues about present identity. Stuart Hall has suggested that cultural identity is the outcome of a process whereby common histor-ical narratives of the past play an essential role in determining a collec-tive identity and individuals define themselves therefore by reference to those narratives. This identity is founded on collective experience, a sense of the imagined past and the creation of a narrative of difference.[1] As part of this it will consider whether narratives of women had ideological roles to fulfil as symbols of Welsh nationhood.

Philippa Levine points out in her study of eighteenth-century Britain, *Gender and Empire*, that in colonial societies the way that women were written about was shaped by an idea that women were defined by and managed by men. Although we cannot see medieval Wales as a colonial society in the modern conception of the term as discussed by Francis James West,[2] nevertheless the portrayal of Nest and other women in the histories of Wales in the eighteenth and nineteenth centuries presented them as a separate category whose futures were shaped by men. Commentators saw the process of the takeover of parts of Wales by the Normans as complex. Such views may well have included conceptions of inferiority based on ethnicity but this was complicated by ideas about gender in the writings of nineteenth-century historians and commentators on Wales. Thus more extreme views of ethnicity and oppression as the twin engines of Welsh subordination to England also incorporated ideas about gender and identity. Identity is as much a matter of 'becoming as of being': it is a historical process, not a 'stable, unchanging and continuous frame of reference', in Hall's words, and is produced by 'people's positioning in the narratives of the past'.[3] Other scholars also stress the flexibility and mutability of notions of identity; Kathleen Wilson, for example, argues that Britishness and Englishness were not static but mutable and were centrally founded on ideas about difference, and that such identities constructed paradoxical meanings. For Wilson, aristocratic women who acted outside accepted conventions if they had extramarital sex paid a heavy price even if they had won some freedom.[4] Wilson puts gender central to the developing discourse of nation and empire and this pinpoints a core motif in writings on medieval women in Wales. Thus narratives of the past are intrinsic to the creation of identity, and gender is implicit within such narratives. In a sense we have come full circle here – modern theorists have merely stated what medieval chroniclers clearly knew, that the past informed the present and they interpreted it according to their notions of identity. Thus Nest's story and others' were incorporated into texts, on occasion, and reinterpreted because Welsh identity in the past was felt to be the key to explaining Welsh identity in the present. This sense was thus produced by writers positioning Nest within the past for whom her history was crucial to the narrative of Wales: categories of difference based on ideas about gender melded with concerns about Nest's ethnicity, which in turn interacted with Celticism.

The social, political, economic and ideological changes of the late seventeenth and eighteenth centuries were influenced by the creation of empire. Britain emerged as a colonial power linked to the rise of empire, slavery and the Enlightenment. Certainly, Wales underwent ideological, social, industrial and political changes from the late seventeenth century and through the eighteenth century. As Geraint Jenkins has pointed out, Welsh remembrancers had a key role to play in shaping a sense of Welsh national identity in the eighteenth century.[5] Wales underwent cultural transformations, and Prys Morgan has suggested that Wales underwent a cultural renaissance which provided new heroes, for example Dafydd ap Gwilym, Twm Siôn Cati and Madoc.[6] The way that the Nest story was recorded, or not, by remembrancers, writers and commentators on Wales should therefore be placed into a context which acknowledges the importance of ideas about gender, women and nation. Nest is only briefly mentioned in the writings of Nathaniel Crouch, who published under the pseudonym Robert Burton. In his *The History of the Principality of Wales*, first published in 1695 and influential well into the eighteenth century, Nest appears in the context of the ancestry of Gerald of Wales as the daughter of Rhys of Deheubarth, and mother of Angharad, mother of Gerald. Gerald's uncle 'David, the second bishop of St David's' is also mentioned. The Welsh ancestry of Gerald is stressed; Nest's husband Gerald of Windsor does not appear in the narrative. Nest appears in the text as an ancestral figure and the tale of her abduction is absent from this narrative. Crouch was interested in the princes of Wales and expends considerable energy on the arrival of the Normans in Glamorgan, influenced by the narrative of the arrival of the Normans in Glamorgan as portrayed in Rice Merrick's work.[7] Crouch notes the Welsh–Saxon interactions and details the Norman conquest of England, conflict between the English and the Welsh and, drawing on Gerald of Wales, states that Flemings were settled to keep the Welsh in obedience. His sympathy for the Welsh resistance to Norman incursion is evident. He states that Normans in Anglesey under the command of Hugh de Montgomery, earl of Shrewsbury and Hugh, earl of Chester in 1095 'executed great Cruelty on the People, cutting off the Hands and Noses, and Arms of the Resisters, sparing neither Age, Sex nor Place, Sacred or Profane from Destruction'.[8] The narrative focuses upon the princes and their interactions with the English crown, and there are only brief mentions of the role of women. For example, Joan, wife of Llywelyn, is mentioned in the context of a brief discussion of Llanfaes Priory, Anglesey, where 'a Daughter of king John and the son of a Danish king' were buried.[9] The story of her alleged adultery, so prominent in the *Brut*, is not mentioned.

While Crouch's mentions of Nest of Deheubarth are limited, the story of Nesta, the wife of Bernard of Neufmarché, is given in some detail. He states that Nesta had been 'debauched' by 'a young gentleman'. Her son 'Mahel, having got this gallant into his hands, used him very severely, at which Nesta being enraged, came into open court, and on her oath before Henry II, publicly deposed that Mahel' was not the legitimate son of Bernard of Neufmarché but 'begotten on her in Adultery'.[10] The slim volume is a pared-down history of Wales and therefore the inclusion of the details of Mahel is all the more prominent. The author acknowledged that he had not included the history of Boudicca and other remarkable women, and so had published a separate book on *Female Excellency, or, The Ladies of Glory*, in 1688. This book was probably modelled on Thomas Heywood's *The Exemplary Lives and Memorable Acts of Nine of the Most Worthy Women of the World: Three Iewes, Three Gentiles, Three Christians* published in 1640.[11] The address to the reader in Crouch's (alias Burton's) *Female Excellency* states that 'Though women . . . have been commonly reckoned incapable of noble undertakings from which God and nature hath no more excluded the Feminine than the Masculine part of Mankind yet it will be a little hard to pronounce that they really are so.' The author suggests that men are given advantages through 'Education, Learning and Arts' and 'if women had the same helps I daresay they would make as good return'. The nine biographies were selected because the women had been 'renowned for either virtue or valour' and include biblical and historical examples, such as Marianne, wife of King Herod, Boudicca and Clotilda, queen of France.[12] Thus there is a recognition that women had had a role to play in the historical/legendary past, but more than this, there is a belief that the divine and natural order which had caused women to be seen as inferior could be overturned through education. This attention to the beneficial effects of 'Education, Learning and Arts' suggests that there was an awareness that gender differences were culturally constructed, and were linked to 'performance' of deeds, but could be changed. Such ideas were here expressed in the language of moral relativism. As such there was an awareness that gender differences were socially constructed even though the language used is that of natural moral qualities. The gallery of women presented is of course made up of chosen exemplars, yet it is significant that such ideas were articulated in the late seventeenth century. It is worth briefly considering Crouch's works more generally in order to set his views of women into context. Crouch published many historical works and he produced simplified, abbreviated versions of more complex works which made them more freely available to a less educated, less wealthy readership. His books were reprinted many times in the eighteenth century, suggesting the lasting popularity and influence of his works.[13] It has been suggested that the presentation, reception and production of his texts indicate that Crouch wrote for 'the people', that is the relatively uneducated public.[14] There has been some debate among scholars of eighteenth-century literature over the extent to which the popularisation of history represented the imposition of a cultural form and ideology by the ruling elite upon their subordinates, and Mayer argues that Crouch's writings suggest that the popularisation of history by the lower orders may well be an appropriation of power.[15] Crouch understood the importance of gender to power relations; he commented on the cultural construction of gender and was able to see that the social reality of female subordination was perpetuated in part by the exclusion of women from the beneficial effects of education. His historical writing on *Female Excellency* reflected these perceptions, and indeed in some ways perpetuated them. The fact that he published a volume on 'Female Excellency' shows that he believed that women had played important roles in history. Thus in, for example, his narrative of Wales, he drew upon the writings of Gerald of Wales and modelled an image of women that was directly derived from Gerald's views about women. Crouch's views were generally positive since he saw women as subordinated but potentially redeemed through education, and such ideas informed his writings on Wales. It may well be that the period from the late seventeenth century into the eighteenth century saw ideological shifts in the perception of women, men and gender as Kathleen Wilson suggests. Further, Wilson argues that women had 'key conceptual, ideological and practical roles to play in the projects of nation- and empire-building' since their bodies 'served as symbols of national virtue and martial potency for much of the century'.[16]

Such gendering of the Welsh past has been related to narratives of the Celts as the original Britons and the rise of Celticism within a context of narratives of the British Empire. In the case of Wales, this goes back to Theophilus Evans's *Drych y Prif Oesoedd* ('Mirror of the primitive ages') of 1716 which saw the history of Wales as a story of conquest and resistance, heroic defeat and triumphs against foreign invasions. It was the first history of Wales in Welsh and was immensely popular, five editions being printed in the eighteenth century and sixteen in the nineteenth.[17] Such ideas were then taken up further in the age of Romanticism by such writers as Edward Davies and Iolo Morganwg. The latter's forgery, the *Brut Aberpergwm*, elaborates the account of the Christmas feast by saying that Owain *saw* Nest there and was quite smitten.[18] Thomas Price (Carnhuanawc) in *Hanes Cymru, a Chenedl y Cymry, o'r Cynoesoedd hyd at Farwolaeth Llewelyn ap Gruffydd* ('History of Wales to the death of Llywelyn ap Gruffudd'), written between 1836 and 1842, is more brief. He does not describe or imply rape, though he claims that Owain *saw* Nest at the feast, and refers to 'Owain and his vile companions' breaking into the castle. This element of criticism becomes clearer in later works.[19] For example, Gweirydd ap Rhys's *Hanes y Brytaniaid a'r Cymry* (1872) condemns Owain's action as typical of the immorality of the old aristocracy of Wales and cites *Brut Aberpergwm*; but the note continues that the oldest chronicles say he only *heard* of her beauty and manners. He doesn't explicitly say Owain raped Nest, but does claim that he was driven by lust to 'enjoy' her and that he 'subdued' her; he also adds a note that he strongly suspects Nest was complicit in the whole affair.[20]

An essential part of this interpretation is the idea of the history of Wales in a British context, and Anglophone writers romanticised the history of 'Celtic' Wales. Some saw the Norman conquest as a positive force: for example, *The Modern Universal British Traveller* published in 1779, written as a guide to 'great Britain', portrayed the Welsh as sexually degenerate since they did not become a 'civilised people' until 'many years after the Norman Conquest', and at the time of the Romans had been a 'rude, ferocious and lascivious' people without 'the least regard to chastity'; women were controlled 'in common . . . if a female was seduced no regard was paid to it'. Further it stated that the Act of Union abrogated all laws and customs 'not agreeable to those of England'. Wales since then 'has assumed a new form': religion has been spread among the poor, so that the Welsh have become 'as rational and civilized as their neighbours the English'.[21]

Published in the second half of the eighteenth century, Benjamin Martin's *Introduction to the History of the Principality of Wales* described the topography, towns and ancient sites of Wales and included historical material as well as ethnographic details. Martin admired the Welsh towns such as Carmarthen which he found to be 'well-built, populous, polite and flourishing' and noted that Caernarfon shared these characteristics and that the residents were 'reputed to be very courteous to strangers'. He recorded that at Wrexham 'It is pleasant here to see the Welch Ladies come to market in laced hats, with their hair hanging in ringlets down their shoulders, with scarlet or blue cloaks, many of them leading a greyhound like the Amazonian Huntresses.'[22] Martin approved of the Norman conquest of Flintshire and the subjugation of Wales by Edward I, and condemned the 'ridiculous stories' associated with the veneration of St Winifrid at her shrine in Holywell.[23] For Martin, Wales was a country from which the Tudors had originated. Conquest by the English had benefited the Welsh, and the Welsh remained different.

Martin's presentation of selected brief historical anecdotes was that of an English protestant who was at ease with the history of a country which he acknowledged had its own historical trajectory that had been shaped by conquest by the English. His work is less a history of Wales than a narrative of contemporary Wales, and its interest in topography and its descriptive structure anticipated the later works of eighteenth-century travel writers such as William Bingley's *A Tour round North Wales*.[24] Bingley's *Tour* described towns, landscapes and scenery in romantic terms, yet, inspired by a harpist that he heard in Porthaethwy (Menai Bridge), Anglesey, he reflected on the conquest of Wales in poetical and prose forms in which he castigated a 'cruel tyrant' from whom virtues would not protect his soul from 'nightly fears, Cambria's curse, Cambria's tears'. Bingley commented that he had overlooked the 'perhaps necessary, though most cruel, policy of Edward I who had destroyed a race of men' who were capable of creating music that caused such a strong response in the listener.[25] Such travel writings were influential in creating a view of Wales, and Bingley saw the repression of Wales by conquerors in a romantic and gendered way.

In the late eighteenth and early nineteenth centuries the genre of travel writing underwent development. Literary scholars and historians have begun to evaluate the genre in terms of its key features including narrative structures, developments and content. For example, Carole Fabricant argues that the growth in travel literature was related to an increased interest in the figure of the traveller in popular literature, the spirit of scientific enquiry and the importance of the Grand Tour and travel within Britain (not least in the Lake District, Scotland as well as Wales, c. 1795–1815, when opportunities abroad were limited by war) and was stimulated by the growth in European travel.[26] Elizabeth Bohls stresses the importance of imperial expansion and the ongoing development of a British ideology. She goes further than Fabricant in her analysis of travel literature and considers links between the literary development of the novel and travel literature to suggest that novels and travel literature shared common epistemological, rhetorical and stylistic strategies. Bohls's key insight is that travel literature and novels were marked by an inter-est in contacts between cultures and that in the eighteenth century they explored 'the meaning of Englishness, in an age of imperial expansion and intra-British negotiation and consolidation'.[27] For Bohls domestic (meaning British) and exotic (meaning overseas) travel were inextricably linked. Travel writing derived from such journeys formed a discourse which had various strands, including antiquarian, economic and aesthetic aspects. This discourse, Bohls suggests, served as an outlet for debate over the meaning of 'Britishness', and crucially played an important role in the 'consolidation of the new sovereign territory of the United Kingdom between the Acts of Union with Scotland (1707) and Ireland (1801)'.[28] Thus there was a changing cultural, economic, political and ideological context within which the genre developed. Scholars have debated how travel writing developed, and Batten, for example, argues that with the advent of picturesque tourism in the 1770s and 1780s the genre changed and Romantic writers endeavoured to generate an emotional response from readers who sought 'pleasurable instruction'. Batten argues that as travel writing developed and the influence of the Romantics waned, travel guides developed from entertaining travel literature to be more instructive, factual and less autobiographical, and that this in turn led to the diversification of the genre.[29] More recently, Nigel Leask has argued that the change in travel writing from scientific and literary travel occurred after 1790–1820.[30] Whilst this debate is important for understanding developments of the genre, for our purposes it is important to note that travel writing was affected by literary changes more generally. Wales too was the subject of travellers' accounts and these developed in a similar context as travel writings more generally. Travel writings on Wales need to be understood in a framework which takes account of the development of travel literature, the broader literary developments of the period, including the Romantic period 1780–1830, and the ongoing importance of ideologies of empire which coincided with a Welsh intellectual renaissance in the eighteenth and nineteenth centuries. The Romantic period saw the development of picturesque tourism in Britain generally, and tourists to Wales published books and guides which presented a view of Wales which, in the scope and range of material discussed, was reflective of approaches to travel literature in Britain generally. Bohls suggests that the concept of inter-cultural experience was key to travel literature. The awareness of cultural differences was suffused with an awareness of class, gender and ethnic differences. For example, George Lipscomb, writing at the start of the nineteenth century, was pleased by 'the docility of temper and assiduity to please' of a barmaid who had reached 'the superior accomplishment of her station'. She was taken to represent 'the general characteristics of the Welch nation', but as a whole the Welsh were prone to be 'obstinate cherishers of superstition'.[31] Lipscomb's positive view contrasts with that of Benjamin Heath Malkin, writing in 1807, who argued that the Welsh way of life was 'coarse in the extreme' and that the Welsh language was 'causing great injury to religion and law'.[32] English Protestantism was here in conflict with the resurgent Welsh language, culture and religion.

However, there is considerable scope for scholars to analyse travel writing as it relates to Wales and in particular the way that broader socio-economic historical contexts and interactions of gender, culture and social status shaped the genre, although, as Geraint Jenkins has pointed out, tourists who visited Wales found it full of myths and legends.[33] As Hywel Davies has clarified, superstitious beliefs were an integral part of English travel writers' view of the people and landscapes of Wales. Wales in a British context was an important element of Welsh travel writers' writing on Wales.[34] In the following analysis, travel literature, including picturesque tourism, will be examined in a context which considers the way that women, in particular prominent women, such as Nest or Gwenllian, were portrayed in the genre.

Picturesque tourism may have been inspired by the desire to see natural landscapes or 'romantic beauties', and some were content to record the details of their journeys and travels in their private diaries.[35] Other writers also included historical material in their published works. Henry Penruddocke Wyndham, for example, who published *A Gentleman's Tour through Monmouthshire and Wales* in 1775, which was republished in 1881, wrote to inform the reader of 'the romantic beauties of nature' which were 'extravagant in the principality ... and they are scarcely to be conceived'.[36] His sources included the 'very useful' Gerald of Wales and Caradoc of Llancarfan.[37] For Wyndham the 'subjection of Wales is esteemed a most happy circumstance by every reasonable Briton'. He dismissed Welsh custom and law, such as *galanas*, as the cause of 'civil and domestic broils', and presented a view of medieval Wales as a country which 'became a scene of the most woeful anarchy and everyone lived in perpetual jealousy'. Wyndham articulated a colonialist view whereby independence was destroyed by internecine wars rather than by conflict with the English.[38] The Welsh were therefore culpable for their own defeat by the English. Other writers also utilised earlier sources in their writings. James Baker's *A Picturesque Guide through Wales*, published in 1795, included material drawn from Geoffrey of Monmouth in his discussion of the River Severn, for example, and also a version of the 'twelve knights of Glamorgan' in which he expressed approval for the Norman settlement. He mentions Nest in the context of her marriage to Gerald of Windsor and as the progenitor of the 'Geraldines so famous in Irish history': but no more.[39]

The importance of the conquest of Ireland by Nest's descendants also features prominently in the late-eighteenth-century writings of a Pembrokeshire bookbinder and bookseller, William Wilmot. Wilmot noted the abduction of Nest in a version which closely follows the *Brut* and other sources dependent upon it. Wilmot presented a pro-Norman view, calling Gerald of Windsor 'a brave and prudent man', while Owain's accomplices were a company of 'wild headstrong youths', a phrase redolent of the language of the *Brut*, yet Wilmot adds that they were 'notorious'.[40] The abduction narrative was part of the narrative of Pembrokeshire in Wilmot's local history at the end of the eighteenth century, and its essential themes – Nest's beauty, her actions to save Gerald, her role as an ancestral figure and so on – were intact and incorporated into the writings of a local historian. The narrative had entered the consciousness of a local historian and this in turn is evidence that he had access to sources such as the *Brut*. Wilmot recorded the narrative as part of the historical past, and his view is remarkably reliant on the chronicle and does not embellish or add to the narrative in the form of myth-making or invention.

Benjamin Malkin, in *The Scenery, Antiquities and Biography of South Wales*, published in 1807, showed an awareness of the dangers of myth-making and the problem of historicity but nevertheless accepted the Arthurian legends as fact. He also incorporated a positive view of the Normans and approved of the Norman conquest of Glamorgan. Malkin alleged that the conquest of Glamorgan had been caused by Iestyn ap Gwrgant's rape of the daughter of Llywelyn ap Sisyllt and his rapes of other Welsh women.[41] Malkin here repeats the trope of the lawless Welsh who were undone by the inability of the Welsh male elite to behave properly, and presented a view of the Normans as a civilising, progressive force.

Travel literature presented a view of Wales which was just as fictive and constructed as that of novels, but which assumed the guise of reported fact. Thompson has argued that the Romantic movement was an authorising vehicle for male poets and writers whose work reflects a masculine agenda through the adoption of 'representational and interpretative strategies'.[42] Within the genre, kidnapping and captivity scenarios were seen as romantic. Given this, it is likely that writers such as those who drew on the narrative of Nest did so not because they saw her as a proto-nationalist heroine who chose Owain over her Anglo-Norman husband, but because her abduction was interpreted as a romantic affair. Its portrayal in travel writing and local histories therefore contributed to a romantic view of Wales and its history, but also constructed the relationship between Nest and Owain as a romantic event. Nevertheless it is essentially a male-authored view of Wales, where historical reference to Nest captured the essence of the tensions at the heart of interpretations of the past. Similarly, the portrayal of the relationship between Joan and William de Braose became romanticised in later accounts.

Other writers also included anecdotes and historical references in their works. For example, in 1804 John Evans published his views on south Wales written after his tour of the region during 1803.[43] His writing is varied and descriptive and melds historical knowledge with observations about the topography, towns and people. Evans was a patriot, asserting that 'Wales may be called a historic country',[44] and wrote to argue that Wales was a country with a separate history. He argues that the inhabitants of south Wales fought with 'consummate skill and determined bravery' when they confronted the Romans and sees the rule of law and harmonious social relations as key to the benefits of the present, as well as the fact that 'protection and liberty' were the 'inalienable right of Britons'.[45] As an example of this he portrays the resistance and death of Gwenllian, the wife of Gruffudd ap Rhys, in a context which suggests that Gwenllian's beheading was an uncivilised act. He noted that Gwenllian 'roused the spirit of her friends' and states that her beheading was 'an act so savage, even without precedent in those brutal times'.[46] Here the Britons, or Welsh, are the 'civilised' forces; the Normans are savage and brutal since they beheaded a woman. This link with morality and the inclusion of women in his discourse is also explicit in his portrayal of Nesta, wife of Bernard of Neufmarché. He states that she was a woman who perhaps 'has never had her equal for outrageous infamy. Possessed of a most abandoned and vengeful spirit, she publicly sacrificed her own character to disinherit her own son of lawful patrimony.'[47] Of course the tale conflicts with contemporary ideas about male primogeniture based on legitimacy since Nesta acted to prove that her son was illegitimate and thus she 'sacrificed' her character. Wales was thus seen as a romantic, beautiful country and such ideas were central themes in early nineteenth-century writers' views on Wales. However, Evans's views were also informed by ideas about gender which were blended with Celticism: in his view the Welsh were the 'warlike Britons' who defended the liberty of the nation against Norman invaders. Like other commentators, Evans relied on the views of Gerald of Wales. Gerald had expressed similar views about Nesta, the wife of Bernard of Neufmarché, and also discussed Gwenllian, the wife of Gruffudd ap Rhys, and had little to say about his grandmother, Nest of Deheubarth, except to note her genealogy, and Evans included this detail.[48]

George Nicholson's *The Cambrian Traveller's Guide*, first published in 1808, noted that Carew castle was one of the royal demesnes of the princes of Wales and was given as dowry to a 'daughter of Rhys of Deheubarth', Nest, along with seven other manors when she married Gerald of Windsor.[49] Nicholson does not mention the abduction tale, but given that it is rare for individuals to be named in the *Guide* it is of note that Nicholson mentions her but does not comment on the abduction tale. *The Cambrian Traveller's Guide* is a rich source for the historian of early nineteenth-century Wales and is full of topographical descriptions and notes on fauna and flora, the inhabitants of Wales, their towns, villages, roads, rivers and houses. It is representative of late-eighteenth- and early nineteenth-century travel literature during the Romantic period and aims to educate and inform the reader, and deploys a wide range of material. The *Traveller's Guide* is ordered alphabetically and the first entry concerns Aber (Abergwyngregyn, Gwynedd), 'a pleasing little village'. The description includes details about ferries, the topography, and natural features including the waterfall near the village which is still a notable local beauty spot. The entry is full of details concerning Joan, daughter of King John, her husband Llywelyn and her relationship with William de Braose. Nicholson discusses the relationship between Joan and William de Braose in romantic terms. He relates how Joan had 'commiserated' with William de Braose on his situation as a prisoner at Llywelyn's castle at Abergwyngregyn and that she was won over by William's 'manners and address' but also by the 'deceit' of William. Thus Joan engaged in 'facts of inconstancy and intrigue'. Llywelyn, on discovering the relationship, changed from a 'friend' to William to a 'fiend': he was hanged on Llywelyn's orders and was thus 'a victim of treachery and love'. After this Nicholson states: 'Yet did not the barbarity of Llywelyn end here; the ultimatum remained, with which he intended to glut his revenge.' Llywelyn is then portrayed as a man who cruelly taunted Joan after William's execution: 'While the knight hung', Llewelyn took the princess to a window, from which was 'a full view of the gallows'. Nicholson presumably drew on local traditions in his description of Abergwyngregyn; he states that 'at the neighbouring cottages, near the foot of this mount [where William was hanged], tradition retains Llewelyn's question and the lady's answer in Welsh'. Nicholson relates that Llywelyn 'sarcastically smiled' and asked Joan what she would 'give' to see William, and she replied that she would give 'Wales and England and Llywelyn' to see de Braose. Nicholson also states that he was shown a man-made cave where William was allegedly kept while he awaited execution. Nicholson recorded traditions associated with the royal castle at Abergwyngregyn which suggests that the details were still remembered in the village nearly six hundred years after the events allegedly occurred. The entry is unusual because the descriptive aspects of the detail are full, and the emotive language used is distinctive. Nicholson drew on local traditions when he compiled his *Guide*, including romantic and legendary material associated with objects such as standing stones. For example, in his entry on Anglesey he notes that near the house of the Panton family at Pentraeth were two standing stones which had 'wrought a marvelous story'. He relates that the poet Einion ap Gwalchmai fell in love with 'the young Angharad, but unfortunately he had two competitors to contend with'. The matter was resolved by Angharad who declared that she would marry the man who won a leaping competition. Nicholson's description does not clarify that the standing stones were placed to mark the size of Einion's winning leaps, yet he tells us that Einion won the competition. He further records how Einion, who had had 'occasion to leave the country', returned to find that the 'faithless Angharad' had 'married another'. Einion took to his harp to console himself. Nicholson is, however, aware that local traditions could be speculative and open to doubt. He indicates, 'after this recital . . . if we may be allowed to descend to common sense', that the stones may have been 'druidic' monuments.[50] Nicholson was interested in the fate of the Welsh nation: his description of Llywelyn and Joan suggests some hostility to the Welsh, here written as a more hostile view of Llywelyn in the context of events and their association with locality, and he tied tradition and memory to place.

Nicholson was interested in local traditions, and his interest in marriage customs is evident in the diversionary mini-narratives that he deploys. For example, he records a superstitious practice which was current in Crickhowell in south Wales (then Breconshire, now Powys). He relates how a tradition, associated with the well of St Cenau or Kyne, which was renowned for its medical qualities, was also locally reputed to have powers especially applicable to newly-weds in which the first of the couple to drink from the well after the marriage ceremony was supposed to have 'government of the house for life'. He then includes a tale about a groom who was outwitted by his wife who had taken a vial of the water with her to the wedding ceremony; he ran to the well after the ceremony only to find his wife 'in the church porch in a state most tranquil' and admitting her strategy.[51] Nicholson also included details of a marriage custom that allegedly occurred in 'Cardiganshire' which involved community participation in what may be termed a ritualised fake abduction, called a 'bidding'. This 'curious custom' took place a week before the wedding in church and began with the calling of the banns. A bidder (*gwahoddwr*) then went from house to house holding a 'long pole with ribbons flying at the end of it'. Nicholson relates how an invitation to the community was spoken and all members were invited to attend. It is apparent that there were customary actions which occurred in a specific order and with precise actions, for example the specific days for the removal of furniture into the newly-weds' house were stated, and the giving of prenuptial gifts by wedding guests was described as 'an ancient British custom'. Events culminate when '80 or 100' of the 'friends of the man [the groom] come all on horseback, to the cheese and ale', a key event in the customary events leading to the wedding. After this, '10 or 20 of the best mounted go to the intended bride's house to demand her'. It is clear that the bride is expecting this but appears 'uncomplying'. Subsequently each side's poets participated in events: 'Welsh poetry is employed by way of argument, one party being within the house and other without, abusing each other much.' Nicholson clarifies that events then take a more dynamic turn: 'Several persons then deliver orations on horseback demanding the daughter from the father who are answered by persons appointed for the purpose.' The 'guests' are then welcomed in by the father of the bride and offered refreshments. The girl mounts behind her father, mother or friend on the swiftest horse 'who then pretend to run away with her like mad folks in any direction'. The girl rode pillion, and this continued until the horse tired or the bride became 'impatient' and consented to go. The parties then went to church and after the ceremony the wedding reception was held at the house of the newly-weds. Further events occurred, such as the specification that the newly-weds stay at home on the day following the wedding in the church, and there was an auction of the cheese left over from the wedding feast. The whole ceremony concluded the following Sunday when the couple were escorted to church by the company who had been involved in the various stages of the marriage customs.[52] It is of note that Theophilus Jones noted similar customs in his *History of the County of Brecknock*.[53]

The detail concerning marriage customs is of note because Nicholson constructed a view of Wales within the *Guide* which was centrally focused on topographical descriptions. The inclusion of details concerning early nineteenth-century marriage customs is suggestive of an ethnographic interest, and part of a wider characterisation of the Welsh. That the custom was recorded in south-west Wales where Nest's abduction allegedly occurred is an interesting congruence which serves to create an image of local Welsh customs as distinctive and uncontrolled within a prescribed framework. The marriage custom is a socially sanctioned and carefully constructed performance which served to reinforce social cohesion. The element of the mock-resistance to the wedding and the chase of the bride by friends of the groom is suggestive of coercion and abduction, which is oddly set against a series of prescriptive local customs that are community based and inclusive. There is evidence to suggest these traditions may have survived into the late nineteenth century, or possibly the early twentieth. R. W. Thompson, a journalist who travelled through Wales in the late 1930s, published reports of his experiences in Wales. He records how he met an old man in a Carmarthenshire pub who told him that he had seen similar events in the area earlier in his life. Thompson's book, *An Englishman Looks at Wales,* was a collected work built on his newspaper articles that he had published weekly in the *Sunday Graphic*.[54] The ethnographic material in Nicholson's guide constructed the Welsh as different, and such ethnographic material is a feature of early travel writing. His guide was intended to be comprehensive, the title-page claimed to note all features of Wales and was the result of 'comprehending histories and descriptions' of all notable features from cities, towns, abbeys, churches, ferries, forts, forests, cromlechs, lakes, ancient roads, battlefields, 'the whole interspersed with biographic notices', to mineralogy, botany, commerce, trade and roads, among many other specific items. His wide interests extended to 'remarks on the commerce, manufactures, agriculture, and manners and customs of the inhabitants'. Thus the biographic details concerning Joan, the comment on Llywelyn and the interest expressed in the extended entry are part of Nicholson's objective to be comprehensive and informative. Yet his apparent factual approach belies a critical and hostile approach to the Welsh. Llywelyn is portrayed as barbarous and Joan is 'the frail princess'. Nicholson draws on contemporary views of women as the weaker sex to justify her adultery. William de Braose is 'the Knight' while Llywelyn is a 'fiend'.

Nicholson's 1808 *Guide* was a success and was reprinted and expanded in 1813 and reprinted in 1840. He listed his sources, which included Thomas Pennant's '*Tour Through Wales* . . . Bingley's *Tour through North Wales* . . . [and] Malkin's *Scenery of South Wales*', and suggested that his guide was timely since there was no comprehensive travel guide for tourists in Wales. Pennant, he argued, was 'the first modern traveler in Wales',[55] while Wyndham's *Tour* (1781) 'first awakened the attention of the English to Welsh scenery and encouraged an inclination for excursions'.[56] Thus Nicholson's list of sources is evidence that he positioned himself as a serious writer and drew on previous approaches. His views of Joan and marriage practices in particular reflect contemporary prejudices and concern with virtue based on ethnicity. Joan was excused as a frail English princess who fell in love with an English knight, Llywelyn was a Welsh anti-hero, a 'fiend' who behaved barbarously. The portrayal of Joan and Llywelyn is not simply reportage, it is a subtle construction of a view which depicts the Welsh elite as barbarous and uncivilised and thus inferior. The material which describes marriage customs that involved mock abductions emphasises social ties and communal vibrancy which mark the participants as different.

Hywel Davies has argued that English travel writing on Wales provoked a Welsh response by writers such as Theophilus Jones. Jones wrote to 'correct' inaccuracies in tourists' accounts and wanted to portray Wales more accurately. He produced a wide-ranging view of Wales and its history. His portrayal was based on observations of the topography, customs, history, language, agriculture and people of Wales. He also articulated a sense of the Welsh in a British context in a complex portrayal of interconnecting identities.[57] Jones published his *History of the County of Brecknock* in two volumes in 1805 and 1809 and it was reprinted as a single volume at the end of the nineteenth century. His view of the Norman conquest was complex and he carefully nuanced his interpretation of key events of the early Norman advance into Wales with an awareness of the importance of ethnicity. For example, he noted that Rhys ap Tewdwr had received help from 'the wild Irishman' whom he sees as representative of ethnic tensions: 'The epithet uniformly conferred by the Britons upon this Hibernian unequivocally marks their opinion of his character and manners, and shews that they considered him no higher in the scale of human beings than we now do the Ourang Outang' whose 'wild manners' were soon civilised by the '*Celtic savages*'. He does not discuss Nest, but notes that the site of the battle between Iestyn ap Gwrgant and her father Rhys ap Tewdwr was memorialised in the name as 'Bodwiggied'.[58] Few women are mentioned in the context of the Norman interactions with the Welsh, although he condemns the adultery of the wife of the Norman Bernard de Neufmarché. She was 'Nest grand daughter of Griffith ap Llewelyn prince of North Wales, a lady who does no credit to our country or his choice'; he condemns her actions during her affair with her husband's vassal which were 'machinations and vile arts'.[59] He notes the complexity of tracing genealogical descent for families with roots in late-medieval Wales without comment: he states that Sir Roger Vaughan of Tretower 'the third son [of Roger Vaughan who fought at Agincourt] is almost intitled to be considered as the head of a tribe; for his issue by different women, whether wives or concubines is by no means clear, nor does it seem to have been very material in his time, were so numerous, that they are with difficulty followed'.[60] Yet in his discussion of the early phases of the Norman conquest and the conflict between Rhys ap Tewdwr and 'Iestyn ap Gwrgan lord or prince of Glamorgan' he argued that the conflict was probably caused by disputes over boundaries, and thus refuted the views of 'others' who had argued that the dispute was related 'to a jealousy entertained by Jestin, who accused Rhys of too great intimacy with his wife'. Jones wrote 'this however is improbable, if not absurd'. Jones argued, on the other hand, that the fault lay with Iestyn who was 'a most abandoned character, dissolute in his morals and oppressive in his government, debauching, either by open violence or secret intrigue, the wives and daughters of his neighbours'. Thus Iestyn was to blame for the death of Rhys, the 'subjugation' of his country, for leaving Wales a prey to 'foreigners', and his sexual promiscuity was thus a moral failing for which he was condemned.[61] The publication of S. R. Meyrick's, *The History and Antiquities of the County of Cardigan* in 1808, like Jones's *History of the County of Brecknock*, is indicative of the new interest in county histories which included a broad range of material. He notes the abduction of Nest, which he dated to 1107, and did so without passing any comment on the morality of Nest. His interest lay in providing historical interest to his descriptions. The abduction is discussed in an entry relating to Cardigan castle, and Meyrick notes the impact of events. Nest is mentioned only as the wife of Gerald, who was abducted; there is no mention of sexual congress, only that Owain was motivated by love. Meyrick appears to have been dazzled by the idea of a magnificent feast: 'when we consider the magnititude of the preparations, the nature of the ceremonies, the number and quality of the guests, and the serious consquences which ensued . . . the castle must have been of some magnititude'. He notes that Cadwgan ap Bleddyn was 'innocent' and that Owain was killed by Gerald of Windsor in 1114 because of the abduction of Nest.[62]

Fenton's *Historical Tour through Pembrokeshire*, published in 1810, presented a more detailed view of the context of the abduction and suggested that the marriage of Nest and Gerald occurred after Nest had been Henry's concubine. Nest's beauty is seen as the cause of the abduction, but the marriage between Nest and Gerald is presented as an attempt by Gerald to secure a position for himself by rights gained to Nest's dowry, rather than merely being reliant on the will of Henry I. Fenton thus situated the abduction in the hard realities of the political context of the early twelfth century, and noted the improvements made at Carew which witnessed the abduction, the 'night adventure'. There is no criticism of the abduction, but the burning of Carew was conducted by 'that profligate cheiftain Cadwgan ap Bleddyn, and his rake-hell companions, when he carrried off Nesta, the governor's wife, of whose beauty he had heard with such extravagant praise'. Fenton corrected his error later when he stated that Owain then abducted Nest.[63]

Jones, Fenton and other writers drew on the medieval past for material and as such the medieval past was part of a contested narrative in which prominent women were portrayed. Travel literature melded contemporary observations on a diverse range of subjects, including historical material, which aimed to educate as well as entertain its readers, and women were incorporated into these narratives and served a variety of functions within texts. Historians too turned their attention to Wales in the middle ages and, like travel writers, romanticisation and national interests were central. Gender informed these texts, and the narratives of women such as Nest, Gwenllian (d. 1136) and Joan were incorporated into a view of Wales in order to cast reflections on Wales and the Welsh. The following discussion will consider Anglophone travel writing. Such texts could be popular, for example William Warrington's *History of Wales* was first published in 1786, and subsequently republished in 1788, 1791, 1805 and 1823.[64] Warrington argued that the history of the people of Wales was 'single and original in the annals of the world'. The Welsh, he argued, were 'distinguished by their independency of spirit defending for ages the rights of nature and liberty'. Warrington clarified that he wrote as an Englishman whose work was partisan to the Welsh as 'a voluntary tribute of justice and humanity as a cause of injured liberty'.[65] He noted the many internecine disputes of Welsh medieval history and the 'spirit and genius' of the Welsh. He was partisan in support of the Welsh and their struggle against the Normans, and thus saw the Welsh resistance to William Rufus as a cause whereby the Welsh, a 'gallant people', recovered their 'ancient character'.[66] Warrington included details on Nest's abduction in an account which is close to that of the *Brut*, but which is romanticised and slightly embroidered; Nest is the 'Lady' whose 'beauty and elegance', 'it was said, exceeded those of any lady in Wales'.[67] The narrative has the key turning points and elements of the abduction tale: Warrington describes Owain's followers as wild companions, for example, and states that Nest's beauty in reality exceeded the tales that had been told at Cadwgan's feast. He does not report Nest's speech as portrayed in the *Brut*, but does state that it was her initiative which saved Gerald. Further, Warrington casts doubt on the nature of the abduction and Nest's response to Owain: 'whether she yielded to the violence of her lover from choice or from necessity, is uncertain'.[68] Warrington noted that Gruffydd ap Rhys, Nest's brother, had returned from exile in Ireland and had stayed with Nest for two years. At the point where this enters the narrative he reiterates that Nest was married to Gerald of Windsor and that through this marriage Gerald had secured south-west Wales. Further, Warrington notes that Nest had been a mistress to Henry I and states that she had had two children by him, one of which was Robert, earl of Gloucester. He then further clarifies that she was 'the same person, whose beauty had so lately excited Owain the son of Cadwgan to the act of violence already mentioned'.[69] He therefore portrays Nest's narrative as integral to the unfolding of political instability in south-west Wales, and this was underpinned by her family connections.

Warrington relied on William Wynne's 1697 *History of Wales*, which was essentially a version of David Powel's 1584 work *The Historie of Cambria, now called Wales*. Wynne is clear, in his portrayal of the attack on Cenarth Bychan, that the burning of the castle was deliberate, as was the ravaging of the countryside which the abductors passed through as they fled Deheubarth, a view which of course ultimately derives from the *Brut*.[70] Warrington thus deviated from the version presented in Wynne, perhaps suppressing this in his desire to portray the Welsh resistance to the Normans in a positive way. Warrington's text shows that the abduction of Nest was integral to the narrative of Norman advance into Deheubarth and thus part of a wider narrative of Wales in the early English-language texts on medieval Welsh history. Warrington noted the political context of the marriage of Llywelyn ap Iorwerth to Joan, daughter of King John, in 1205 and her intercession with John following Llywelyn's revolt in 1210–11.[71] Warrington utilises the language of empire to describe Wales, the 'remnant of the British Empire', writing that the Welsh 'poured down devastation and vengeance on the heads of their hated oppressors'.[72] His use of imperial imagery serves to underpin the portrayal of Wales as a nation cast down but resilient. This is a clear critique of what he perceived to be English oppressiveness; and his use of the term 'British Empire' is evocative of a lost ancient Britain. In his 1786 edition he portrayed the affair between Joan and William de Braose as an 'injury of all others the most poignant'.[73] In the revised 1823 edition he cast doubt on the affair but felt that the latter's death was 'justly due' because of 'a life, deeply tinged by perfidy, and marked by the bloody traces of a spirit the most cruel and ferocious'.[74] Joan's marital fidelity was thus an important component in the portrayal of the effectiveness of Llywelyn's rule. Warrington therefore wrote a positive view of Wales and saw the struggle for liberty against the Normans as key to understanding the dynamics of Welsh political history. Within this narrative the abduction was portrayed in an ambivalent way. Such ambivalence affected the way that Philip Yorke portrayed Nest and the abduction in his *The Royal Tribes of Wales*, published in 1799, which drew directly on Warrington's work.[75] Thus the romanticisation and ambivalence concerning Nest in Welsh medieval history was an important element in late-eighteenth- and early nineteenth-century texts, and was part of a narrative of Wales and its resistance to the Norman conquest.[76] These latter themes of course first appeared in the *Brut y Tywysogion* and were perpetuated through the early modern period, to be resurrected in later Welsh history and adapted to suit contemporary concerns.

A year later than Warrington's reprint, in 1824, John Jones published his *The History of Wales, Descriptive of the Government, Wars, Manners* ... His view of Wales, which noted the internecine disputes, condemned the internal wars of the native princes which he thought had been 'as many crimes to Cambria, because they had spirit without power'. Jones either did not know of, or ignored, Nest's story, but did include details of Gwenllian's death in 1136. Huw Pryce has noted that John Jones expressed some 'patriotic' sentiments but was highly critical of the Welsh ideas about government and their willingness to rebel.[77] Jones, while he condemned the Welsh leaders as traitors to the English king, excused the Welsh rebellions, since he argued the Welsh had been forced to rebel due to the tyranny of the English: 'the kings of England by imposing on the princes by force, tyrannical conditions of tenure, had no right to expect performance of treaties because there can be no binding contract in any case where either of the parties is not in the full liberty and exercise of volition'. Thus, although he wrote of the Welsh in sympathetic and positive ways, seeing racial differences constructed through appearance, language, pastimes and character, and although he is critical of the Welsh 'hurriness of manner', he excuses rural unruliness by reference to the enclosure acts 'which have thrown over the mind of the peasant'.[78] His views were indeed 'patriotic' in places, as Huw Pryce has shown, though he also presented a positive view of the Normans arguing that the imposition of feudalism by the Normans and their roles as 'artificers and husbandmen' had been beneficial to Wales. Jones presented a view of Wales which distinguished between the Normans and the Welsh elites and he attempted to clarify and contextualise his views by recourse to ideas about liberty and tyranny. These contexts underpin his portrayals of Gwenllian and Nesta, wife of Bernard de Neufmarché. Their stories are part of a wider narrative about the history of Wales in which women in general play little role. Yet when their portrayals in his narrative are constructed it is by recourse to moral comment and stereotyping, which also became part of the fabric of Welsh identity. Thus the story of Gwenllian (d. 1136), wife of Gruffudd ap Rhys, as a victim of male violence became an integral part of the story of Welsh resistance to Norman activity. The violence meted out to Gwenllian on the battlefield was seen to be representative of Norman violence and was a leitmotif of nineteenth-century writings on the history of Wales. Such views are evident in Eliza Constantia Campbell's 1833 *The History of Wales*, which was written for use in schools. Distinctly patriotic and written in a brief form, it discussed the Norman encroachment and Welsh resistance and in general praised Welsh leaders, but the abduction narrative is not featured.[79] Jones's views suggest the ongoing importance of the writings of Gerald of Wales to nineteenth-century commentators. For example, Bernard Bolingbroke Woodward's *History of Wales*, published in 1853, was throughout heavily influenced by Gerald of Wales, but he also drew on *Brut y Tywysogion*. He mentions Nest's abduction and notes that Nest had 'been the king's mistress', and his version is reliant on the *Brut*. He also noted the death of Gwenllian in 1136, saying she was put to death 'as an example'.[80]

A year later, in 1854, T. J. Llywelyn Prichard published *The Heroines of Welsh History: Comprising Memoirs and Biographical Notices of the Celebrated Women of Wales*.[81] The book is dedicated to 'the virtuous votaries of True Womanhood, in all its graces, purity and excellence as contra-distinguished from the fantastic fooleries and artificial characteristics of fine ladyism in the middle walks of life'.[82] The latter comment is a criticism of middle-class manners and perhaps is intended as a critique of modernism; it may also have been part of a reaction to the negative comments that were made by education commissioners in the 1847 *Report into the State of Education in Wales*, which became known as *Bard y Llyfray Gleision* or 'Treachery of the Blue Books'.[83] The attributes of 'fine ladyism' are ill-defined, yet it is clear that the lives of Welsh women were of importance to Welsh history. Not all contemporaries would agree: women are rarely mentioned in the Welsh-language encyclopaedia *Y Gwyddoniadur Cymreig* that was published in the mid-nineteenth century and includes entries on many prominent individuals; Nest is not mentioned, and neither is Owain ap Cadwgan. Thus there are entries relating to famous Welshmen, and a few legendary women appear, but the role of women within Welsh history is, in general, ignored.[84]

Prichard uses examples of women from the medieval past to critique women in the present. The book has a biographical approach and considers a broad range of women from all social categories across the historical past including 'Actresses of celebrity born in Wales'; 'the princess Elfleda' or Æthelflæd (d. 918); Angharad, the daughter of Meredith ap Owain (d. 998); 'Angharad the Nun', the *first love* of the poet Dafydd ap Gwilym' (*fl.* 1330–50); 'Bella the Fortuneteller'; the 'Lady Hawys Gadarn', who lived in the fourteenth century; Matilda de la Haie (d. 1210); Gwenllian (d. 1136), wife of Gruffudd ap Rhys (d. 1137); Joan, princess of Gwynedd (d. 1237), wife of Llywelyn ab Iorwerth; Mistress Trevor Hanmer (who lived during the civil war period); and the contemporary 'beauties of Anglesey', as well as women from the legendary past, for example, the ladies of the court of King Arthur.[85] In his preface, Prichard stated his intention to write another volume since 'we are far from approaching a state of exhaustion' on the subject of 'worthies'. This would have included, among others, Nest, who is described as 'the Princess Nest, daughter of Prince ab Tewdwr, mistress of king Henry I and mother of the learned Robert of Gloucester'.[86] This additional volume never appeared, however. *Heroines of Welsh History* reflects the nineteenth-century interest in medievalism and hero-worship and is laced with moral values, presenting individual women in stereotypical ways.[87] Princess Joan, for example, is described as 'very beautiful in person, and captivating in manners, and . . . she completely enslaved the Cambrian prince by the fascination of her charms'.[88] For Prichard, Llywelyn's 'infatuation' caused him to overlook the illegitimacy of her birth. He argues that it is hard to explain how the Welsh could accept the marriage of Joan and Llywelyn given that they were 'a people of such violent prejudices and high national pride . . . who especially branded illegitimacy of birth as a personal disgrace'. Prichard links national pride to a moral code which is more representative of nineteenth-century values than an understanding of the medieval past. More than this, however, Prichard romanticises the union between Joan and Llywelyn and in so doing places less emphasis on the political importance of the marriage. The gaze of the nineteenth-century romantic commentator therefore trivialises the union into a love match and demonstrates a lack of perspicacity on the part of the author with his failure to appreciate the medieval past on its own terms. Prichard condemned Joan because of her relationship with William de Braose, describing her as 'one of the most unpopular female sovereigns of Wales' because of her 'faults of character', which were not 'redeemed by high talents, private virtues nor imputed amiability of disposition'. In contrast to this negative view of Joan, Prichard presents positive portrayals of Æthelflæd (d. 918), the daughter of King Alfred of Wessex. Æthelflæd married a Mercian and after the death of her husband ruled in her own right as 'Lady of the Mercians', and it is generally accepted by historians that she was an effective military leader. Prichard tells us that 'this terrific warrior queen of the Saxons came among the Welsh only to shed their blood . . . and cast the chain of captivity on all . . . yet she shall have fair play at our hands . . . [She was] as masculine in frame as she was intrepid in mind.'[89] His view was perhaps influenced by the twelfth-century chronicler Henry of Huntingdon, who stated that Æthelflæd was 'the dread of men' and 'worthy of a man's name' and praised her as a 'mighty queen and a king' in his *History of the English People* completed in 1145.[90] Prichard states that he would 'deal' with

Æthelflæd fairly since previous portrayals had been unjust. Æthelflæd is described in gendered terms related to her physique: she was 'masculine', and this is then tied in with her mental prowess as 'intrepid' of mind, with her physical appearance validating her mental ability. As part of the defence of Wessex, King Alfred had reorganized the system of forti-fied settlements known as 'burhs'. Æthelflæd took this policy to Mercia, but the impact of this upon Wales is less clear.[91] Given that Prichard was writing a history of Welsh heroines, it is odd that he included Æthelflæd, a Mercian who was in conflict with Welsh kingdoms. This suggests that his biographies were selected not only because they represented nation-alist imperatives, but because they exemplified the types of character-istics that he wished to promote, while having some connection to Wales or Welsh history. Prichard presented a passionate view of Welsh history: women are portrayed in stereotypical ways, and he condemns Welsh, Norman and English royal abuse of women who were victims of war in his portrayal of Angharad the wife of Hywel ab Edwin, who was the grandson of Hywel Dda. In a passage which condemns the way that Gruffudd ap Llywelyn took Angharad as his concubine after the defeat of her husband in 1038, Prichard attacks the views of Lord Lyttleton who had condoned Gruffudd's actions. Prichard, citing Walter Scott, remarked that 'parallel cases of atrocity may be cited done by English heroes, "of the gentle Norman blood"'. Prichard then uses the example of Nest to critique Anglo-Norman royal lordship, stating that Nest's 'pitiable help-lessness' after the death of her father, 'the flight of her brothers for their lives, from those who were thirsting for their blood, the utter destruction of her paternal home' and her general situation gave her 'no protection against the lustful barbarity of the Anglo-Norman king' who made Nest his concubine.[92] Nest is thus portrayed as a victim of royal rapacity and of events beyond her control.

The Heroines of Welsh History is a collective biography of women who were included because they were seen to have had an impact on, or could be connected to, the trajectory of Welsh history, whether Welsh or Anglo-Norman, legendary or real. It has been suggested that collective biographies were utilised by groups or individuals who wished to con-struct their own or national identities. His choice of genre, a biograph-ical approach, is representative of an exemplary approach to history which had enjoyed a long tradition reaching back to antiquity. It was thus written in a well-established biographical tradition.[93] This context in part clarifies the objective of Prichard's *Heroines of Welsh History*. Its novelty lay in its emphasis on the place of women within Welsh history who were seen to be an important part of that narrative but the language used constructs the women, with connections to Wales, as models of behaviour as a way of critiquing the present. Overall the book is indicative of the increasing interest in Welsh culture and history in the nineteenth century and suggests that there was a readership who would be interested in the 'heroines' of Welsh history. His Welsh national patriotism was a key theme in his descriptions, and through a Scottish connection was part of a constructed vision of the past greatness of medieval Wales and the Welsh as key in the creation of Britain. Prichard claimed that the Stuart dynasty in Scotland could trace its descent from Gruffudd ap Llywelyn through a daughter, Nest, when she had an affair with Fleance, the son of Macbeth of Scotland. His dismissive tone and hostility to Scottish nationalism is evident: 'it is really pitiable – more than pitiable – it is truly laughable to witness the pride of Scotch nationality' that was founded on 'a criminal amour based on illegitimacy'.[94] The volume only discusses contemporary women in rural settings such as 'the beauties of Anglesey', who are described in a very positive way, which is again suggestive that Prichard distrusted modernity since such 'beauties' were to be found in rural, undeveloped areas of Wales. Prichard's great literary success came with his *The Adventures and Vagaries of Twm Shon Catti, Descriptive of Life in Wales: Interspersed with Poems*, first published in 1828, and thanks to its popularity reproduced in many forms subsequently.[95] Prichard was a patriot who identified with and held a romantic view of the history of Wales which was as a rural Welsh past. His view of women, or heroines, in that Welsh history situated them in rural Wales, and it could be argued that he was representative of the intelligentsia who sought a Welsh rural past as a vehicle for Welsh patriotism in the face of the vast social and economic changes that were affecting parts of Wales with the onset of industrialism. Twm Siôn Catti, the 'Welsh Robin Hood', was equally a vehicle for the expression of his distrust of modern Wales.

Such themes are also evident in Jane Williams's 1869 *History of Wales*. Williams conceptualised the history of Wales from 1091 to 1240 in terms of a clash between peoples, 'the Cymry and the Normans'. Her patriotic views are evident in her writings on contemporary Wales and its history. As Gwyneth Tyson Roberts has pointed out, Williams wrote to discredit and demolish the perjorative views of the Welsh that were presented in the 'Blue Books', and she wrote as part of the broader reaction by contemporaries.[96] Her patriotism led her to envisage the Welsh as a Cymric people who were 'a prey to the despoilers', who had fought courageously against Norman invaders, but were undone by 'selfish rivalry and perverse ambition'.[97] Jane Aaron has pointed out that Williams knew the didactic value of history and argues that as part of the reaction to the Blue Books idealised images of Welsh women were created in, for example, contemporary poetry, which created an image which was 'defined by English notions of respectability'. As Huw Pryce has commented, she saw the Norman conquest of Glamorgan as a pivotal event in Welsh history.[98] More than this, however, Williams was sensitive to the contribution of women to the trajectory of the medieval past, in an approach which owes much to sixteenth- and seventeenth-century writers, portrays sympathy for the Welsh in the face of Norman activity in Wales, and characterises the Welsh as a passionate people who struggled to come to terms with Norman settlement in Wales. This is emphasised through commentary on the marriage of Cadwgan ap Bleddyn with the daughter of Picot de Say, 'a Norman baron who had acquired lands in Wales with which she was endowed'. Williams states that 'Her influence may have tended to soften the pangs of that political submission which circumstances extorted from Cadwgan.' The Normans were an 'impenetrable barrier to his martial career', but the 'head, heart, and hand of this illustrious man were ever occupied in striving to promote the welfare of his people'. Her portrayal of the abduction of Nest is based on the *Brut* yet is also embellished. Williams used emotive language to describe the abduction episode in terms of Owain's lapse of judgement: 'Owen . . . a renowned warrior, yielded up his reason and his conscience to a frantic passion for the Princess Nest.' Nest appears as the victim of a false promise from Henry I, 'some years before [she had] been seduced while a hostage, and under pretence of marriage'.[99] This portrayal of Nest as deceived is an explanatory device which is a novel element in the development of explanations of her predicament. It is indicative of nineteenth-century morality and attitudes to marriage and illegitimacy, and is, further, a portrayal of Nest as a victim of abusive royal lordship. Williams goes on to state that Owain was aware of the sexual relationship between Henry I and Nest and through this knowledge was 'steeled against compunction by a recollection of Norman wrongs'. Thus Henry's morally dubious behaviour militated against any doubts that Owain might have had, since the abuse of Nest by Henry was set into a broader context of Norman abuse of Wales and the Welsh generally. Williams suggests that Henry's wrongdoing against Nest was therefore used by Owain to justify his offence. Williams then goes on to brand Owain's companions as 'a band of fourteen roisterers' who set fire to Gerald of Windsor's castle at Pembroke and carried away Nest and his children. Williams portrays Cadwgan ap Bleddyn as having 'rebuked his moral madness'. She argues that Owain was initially defiant, but ultimately 'with Nest's entreaty' sent the children back to Gerald of Windsor. The royal response to the abduction is evocatively described: 'like wildfire in a forest, the kindling flames of retribution spread with devastating fury throughout Dyfed, Ceredigion and Southern Powys. In the former, Gerald of Windsor and his followers raged.' Thus the abduction episode was placed into a context of Welsh patriotic resistance to Norman invasion, and Owain's role as the cause of the retribution and devastation that followed is explained in terms of a passionate escapade. Nest was key to the event. The real immorality was committed by Henry I and his relationship with Nest was thus duplicitous. Nest is portrayed as a fallen woman whose seduction by Henry I on the pretence of marriage is foregrounded with other unspecified 'Norman wrongs'. Further, Williams does not mention Nest's role in facilitating the escape of Gerald of Windsor from the castle nor the sexual congress of Owain and Nest. The role of Cadwgan ap Bleddyn as an elder figure who rebukes his son's behaviour is a central feature of the abduction tale. The motif serves to remind the reader that Owain's behaviour was condemned by the Welsh as well as the English for his moral lapse of judgement which caused the subsequent retribution in Ceredigion. The suggestion that Nest was seduced by Henry 'while a hostage' has a didactic purpose. Fundamentally it serves to augment a sense of 'Norman wrongs' and thereby provides some justification for Owain's response. Williams's view is thus that Nest, a Welsh princess, was seduced by an English king while in his power as a hostage. This seduction was an affront to the Welsh nation since Nest is an embodiment of Wales through her royal status. It therefore casts Owain's response as a patriotic act of resistance as well as a Romantic episode. It thus enhances the patriotic portrayal of Owain's resistance and explains Nest's sexual past which was the result of broken promises and abuse by Henry I. This is a further development of a stereotype, that of the passionate Welsh patriot whose lack of control caused the downfall of the Welsh.

Recent views on Williams's methodology and general approaches have been less favourably mixed. Evans, for example, criticised Williams for her unfocused writing style and that she lacked analytical insight.[100] Williams had an interest in women in particular and her publication of *The Literary Women of England* in 1861 is symptomatic of this. Further Williams's methodology in her work on Welsh women was sensitive to the different traditions of the transmission of knowledge, through formal means which were historically male-dominated and through informal, or oral, means which were used by women.[101] More recent scholars, such as Elisabeth van Houts, have begun to address such issues[102] within a more developed analytical framework. Williams is an example of an 'amateur' female historian, and, as Smith has pointed out, the emergence of 'high amateurism' had, by the end of the nineteenth century, created a body of work which had expanded the boundaries of historical research and took account of a broad array of historical sources, and such work had partly been inspired by ideas on the degeneration of the aristocracy which in part were anti-modern.[103] Jane Williams recognised that the way that knowledge was transmitted affected how history was written, in particular her use of oral sources while within a context of 'high amateurism', and although not systematic nor methodologically coherent, as Evans suggests, nevertheless was an attempt to enrich the paradigms of the Welsh historical past. Her *History of Wales* presented a view of Nest that was derived from the *Brut* and explained the abduction in terms of Owain's inability to control his passion. Thus she was sensitive to the way that knowledge dissemination could reflect gender issues. Her portrayal of Nest is evidence that she was aware that Nest was open to criticism, and this explains the care she took to clarify the wrongdoing by Henry I. This indicates that she was aware that contested power over Nest's body was central to the explanation of the Norman conquest. In particular her concern to excuse Nest as a victim of abuse by Henry and the lapse of judgement by Owain is suggestive that she was aware that Nest was potentially a source of embarrassment in Welsh history, yet her body was a contested site of male interest and therefore significant to the course of Welsh history.

The emphasis on male passion underpinned the portrayal of the abduction in Edward Laws's *The History of Little England beyond Wales*, published in 1888.[104] Laws saw the abduction of Nest as a 'rascally deed' and pondered that 'it seems strange that a band of Welshmen should have been able to gain admittance at dead of night into the principal English fortress of West Wales'. Laws describes Nest as 'the fairest of the fair' who had 'enslaved the English king' and now 'was wife to the robber chief Gerald of Windsor'. Fired by the bards, Owain was determined to 'wrest the Kymric Helen from her foreign lord'. This is the clearest indication of a nationalist reading of the marriage and abduction of Nest. Without doubt the language used is romanticised, evocative and thrilling, and Laws embroidered the tale, evidently based on a reading of *Brut y Tywysogion* and augmented by the *Annales Cambriae*, with additional details. Like earlier commentators, Laws places the marriage and abduction firmly in a context of Norman/Welsh hostilities, and his view deviates little from the established narrative. But Laws's firm anti-Norman view was underpinned by a portrayal of Nest as a legendary beauty in the mould of Helen of Troy. This provided two linkages for her story:

first, with Homeric heroic and epic tragedy and, second, with the origin-myth of the Welsh in a classical past. Both are key to his construction of an image of the Welsh as heroic resisters of Norman atrocity. This also represents an important explicit link made by later scholars between Nest and Helen of Troy and represents therefore a key stage in the evolution of the tale. Essentially, this portrayal by Laws is concerned with the historical identity of the Welsh in the medieval past, and Nest's abduction is the vehicle by which he presents a gendered, romanticised view of a contested period in Welsh history. Patriotic pride and a developing narrative based on a nationalist view of the past therefore informed his approach, which in this respect represents a development of the views of earlier nineteenth-century writers. The narrative of conquest as symbolised by Nest was changing. She had become the Welsh Helen of Troy, and thus an evocative and powerful image was coined to perpetuate a nationalist view of the Normans and the resistance to them in south-west Wales. Laws thus deployed a classical allusion to enhance the image of Nest as a legendary beauty. Although the comparison may well be reflective of a classical education, and Laws does not explicitly link the comparison to the origins of the Britons, it is nevertheless an evocative conception which became a powerful motif in the way that Nest was portrayed.

The long-term development of the discourse of Celticism continued to have a gendered aspect. Within this discourse the influence of Matthew Arnold is pivotal. Writing in the 1860s, Arnold suggested that Celtic nations were inferior because they were more romantic and intuitive with purer blood and that the history of Wales had been directly affected by conflict with more masculine, rational Saxons.[105] Arnold wrote in defence of Celtic Wales in response to an attack in *The Times* which had stated that Welsh 'was the curse of Wales'. Arnold explicitly argued that Celts were more prone to emotional responses to events, which he gendered feminine, and that this accounted for the failure and defeat of Celtic societies. Further, Arnold portrayed an almost symbiotic relationship between Celtic society and England and this was related to contemporary ideas where Saxon Englishmen saw themselves as possessing the marginalised Celt who was feminised and thus portrayed as weaker than the English, and a key aspect of this was that the Celtic men were less able to control themselves. Arnold certainly portrayed an image of the 'noble savage' who loved nature but was thereby immature and irrational and 'prey to the spell of the feminine'; further, 'rapine [was] implicit in his sentiments'.[106] The influence of such views can be measured in the later populist travel literature on Wales – and in the views of Thompson, who portrayed a sense of Wales as different, with an identity which was founded on romantic and historical differences related to a Celtic identity. Further, such writings commented on Wales and modernity as well as noting the romantic past in texts which were written for tourists to encourage visitors to Wales. In such texts Wales became a consumer product and identity, as difference was key in which Wales was defined as a feminised landscape.[107] Thus Nest served at once as a symbol of the Welsh nation in the writings of nationalists, and also as a symbol of Welsh women and their vulnerability to the vagaries of political contexts in the middle ages, as well as a vulnerable woman in the writings of those who saw Wales as feminised and 'Celtic'.

Patriotism inspired O. M. Edwards to publish his popular *History of Wales* in 1901. Edwards presented a view of Nest as key to understanding the causes of war between Henry I and Cadwgan ap Bleddyn. Edwards was sensitive to the complexities of the uneasy political climate of the early twelfth century and presented the differences in the ways that different areas in south Wales interacted with the Normans. Thus while Morgannwg is stated to have begun the process whereby 'Normans and Welsh were beginning to form one people', Gruffudd ap Cynan and Cadwgan ap Bleddyn 'found themselves supreme in the still unconquered parts of Wales'. Although unconquered, such rulers were not unaffected by the Norman advance into Wales: Edwards argues that Cadwgan was anxious to be 'at peace with the king' and yet states 'the hope for peace disappeared on account of the fatal beauty of Nest. King Henry had entrusted Pembroke to the Gerald who had defended it so well. Now this Gerald's wife was the daughter of Rees ap Tudor the last king of Deheubarth, and was famous for her beauty. She had been the ward of Henry I, after her father's death, and had been deeply wronged.' Edwards thus suggests that the major wrong done to Nest was enacted upon her while a ward of Henry, thus he implies that her liaison with Henry was an abuse of her by her royal guardian. The narrative follows the main characteristics of the story as presented in *Brut*: Owain ap Cadwgan prior to the feast at Cadwgan's court had already 'been a firebrand in Powys'. He does not mention the alleged sexual intercourse between Owain and Nest. He states that Owain 'carried Nest away' and that he 'would not restore' her even though the events had put his father Cadwgan into 'abject terror' who 'tried to turn away the king's wrath'.[108] He mentions Nest as a source of support for her brother Gruffudd, who sometimes stayed with Nest at Pembroke, and further notes that Gerald of Windsor killed Owain since he 'remembered old wrongs' and as a result killed the man 'whom the Welsh had regarded as the champion of their freedom, and whom Henry the First had regarded as the means of ruling the Welsh in peace'.[109] The portrayal thus presents Owain in a positive way and does not comment on the morality of the abduction. It presents the abduction tale as part of a patriotic view of Wales and the course of Welsh history.

Such views also informed J. E. Lloyd's pivotal *A History of Wales from the Earliest Times to the Edwardian Conquest.*[110] Lloyd is one of the earliest, and most influential, modern writers on medieval Wales, his 1911 narrative of Wales being based on painstaking historical enquiry and an understanding of the medieval record which set the parameters of the debates on the history of medieval Wales for much of the twentieth century.[111] Lloyd is considered to be a key text for understanding the emergence of the historiography of Wales. He saw nationality as an enduring theme in Welsh history, and historians still debate the importance of nationality.[112] Lloyd saw the processes of conquest and settlement, and Welsh reactions to these, as key determinants of the emergence of the nation. According to Pryce, Lloyd wrote Romantic nationalist history with the purpose of revitalising interest in the Welsh past.[113] Such romanticism made the Welsh past acceptable.[114] It was a view which accepted the portrayal of Nest within the *Brut* unquestioningly and even developed it since the abduction narrative fitted with his overall Romantic nationalist approach which saw the Norman Yoke as particularly detrimental to Welsh identity. Lloyd inscribed Nest as a gendered symbol of Welsh patriotism whose fate was inextricably linked to her nation and kin. While these were central to the political context of twelfth-century Deheubarth and Wales, the deeper resonances of the narrative of the abduction, such as the importance of abduction in origins legends of kingdoms, did not feature in Lloyd's analysis. Lloyd wrote during a period when a cultural renaissance in Wales fostered cultural nationalism and when the scaffolding for shaping the agenda of Welsh scholarly enquiry emerged. K. O. Morgan (and others) suggested that at the end of the nineteenth century the industrialisation of south Wales and the resultant creation of wealth brought profound social and cultural changes to Wales. With the foundation of the University College in 1872 at Aberystwyth, Cardiff in 1883 and Bangor in 1884 the institutions for a 'national renaissance' which articulated a Welsh sense of identity were created. Within this context, Lloyd's analysis of the debate about the importance of the history of medieval Wales and the Norman conquest was part of the search for a distinct Welsh identity. More recent academic scholarship has moved a long way from the concerns of nineteenth- and early twentieth-century historians.

It is certainly evident that travel writers in Wales from the 1780s to the 1830s did not directly address, although they may have been indirectly stimulated by, the processes of industrialisation and the experience of non-rural and urbanising Wales. The genre, during the Romantic period, in general did not lend itself to the inclusion of such material. Travel writing and eighteenth- and nineteenth-century views of Wales, such as Nicholson's views or those of Warrington, certainly reflect the importance of race and nation, class and geography. Such writers inspired later travel writers and created a narrative of Wales which was inspired by history real and imagined, Romanticism and landscape. Yet they also represented a gendered ordering of that past where chosen categories of women, or selected examples, such as Nest or Joan, were placed into a historical narrative which was reinterpreted and rewritten within an approach which looked back towards the medieval past as authentic. Such approaches were continued into the twentieth century.

The Norman invasions and their impact upon Wales were therefore reinterpreted and remade by later writers, and prominent women such as Nest were essential elements in this narrative. Travel writers drew on such narratives, and included information drawn from local sources and traditions and incorporated ethnographic material to inform their accounts. By the end of the nineteenth century, with the publication of histories such as that of J. E. Lloyd, a narrative about the fate of the Welsh nation was well established, and women, such as Joan or Nest, within this narrative, were consigned to Romantic symbolic roles as victims within a (mostly) male discourse. Nest, in an epithet that was to inform later narratives of Wales, was transformed into the 'Helen of Wales' in the late nineteenth century. This was, in part, a reflection that the search for an understanding of the Welsh medieval past was founded on classical models of conquest which in turn modelled a narrative that held that Nest's abduction had had tragic consequences for the fate of the developing Welsh nation. The construction of this was based on a nationalist reading of a key source which portrayed events in a symbolic and gendered way. The resilience of this image in a plurality of sources examined here suggests that the motif was a central part of the construction of understandings of the Welsh medieval past.

Thus it can be argued that narratives of the past are intrinsic to the creation of identity and, just as modern theorists have debated identity, in reality they have theorised what medieval chroniclers clearly knew: that the past informed the present, and they interpreted it according to their own notions of identity. Thus Nest's story, or narratives about other women, were repeated and, on occasion, reinterpreted because Welsh gendered identity in the past was felt to be the key to explaining Welsh identity in the present. This sense was thus produced by writers positioning Nest within the past in which her history was crucial to the narrative of Wales. This debate was conducted within a context of a broader debate about Britishness and Englishness, as Wilson suggests, but also about Welshness within that broader debate. Such identities may not have been stable but they were constructed around a sense of a historical past which was romanticised and, crucially, gendered, and this interacted with social status. Thus Nest's abduction was an essential part of the narrative of Norman success in Wales and Welsh resistance. It featured women as conduits of instability through their sexual attractiveness which thereby caused the Welsh male elite to respond inappropriately with devastating consequences. This conquest was portrayed as sexual conquest or, rather, women appear as objects of male desire whose bodies were responsible for political catastrophe. We can see these themes recurring in the narrative of the conquest of Ireland and also in the narrative of the 'Twelve Knights of Glamorgan' as it developed from the early modern period and was revisited in later writings. Thus, as writers defined and debated ideas about Wales in the British context, gender and ideas about the medieval past were an intrinsic part of that discussion.

Notes

1 Stuart Hall, 'Cultural identity and diaspora', in Nicholas Mirzoeff (ed.), *Diaspora and Visual Culture: Representing Africans and Jews* (London: Routledge, 2000), pp. 222–37, at pp. 223–5.

2 Francis James West, 'The colonial history of the Norman conquest?', *History*, 84 (1999), 219–36; compare Chris Williams, 'Problematizing Wales: an exploration in historiography and postcoloniality', in Jane Aaron and Chris Williams (eds), *Postcolonial Wales* (Cardiff: University of Wales Press, 2005), pp. 3–22. Williams argues that following the death of Llywelyn ap Gruffudd (1282) and the Acts of Union (1536) 'Wales stood in something of a colonial relationship' to England, *ibid.*, p. 4.

3 Hall, 'Cultural identity and diaspora', pp. 222–3.

4 Kathleen Wilson, 'Empire, gender and modernity in the eighteenth century', in Philippa Levine (ed.), *Gender and Empire* (Oxford: Oxford University Press, 2004), pp. 14–45, at p. 14.

5 Geraint H. Jenkins, 'Wales in the eighteenth century', in H. T. Dickinson (ed.), *A Companion of Eighteenth-Century Britain* (Oxford: Blackwell, 2002), pp. 392–402. For a more general discussion of eighteenth-century literature in Wales, see Sarah Prescott, *Eighteenth-Century Writing from Wales: Bards and Britons* (Cardiff: University of Wales Press, 2008); A. O. H. Jarman and Gwilym Rees Hughes (eds), *A Guide to Welsh Literature* (7 vols, Cardiff: University of Wales Press, 1992–2000), vols 3–5.

6 Prys Morgan, *The Eighteenth Century Renaissance* (Llandybie: Christopher Davies, 1981), pp. 119ff.

7 R[obert]. B[urton]. [i.e. Nathaniel Crouch], *The History of the Principality of Wales: In Three Parts . . . Together with the Natural and Artificial Rarities and Wonders in the Several Counties of that Principality* (London: printed for Nathaniel Crouch, 1695). See previous chapter for discussion of the significance of Merrick.

8 B[urton]., *History of the Principality*, pp. 50–3.

9 B[urton]., *History of the Principality*, p. 130.

10 B[urton]., *History of the Principality*, p. 134.

11 Thomas Heywood, *The Exemplary Lives and Memorable Acts of Nine of the Most Worthy Women of the World: Three Iewes, Three Gentiles, Three Christians* (London: printed by Thomas Cotes, for Richard Royston, 1640). This consisted of short biographies of nine women, including Boudicca, legendary women and Queen Elizabeth. An earlier work by Richard Johnson had a similar 'nine worthies' format: Richard Johnson, *The Nine Worthies of London Explaining the Honourable Exercise of Armes, the Vertues of the Valiant, and the Memorable Attempts of Magnanimious Minds. Pleasant for Gentlemen, not Vnseemely for Magistrates, and most Profitable for Prentises* (London: by Thomas Orwin for Humfrey Lownes, 1592).

12 Robert Burton [i.e. Nathaniel Crouch], *Female Excellency, or, The Ladies of Glory Illustrated in the Worthy Lives and Memorable Actions of Nine Famous Women, who have been Renowned either for Virtue or Valour in Several Ages of the World . . . : The Whole Adorned with Poems and the Picture of each Lady* (London: printed for Nath. Crouch . . . , 1688), pp. 1–6.

13 Jason Mc Elligott, 'Crouch, Nathaniel [Robert Burton] (*c.*1640–1725?)', *ODNB*.

14 R. Mayer, 'Nathaniel Crouch, bookseller and historian: popular historiography and cultural power in late seventeenth-century England', *Eighteenth-Century Studies*, 27 (1993–94), 391–420, at p. 395.

15 Mayer, 'Nathaniel Crouch', p. 419.

16 Wilson, 'Empire, gender and modernity', pp. 19–20.

17 Discussed e.g. in G. H. Jenkins's chapter in Jarman and Hughes (eds), *Guide to Welsh Literature*, vol. 4; and see Geraint H. Jenkins, 'Evans, Theophilus (1693–1767)', *ODNB*.

18 'Brut Aberpergwm', in Owen Jones, Edward Williams and William Owen, *The Myvyrian Archaiology of Wales Collected out of Ancient Manuscripts* (3 vols, London: printed by S. Rousseau for the editors and sold by Longman & Rees, 1801–7), pp. 685–715, at pp. 669–70; Prys Morgan, 'Williams, Edward (1747–1826)', ODNB; for discussion see David E. Thornton, *Kings, Chronologies, and Genealogies: Studies in the Political History of Early Medieval Ireland and Wales* (Oxford: Unit for Prosopographical Research, Linacre College, 2003), pp. 10–11.

19 Thomas Price, *Hanes Cymru, a Chenedl y Cymry, o'r Cynoesoedd hyd at Farwolaeth Llewelyn ap Gruffydd; Ynghyd a Rhai Cofiaint Perthynol i'r Amseroedd o'r Pryd Hynny i Waered* (Crughywel: Thomas Williams, 1842), p. 514. J. E. Lloyd, 'Price, Thomas (1787–1848)', rev. Brynley F. Roberts *ODNB*.

20 Gweirydd ap Rhys, *Hanes y Brytaniaid a'r Cymry: Yn Wladol, Milwrol, Cymdeithasol, Masnachol, llenorol, a Chrefyddol, o'r Amseroedd Boreuaf hyd yn Bresennol* (2 vols, London and Caerlleon: William Mackenzie, 1872–74), ii. 35.

21 David Llewellyn Rees, *The Modern Universal British Traveller: Or, a New, Complete, and Accurate Tour through England, Wales, Scotland, and the Neighbouring Islands / Comprising all that is Worthy of Observation in Great Britain. And Containing a Full, Ample, and Circumstantial Account of Every Thing Remarkable in the Several Cities,*

Boroughs, Market Towns, Villages, Hamlets, &c. Throughout the Kingdom ... being the Result of an Actual and Late General Survey of the Whole Kingdom. And Including Various Maps, Corrected from the Latest Observations, a Collection of Landscapes Views, &c. that make an Admirable Groupe of Elegant Copper-plate Prints ... / The Articles Respecting England, by Charles Burlington, Esq. Such as Relate to Wales, by David Llewellyn Rees, Gent. And those Descriptive of Scotland, by Alexander Murray (London: printed for J. Cooke, 1779), pp. 646–7.

22 Benjamin Martin, *Introduction to the History of the Principality of Wales* (London, 1763), pp. 354, 357, 379.

23 Martin, *Principality of Wales*, pp. 380–1.

24 William Bingley, *A Tour round North Wales, Performed during the Summer of 1798: Containing not only the Description and Local History of the Country ...* (London: sold by E. Williams (successor to the late Mr. Blamire); and J. Deighton, Cambridge. Printed by J. Smeeton, 1800).

25 Bingley, *Tour round North Wales*, p. 142.

26 Carole Fabricant, 'Eighteenth-century travel literature', in John Richetti (ed.), *The Cambridge History of English Literature 1660–1780* (Cambridge: Cambridge University Press, 2005), pp. 707–44, at p. 720. There is no discussion of Wales, although Scotland and Ireland are discussed.

27 Elizabeth A. Bohls, 'Age of peregrination: travel writing and the eighteenth-century novel', in Paula R. Backscheider and Catherine Ingrassia (eds), *A Companion to the Eighteenth-Century English Novel and Culture* (Oxford: Blackwell, 2005), pp. 97–116, at pp. 97–8.

28 Elizabeth A. Bohls, *Travel Writing 1700–1830: An Anthology* (Oxford: Oxford University Press, 2005), p. xxvi.

29 Charles L. Batten, *Pleasurable Instruction: Form and Convention in Eighteenth-Century Travel Literature* (Berkeley, Los Angeles and London: University of California Press, 1978), p. 29.

30 Nigel Leask, *Curiosity and the Aesthetics of Travel Writing, 1770–1840: 'From an Antique Land'* (Oxford: Oxford University Press, 2002), p. 7.

31 George Lipscomb, *Journey into South Wales, through the Counties of Oxford, Warwick, Worcester, Hereford, Salop, Stafford, Buckingham, and Hertford; in the Year 1799* (London: T. N. Longman & O. Rees, 1802), pp. 114, 175.

32 Benjamin Heath Malkin, *The Scenery, Antiquities and Biography of South Wales* (2 vols, London: Longman, Hurst Rees and Orme, 1807), ii. 29.

33 Jenkins, 'Wales in the eighteenth century', p. 399.

34 Hywel Davies, 'Wales in English travel writing 1791–8: the Welsh critique of Theophilus Jones', *WHR*, 23 (2007), 65–93.

35 'Narrative of a tour through Wales by an anonymous English Gentleman, [1701×25]', NLW MS 18943B; Diary of a Journey into Wales A.D. 1789, NLW Cwrtmawr 1 (C) MS 199B; An account of three tours, by an English gentleman, accompanied by Mr and Mrs William (?) from Hereford ... 1787, NLW MS 9352A; 'Walk through South Wales: an account of a tour made in October 1819 by William and Sampson Sandys, lawyers of London, with a number of sketches by WS', NLW Cwrtmawr 393 C.

36 Wyndham, Henry Penruddocke, *A Gentleman's Tour through Monmouthshire and Wales, in the Months of June and July, 1774 ...* (London: printed for T. Evans, 1775; new edn 1881), p. i.

37 Wyndham, *Gentleman's Tour*, pp. 8–11, 46.

38 Wyndham, *Gentleman's Tour*, pp. 47–9.

39 James Baker, *A Picturesque Guide through Wales and the Marches* (2nd edn; Worcester: printed and sold by J. Tymbs; sold also by Robson; Ottridge; White; Rivingtons; Richardson; and at Taylor's architectural library, London, 1795), pp. 9, 81–3.

40 'A Tour thro' Pembrokeshire: Or a concise Account of Whatsoever in that County deserves the attention of the Traveller . . .', Pembrokeshire Papers, NLW MS 1406E, fo. 7.

41 Malkin, *Scenery, Antiquities and Biography of South Wales*, i. 59–65.

42 Carl Thompson, *The Suffering Traveller and the Romantic Imagination* (Oxford: Clarendon Press, 2007), p. 6.

43 John Evans, *Letters Written during a Tour through South Wales in the year 1803 and at other Times Containing Views of the History, Antiquities and Customs of that Part of the Principality, and Interspersed with Observations on its Scenery, Agriculture, Botany, Mineralogy, Trade and Manufactures* (London: printed for C. and R. Baldwin, New Bridge-Street, 1804).

44 Evans, *Letters*, p. 28.

45 Evans, *Letters*, pp. 26–8.

46 Evans, *Letters*, p. 200.

47 Evans, *Letters*, pp. 367–8.

48 Evans, *Letters*, p. 262.

49 George Nicholson, *The Cambrian Traveller's Guide in Every Direction; Containing Remarks made during many Excursions, in the Principality of Wales and Bordering Districts, Augmented by Extracts from the Best Writers* (Stourport: George Nicholson, 1808), p. 109; (2nd edn, London: Longman, Hurst, Rees, Orme & Brown; Sherwood, Neely, & Jones; and Baldwin, Cradock & Joy, 1813), p. 342.

50 Nicholson, *Cambrian Traveller's Guide* (1813), p. 67.

51 Nicholson, *Cambrian Traveller's Guide* (1813), p. 430.

52 Nicholson, *Cambrian Traveller's Guide* (1813), pp. 342–3.

53 Theophilus Jones, *A History of the County of Brecknock in Two Volumes* (Brecon: North, William and George, 1805–9), p. 142.

54 R. W. Thompson, *An Englishman Looks at Wales* (Bristol: Arrowsmith, 1937), p. 9.

55 Nicholson, *Cambrian Traveller's Guide* (1808), pp. i–iv. See Thomas Pennant, *A Tour in Wales* (London: printed for Benjamin White, 1784).

56 Nicholson, *Cambrian Traveller's Guide* (1808), p. iii.

57 Davies, 'Wales in English travel writing', p. 89. Jones, *History of the County of Brecknock* (1898).

58 Jones, *History of the County of Brecknock*, ii. 662–3.

59 Jones, *History of the County of Brecknock*, i. 96–8.

60 Jones, *History of the County of Brecknock*, ii. 188.

61 Jones, *History of the County of Brecknock*, i. 86.

62 S. R. Meyrick, *The History and Antiquities of the County of Cardigan Collected from the Few Remaining Documents which have Escaped the Destructive Ravages of Time, as from Actual Observation* (London: printed by T. Bensley, for Longman, etc., 1808), pp. xxxi, 95.

63 Richard Fenton, *A Historical Tour through Pembrokeshire* (London: Longman, Hurst, Rees & Orme, 1810), pp. 249–50 (Carew as Nest's marriage portion), 367–9 (abduction),

376 (Henry I and his suspicion of Gerald on account of his hospitality to Gruffudd ap Rhys, Nest's brother).

64 William Warrington, *The History of Wales in Nine Books: With an Appendix* (London: printed for J. Johnson, 1786; 2nd edn 1788; 3rd edn 1791); 4th edn as *The History of Wales, in Nine Books: With an Appendix* (2 vols, Brecon: W. Williams, 1823).

65 Warrington, *History of Wales* (1786), pp. v–vii.

66 Warrington, *History of Wales* (1786), Book 5, p. 261.

67 Warrington, *History of Wales* (1786), Book 5, p. 270.

68 Warrington, *History of Wales* (1786), Book 5, pp. 270–1.

69 Warrington, *History of Wales* (1786), Book 5, pp. 281, 287.

70 Caradoc, of Llancarvan, *The History of Wales Comprehending the Lives and Succession of the Princes of Wales, from Cadwalader the Last King, to Lhewelyn the Last Prince of British Blood . . . by William Wynne* (London: printed by Mary Clark, for the author, and are to be sold by R. Clavell, 1697), pp. 129–30; *Brut, Peniarth MS. 20* (1952), pp. 28–9.

71 Warrington, *History of Wales* (1786), Book 7, pp. 356–7, 361.

72 Warrington, *History of Wales* (1786), Book 7, pp. 361–2.

73 Warrington, *History of Wales* (1786), Book 7, p. 384.

74 Warrington, *History of Wales* (1823), Book 7, vol. 2, p. 61.

75 Philip Yorke, *The Royal Tribes of Wales* (Wrexham: printed by John Painter, 1799), p. 33.

76 See also the erection in 1808 by Thomas Bulkeley of a grotto to incorporate the remains of the tomb of Princess Joan, transferred to his house at Baron Hill; the inscriptions emphasised that the time spent by her tomb as a horse-watering trough might trigger reflections on the 'transitory nature of all sublunary distinctions': Neil Fairlamb, *The Viscount and the Baron: The Life and Times of Thomas James Warren Bulkeley 1752–1822 Viscount Bulkeley of Cashel and Baron Bulkeley of Beaumaris* (Carlisle: Bookcase, 2009), pp. 152–4. There is an engraving of the grotto in BL, Add. MS 36,396, fos. 124–5.

77 Huw Pryce, 'The Normans in Welsh history', *ANS*, 30 (2008 for 2007), 1–18, at p. 10; H. Pryce, *J. E. Lloyd and the Creation of Welsh History: Renewing a Nation's Past* (Cardiff: University of Wales Press, 2011).

78 John Jones, *The History of Wales: Descriptive of the Government, Wars, Manners, Religion, Laws, Druids, Bards, Pedigrees, and Language of the Ancient Britons and Modern Welsh, and of the Remaining Antiquities of the Principality* (London: J. Williams, 1824), pp. 67–8.

79 E. C. Campbell, *The History of Wales: Containing some Interesting Facts concerning the Existence of a Welsh Tribe among the Aborigines of America Arranged as a Catechism for Young Persons by a Lady of the Principality* (Shrewsbury: [printed by John Eddowes], 1833), pp. 36–7 (her coverage of the Normans and the early twelfth century to 1137).

80 B. B. Woodward, *The History of Wales: From the Earliest Times, to its Final Incorporation with the Kingdom of England; With Notices of its Physical Geography, and Mineral Wealth; and of the Religion and Literature, Laws, Customs, Manners, and Arts of the Welsh* (London: Virtue and Co., 1853), pp. 252–3, 263.

81 T. J. Llewelyn Prichard, *The Heroines of Welsh History: Comprising Memoirs and Biographical Notices of the Celebrated Women of Wales* (London: W. and F. G. Cash, 1854).

82 Prichard, *Heroines of Welsh History*, p. iii.

83 Jane Aaron, *Nineteenth-Century Women's Writing in Wales: Nation, Gender and Identity* (2nd edn, Cardiff: University of Wales Press, 2010), ch. 3. Huw Pryce suggested to me a further context of writing about heroes, sparked especially by Carlyle in England – e.g. [R. J. Derfel], 'Cymru yn ei chysylltiad ag enwogion' [Wales in its relationship with heroes], *Y Traethodydd* (1855), 322–59.

84 *Encyclopædia Cambrensis: Y Gwyddoniadur Cymreig: Duwinyddiaeth, Athroniaeth, a Henafiaethau* (10 vols, Dinbych: Thomas Gee, 1858–79); for example, vol. 10 has entries for Gwynwhwfar (Guinevere), Gwenllian, Gwenddolen and Gwladys Ddu, daughter of Llywelyn ab Iorwerth, at pp. 613–14, but there are in general few entries for women. My thanks to Huw Pryce for drawing my attention to the *Gwyddoniadur Cymreig*.

85 Prichard, *Heroines of Welsh History*, pp. 11–14 (actresses), 42–60 (Angharad, the daughter of Meredith ap Owain), 61–5 (Angharad the Nun), 83–5 (Bella the Fortuneteller), 267–78 (Lady Hawys Gadarn), 442–56 (Matilda de la Haie), 325–77 (Gwenllian), 509–34 (Joan), 457–80 (Mistress Trevor Hanmer), 23–9 ('Anglesea Beauties'), 71–82 (Ladies of King Arthur's court).

86 Prichard, *Heroines of Welsh History*, pp. viii–ix.

87 W. E. Houghton, *The Victorian Frame of Mind 1830–1870* (New Haven: Yale University Press, 1957); S. L. Barczewski, *Myth and National Identity in Nineteenth-Century Britain: The Legends of King Arthur and Robin Hood* (Oxford: Oxford University Press, 2000).

88 Prichard, *Heroines of Welsh History*, pp. 507–34, at p. 507.

89 Prichard, *Heroines of Welsh History*, pp. 229–37.

90 Henry of Huntingdon, *Historia Anglorum: The History of the English People*, ed. and trans. Diana Greenway (Oxford: Clarendon Press, 1996), pp. 304–9.

91 For Æthelflæd and use made of her in earlier sources, see Pauline Stafford, '"The annals of Æthelflæd": annals, history and politics in early tenth-century England', in Julia Barrow and Andrew Wareham (eds), *Myth, Rulership, Church and Charters: Essays in Honour of Nicholas Brooks* (Aldershot: Ashgate, 2008), pp. 101–16. For Alfred and Mercia, Simon Keynes, 'King Alfred and the Mercians', in M. A. S. Blackburn and David N. Dumville (eds), *Kings, Currency and Alliances: History and Coinage of Southern England in the Ninth Century* (Woodbridge: Boydell, 1998), pp. 1–46.

92 Prichard, *Heroines of Welsh History*, p. 46.

93 David Bates, Julia Crick and Sarah Hamilton, 'Introduction', in David Bates, Julia Crick and Sarah Hamilton (eds), *Writing Medieval Biography, 750–1250: Essays in Honour of Professor Frank Barlow* (Woodbridge: Boydell, 2006), pp. 1–13, at pp. 6, 12.

94 Prichard, *Heroines of Welsh History*, pp. 563–4.

95 T. J. Llewelyn Prichard, *The Adventures and Vagaries of Twm Shon Catti, Descriptive of Life in Wales: Interspersed with Poems* (Aberystwyth: printed for the author by J. Cox, 1828). See Daniel Huws, 'Twm Siôn Cati', *The Carmarthenshire Antiquary*, 45 (2009), 39–45.

96 Gwyneth Tyson Roberts, *The Language of the Blue Books: Wales and Colonial Prejudice* (Cardiff: University of Wales Press, 2011), pp. 1, 210–14.

97 Jane Williams, *History of Wales Derived from Authentic Sources* (London: Longmans, Green, and Co., 1869), p. 199.

98 The 'Blue Books' was the name given to the 1847 *Report of the Commission of Inquiry into the State of Education in Wales* which was intended to facilitate greater Parliamentary control of Welsh education. The report, composed by monoglot English commissioners, condemned the Welsh for their lack of education and moral failures. Aaron, *Nineteenth-century Women's Writing*, pp. 74–87. Huw Pryce, 'Modern nationality and the medieval past: the Wales of John Edward Lloyd', in R. R. Davies and Geraint H. Jenkins (eds), *From Medieval to Modern Wales: Historical Essays in Honour of Kenneth O. Morgan and Ralph A. Griffiths* (Cardiff: University of Wales Press, 2004), pp. 14–29. Neil Evans, 'Finding a new story: the search for a usable past in Wales, 1869–1930', *Transactions of the Honourable Society of Cymmrodorion*, new ser., 10 (2004), 144–62; note Jane Williams's defence of the Welsh against the aspersions cast on them in the 1847 'Blue Books': Roberts, *Language of the Blue Books*. Geraint H. Jenkins, 'Clio and Wales: Welsh remembrancers and historical writing 1751–2001', *Transactions of the Honourable Society of Cymmrodorion*, new ser., 8 (2001), 119–36, argued that J. E. Lloyd saw Williams's work as 'a landmark in Welsh historiography', *ibid.*, p. 126.

99 Williams, *History of Wales*, pp. 199–200.

100 Evans, 'Finding a new story', notes that Williams emphasised the bravery of the Welsh and their sufferings under the Norman Yoke, at pp. 147–9.

101 Jane Williams, *The Literary Women of England including a Biographical Epitome of all the Most Eminent to the year 1700; and Sketches of the Poetesses to the Year 1850; with Extracts from their Works, and Critical Remarks* (London: Saunders, Otley, & Co., 1861). Deidre Beddoe, 'Williams, Jane [known as Jane Williams Ysgafell] (1806–1885), historian and writer', *ODNB*.

102 Elisabeth M. C. van Houts, *Memory and Gender in Medieval Europe, 900–1200* (Basingstoke: Macmillan, 1999).

103 Bonnie G. Smith, *The Gender of History: Men, Women and Historical Practice* (Cambridge, MA and London: Harvard University Press, 1998), pp. 156–7.

104 Edward Laws, *The History of Little England beyond Wales: And the Non-Kymric Colony Settled in Wales* (London and Tenby: George Bell and Sons, 1888).

105 Matthew Arnold, *On the Study of Celtic Literature* (London: Smith, Elder and Co., 1867). This is available as 'On the study of Celtic literature', in *The Complete Prose Works of Matthew Arnold*, III: *Lectures and Essays in Criticism*, ed. R. H. Super (Ann Arbor, MI: University of Michigan Press, 1962), pp. 291–395.

106 Arnold, *On the Study of Celtic Literature*, p. 65.

107 Pyrs Gruffudd, David T. Herbert and Angela Piccini, 'In search of Wales: travel writing and narratives of difference, 1918–50', *Journal of Historical Geography*, 26 (2000), 589–604, at p. 600.

108 O. M. Edwards, *A Short History of Wales* (London: T. Fisher Unwin, 1906), pp. 70–1.

109 Edwards, *Short History of Wales*, pp. 76–8. According to Neil Evans, Edwards wrote a 'simpler story' and his narrative was shaped by a sense of the geographical impact of the Welsh topography upon its history ('Finding a new story', pp. 150–1). Edwards's views about the role of Wales within a British Empire have been discussed by Evans, who drew on the work of Aled Jones and Bill Jones, 'Empire and the Welsh press', in Simon J. Potter (ed.), *Newspapers and Empire: Ireland and Britain, c. 1857–1921* (Dublin: Four Courts Press, 2004), pp. 83–91.

110 J. E. Lloyd, *A History of Wales from the Earliest Times to the Edwardian Conquest* (2 vols, London: Longmans, Green, and Co., 1911). This appeared as a third edition in 1939 with a new Introduction and supplementary bibliography with changes to notes, although the main text remained unchanged. See Pryce, *J. E. Lloyd*, pp. xvi, 64, 126.

111 Pryce, 'Normans in Welsh history', p. 12; see also Pryce, *J. E. Lloyd*, pp. 170–6.

112 Pryce, 'Modern nationality', p. 29.

113 Pryce, 'Modern nationality', p. 15; Pauline Stafford, 'Historiography', in Pauline Stafford (ed.), *A Companion to the Early Middle Ages: Britain and Ireland, c.500–c.1100* (Chichester; Malden, MA: Wiley-Blackwell, 2009), pp. 9–22, at p. 10; Pryce, *J. E. Lloyd*, p. 176.

114 Pryce, *J. E. Lloyd*, p. 168.

6

Constructing Nest in the twentieth and twenty-first centuries

THE NARRATIVE OF Nest as a romantic tale which is blurred by hard political realities has inspired creative writers and populist interpretations of modern Wales. Such interpretations are derived from late-nineteenth-century interpretations of the Welsh medieval past, especially that of Edward Laws (1888) later endorsed by Lloyd (1911). The importance of Nest as the 'Helen of Wales' as a narrative which interlinks with a broader theme of Welsh resistance to Norman incursion relates to Victorian Anglo-Saxonism. Interpretations of medieval Wales and the role of prominent women from the Welsh medieval past exert a fascination on the popular imagination within contemporary Wales. For example, in a recent edition of its membership magazine, Cadw, the Welsh Assembly government's historic environment service, informed its readers of the launch of public consultation on an initiative to create a battlefields register for Wales. The article stated that 'battles are iconic events in Welsh history', citing examples of battles including those involving Owain Glyndŵr at the start of the fifteenth century and the 1797 French landing at Fishguard. The first example given is, however, that of the battle in 1136 in south-west Wales and the Welsh response to Norman activity and castle-building at Kidwelly. During this battle Gwenllian, wife of Gruffudd ap Rhys of Deheubarth and daughter of Gruffudd ap Cynan, was killed, and the article suggests that 'The defeat and subsequent beheading of this Welsh "Joan of Arc" has passed into folk memory,' since the site of the fighting is memorialised by a farm named Maes Gwenllian.[1] Evidence for the battle rests with Gerald of Wales's description in his writings on Wales.[2] Thus the first example given to illustrate the importance of battlefields in Welsh history involves 'a native Welsh princess' who is then described as a symbol and bearer of national hopes. The article's reference to Joan of Arc is symptomatic of a wider inscription of women as bearers of nationhood: the implication here is that Gwenllian fought for 'Wales' against the Normans, whereas in reality Gwenllian fought for the independence of Deheubarth, the hereditary lands of her husband, Gruffudd ap Rhys, Nest's brother, against the Normans. As such this interpretation fits into a framework in the modern interpretation of medieval Wales – that of a nation which stoutly resisted foreign invaders, whether Norman in the twelfth century, or English in the thirteenth century or later – and which misunderstands the political context of the early twelfth century.

The following discussion will consider how medieval Welsh women have been portrayed in more recent popular literature and modern media, and set this into a discussion of more formal academic historiography. It will do so by focusing upon a few case studies to analyse ways that individual women have been portrayed and consider what this can tell us about conceptions of the roles of women in the past. The analysis will consider the place that Nest occupies in late-twentieth- and twenty-first-century portrayals of the Welsh medieval past and will begin to suggest ways that the significance of this for our understanding of the imagined past of twentieth-century and contemporary Wales can be discussed. It will consider a range of evidence including travel literature, histories, and more recent sources such as media coverage, the internet and presentations at Welsh historical sites associated with Nest. Beginning with an analysis of the way that Nest was constructed in early twentieth-century popular history, it will suggest ways that the essential elements of the narrative were popularised in different media and for different purposes. This will facilitate a discussion of the importance of her role in purveying a romantic view of the past, noting the links made between gendered images and national perspectives.

In 1905 Arthur Owen Vaughan, under the pseudonym Owen Rhoscomyl, published his *Flame Bearers of Welsh History*. The book was written for use in Welsh schools, and its avowedly nationalist purpose within a British context was predicated on racial and gender stereotypes. Vaughan's view, as evidenced in *Flame Bearers*, was based on a romantic interpretation of Welsh history and is evidence of the popular conception of the Welsh medieval past as essentially a heroic struggle against foreign oppressors. The preface states that 'No Welsh boy can read well the history of his ancestors – so stirring a record of so stubborn a race, such a good, grim fighting race – without feeling that it is good to be a Cymro. And once he feels *that* he will go on to feel that it is good to be a Briton too.' The intention of the text was that 'No Welsh boy need ever again go to the history of other peoples for a record of stirring deeds and struggles.'[3] The book offers a simplified history of Wales from prehistory to the late medieval period. It presents the chronology through a biographical approach which is framed around a belief in the heroic and just resistance of the Welsh, or 'Cymro', to outsiders. The book was written for the education of boys, and few women appear in the text; when they are included in the narrative they appear in decisive roles and the portrayal is romanticised. For example, Nest of Deheubarth is described in romantic and stereotypical terms as a great beauty in a passage which portrays her in a more decisive and politicised role. She is assigned a pivotal role in the narrative of her brother's evasion of capture by Gruffudd ap Cynan who had colluded with Henry I to capture him. Nest is described as a key supporter of her brother Gruffudd in his return to Wales following his exile in Ireland. She was a 'Princess of wondrous beauty' who warned her brother of the promise made by Gruffudd ap Cynan to Henry I to betray her brother. As a result of the warning, Gruffudd only just managed to escape to Aberdaron, avoiding Gruffudd ap Cynan's men.[4] The portrayal is based on an interpretation of passages in the *Brut* which narrate the actions of Nest's brother, Gruffudd ap Rhys, following his return to Wales after his exile in Ireland.[5] Vaughan assumed that the *Brut's* reference to 'those who loved Rhys' referred to Nest, an assumption not made by more academic historians such as Edward Laws or later J. E. Lloyd.

This romanticised interpretation of Nest underpins Vaughan's portrayal of Nest in a further chapter. Vaughan states that 'There are many princesses in history, but there is not one of them who could have been so fair and sweet as Nest. It seemed as if no man could see her without falling in love with her.' Her marriage to Gerald of Windsor, possible marriage with Stephen, constable of Cardigan, and her relationship with Henry I are noted, as is the abduction by Owain ap Cadwgan in a romanticised interpretation. These details concerning Nest are included in a chapter relating to Gerald of Wales which emphasises her as an ancestral figure. Yet this depiction is extended to include her role in the transmission of superior ability at war: 'It seemed, in truth, as if no man could be descended from her without being a gallant fighter.'[6] The imperialistic image of the descendants of Nest as the conquerors of Ireland is of course derived from the writings of Gerald of Wales but is extended to include implicitly an emphasis on race and the role of the female ancestor as a genetic conduit of martial ability. The abduction is described as an act which was effected 'in defiance of all the land'. Nest's beauty was to blame: 'The fame of her loveliness and charm went through the land, causing long war and bloodshed about her.' Although Vaughan strikes a patriotic tone, the abduction is not portrayed as an episode of resistance to the Normans. It is revealed as evidence of Owain's passion, for which he was not to blame since his actions were caused by Nest's beauty. The repercussions and political context are not fully clarified, and he erroneously placed the scene of the abduction at Pembroke castle.

Romantic and emotive themes reoccur throughout the book and are central to the portrayal of women. For example, the marriage of Gruffudd to Gwenllian, daughter of Gruffudd ap Cynan, is portrayed as a love match, and her death and defeat at Kidwelly in 1136 is presented in an embellished and romanticised account. The death of Gwenllian on the battlefield is seen as the cause of Welsh revenge attacks. The Normans are portrayed as unheroic and unchivalric: 'No pang of generous thought for her womanhood softened them; no flash of admiration for her heroic spirit moved them. There over the corpse of her son, they hewed off her head.' Gwenllian is the only woman who is the subject of an entire chapter. A central theme of the chapter is Welsh patriotic resistance to the Normans, and Vaughan takes an almost celebratory tone when writing of Welsh revenge: 'long long did the Norman widows curse the name of Maurice de Londres, the leader of the Norman forces which defeated Gwenllian'. This approval for Welsh ferocity against a Norman foe is extended to cast reflections on the efficacy of Welsh resistance and its role in Welsh history: 'Had every deed of Norman savagery been as terribly avenged as was the murder of Gwenllian, there would have been few Normans left to work ruin on our land.'[7] The book as a whole romanticises Welsh history and melds history and myth with stereotypical images of the elite as bearers of national history or the history of 'Wales'. The chapter on Gwenllian and the entries which concern Nest confirm Vaughan's stress on the importance of gender, race and imperialism as key to the popular understanding of that history. Vaughan casually accepts and celebrates revenge and violence in that history as part of the portrayal of the medieval period. His view of 'our history' is part of his British imperial project: the Normans are represented as foreign interlopers who skewed Welsh history within Britain and caused the trajectory of that history to change. Overall, *Flame Bearers of Welsh History* presented a nationalistic, romanticised view of the medieval past in which stereotypical images of romantic heroines that portrayed gendered ideas were utilised to convey ideas about the vibrancy and importance of that history.

This view of the medieval past was central to Vaughan's interpretation of Welsh history. Vaughan played a key role in the National Pageant of Wales in 1909 at Cardiff castle which celebrated Welsh history. Hywel Teifi Edwards has argued that scholars have been dismissive of the event, and suggests that Dai Smith's interpretation of it as an 'overblown Edwardian fantasy' is too dismissive.[8] Yet Smith put the pageant into a solid perspective which takes as its central axis the argument that 'Wales' as an entity was imagined and produced in the context of the social, political and economic changes of the nineteenth century which were a result of the industrialisation of Wales, the growth of nonconformity and the changes in education and literacy which affected the mental landscape of Wales. Smith emphasised the consensual nature of the event which represented a Wales that had been produced during the nineteenth century and which in effect saw history as a continuous thread. National identity was implicitly connected to the British Isles and the pageant defined Wales and its identity through its presentation of Welsh history.[9] The pageant was an event which took liberties with Welsh history from the end of the Roman occupation to the Acts of Union in 1536, in order to present a romanticised, nationalistic and elitist view of the past through performance. That it had some measure of popular support in Cardiff among working people is evident since over 5,000 individuals participated in various performances. Participants included members of the socially elite gentry families, the Lord Mayor of Cardiff, city councillors and council officers, as well as a diverse range of people including over 500 rugby players and school teachers and their pupils.[10] The pageant was intended to showcase the vibrancy and importance of the Welsh medieval past and its role in British imperial history.[11] The involvement of rugby players who were specifically named in publicity material in the *Western Mail* was an attempt to gather popular support.[12] The event was not a success, however, as Edwards points out: it left over £2,000 in debts.[13] These losses can partly be explained by poor weather in the first week, but this does not explain the lack of interest within Wales for the affair. The pageant represented a view of Wales which failed to capture the popular imagination. It was selective in its presentation, and the lack of support for it suggests that it was out-of-step with the social, economic, political and cultural realities of contemporary society. Further, it presented a romantic, fanciful and deeply gendered perspective of the Welsh past which was elitist in conception and performance. The narrative of Welsh history presented at the pageant was created by Vaughan, who, with George Hawtrey, co-authored the *Book of Words*, a handbook to the pageant, under the pseudonym 'Owen Rhoscomyl'. The purpose of the pageant was to be 'a National, not a local, Pageant'.[14]

The pageant freely reinterpreted Welsh history and the role of women within it in romantic terms. The *Book of Words* states that Nest was 'a lady of extraordinary beauty and wonderful charm' and that 'She no less than Helen of Troy, Cleopatra, and Mary Queen of Scots, was the cause of endless trouble among her admirers.'[15] This latter boast not only portrayed Nest as a great beauty but also placed her into a world-famous context: thus the history of Wales itself was elevated by her beauty. The mention of her as the 'Helen of Wales' suggests the migration into 'popular' understandings of Welsh medieval history of a parallel which had been first conceptualised by Edward Laws in 1888.[16] Nest's abduction was not part of the pageant; the *Book of Words* declared: 'We make no attempt in this scene to show any special incident in the life of Nest.' This lack of detail concerning Nest is indicative that her abduction was not seen as an appropriate episode for the pageant, since it would have visibly represented Welsh disunity as well as morally questionable actions and behaviour. Instead, the episode which represented Nest displayed her with her maidens and then a succession of men including Gerald of Windsor, Owain ap Cadwgan and Stephen constable of Cardigan, as well as 'the king's favourites, assorted knights, warriors and jesters'. A photograph of the scene appeared in the *Western Mail* and featured the principal actors.[17] Her role as an ancestral figure is also mentioned in the *Book of Words*. This contrasts with the scene which portrayed Gwenllian, the wife of Gruffudd ap Rhys, Nest's brother. Gwenllian is described in the *Book of Words* as 'Gwenllian, the heroine, whose story is so well known to every child in Wales'. There was a brief re-enactment of the defeat of Gwenllian in 1136 and the Welsh response to her death, and Gwenllian was portrayed in white romantic robes.[18] The *Western Mail* provided free publicity for the event and published over two full pages of photographs of the scenes of the pageant in one edition; the newspaper had features about the pageant on several days. This event was a performed, imagined and reconstructed narrative of the history of Wales which inculcated a sense of a lost heroic Welsh past and conformed to contemporary gender stereotypes. Thus, most scenes which include women portrayed the women of the elite as wives and mothers in supportive and decorative roles, while working women were dressed as nameless, generic, decorative and supportive 'fairies'. The narratives of Nest and Gwenllian were thus included as women of the elite whose roles were shaped by such imperatives. The pageant's core theme was the importance of the medieval history of Wales to the Welsh national present, and women's roles were inscripted into this view of the past in gendered ways which were essentially decorative and symbolic of Welsh unity. Thus the pageant took the form of 'Episodes' which were scripted and rehearsed, some with various scenes. The chosen episodes were acted out, some with dialogue, and some had multiple scenes to clarify the chronology. The opening episode featured a parade of individuals who personified and thus represented the counties of Wales; they followed the marchioness of Bute, who represented 'Dame Wales', and were in turn followed by a parade of fairies. 'Dame Wales' then spoke, with each 'county' claiming their 'hero'; for example, 'Flint' claimed King Arthur, while 'Pembroke' claimed 'Harry Tudor, Gerald the Cymro and Nest', to which 'Carmarthen' responded 'What nonsense! Nest belongs to me! Gwenllian also'. Episode One concerned Caradoc *c.* AD 50, and subsequent episodes focused on various individuals or themes, such as 'the coming of the Cymry' or Rhodri Mawr and his seven sons or Hywel Dda. Nest and her sister-in-law Gwenllian were the only women from the Welsh historical past who were given their own scenes in the pageant, scenes which portrayed the Norman advances into Wales and Welsh resistance to it.[19] Other women of the elite were represented throughout in other scenes as wives or daughters of powerful rulers, and the pageant contained over 1,000 fairies who were included in most scenes.

Thus elite women served as emblems of national pride in the national pageant, but also in the writings on Wales in the early decades of the twentieth century in the popular understandings of the medieval past, and this impulse can be seen in modern Wales. The activities of a society, founded in the late twentieth century, dedicated to the memory of another Welsh princess, Princess Gwenllian, the daughter of Llywelyn ap Gruffudd (d. 1282), help demonstrate the significance of this. The Gwenllian Society, formed in 1996, according to its web page exists solely to 'restore the memory' of Princess Gwenllian and to commemorate her. A plaque commemorating Gwenllian was erected in 1993 at Sempringham on the initiative of Byron Rogers. The society, after meetings with the representatives of Snowdonia National Park, had a plaque erected near the peak of Snowdon in 2007. Furthermore, on Saturday 26 September 2009 at an official ceremony, attended by the then first minister Rhodri Morgan, held at the Bulkeley Hotel, Beaumaris (Anglesey), which had been organised by the Gwenllian Society, a mountain in Snowdonia hitherto known as Carnedd Uchaf in the Ogwen Valley was renamed as Carnedd Gwenllian. The Gwenllian Society argued that renaming a mountain after her was a way of 'bringing her home' and its website states that the ceremony which formally renamed the mountain was conducted by the Welsh Assembly Minister of Culture Alun Ffred Jones. Further, Lord Elis-Thomas, the Welsh Assembly's Presiding Officer, 'welcomed Gwenllian's name back from her outcast prisoner existence'.[20] As part of the campaign to raise awareness of the event, Gwenllian's life had been reported in various media, including BBC local radio, and local and regional press, such as, for example, *The Leader*, a local paper which serves Flintshire. This paper's version of her story featured as a lead headline on its front page under the headline 'Our lost princess', complete on one side of the headline with a misty, romantic-focus photograph of a girl and on the other a photograph of the commemorative headstone at Sempringham for Gwenllian. Inside, the paper described Gwenllian's life and incarceration in the nunnery at Sempringham at the orders of Edward I after the defeat in battle of her father under a sub-headline 'Our lost princess ... locked away for 50 years ... wiped from the pages of history'. The main story is complete with images of her memorial stone and a pen-and-ink drawing of a nun at a romanesque door.[21] The article strikes a romantic and patriotic tone throughout: Gwenllian lived 'the saddest of lives' as one who 'could not speak her native language and was never even taught to spell her own name'. The portrayal of Gwenllian as an infant victim of Edward I is consolidated within the article which states that she was the 'last true Princess of Wales', who 'was lost to her people and her nation for 700 years': she was 'like a butterfly that never took flight' and 'lived and died in a cocoon'. Her tale also features on the 'Castlewales' website, complete with an image of the modern tombstone at Cwmhir Abbey and the commemorative stone in Lincolnshire.[22] The latter two quotations were from Malt Anderson, who formed the Gwenllian Society, and shows that the impulse behind this twenty-first-century commemoration is a nationalistic sense of a Welsh medieval past deprived of its proper place in modern understandings of that Welsh medieval past. It conveys a romanticised imagined view of a female victim of English oppression and a sense of justice being done in the present for past mistakes. It is intriguing, however, that there is a sense of commemoration of the nation through female victimhood, where Gwenllian is seen as the last 'true' princess of Wales. Here the Welsh medieval past of victimisation at the hands of Edward I is also a narrative of female oppression which is memorialised in more modern twenty-first-century Wales.

This recently created link between a mountain and Gwenllian is illustrative of the continued importance of the mountains of Wales to its identity; scholars have argued that the Welsh landscape is intrinsic to ideas about the essence of Wales and has defined its history.[23] Katie Gramich, in a study of twentieth-century writings of women in Wales, has argued that the historical processes by which people shape landscapes caused an internalisation and identification of ideas about the landscape and these in turn create a relationship between land and mentality. Gramich argues that such 'ethnoscapes' and the way that they relate to women are significant.[24] Gramich therefore uses an idea imported from modern anthropological approaches which has its origins in the work of Arjun Appadurai. Appadurai extends the analysis offered by Benedict Anderson's thesis on the importance of imagined communities and the central role of the invention of the printing press. Appadurai provides an analysis which sees connections between communities that take different forms, such as ethnoscapes, or technoscapes for example, to explain global imagined communities.[25] By contrast, the imagining of the Welsh medieval past is about the specific, localised identity of the Welsh within Wales. The relationship between land and mentality, and the construction of the role of women within understandings of the Welsh medieval past, are related to ideas about women as enduring symbols of the nation: such ideas, then, are recast within ideas about ethnoscapes. Anthony D. Smith discussed these ideas about the link between ethnicity, landscapes and nation to argue for the long-lasting nature of such ideas upon mentalities.[26]

The renaming of Carnedd Uchaf as Carnedd Gwenllian is evidence of these ideas represented in an act of modern remembrance of the medieval past. It is perhaps best understood as an attempt to create a modern understanding and commemoration of a difficult period in Welsh history. For the Gwenllian Society it inherently embodies a sense of righting past wrongs and, more specifically, the society sees the commemoration as a 'home-coming', since, according to the society, other neighbouring mountains are named after her mother, father and uncle.[27] However, it is far from clear that the peaks named Carnedd Llywelyn, Yr Elen and Carnedd Dafydd are linked to Gwenllian's family. The editors of the *Dictionary of the Place-names of Wales*, a definitive scholarly guide, indicate that although it is possible that Carnedd Llywelyn, for example, may commemorate Llywelyn ap Iorwerth (d. 1240), and Carnedd Dafydd could possibly be named for his son who died in 1246, it is by no means certain.[28] Some popular awareness of the lack of certainty regarding the naming of these mountains has resulted in limited debate about the renaming, given the ambiguity of the provenance of the names.[29]

For our purposes the renaming of the mountain is perhaps evidence of the projection of modern ideas about the place of the aristocratic elite of medieval Wales as symbolic of the 'nation' of a united Wales. Such a conception of the past within this example of an imagined, and consciously created, modern interpretation combines a sense of land and history in which a woman, and family connections, are central. It has much to tell us about modern conceptions of the place of elite women in the history of Wales as symbols of oppression by the English. Gwenllian is an elite woman who is almost entirely passive, whose importance stems from her ancestry and her family. Further, the focus on the elite of Wales as symbolic of Wales as a whole privileges the role of the medieval military elite in the trajectory of the history of Wales. It promotes a view of the past which has much to tell us about modern conceptions of the medieval past through the romanticisation and promotion of female victimhood in the cause of promoting a nationalistic interpretation of the medieval Welsh past. Such ideas were important in the early material published as part of this campaign. As part of the early campaign for a wider recognition of the importance of Gwenllian in 1991, Byron Rogers published an article discussing Gwenllian in *The Guardian*.[30] Rogers's article is primarily concerned with Gwenllian's life, and her incarceration at Sempringham is central; he also notes that the 'little boys of Gwynedd' were not placed in Sempringham but were imprisoned.[31] For Rogers this proves that 'the Welsh children were already history and for them Sempringham was the dustbin of Welsh history'. Rogers was writing a discursive piece for a national broadsheet and deployed emotive language, and the fate of Gwenllian is seen as key to understanding Edward I's policy towards Wales. Thus Gwenllian's fate is written as a story of national significance and this is related to her position as the heiress to Gwynedd as heir to the 'last' prince of Wales. In this early phase of the campaign Gwenllian serves as a passive symbol of English oppression of the Welsh elite in the medieval past, whereas, by contrast, Nest serves as an active, adult symbol of a Welsh past that is romantic, where adults make choices, take action and exert their will on events. Gwenllian's narrative, which depicts a passive child-victim, serves to show the harsh, brutal aspects of the medieval period and English oppression.

Resistance to such 'English' oppression has informed views of other Welsh medieval women. As we have seen, Gerald of Wales preserved the memory of his great-aunt, Gwenllian, the wife of Gruffudd ap Rhys of Deheubarth and Nest's sister-in-law, and secured her place in the history of south-west Wales as part of the narrative of the Welsh response to the Normans.[32] Rhoscomyl's views of Gwenllian demonstrate the ways key features of the narrative created by Gerald, her manner of death, her role in battle and her resistance to the Normans, were taken up by later writers. Her story had by the nineteenth century become a powerful motif, and there has been a long-standing interest in her narrative which featured in earlier romantic travel writing as discussed in the previous chapter,[33] but it was also current in 1930s Carmarthen, as is evidenced by a brief reference to her in R. W. Thompson's travel-book *An Englishman*

Looks at Wales. Most of the book originally appeared as a series of news-paper articles which he eventually published in book form. He reveals his own negative images and stereotypes of the people of Wales and its language, but his work overall portrays a positive image of both rural and industrial Wales. Thompson describes Wales and its people from the perspective of an outsider and often remarks on the hospitality and friendliness of the Welsh. He clearly formed a very positive opinion about Kidwelly and its castle. He notes how it was a topic of conversation with some old Welshmen in a pub in Carmarthen, one of whom asked him, 'Did you see the tomb of Princess Gwenllian?' Thompson asked the old man if Kidwelly was her castle; the old man did not know, pointing out, 'It's a thousand years ago – and I'm not so old.'[34] Gwenllian's resistance has also had some exposure in national newspapers: for example, describing her as the daughter of 'the king of North Wales', Roger Dobson discussed the events of 1136 in *The Independent* newspaper in January 1997. The article reported the suggestion by Andrew Breeze that Gwenllian was possibly 'the first British woman author', and it included the scept-ical views of Rhiannon Evans and Sioned Davies.[35] The Norman conquest and Gwenllian's attempt to resist the Norman Maurice of London are part of the local identity of Kidwelly: memories of her and her resistance have become part of local marketing literature. A website hosted by the Kidwelly Town Council which features a page on the history of Kidwelly includes details of the early history of the town as well as the defeat of Gwenllian. The passage ends with 'Hail Gwenllian – Kidwelly's unequi-vocal heroine after 900 years!'[36] The website also includes details con-cerning the location of Maes Gwenllian (Gwenllian's field), the alleged site of the battle. This is possibly the only battlefield in Britain which is named after a woman. Pride in Gwenllian's resistance is fundamental to the presentation of the town in contemporary Wales. It suggests the importance of the medieval past to the local identity, and her active role in the defence of her castle and lands contrasts with the passive identity, in modern constructions, of Gwenllian the daughter of Llywelyn ap Iorwerth.

The association with Gwenllian at Kidwelly is founded in historical sources, especially Gerald of Wales, who is the key source for Gwenllian's defeat and beheading. The identification of person with place is an important aspect of tourist and heritage literature and as such is a com-monplace enough aspect of tourism. Such claims, spurious or otherwise, then may form part of the appeal of heritage sites and may serve to identify and define a heritage site. The characterisation of Wales as dif-ferent and romantic was tenacious; Mrs Rodolph Stawell's *Motor Tours in Wales* drew on historical, topographical and ethnographic material. The abduction of Nest appears in the narrative and is introduced into the text in a section which discusses Manorbier castle. Stawell draws on Gerald of Wales and his portrayal of Gerald of Windsor who deceived besiegers of his castle by throwing animals over the walls.[37] Stawell states that there is some uncertainty over the location of the abduction of Nest and suggests that Nest, being 'less discreet than her husband, apparently, was carried off by a Welsh prince, not without encouragement from the lady'. Stawell then explains: 'But when one hears that the discreet Gerald escaped on this occasion by creeping down a drain-pipe, one feels that there was some excuse after all for Nest.'[38] Stawell here draws on the portrayal of Gerald's shameful escape which is seen as a justification for Nest's decision to encourage Owain.

In the 1930s motor tours began to be popular with the middle classes as cars became more affordable and available, and in turn this generated travel guides. There is a certain congruence with the pattern of development of the narrative of Gwenllian in that a travel writer, publishing in the 1930s, brought the story of Nest to the attention of a wider public at around the same time. Henry Morton's 1932 volume *In Search of Wales* includes details about Nest's abduction and associates her with the manor house at Eglwyseg (Denbighshire).[39] The abduction is juxtaposed with and follows details about the 'Ladies of Llangollen'. These two young Irish women fled Ireland to avoid marriage, setting up home near Llangollen and becoming famous in nineteenth-century Britain, visited by a variety of well-connected and well-known individuals. Their house, Plas Newydd, became, and remains, a part of the tourist trail associated with Llangollen. Morton's version of the abduction of Nest is very close to that first originated in the *Brut*. It contains motifs which are central to the well-established narrative: the origination of events at a feast of Cadwgan ap Bleddyn, the visit by Owain and the raid on Cenarth Bychan. Morton obliquely references formal and popular history, as seen in the writings of Laws, Lloyd and Rhoscomyl, when he states that Nest was the 'Helen of Wales', and criticises the abduction since it would 'plunge Wales into war and deny those still independent regions in the north the peace they so desperately needed'. Morton embellishes his version for literary effect; for example, he argues that after the abduction of Nest and her children all were 'soon galloping like madmen for Powys'. He states that while Nest and Owain hid in the hunting lodge at Eglwyseg 'the whole of Wales and the Border Marches were on fire'. Morton's account is attenuated, he does not mention that Owain was later killed by Gerald of Windsor, and he romanticises Nest's role in Welsh history:

'So Nesta, the Beautiful, passes across a page of Welsh history like a figure in the mist.' Yet he notes that Nest was the central ancestral figure of 'those stormy knights who conquered Ireland under Strongbow'. Morton comments on the link between people and place in terms of memory and its importance in romantic terms: 'Any place in which men and women have felt deeply retains a pathetic significance. It seems almost as if some part of their passion has scorched the earth. We shall never know if Nesta loved her stormy prince.'[40] Morton was a prolific populist writer who has been termed the most successful travel writer of the twentieth century and who insisted that his books should remain priced at an affordable level. His book on Wales was the fourth in a series of 'In search of' volumes, which had begun with the volume *In Search of England* and had been followed by books on Scotland and Ireland.[41] Given his evident popularity, his book on Wales was written to a formula which had already proved commercially successful and it is thus arguable that he was responsible for bringing the romanticised view of Nest's abduction to a wider audience. It has been suggested that, deeply Christian, Morton had an antipathy to the effects of the industrialisation and urbanisation upon Britain, a strong love of the countryside and a firm conviction in the importance of the continuities of British history as a way to renew the 'national character'.[42] Travel writing in the 1930s was a genre which underwent developments reflective of broader political and cultural contexts.[43] Wales in the 1930s, like the rest of Britain, dealt with the impact of the Depression and mass unemployment, and some areas faced near starvation.[44] Yet such contemporary realities are absent from both Morton and Thompson's narratives. Morton's views on Wales are not only reflective of his overall approach to the history of the British Isles, but also show an understanding of the importance of local tradition which encapsulated ideas about identity and place linked through tangible objects. The Nest abduction narrative for Morton is an example of the use of local traditions by writers to inform a narrative of the past which was romantic, and essentially chronologically distant from the realities of twentieth-century Wales which faced many economic, social and political challenges. Morton suggested that Nest was linked with the site near an Elizabethan manor house in Eglwyseg within the area in the north of Powys which became known as Powys Fadog after the split of the kingdom after 1160. A key element of this tradition is that the extant house was built on the site of a former hunting lodge of the princes of Powys, including houses like the one in question, Plas Uchaf. The romantic association of Plas Uchaf as a refuge for Owain after the abduction of Nest has been repeated in other modern print media. *Country Quest* magazine had a feature on Plas Uchaf in 1986 which included details of Nest and Owain at the site, and the narrative has been replicated in a relatively modern guide book to walks in the Llangollen area.[45] Further, the association has been perpetuated in modern media such as internet sites.[46] This is all suggestive that local folklore has its attractions for modern readers, and is indicative that Nest's abduction has been cast as a romantic escapade but which has penetrated modern consciousness through print and computer media. The tale adds historic interest and locates Nest and Owain in a narrative which is romantic and localised, marginalised to heritage tourism. The narrative of the abduction within a framework that takes account of the Norman impact upon Wales, which is central to the *Brut*, and which informed earlier antiquarian writings, has been lost: instead it is reinterpreted and remains a bite-size, popularised and reinterpreted remnant of a grand narrative of Welsh history.

The association of Nest and Owain at Plas Uchaf is, however, a modern invention. There is no evidence of any tradition recording the association earlier than the twentieth century. Two articles on the locality in *Archaeologia Cambrensis* in the mid-nineteenth century, for example, do not mention Nest and Owain at Plas Uchaf, although they do refer to a Prince Llywelyn sleeping still in a cave. The association may have its roots in a misinterpretation of genealogies recorded in the sixteenth and seventeenth centuries.[47] Nevertheless it is instructive that a relatively late misinterpretation should be taken up and replicated in modern publications and it is evidence of the appeal of the narrative to more modern audiences. The association of Nest with a specific location relates to ideas about the fusion of gender, ethnicity and landscape within Wales. The creation of a link with Nest at Plas Uchaf is indicative of Morton's view of the importance of the Welsh medieval past since his presentation of the abduction narrative magnifies it into an event of all-Wales significance that therefore assumes 'national' proportions. Morton is a key representative of travel writers who saw links between landscapes and races, but who also fused a narrative of modern Wales and its historic past.[48]

Morton's writings, like Stawell's before him, were a commentary on Wales which was part of a wider discourse on Welsh identity conducted in the context of vigorous debate on Welsh nationhood during the interwar period. Travel writing had various functions in this context and it was part of the construction of Wales as different in popular texts in which Wales as a tourist destination was created, founded on, in part, understandings of Welsh history and heritage. If such representations in popular texts had elements of myth-making or even of simple mis-understandings, they constructed Wales as romantic and intriguing. Nest appears in such writings within the motifs established in the *Brut*: Gwenllian's tale was recycled as it was borrowed from Gerald of Wales, and such tales in Morton's work, or that of Stawell, are reflective of a deliberate construction of Wales and its meanings which saw the role of women in its history as romantic yet decisive and unique.

*****

The site of the abduction of Nest remains unknown, since the *Brut* refers to the castle of 'Cenarth Bychan', at present still unidentified. This uncertainty has allowed for the association of Nest with several key heritage sites in south-west Wales, at Carew, Cilgerran and Pembroke castles. Carew castle in Pembrokeshire and Cilgerran castle in Ceredigion both have promotional material which discuss Nest as the 'Helen of Wales' and associate the castle with the site of the abduction. Carew, managed by the Pembrokeshire Coast National Park Authority, produces educational material about the castle which features Nest's story as well as other items such as A4 and A3 colouring sheets of 'Princess Nest' for children. Nest also features over four pages in a book, *Carew Castle*, produced for children. The Authority also maintains a website which features Nest and Gerald of Windsor among 'Carew Castle's Characters', a page which provides information about prominent historical figures associated with the castle.[49] The official Carew guidebook produced for the general public has a full-page feature on Nest and the abduction with an illustration derived from an early fourteenth-century French romance. Other materials include a website which also has dedicated pages that feature Nest and asserts that Carew was her 'true home', that she was kidnapped not unwillingly, was held prisoner at Cilgerran castle for six years and that her ghost haunts the castle grounds.[50] The laminated leaflets which are given to visitors to guide them around the remains and which clarify the various phases of construction and so on, specifically label the garderobe in the twelfth-century remains of the Old Tower as the site where Gerald of Windsor escaped. Further there has been some relatively recent local community involvement in the commemoration of Nest at Carew. A local youth club designed and installed a mock stained-glass window in the late-thirteenth-/early fourteenth-century chapel prominently featuring Nest. Nest is therefore integrally associated with the history of the castle in its promotional literature. Cilgerran on the other hand is owned by the National Trust and managed by Cadw, which also produces promotional material. Its guidebook to Cilgerran provides an overview of the chronological development of the site and mentions Nest and her marriage to Gerald of Windsor in the main text. Further, the guide includes a full-page inset on 'Nest: The "Helen of Wales"', complete with a quotation from the *Brut* and an illustration from the early fourteenth-century manuscript which also features in the guide to Carew.[51] Although the official guide does not posit Cilgerran as the site of the abduction, other promotional literature is more forthright. Nest and the abduction appear on promotional merchandise, including a tea towel which lists significant dates in the life of the castle, and her name appears on a mug which lists important words associated with the history of Wales, among a seemingly randomly selected set of words such as 'slate', and 'Owain Glyndŵr'. Thus this small but very telling detail suggests the elevation of Nest's name in popular understandings of the history of Wales to a stature approaching that of Owain Glyndŵr. The website of Cadw provides information about visitor sites and as of January 2011 made no mention of Nest and the abduction.[52] Yet the abduction narrative is associated with Cilgerran in internet sources and as such there is evidence that it retains an appeal, and the growth of the internet has facilitated this spread and development of the narrative. For example, Britainexpress.com, a website which offers travel information and details of sites of interest throughout Britain, suggests Cilgerran was the site of the incident and that Nest arranged the abduction so that she could 'get rid of her husband'; the entry for Carew does not mention Nest.[53] The website Castlewales.com associates Carew as the dowry of Nest when she married Gerald of Windsor.[54] It identifies the abduction with Cilgerran castle and has a link to a page about Nest, the 'Helen of Wales', which has an image and text derived from the Cadw official guidebook.[55] The original image is derived from a manuscript in the British Library which is an early fourteenth-century manuscript of an Arthurian romance.[56] It has been used as an illustration associated with Nest on the information boards at Pembroke castle, the cover of Kari Maund's book and in the guidebook to Cilgerran and Carew castles.[57] It is indicative of the visual power of this image when linked with the enduring appeal of Nest's abduction which is thus authenticated by recourse to a medieval image derived from a French romance. The image is cleverly deployed to illustrate the narrative and this has been facilitated by the emergence of modern media. Nest has thus become associated with key heritage sites in south-west Wales, and even perhaps the subject of friendly rivalry between Carew and Cilgerran as they vie to be the authentic location of the abduction. The abduction motif has thus become an aid to marketing the castles at Carew and Cilgerran, and the accessibility of Nest's story in modern media reveals its enduring appeal and the way that the internet facilitates the spread of ideas and tropes. Such themes are again apparent in the presentation of the history of Pembroke castle, owned by the Pembroke Castle Trust, which also includes information about the abduction in some of its promotional materials. In particular it has a number of detailed information boards which present the origins and chronology of the site from its early beginnings to the modern period. Key phases of development are highlighted on separate boards, and important political events are discussed, including the birth there of Henry Tudor in 1457, and the castle's fortunes during the civil war. Nest's narrative and family connections are featured on an information panel which, at its centre, provides a genealogical chart with Nest at its heart. Her various alliances/marriages and children are portrayed and the abduction narrative features prominently. The guidebook to the castle does not mention the abduction, however, but it does include the same genealogical chart and locates the marriage of Gerald of Windsor within a narrative of the development of Pembroke castle caused by the Norman invasions of Pembroke and the creation of the lordship of Pembrokeshire.[58] In the old gatehouse there is an education room which invites visitors to sit and watch a film of the history of the castle. In the same room, opposite the door, is a cabinet of dolls dressed as the 'Ladies of Pembroke castle'. These dolls at Pembroke serve as a metaphor for modern understandings of medieval women: Nest is represented in this gallery of dolls, dressed in costume near two children. These dolls – playthings in a cabinet – are decorative, but not part of the main exhibition, relegated to a separate display of little 'serious' intent. They are representative of popular interest in the costume and decoration of medieval women, perhaps a timid reminder of the very real lives lived in difficult and politically charged contexts. Within the main displays there are, by contrast, few female mannequins, and the portrayal of the chronology of the castle is charged with associations with war and conflict. The dolls in a separate display serve as a metaphor of how, until relatively recently, the history of medieval Wales was seen as male gendered at such sites. Thus three key heritage sites in south-west Wales include detailed information about Nest and the abduction within a context of information concerning the political chronology and development of the sites. The abduction narrative, with Nest constructed as 'Helen of Wales', is an interesting and historically validated narrative which gives colour and romance to chronological approaches to the past.

*****

There is some evidence to suggest that the name 'Nest' when used to name a fictional character in plays and poetry became synonymous with a beautiful Welsh princess figure who inspired love in male characters and who was involved in high political drama. Thus the use of the name by writers served to evoke romantic and dramatic associations. This can be seen, for example, in a tragedy written by Robert Eyres Landor in 1841 in which a 'Nesta' is the inspiration for her lover Ivor to fight for the cause of the Welsh. The play is set in late-thirteenth-century Wales and the Edwardian conquest.[59] The poet Glyn Jones (d. 1995) wrote a poem called 'Gerald's wife' which is based on Nest's abduction. His poem presents an ambiguous view of the abduction. The first stanza has a dramatic imperative:

> Raising a shout, Prince Owen rides out,
> Leading our Powys Lads, faithful and stout;
> Sun on each breast, bound for the West,
> Fifteen blades ride out to the raping of Nest.

Yet the poem also implies that the abduction was consensual, as it ends with a scene whereby the raiding party ride:

> Across Ceredigion, with daffodils blooming –
> Owen and Nest, her head on his breast,
> Laughing with Gerald of Windsor for jest.

This poem therefore conforms to the narrative which stresses Nest's consent and plays on the affection between Nest and Owain.[60] Jones also wrote a poem called 'The death of Prince Gronw' in which a certain Nest appears as the beautiful but unfaithful female whose affair with another man caused the death of the prince. She is murdered in a revenge attack and her attacker in turn is murdered by the brother of the prince.[61] Thus the romance elements of the narrative were incorporated by Jones, and although the view of 'Gerald's wife' begins as if the abduction was a rape, it ends with an allegation of consensuality. Such ambiguity is unusual in the constructions of Nest in many modern interpretations, where romance and consensual themes predominate.

Such romance elements have therefore dominated creative fiction which reinterprets and constructs Nest as a romantic heroine in modern literature. The narrative of Nest inspired creative writers during the twentieth century in both English and Welsh. Geraint Dyfnallt Owen published two novels in Welsh about Nest; the first, *Nest*, was published in 1949, and the second in the series, *Dyddiau'r Gofid* ('Days of anxiety'), in 1950.[62] Owain is portrayed as a man who respects the teaching of the

Church, and Nest as a romantic heroine. Commercial Welsh-language publishing in Wales underwent a period of crisis in the post-war years until the mid-1950s.[63] Given this difficult context of Welsh-language publishing, Owen's work is suggestive of the appeal of Nest as a commercial project for the publishers even in challenging times. Eleanor Fairburn's *The Golden Hive*, published in 1966, was the first English-language romantic novel about Nest. It portrays Nest as a beautiful heroine who was unwillingly abducted by Owain and stayed loyal to Gerald of Windsor. Geraint Owen in a positive review of this reinterpretation of Nest, which appeared in the *Welsh History Review*, noted that the publication of *The Golden Hive* had stepped 'into the breach' left by scholars who had treated Nest in a 'niggardly fashion'. Owen argued that her narrative had disappeared from Welsh history since Lloyd described her as the 'Helen of Wales' in the early decades of the twentieth century. Further, Owen suggests that Fairburn's Irish descent and residency for a period near the Welsh Marches may explain her interest in Nest.[64] The year 1966 thus marks a turning point in the narrative of Nest, where a creative reinterpretation of her life was published and brought to the attention of an academic audience through a scholarly review, and coincidentally this was a significant period in Welsh politics since Plaid Cymru won the by-election in Carmarthen later in 1966 after the Labour victory in the General Election in March earlier in the year. In the period when modern feminist scholarship emerged during the 1970s, other novelists produced romanticised books based on Nest, three of which were published during the decade, and another was published in 1981.[65] Anne Bell's portrayal of Nest reinterpreted her as a more modern heroine who skilfully managed Henry I and her husbands, and who was a key figure in the political life of Wales. It further utilises stock images, for example of noble Saxons who integrate with Norman life but retain a sense of their past. The romantic tragedy *Lion Rampant*, by Bernard Knight, cast Nest as a dutiful mother and wife who was loyal at heart to the cause of the Welsh but victim to political events beyond her control, and presented Owain as a Welsh hero. This was first published in 1972 and recently returned to print as a 'print on demand' publication. Part of the appeal of Nest as a subject is summed up in the 'author's note' to Knight's *Lion Rampant* where he argues for the historicity of the narrative: 'Most of the events described in this book actually happened.' Thus it is the authenticity of the key events based on a narrative derived from the *Brut* which inspired Knight. More recently Nest has been the subject of renewed interest by creative writers. In 2004 Nest was the subject of another work of romantic fiction, and she inspired a volume of poetry which was completed as part of an MA in literary studies in 2005.[66] Populist articles in *Country Quest* and, more recently, *Cambria* magazines have also appeared.[67] This interest in Nest can partly be explained by a popular interest in medieval women more generally. This can be seen, for example, in the publication of Deborah Fisher's *Princesses of Wales* in 2005. Although this work includes summaries of the lives of Nest of Deheubarth, her sister-in-law Gwenllian, Joan, daughter of King John and Gwenllian the daughter of Llewelyn ap Gruffudd, the lives of late-medieval and more modern women are detailed in much more depth.[68] The book is symptomatic of a broader interest in the concept of the 'princesses' of Wales which is founded upon a yet wider interest in women's history more generally. In a more academic frame, if still clearly aimed at a popular audience, Kari Maund's study of Nest and the context of her narrative admirably put Nest into a critical framework which takes account of the contemporary politics of Norman and Welsh conflicts in the eleventh and twelfth centuries.[69] The growth in academic study of medieval women such as Nest is reflective of the growth in first-wave feminist studies and women's history since the 1970s which has then in turn inspired the study of medieval Welsh women. Therefore it may be argued that over the past century Nest's narrative became a simplified tale of Welsh nationhood which was one of resistance to the Normans and English. Nest has therefore in the past century rapidly become a romanticised figure helping to construct an uncomplicated view of Welsh nationhood in its resistance to the Normans and English. She has done so as social and more narrowly historiographical trends have turned our attention towards the significance of women's involvement in events which have been seen as traditionally gendered exclusively male – whether this was the case or not. This self-conscious rediscovery has interacted intriguingly with the underlying continuities in the transmission of the story, both locally and regionally in Wales and in more formal accounts. And it has made itself felt across a very broad canvas, from travel writing, through the interpretation of heritage sites and into popular fiction. The breadth and depth of the culture of Welsh popular historiography has the role of women, and in particular of Nest, written right through it.

Notes

1 'Towards a battlefields register for Wales', *Heritage in Wales*, 46 (Summer 2010), 5. The initiative is part of CADW's £19m Heritage Tourism Project; the first phase, 2009–15, aims to conserve and promote heritage associated with the Welsh princes and to develop heritage sites in Wales to encourage tourism.

2   See chapter 2, p. 62–4 for further discussion.

3   Owen Rhoscomyl [Arthur Owen Vaughan], *Flame Bearers of Welsh History: Being the Outline of the Story of the 'Sons of Cunedda'* (Merthyr Tydfil: Welsh Educational Publishing Co., 1905).

4   Rhoscomyl, *Flame Bearers*, p. 139.

5   *Brut, Peniarth MS 20* (1952), p. 39. See chapter 1.

6   Rhoscomyl, *Flame Bearers*, pp. 164–5.

7   Rhoscomyl, *Flame Bearers*, pp. 143–8.

8   Hywel Teifi Edwards, *The National Pageant of Wales* (Llandysul: Gomer, 2009), p. 191.

9   Dai Smith, *Wales: A Question for History* (Bridgend: Seren, 1999), pp. 90–3.

10 Edwards, *National Pageant*, pp. 7–9.

11 Edwards, *National Pageant*; Hywel Teifi Edwards, 'Owen Rhoscomyl (1863–1919) a "Rhwysg Hanes Cymru"', *Transactions of the Honourable Society of Cymmrodorion*, 13 (2007), 107–33.

12 The *Western Mail*, 23 July 1909, had a front-page advertisement which specifically named Percy Ruse and other rugby players but made no mention of the role of elite individuals such as the marchioness of Bute or the Lord Mayor of Cardiff.

13 Edwards, *National Pageant*, p. ix.

14 G. P. Hawtrey and 'Owen Rhoscomyl', *Book of Words* (Cardiff: Western Mail, 1909), preface.

15 Hawtrey and 'Rhoscomyl', *Book of Words*, pp. 30–1.

16 See chapter 5.

17 *Western Mail*, 27 July 1909, p. 3. There was also a photograph of the scene which included Nest in a pamphlet published by the official photographer of the pageant; C. Corn, *Pageant Pictorial* (Cardiff: E. Rees, 1909), p. 7.

18 Hawtrey and 'Rhoscomyl', *Book of Words*, pp. 33–4. Edwards, *National Pageant*, p. 131.

19 Hawtrey and 'Rhoscomyl', *Book of Words*, 'Scene 3', 'Nest daughter of Rhys ap Tudor', pp. 30–1, 'Gwenllian and the Avengers', pp. 33–4; Edwards, *National Pageant*, pp. 130–1.

20 http://www.princessgwenllian.co.uk/tpgscg.htm. For Byron Rogers's interest in the topic, see *The Lost Children* (Tregynon, Newtown, Powys: Gwasg Gregynog, 2005); *Me: The Authorised Biography* (London: Aurum Press, 2009), p. 269 (Rogers's daughter, Bethan Gwenllian).

21 'Our lost princess . . .', *The Leader* (15 September 2009), pp. 27–8, profiled under the section 'Way back when' which is a 'trip into our past every Tuesday'.

22 http://www.castlewales.com/gwen.html. At http://www.castlewales.com/pen.html.

23 For a modern discussion of this, see Neil Evans, '"When men and mountains meet": historians' explanations of the history of Wales, 1890–1970', *WHR*, 22 (2004), 221–51, at pp. 222–6, and for discussion see pp. 183–4n.109 above. For a recent restatement of similar themes in the early medieval European context, see C. Wickham, 'Medieval Wales and European history', *WHR*, 25 (2010), 201–8, which restates an accepted view that the mountains of Wales caused political fragmentation, at p. 204.

24 Edwards, *Short History of Wales*; Katie Gramich, *Women's Writing in Wales: Land, Gender, Belonging* (Cardiff: University of Wales Press, 2007), p. 149; for an early twentieth-century example of this view of the importance of geography see the opening remarks of O. M. Edwards, *A Short History of Wales* (London: T. Fisher Unwin, 1906), p. 1.

25 Arjun Appadurai, 'Disjuncture and difference in the global cultural economy', in Jane Evans Braziel and Anita Mannur (eds), *Theorising Diaspora: A Reader* (Oxford: Blackwell, 2003), pp. 29–48, at p. 31; see also *idem*, *Modernity at Large: Cultural Dimensions of Globalization* (Minneapolis: University of Minnesota Press, 1996), for more explanation of ethnoscapes.

26 Anthony D. Smith, *Myths and Memories of the Nation* (Oxford and New York: Oxford University Press, 1999).

27 A spokesperson for the Ordnance Survey stated, 'As agreement has been reached, we are delighted to reflect the name change and to be playing a role in reuniting Princess Gwenllian with her father, mother and uncle among the mountain peaks of her homeland.' The agreement to change the mountain's name was after consultation with the National Trust and Snowdonia National Park. Reported on the BBC Wales news web page 28 September 2009.

28 Hywel Wyn Owen and Richard Morgan, *Dictionary of the Place-names of Wales* (Llandysul: Gomer, 2007), pp. 72–3.

29 http://www.snowdonia-active.com/news.asp?newsid=670; http://www.grough.co.uk/magazine/2009/09/22/welsh-peak-will-bear-name-of-lost-princess.

30 Byron Rogers, 'Dateline, November 11th 1283 "The lost children"', *The Guardian*, 27 July 1991, p. 20.

31 See above, p. 105.

32 See above, pp. 62–4.

33 See above, pp. 156, 165–6.

34 R. W. Thompson, *An Englishman Looks at Wales* (Bristol: Arrowsmith, 1937), p. 58.

35 Roger Dobson, 'Is this Welsh princess the first British woman author?', *The Independent*, 11 January 1997; http://www.independent.co.uk/news/is-this-welsh-princess-the-first-british-woman-author-1282555.html. See chapter 1, pp. 26–8.

36 http://www.kidwelly.gov.uk/kidwelly-history.html.

37 See chapter 2 pp. 50–1 for further discussion.

38 Mrs Rodolph Stawell, *Motor Tours in Wales and the Border Counties* (London: Hodder and Stoughton, 1908), pp. 201–2.

39 H. V. Morton, *In Search of Wales* (London: Methuen, 1932), pp. 28–30. The story appears on Wikipedia; see also http://uk.ask.com/wiki/Eglwyseg, which is very similar to the Wikipedia version, as well as other sites such as ancientsites.com at http://www.ancientsites.com/aw/Places/Property/1211757.

40 Morton, *In Search of Wales*, pp. 29–30.

41 C. R. Perry, 'Morton, Henry Canova Vollam (1892–1979)', *ODNB*.

42 Perry, 'Morton'.

43 Bernard Schweizer, *Radicals on the Road: The Politics of English Travel Writing in the 1930s* (Charlottesville and London: University Press of Virginia, 2001).

44 There has been some historical debate about Wales in the interwar period, see Kenneth O. Morgan, *Rebirth of a Nation: Wales 1880–1980* (Oxford and Cardiff: Clarendon Press and University of Wales Press, 1981), pp. 220–40, which argues that Wales was devastated by the effects of the Depression; Gwyn A. Williams, *When was Wales? A History of the Welsh* (Harmondsworth: Penguin, 1985), p. 86, also stresses the economic and social dislocations of the period, at pp. 252–3; while Steven Thompson's *Unemployment, Poverty and Health in Interwar South Wales* (Cardiff: University of Wales Press, 2006), for example, posits a more complex view.

45 Howard Knox-Mawer, 'The house at World's End', *Country Quest*, 27 (1986), 28–9; David Crane, *Walks through the History of Rural Llangollen* (Wrexham: Bridge Books, 2000), p. 27.

46 Morton, *In Search of Wales*, pp. 28–30. The story appears on Wikipedia; see also http://uk.ask.com/wiki/Eglwyseg, which is very similar to the Wikipedia version, as well as other sites such as ancientsites.com at http://www.ancientsites.com/aw/Places/Property/1211757.

47 A. B., 'Notes on the antiquities and etymology of Eglwyseg, Denbighshire', *Archaeologia Cambrensis* (1865), 133–6; *idem*, 'Additional notes on Eglwyseg', *Archaeologia Cambrensis* (1865), 369–70.

48 Pyrs Gruffudd, David T. Herbert and Angela Piccini, 'In search of Wales: travel writing and narratives of difference, 1918–50', *Journal of Historical Geography*, 26 (2000), 589–604, at pp. 599–601.

49 http://www.pembrokeshirecoast.org.uk/default.asp?PID=306; http://www.pembroke shirecoast.org.uk/default.asp?PID=262.

50 Pembrokeshire Coast National Park with acknowledgement to the Department of Archaeology, University of Wales Lampeter, *Carew Castle: Souvenir* Guide (Pembrokeshire Coast National Park, n.d.); http://www.pembrokeshirecoast.org.uk/default.asp?PID=353; it at one time had fun activities for children including one where Nest appeared in a 'who am I' game, as allegedly the mother of twenty-one children.

51 John B. Hilling, *Cilgerran Castle, St Dogmaels Abbey, Pentre Ifan Burial Chamber* (Cardiff: Cadw – Welsh Historic Monuments, 1992; new edn 2000), p. 4.

52 http://www.nationaltrust.org.uk/main/w-cilgerrancastle; http://www.cadw.wales.gov.uk/default.asp?id=6&PlaceID=53.

53 http://www.britainexpress.com/attractions.htm?attraction=455: 'It is thought to have been the home, in the early 1100's, of Nest, the "Helen of Wales", who arranged to be kidnapped by her cousin Owain, who had fallen in love with her.'

54 http://www.castlewales.com/carew.html.

55 http://www.castlewales.com/nest.html.

56 British Library, Add. MS 10292, fo. 96r. This manuscript forms part of three bound volumes of the Grail cycle of which MS 10292 is the first volume; see British Library, Add. MSS 10292–4.

57 K. L. Maund, *Princess Nest of Wales: Seductress of the English* (Stroud: Tempus, 2007); Hilling, *Cilgerran Castle*, p. 4; Pembrokeshire Coast National Park, *Carew Castle*, p. 4.

58 Neil Ludlow, *Pembroke Castle: Birthplace of Henry Tudor* (Pembroke Castle Trust, n.d.), pp. 3–5.

59 Robert Eyres Landor, *The Earl of Brecon: A Tragedy in Five Acts; Faith's Fraud: A Tragedy in Five Acts; The Ferryman: A Drama in Five Acts* (London: Saunder's and Otley, 1841).

60 Glyn Jones, 'Gerald's wife', in *The Collected Poems of Glyn Jones*, ed. Meic Stephens (Cardiff: University of Wales Press, 1996), p. 168.

61 Glyn Jones, 'The death of Prince Gronw', in *The Collected Poems of Glyn Jones*, ed. Stephens, p. 169.

62 Geraint Dyfnallt Owen, *Nest* (London: W. Griffiths a'i Frodyr, 1949); *idem*, *Dyddiau'r Gofid: Yr ail I Nest* [*Days of Anxiety: Nest, the second volume*] (London: W. Griffiths a'i Frodyr, 1950).

63 Gwilym Huws, 'Welsh language publishing 1919 to 1995', in Philip Henry Jones and Eiluned Rees (eds), *A Nation and its Books: A History of the Book in Wales* (Aberystwyth: National Library of Wales, 1998), pp. 341–53, at p. 341.

64 Geraint Dyfnallt Owen, 'Review of *The Golden Hive*', *WHR*, 3 (1966–67), 321–2.

65 Bernard Knight, *Lion Rampant: The Story of Owain and Nest* (London: Hale, 1972); Margaret Orford, *The Royal Mistress* (Swansea: Davies, 1976); Anne Bell, *Daughter of the Dragon* (London: Hale, 1978); Margaret Mackinley, *The Pawns of Kings* (London: Hale, 1981).

66 Bryan Alderson, *Nest: A Novel Based on the Life of the Twelfth Century Welsh Princes* (Haverfordwest: Hedgehog Publications, 2004); Carole Jacobs, 'Journey-coat: a collection of poems inspired by Nest, Princess of Deheubarth, in eleventh-century west Wales' (unpubl. MA thesis, University of Wales, Trinity College, 2005).

67 Olwen Davis, 'Princess Nest, the Helen of Wales', *Country Quest* (2007), 32–3; Gwenllian Meredith, 'Princess Nesta ferch Rhys ap Tewdwr of Deheubarth', *Cambria* (2009), 31–3.

68 Deborah C. Fisher, *Princesses of Wales* (Cardiff: University of Wales Press, 2005).

69 Maund, *Princess Nest of Wales*.

7

Constructing beauty, constructing gender

THE IDEA OF Nest as a great beauty has been central to her story in the modern historiography of Wales, and is based on readings and interpretations of *Brut y Tywysogion*. J. E. Lloyd followed Edward Laws's interpretation of Nest as a great beauty in the mould of Helen of Troy.[1] Lloyd's romantic view of the abduction was placed into a political context, and the reference to Homer in Lloyd's *History* saw the event in terms of a heroic and epic tragedy for Wales.[2] More recent scholars have accepted this interpretation of Nest; for example, Gwyn Williams also called her the 'Helen of Wales' in his popular and well-received *When Was Wales?*, as did Brynley Roberts in his survey of Gerald of Wales.[3] Nest's beauty is a central motif in all interpretations of her and is key to the construction of her as the 'Welsh Helen'. Her beauty is emphasised in other genres, such as modern popular interpretations of her in creative fiction. Her inscription as a great beauty is a result of interpretations of the *Brut*, and her beauty authorises the actions of Owain ap Cadwgan's abduction. The following discussion will consider the importance of beauty in selected texts to consider how it was portrayed and its meanings and to analyse how it was used by authors to authorise agency and power.

As I have argued elsewhere, it is generally agreed that the concept of beauty encompassed a complex array of cultural meanings which included ideas about authority and legitimacy.[4] There has been a scholarly discussion about the culturally specific meanings of beauty and its attributes, especially the importance of courtliness and aesthetics, as well as ideas about inner and outer qualities which were tied to ideas about the body derived from a classical writer on medical matters, Galen. It has been noted how specific attributes of beauty, such as flaxen hair, or milky skin, were derived from classical models, became associated with stereotypical descriptions and remained relatively unchanged throughout the middle ages.[5] Stephen Jaeger has shown that beauty as a construct in medieval texts denoted complex associations, which, when applied to the ruling elite, may be related to fitness for office. Further, ideas about proportionality, linked to ideas about proper conduct, were the product of the cathedral schools in the twelfth century and of humanist learning.[6] Descriptions of beauty which demonstrate the importance of the physical proportions of the body encapsulated Galenic ideals about outer physical proportion reflecting inner qualities. Eco has argued that inner qualities and exterior physical appearance were intrinsic to medieval notions of beauty, while Sarah Heller has suggested that beauty was rare and signified social exclusivity.[7] I have argued that such ideas influenced the content of the *Vita Griffini Filii Conani*, which contains descriptions of Gruffudd ap Cynan and his wife Angharad in a text that was composed shortly after the death of Gruffudd in 1137, probably under the patronage of his son Owain Gwynedd. These descriptions are unique examples of the description of a twelfth-century Welsh ruler and his queen/consort. The passage which describes Angharad is remarkable for the close focus on her personal physical and mental attributes and it shares features with the descriptions of Gruffudd. The descriptions have been more fully discussed elsewhere, but the key features of the descriptions of Gruffudd and Angharad are that they serve as models of courtly and royal conduct with a didactic purpose. Given this, the emphasis on exterior appearance as a manifestation of inner qualities serves to illuminate the required and desired qualities in a ruler of Gwynedd and his wife. The following discussion will draw on these approaches and will place them into context by an analysis of contemporary texts, including Geoffrey of Monmouth's *Historia regum Britanniae* and Welsh poetry and literature. It will consider how aesthetics influenced texts and how genre played a role in the way that writers conceptualised beauty. Finally, it will consider whether the portrayal of Nest as a beauty in later texts is evidence of the way that gender has affected the evolution of ideas about nation and conquest in the historiography of Wales.

This discussion is set into an analytical context which takes account of the purpose of the text, the role of beauty as an authorising agent and genre. All of this is considered within a framework which considers how the construction of Nest as a great beauty in interpretations of the *Brut* conveyed social, political and ideological values. This in turn became an essential element of myth-making and romanticism in later interpretations of Nest.

The writings of Geoffrey of Monmouth are an important source for early twelfth-century views, given that Geoffrey's *History of the Kings of*

Britain (*de gestis Britonum*) was completed in the period 1123–39. It was a popular text in the middle ages: there are 217 extant manuscripts which contain versions of the text.[8] Scholars have debated the historical veracity of Geoffrey's writings, and in particular the sources upon which he relied; Geoffrey's assertion that he relied upon an 'old British book' which had been lost by his time has called into question his reliability. Nevertheless as a source for contemporary attitudes to a diverse range of issues, from the conduct of kings, war, politics and society to attitudes to women, Geoffrey is unusually rich and diverse.[9] It is instructive to consider the purpose of Geoffrey's choice of genre and the structure of his narrative. Laura Barefield has suggested that Geoffrey's narrative structure was reinforced by recourse to romance as part of a substructure which was intrinsically part of his overall narrative structure, which itself was founded on historiographical traditions. Further, Barefield suggests that Geoffrey experiments with narrative forms in the context of the uncertainties of succession given the political instability in the period after 1135 when the Empress Matilda contested the claim of her cousin Stephen of Boulogne to the throne of England.[10] Certainly the context of political uncertainty is key to understanding Geoffrey, and the positive image of women more generally is predicated on the contemporary political context. Valerie Flint suggested that Geoffrey's purpose was to parody the writings of monastic authors and that Geoffrey's text is secular in tone and content. Further, she argues that Geoffrey's positive portrayal of women, especially his portrayals of women such as Cordelia, the daughter of king Lear, and Marcia, an alleged female ruler of a kingdom whom Geoffrey suggests codified law, are derived from his knowledge of Welsh tradition.[11] Unfortunately this interesting suggestion is not developed in Flint's analysis, but it is certainly apposite here in the context of understanding contemporary attitudes to women such as Nest. Geoffrey's image of women is complex and deserves greater scrutiny than can be achieved here, but in understanding constructions of beauty in the twelfth century and its relationship to female power Geoffrey's views are instructive. Geoffrey draws on the typical twelfth-century stereotype of powerful women in familial contexts. Yet he also provides a snapshot of a beautiful woman in the brief pen portrait of Estrildis, the captured 'king's daughter from Germany' with whom Locrinus, the eldest son of Brutus, fell in love. Geoffrey tells us that she was captured along with two other 'girls of striking beauty' whom Locrinus 'kept for himself'. Yet Estrildis 'was so beautiful that it was difficult to find her like, neither Indian ivory, new fallen snow nor any lily could surpass her white skin'.[12] These images are complex, and although they draw on conventional stereotypical devices, they nevertheless contain a certain exoticism: his reference to Indian ivory suggests rarity, and purity is evoked in the references to fallen snow. Further, lilies were associated with the Virgin Mary and family lineage in contemporary aesthetics. Geoffrey's descriptions, while drawing on the familiar literary topos of white skin as an indication of beauty, thus contain a mix of allusions to moral qualities which are linked with the literary motifs. Estrildis's beauty caused political dispute, and Locrinus's passion was such that he wanted to become her 'lawful husband' and to 'share his bed with her'. This caused political dispute since he was already betrothed to the daughter of Corineus, Guendolena, whom he eventually married after her father put pressure on him and forced him to honour his previous agreement. Locrinus then kept Estrildis as a secret concubine for seven years, and she eventually gave birth to a daughter Habren. Both Habren and her mother were eventually drowned by Guendolena after the latter's repudiation by Locrinus and her defeat of him in battle. It is clear that family politics and lineage are central to Geoffrey's story, and the two women, bound by their relationship with Locrinus, are central to this. The cause of the dispute, however, is female beauty, which leads Locrinus to wish to marry a foreign captive princess (although she is not given this title by Geoffrey). The delicate political situation is resolved through concubinage and marriage. Marriage was central to the political process and the position of Guendolena depended upon the support of her natal family. Estrildis was a threat to her due to her beauty and the love that she inspired in Locrinus. The beauty of Estrildis is an explanatory motif in the text and the emotional charge of the episode is increased by her death at the hands of Guendolena. Female beauty as a cause of male desire which in turn has political implications is a key component of Geoffrey's depiction of the early settlement of Kent. As such, female beauty as a cause of male sexual response which triggers a political response and long-term damage to the trajectory of a kingdom's history is implicit in Geoffrey's portrayal of the early history of the Saxon arrival in Britain. It is the beauty of Rowena, the daughter of Hengist, a Saxon mercenary in the service of Vortigern, the ruler of Kent, which inspires the latter to fall in love with her at their first meeting. The setting for the meeting is a feast at the court of Hengist which Vortigern visits at Hengist's invitation in order to inspect Hengist's new fortress and the 'knights' that he has sent for from Germany to help Vortigern defeat the Britons. The setting for the fateful meeting follows a banquet, in which Rowena offers a cup of mead to Vortigern. Rowena is described as a woman 'cuius pulcritudo nulli secundur uidebatur', that is, whose 'beauty was unsurpassed'.[13] Geoffrey then states that Vortigern's judgement was impaired because he asked Hengist for Rowena so that he could have sex with her. Hengist noted the lack of judgement that this showed, consulted with his senior advisers, and a deal was struck. Vortigern gave away Kent in return for marriage to Rowena. From this stemmed a sequence of events which ultimately led to the 'Night of the Long Knives' whereby many Britons were killed by Saxons in a treacherous act at a gathering to discuss peace. Rowena is central to the narrative as a conduit of Saxon influence upon Vortigern, as a murderess of Vortimer, her stepson, and as a source of support for Vortigern's policy of utilising Saxon mercenaries and as a source of information for her father on the political situation in Britain when she sends him details about the difficulties faced by the Britons. Rowena then functions as a bridge between two cultures whose influence is damaging to the interests of the Britons, and whose political actions were dictated by her loyalty to her father. Thus the marriage to Rowena, based as it was upon the instant and inflamed sexual desire of Vortigern which was caused by her beauty, is suggestive of the malign effect of sexual desire and alcohol upon the mental capacity of Vortigern. His lapse of judgement resulted in a marriage which inaugurated an inexorable chain of events leading to the defeat of the Britons. Female beauty is thus a potent source of instability in the origin-myth of the English encapsulated by the tale of Rowena. At the heart of Geoffrey's narrative about the matter of Britain was a clear message about political instability which arose in Britain due to Vortigern's inflamed desires in response to female beauty.

The complexities of the political narrative in Geoffrey's work creatively filled in gaps in his sources.[14] His origin-myth of Britain shows how almost from the beginning of the Saxon invasions women were involved as causes of political instability. The dangers of marital strife and the vulnerability of concubines and their offspring are made abundantly clear in Geoffrey's narrative. Love and beauty are deployed as explanatory motifs to explain concubinage and this is related to political instability. Francis Ingledew has argued that Geoffrey eroticises history and that this goes beyond the classical approach of erotics as deployed by Virgil, since eros is admitted into the 'fabric of normative history as a productive, if anxious force'.[15] Erotic motifs galvanise action, but their effect is not always positive. These have clear parallels in the way that the abduction tale of Nest is conceptualised and portrayed. Her abduction is eroticised in interpretations of the *Brut*, which saw Owain motivated by love and passion for her, and this destabilised south-west Wales.

The writers of the *Brut* designed it as a continuation of Geoffrey of Monmouth's work.[16] The literary models deployed, and the diversionary narrative structure with the use of romance sub-narratives, in Geoffrey of Monmouth's work are models of how fluidity in genre was a way of encapsulating uncertainty, or expressing concerns about the core political narrative. By utilising motifs and incorporating different narrative structures, the core narrative has an elasticity which facilitates the expansion of core themes within an overarching narrative frame. Thus, for example, Geoffrey incorporates the story of Guendolena and Estrildis into his tale of Britain and elucidates themes which deal with socio-cultural issues. In this example the female victim of male passion was imprisoned and eventually murdered by the wife of her captor; it is not only a brutal image of the precarious position of concubines, but also shows how such sexual relationships were political dynamite. If John Gillingham's view that Geoffrey's purpose was that of cultural nationalism is accepted,[17] then that cultural nationalism was one which saw sexual politics as a driving force in conquest. This context of understanding the text in terms of political context and genre is a fruitful way to consider how the abduction is written in the *Brut*. Nest's abduction too caused massive dislocation in south-west Wales. To facilitate discussion of this, the *Brut* also deploys a diversionary narrative structure within its overarching themes of the loss of Britain and Welsh polities. The abduction episode functions to facilitate comment on the politics of south-west Wales and its impact on the Welsh political diaspora more generally as well as generating a narrative about the resistance of the Powysian dynasty to the Normans through a focus upon Owain ap Cadwgan, but it also comments on Welsh disunity caused through generational conflict.

The *Brut* portrays Nest as a sovereign princess, whereby she conveys legitimacy to, first, her Anglo-Norman husband and, then, by stealth, to her abductor. If we see Nest in this way the retribution in south-west Wales by the Normans is also symbolic of cultural tensions between old and new orders. This creates tension because if Nest is a symbol of the old order as represented by her father Rhys of Deheubarth, she is representative of a sovereign princess at the mercy of a war leader who seized the political initiative from the Normans through control of Nest's body. The whole episode becomes a seismic cultural battle for legitimacy – Owain represents a warlord, Nest stands as a conveyor of legitimacy, and Henry I and the Anglo-Norman realms represent intrusion and lordship. In retrospect the compilers see the abduction as a pivotal moment, but it has been cast in romantic terms because commentators have misunderstood the symbolism of Nest and the literary models used to convey subtle messages. She is not described as beautiful directly because this is not a romantic episode. It is a moment of change and conquest – and Owain challenges the status quo: it is portrayed as a warning that Henry I and Anglo-Normans will not tolerate challenges. Once again local lordship, the power to effect control, is key, and the genre-shift and episodic nature of the *Brut* facilitate a textual space which allows these anxieties to be represented through an episode which was erotically charged. In this aspect it defines Owain by his lack of control and his hot-headed impulsive nature, and it locates male sexual energy when it intersects with politics as an agent of dramatic force. It is gendered since Owain is inscripted as the dynamic agent of change, and Nest as the passive woman who is acted upon, but who nevertheless exerts agency in her role as a wife and mother but who loses her position. The interpretation of this as a romantically charged, or erotically charged, narrative is related to the way that the episode is framed. Nest's entry into the political narrative is signalled by recourse to poetical declamation at one remove from the reader/listener of the text. We are told that Owain 'heard that Nest, daughter of the lord Rhys ap Tewdwr, wife of Gerald the Officer, was in the said castle' (Cenarth Bychan). We are told only of Owain's love and passion for Nest. The abduction is an episode which deviates from the narrative of the *Brut*, and the diversionary nature of the narrative represents a fluidity in the genre which facilitates comment on the trajectory of Welsh history.

As such, the descriptions of Nest's actions serve as signs of her personal qualities, and may well have encapsulated ideas about the link between exterior beauty and inner qualities. It can be argued that the concept of beauty itself was complex and contained moral judgements and values. Beauty, when placed into a critical context, is more than a simple descriptor in a text, it is a moral motif which underpinned an array of ideas and images which serve to show how personal feeling was intertwined with political response, or, in other words, the personal was political and there was no sense of the boudoir as divorced from political processes. Since beauty as a concept contained ideas which were more than physical attributes, it also conveyed a mix of other qualities. Thus, even the idea of beauty, an attribute which has to be viewed and appreciated by others, is public. Beauty, and the appreciation of it, is thus a public act, and Owain's response to Nest is public, but scholars have presumed that Nest was a great beauty and in so doing they have constructed a concept of beauty within the text which undermines any model of public/private spheres of influence.

In order to examine the above proposition and to clarify the ways that the concept of beauty was understood in Wales, we can consider notions of beauty in a text which is a close contemporary to the 1109 raid. The *Life of Gruffudd ap Cynan* was until recently only thought to have survived in fragments of a Middle Welsh translation (in Peniarth MS 17) of the thirteenth century. Paul Russell has, however, reconstructed the lost twelfth-century Latin original on the basis of the sixteenth-century Latin text in Peniarth MS 434; his convincing argument therefore allows us to treat his text as at least closely allied to one created by a near contemporary of the events of 1109.[18] It has been suggested that the *Life* was written in the period 1137–70 when links between Gwynedd and Deheubarth were closest, Russell proposing an even more precise date of 1137x48 on account of the support expressed for the ambitions of Bishop Bernard of St David's.[19] It was thus composed after Gruffudd's death in 1137, stresses the legitimacy of his rule, and was possibly written to defend his position against allegations of usurpation. Gruffudd had fought his way to become ruler of Gwynedd against aggressive Norman incursions into north Wales. It was written at a pivotal moment in Welsh history when the fortunes of Powys were in the ascendant and Gwynedd faced a resurgent force on its southern borders. The *Life* is a Welsh view of rulership and it is therefore an important source for the study of twelfth-century Welsh political, social and cultural values. Scholars have explored the source from a number of perspectives, including, for example, the audiences for the work, the importance of Hiberno-Norse influences demonstrated in the text, and the role of genealogy.[20] As such the *Life* provides an unparalleled contemporary view of Wales from a Welsh perspective, and is thus a useful contextual source for views of women in twelfth-century Wales. It contains passages descriptive of both Gruffudd ap Cynan and his wife Angharad, who serve as idealised models of a mid-twelfth-century ruler and his wife. We can therefore evaluate the conception of beauty as applied to the Welsh nobility, a conception which may be representative of ideas of beauty as applied to Nest, who was after all a near contemporary of Gruffudd.

The *Vita*, through its focus upon Gruffudd's illustrious ancestry, professed his claim to legitimacy.[21] The *Vita* stresses the importance of both the maternal and paternal ancestral genealogy. Lineage was essential to any would-be claimant to a kingdom.[22] His ancestry is traced through the paternal line to God, whilst his matrilineal descent is traced to the Danish dynasty as far as Olar, son of Haafgar of Denmark. His genealogy was carefully constructed to stress the superiority of Gruffudd's kinship links with Scandinavian and Irish kings as compared to the pedigrees of other Welsh kings as well as those of the Normans.[23] The patrilineal genealogy is traced in a traditional way, each son listed as son of his father, in a continuous line from Adam, son of God. It is also intrinsically part of the historical narrative structure commonly used by chroniclers who included details of genealogy as a way of stressing the status and claims of individuals. This is part of the function of the text: genealogy is part of a narrative structure which underpins the cohesion of patriarchal society. Genealogy reinforces a sense of continuity, and the inclusion of the maternal genealogy is indicative that at the time of composition the maternal pedigree was considered an important part of Gruffudd's claim. It also draws attention to the wider Irish Sea world and Scandinavian influence. As part of his strategy to secure the kingdom of Gwynedd, Gruffudd married Angharad, with her important connections in north-east Wales, while he was being 'tossed about by the variable waves of fate'.[24] His marriage was thus achieved against an unstable background and was an important tool for the symbolic expression of political stability. It is worthy of note that marriage was considered to be the point at which a *juvenes* became a senior. That is, it is a significant part of the male life-cycle and is a device in contemporary sources to signal maturity and stability and responsibility.[25] The *Life of Gruffudd ap Cynan* draws upon the ideas of contemporary cathedral schools and aesthetics to create an image of a modern, European model of rulership. The author drew upon earlier models from antiquity to inform the narrative. The model of Gruffudd and Angharad as king and his queen indicates that contemporary ideals of good rulership incorporated ideas about physical appearance and appropriate behaviour. It was linked to the purpose of the text which served to legitimise Gruffudd's claim; as such a good marriage indicated stability at the heart of the ruling dynasty in the kingdom. Aesthetics inform this image: beauty, with its sense of fitness for office, is an important element in the construction of good rulership which evokes male response but which is far more than a physical description in texts which have an ideological purpose. The legitimation of male strategies is at the heart of the *Life of Gruffudd ap Cynan* and it served as a remembrance for his dynasty. Gruffudd in some ways fulfils a model derived from antiquity. He is an exile who wanders, returns as a conqueror hero, founds a dynasty and fulfils a divine plan.[26] The importance of fate, or divine intervention, is indicated by a passage which shows how prophecy had predicted his return, and the agent for the prophetic discourse is a woman. The biography shows how Gruffudd was born in exile, in Ireland, and his mother 'would often recount to him what kind of man his father had been, and how great he had been, how rich his realm, and how famous a kingdom was owed to him, and also how a cruel tyrant now held it'. The *Life* tells us that this upset Gruffudd and that he 'would often turn these things over sadly in his mind'.[27] Gruffudd spent his youth at his mother's home and with his relatives, and thus it was his mother who transmitted and maintained the memory of the importance of his dynasty and kingdom. Once Gruffudd had the support he needed from the Irish to reclaim his kingdom he sailed to Abermenai and had secret talks with the men of Anglesey. At some point he was visited by a 'wise woman Tangwystl' 'his kinswoman and wife of Llywarch Olbiwch, to greet him and by a certain omen that the kingdom would be his'. Tangwystl then gave him a 'very fine shirt, the best she had, and which had once belonged to Gruffudd, son of Llewelyn, son of Seisyll, who had once been king'.[28] We are told that her husband had once been in control of the treasury for Gruffudd ap Llewelyn. Thus Tangwystl was a political actor at the inception of Gruffudd's bid to claim Gwynedd. She served to articulate a prediction of his success, and enacted the transferral of the political allegiance of her husband when she transferred the shirt, an act which must surely have been deeply symbolic. Gruffudd's mother memorialised Gruffudd's dynastic role and articulated his dynastic past and future claims. Both women articulate such claims; they not only transmit the idea of political power, the text recognises their pivotal roles. They served to memorialise and practically transfer power to Gruffudd. Geoffrey of Monmouth dealt with the matter of Britain, the author of the *Life* dealt with the matter of a dynasty. Both texts articulate the ways in which women were involved in the political processes which cause a response by the male protagonists.

Gwyn Williams argued that the poets were 'the remembrancers of the people': the bardic structures and poetry were complex, traditional and architectural in style, and their main foci were 'praise, morality, exhortation and legitimation'.[29] The twelfth century was the age of the poets of the princes, and during the twelfth and thirteenth centuries the court poets wrote praise poetry for their patrons, the Welsh military elite. Their poetry was composed within strict conventions. Praise poetry took different forms: the eulogy praised the Welsh ruler's life and the elegy praised him after his death.

J. P. Clancy, referring to Nest as 'a notoriously beautiful woman of the early twelfth century, who was the daughter of Rhys ap Tewdwr, the mistress of Henry I, and the wife of Gerald of Windsor, and was abducted by Owain ap Cadwgan, a prince of Powys', suggests she is alluded to in a love poem by Llywarch ap Llywelyn (*fl.* 1173–1220) for a certain

Gwenllian, probably the daughter of Hywel ap Iorwerth of Caerleon. The poet states that 'Nest spoke to me, nothing will come of it.' The poem is in a tradition first exemplified in Gwynedd by the work of Hywel ab Owain Gwynedd (c. 1140–70), 'In praise of fair women' – which also mentions a Nest. Hywel was the illegitimate son of Owain Gwynedd; his mother, Pyfog, was Irish. Clancy argues that it was Hywel who was the chief architect of a new genre of poetry, that of love poetry.[30] It is important that, as Clancy notes, Hywel was able to go beyond the bounds of conventional bardic compositional techniques because of his princely status. This is significant because it suggests that Welsh bardic techniques ossified genres and thus later poetry contains elements of earlier traditions. The innovation offered here, that of Welsh bardic poetry beginning to create love poetry, reflects the general trend towards such a genre within European literary culture.[31] Whether or not Welsh bardic poetry was open to European influence, what this poem suggests for our purposes is that the association of the name Nest with a reputation for great beauty is possibly evident within the extant examples of the first stirrings of love poetry in Wales by the late twelfth century. The work of Hywel, a poet from north Wales whose leaders had defeated Nest's son in battle at Tal Moelfre in 1157, suggests that a bard who could be expected to declaim any virtues in the leaders of the southern kingdoms could nevertheless recognise the model of beauty that Nest provided. While both he and Llywarch ap Llywelyn in their poems were probably referring more immediately to different women by the name of Nest, this is tenuous, but tantalising, evidence of the way the name could perhaps already suggest a model of beauty.[32]

Hywel's Nest is not alone, however. The poem is after all in praise of fair women, and thus gives us a view of the values ascribed to such an epithet. The women, the poet tells us, from north to south Wales 'rule my wordcraft'. There are nine women named, each with their own specific characteristic. Thus we have Gwenllian 'whose praise will come first, summer's glow', and 'Fair Gweirfyl', 'graceful Gwladus, shy girlish bride, The hope of her people'. Then, with 'Bright Lleucu, my darling, laughing', the praise contains within it a threatening note: she is praised 'for lust's sake' but with 'my sword in my hand', and there is a dark warning to her partner: 'Her mate will not laugh when hard-pressed.' Nest is praised in a stanza which emphasises the emotional pain associated with desire:

Great stress that concerns me besets me
And longing, alas that goes with it
For Nest, fair as an apple-blossom
For Perweur, centre of my sin,

Other women are mentioned in turn in the same stanza: the 'pure Generys, who cured not my lust'; Hunydd, for whom Hywel expresses 'concern till doomsday', and lastly Hawis, who was his 'choice for courtship'.

In the last stanza Hywel boasts a catalogue of sexual conquests, and each line of the poem gives us some indication of his attitude to the unnamed conquest. Thus the first line begins 'I had a girl who concurred one day, next; I had two the more is their praise'; his third and fourth conquests were had by 'good fortune'. He states 'I had five of them, fair their white flesh'. Further, he boasts, 'I had six with no shying from sin' – this was a girl from 'a bright white fort' – and his seventh was due to 'earnest effort'. His boast concludes:

> I had eight as reward, prize for praise I sang –
> Best for teeth to guard tongue!

It is possible that the final stanza may refer obliquely to the named women in the previous verses. This impression is strengthened by the way that the praise in the last verse seems to echo that of the previous stanzas. For example, if we consider the references to Nest, she is first called 'fair as an apple-blossom' and is thus the fifth conquest. In the last verse she is perhaps referenced in the words 'I had five of them, fair their white flesh'. The references to Perweur are more obvious. Perweur is first mentioned as the 'centre of my sin' and so likely to be referenced in the line 'I had six with no shying from sin'. The seventh named is Generys, who failed to cure Hywel's lust; in the last verse he writes: 'I had seven, with earnest effort'. When he first mentioned Hunydd he expressed concern for her, the eighth was 'as reward'. It is intriguing then that he silences himself: Hawis is possibly not referenced in the last verse because she was his 'choice' for courtship. The way that the last verse is written could suggest a conflation of attributes blended and attributed to all the women, yet the verse is cleverly constructed within a self-referencing system. This is derived from the progressive structure of Welsh bardic poetry, and is typical of 'lyric poetry', that is, poetry which uses language to express thoughts and feelings of an author in a single situation. Lyrics progress with a radial structure, and there is thus a circularity within early Welsh poetry by which the central themes are revisited and reinforced.[33] Scholars notably attribute these features to earlier poetry of the ninth century, for example as evidenced in *The Gododdin*, which was probably composed about 850 and is concerned with struggles for power in the sixth and seventh centuries.[34] Further, it is accepted that Welsh bards were aware of the influences of troubadour poetry in the twelfth century. Hywel suggests that the traditions of bardic composition were open to the European influence. Hywel was a prince, as the son of Owain Gwynedd, and so his poetry is representative of the views of the secular elite. It is evident that classical awareness affected literary forms in Wales – for example, literary heroes were alluded to in poetry and *Brut y Tywysogion* – although the extent of this influence is hard to judge; certainly it is unclear whether individuals had direct knowledge of specific Latin texts.[35]

This concern with love poetry was not without precedents in Welsh literature. A contemporary of Hywel, the poet Gwalchmai (*fl.* 1130–80), who wrote poems in praise of Hywel's father Owain Gwynedd, was concerned with love, nature and war. His work has been considered to parallel the work not of Anglo-Norman writers, but that of later twelfth-century Provençal poets.[36] The congruence between the thematic linkage of the poetical traditions of two areas, Wales and southern France, places the emergence of love poetry within Wales in a European context. Female beauty is referenced within the work of Gwalchmai: he states that he would not shun strife 'in spite of pain' and that he loved 'a white-cheeked girl's tender glances'.[37]

This twelfth-century poetry conveys a rich mixture of contrasted images of sexual energy and gentle, caring sentiments with the explosive and dynamic images of war within the poetry. As such the emotions conveyed by the poets suggest strong passions juxtaposed with sensitive passages, which draw on stereotypical images of female beauty, for example the references to white skin. Sometimes the observation is acute. For example, in a love poem by Cynddelw Brydd Mawr (*fl.* 1155–1200) for one Efa, he describes her as having 'Hue of snow glowing on Epynt's shores'; she is a 'gold-mantled maid', 'courtly her form in cloak of gold'. She is an 'eloquent princess' and the poet tells us 'He has not seen beauty who has not seen her.' She is wealthy and her jewellery too is impressive: 'beneath a red gem, a red-gold ring'.[38] The poet shows that his admiration for the appearance of Efa includes an awareness of her impressive attire which is of course indicative of her high social status and symptomatic of the appreciation and the importance of exterior appearance in courtly culture.

The importance of appearance and social status in contemporary ideas about beauty can be seen in other literary forms, most notably the tales of the *Mabinogi*. The tale 'How Culhwch won Olwen' is particularly important for the emergence of ideas about beauty in the high middle ages because it is generally agreed that this is one of the earliest tales and contains elements from the eleventh century within it. The tale has been considered by literary scholars interested in many features, but for our purposes the portrayal of female beauty is significant. The tale is principally concerned with the adventures of Culhwch, Arthur's cousin, and how he sought and received the help of Arthur's war-band to perform impossible tasks set by Olwen's father Ysbaddaden Bencawr. The tale contains a lyrical description of Olwen's beauty, yet the trials undertaken by Culhwch are the main focus of the narrative. For our purposes this early literary model of female beauty then conforms to the medieval stereotypical norm as described by Brewer and noted by other commentators.[39] Culhwch's destiny is set by his step-mother who tells him that 'Your side shall never strike against a woman until you get Olwen daughter of Ysbaddaden Bencawr.'[40] Eventually Culhwch meets Olwen. The poem changes rhythm and metre at the point where a lyrical description of her beauty is given. She is described as wearing a 'robe of flame-red silk', a red-gold torque around her neck. Her hair was 'yellower than the flowers of the broom', her skin was whiter than 'the foam of the wave' and her breasts were 'whiter than the breast of a white swan', while her cheeks were 'redder than ... the reddest foxglove'. The association of female beauty with natural images, especially the association of the skin with sea imagery and wild birds such as swans, was also utilised by later poets.

This places Welsh poetry in its contemporary European context, but also provides key insights into many ideas including those about beauty as well as about love and sexual conquest. The women who are objects of praise and desire are mostly obscure. An exception to this is an elegy composed for Nest ferch Hywel. It is the only extant elegy written about a woman. It reveals a complex and intriguing insight into the qualities for which secular noblewomen were praised. The elegy was composed by Einion ap Gwalchmai, who wrote poems in praise of the dynasties of Gwynedd and Powys. The elegy praises Nest for her beauty, eloquence, wit and charm. Laura Radiker has explored the significance of the poem in detail and usefully deconstructs the poem in terms of its bardic technique and provenance to show that the qualities which were valued included a sense of appropriate sexual conduct. Radiker has discussed the poem in terms of understanding contemporary attitudes to secular unmarried noblewomen and she argues that the poem has an emphasis on physical appearance as well as qualities such as youthfulness, beauty and eloquence.[41] In his poetry the poet Cynddelw reveals the attributes for which women were praised: one anonymous girl was a 'dear, high-spirited girl' and the poet images her pale skin by reference to the 'glowing hue of waves'. In 'A love poem for Efa' Cynddelw talks of her pale skin and her deportment: he describes Efa's white skin, imaged as a 'twin of foam on wind-ruffled water', with a 'hue of snow', and she is 'sprightly', 'courtly', with 'a tall form', a 'modest, sagacious, fair-skinned beauty' and eloquent. She is the 'slim girl who will not come to me' and is innocent, 'quiet her conversing' and 'mild-mannered'.[42] Such characteristics are commonplace in medieval writings on women generally, but for our purposes in understanding the Welsh context for such poetry, they show that in this respect the poem places Wales in the mainstream of the trajectory of European influences. The elegy to Nest ferch Hywel serves as a model of perfect maidenhood, as Radiker suggests. The emphasis on comportment within the poem is part of the attributes for which she is praised, and composure and demeanour were important elements in the construction of beauty.

Poets also draw attention to the way that women speak. Hywel ab Owain Gwynedd, for example, praised his 'chosen one' since 'When she speaks' she voiced 'scarcely heard modest words' with 'pure-spoken Welsh part of your wealth'.[43] In the *Brut*, Nest's quick thinking which helped her husband to escape and her composure when she called out to her besiegers as portrayed in the *Brut*, is also suggestive of twelfth-century secular ideals which valued comportment and idealised behaviour.[44] Poets often utilise images which contain associations with light, or luminescence.[45] The idealised image presented in poetry then conforms to European norms when describing female beauty, but the poetical forms in which they are portrayed are representative of Welsh bardic compositional techniques.

The idea of beauty was a construct which had multiple associations in Welsh bardic poetry and was clearly linked with sexual conquest in the examples cited above. The poem is suggestive of contemporary European influences in the humanistic tradition on writers in Wales. This contrasts with the more formal descriptions of Angharad in the *Vita Griffini Filii Conani*, where the physical description of Gruffudd and his consort are associated with claims to legitimate rule. This portrayal of male and female beauty may well be charged with ideas about Gruffudd and Angharad as Welsh rulers and thus hold a particular ethnic resonance, but is, rather, suggestive of European ideas of manners and comportment. The *Vita Griffini Filii Conani* demonstrates that manners and comportment, education and physical appearance were critically important for constructing an image of appropriate rulership.

Finally, it has been suggested by Whetter that genre has an active role in generating a response from authors of texts and their audiences. Whetter suggests 'a genre can usefully be considered a contract creating criteria and expectations for writer and reader alike' and that although genres may have many features, including setting, pace, tone and so on, texts which violate genre may paradoxically reinforce them. Similarly genres are not static.[46] The abduction episode within the *Brut* is central to the construction of a narrative about native responses to outside incursions, which are imaged through Owain and Nest. The episode has been considered to have overtones of romance by Austin and Pollard, but it could be argued that here genre is blurred: the *Brut* is a chronicle which incorporates material that appears to cross genre boundaries, yet this merely shows that the sources upon which the compilers drew were diverse. If we consider Whetter's view it is arguable that the genre of the *Brut* as a chronicle is confirmed by the deviationary nature of the Nest narrative. It is a fuller, more detailed description of events than any earlier episodes, and the pace, tone and setting are varied, rich and evocative. As such the tale is almost a self-contained narrative within the larger chronicle, which may be suggestive of the variety of sources incorporated into the final form and also the mutability of the chronicle form. It suggests that the grand narrative of Wales which forms the bedrock of the *Brut* incorporated different sources and that the genre of chronicle writing itself was capable of development, but the inclusion of such tales did not undermine the essential aim of the *Brut*. It may well require elements of romance because Owain's actions are justified by his love and passion for Nest, but she is not described as a beauty; rather, the descriptions of her actions are explicable as key to forcing the pace of the narrative. She acts to save her husband, but also to secure the release of her children. Her composure is key to the escape of Gerald of Windsor and, given that deportment was an important element in contemporary expectations in the wife of a Welsh ruler, Nest's actions were symbolically powerful within the text as much as practically for what they achieved.

Female beauty as a cause of war of course had a long-standing model in classical literature in the figure of Helen of Troy, and this motif was taken up and used to explain political instability in European literature. Early modern interpretations of Nest cast her in a similar role: thus Humphrey Llwyd writing at the end of the sixteenth century saw her beauty as an integral element in the narrative.[47] Nest serves this function within the *Brutiau*, and, although her beauty is not explicitly stated in the text, the chronicler records that it was hearing of Nest's 'fame' as related by bards at the Christmas feast of Cadwgan, that inspired Owain to act. Nest has been interpreted as a great beauty because of this description. The indirect association with the literary convention of female beauty as a cause of war is localised to south-west Wales but this has a clear purpose. It is a key element in the portrayal of south-west Wales as the crucible of change and reaction following the Norman advances there. Later interpretations of Nest as a great beauty were derived from early modern sources. The importance of beauty as a concept in the twelfth century is that it was a key element in the articulation of ideas about power and its legitimacy: female beauty was a cause of instability in classical texts, and this was alluded to in the *Brutiau*, and reinterpreted later. Beauty as a motif was a complex idea in twelfth-century texts which encapsulated ideas about legitimacy and conduct and as such when deployed by authors was dependent on generic context for meaning. Beauty as a construct had specific purposes in texts which were dependent on socio-historical contexts as much as literary genre. Nest's beauty has functioned as a legitimating trope in narratives which are based on a static view of female beauty in a conception of medieval Wales which is both roman-ticised and sanitised. The tawdry aspects of the abduction as a possible rape have been written out of modern views of the abduction in favour of a rose-tinted nostalgic view of the past which is based on myths.

Notes

1 See chapter 5 for discussion, at pp. 172–4.

2 J. E. Lloyd, *A History of Wales from the Earliest Times to the Edwardian Conquest* (2 vols, London, 1911; 3rd edn, London: Longmans, Green, 1939), ii. 417–18.

3 Gwyn A. Williams, *When was Wales? A History of the Welsh* (Harmondsworth: Penguin, 1985), pp. 67–8; Brynley Roberts, *Gerald of Wales* (Cardiff: University of Wales Press on behalf of the Welsh Arts Council, 1982), p. 10.

4 S. M. Johns, 'Beauty and the feast: the cultural constructions of female beauty and social interaction in twelfth-century Wales', *Proceedings of the Harvard Celtic Colloquium* (2011), 1–14.

5 D. S. Brewer, 'The ideal of feminine beauty in medieval literature, especially "Harley lyrics"', Chaucer and some Elizabethans', *Modern Language Review*, 50 (1955), 257–69; Umberto Eco, *Art and Beauty in the Middle Ages* (New Haven and London: Yale University Press, 1986); Sarah-Grace Heller, 'Light as glamour: the luminescent ideal of beauty in the Roman de la Rose', *Speculum*, 76 (2001), 934–59; C. Stephen Jaeger, *The Envy of Angels: Cathedral Schools and Social ideals in Medieval Europe, 950–1200* (Philadelphia: University of Pennsylvania Press, 1994).

6 Jaeger, *Envy of Angels*, p. 325.

7 Eco, *Art and Beauty*, pp. 9–11; Heller, 'Light as glamour', p. 936.

8 Geoffrey of Monmouth, *The History of the Kings of Britain: An Edition and Translation of De Gestis Britonum (Historia regum Britanniae)*, Latin text ed. Michael D. Reeve, trans. Neil Wright (Woodbridge: Boydell Press, 2007), vii. (Hereafter *HRB*.)

9 There is much debate over Geoffrey's purpose; see Helen Fulton, 'History and myth: Geoffrey of Monmouth's *Historia Regum Britanniae*', in Helen Fulton (ed.), *A Companion to Arthurian Literature* (Blackwell companions to literature and culture, 58) (Oxford: Blackwell, 2009), 44–57; Martin Aurell, 'Geoffrey of Monmouth's *History*

of the Kings of Britain and the twelfth-century renaissance', *Haskins Society Journal*, 18 (2007 for 2006), 1–18; Paul Dalton, 'The topical concerns of Geoffrey of Monmouth's *Historia Regum Britannie*: History, prophecy, peacemaking, and English identity in the twelfth century', *Journal of British Studies*, 44 (2005), 688–712; John Gillingham, 'The context and purposes of Geoffrey of Monmouth's *History of the Kings of Britain*', *ANS*, 13 (1990), 99–118; J. C. Crick, *The Historia Regum Britannie of Geoffrey of Monmouth, 4: Dissemination and Reception in the Later Middle Ages* (Cambridge: D. S. Brewer, 1991); for a general overview see Karen Jankulak, *Geoffrey of Monmouth* (Cardiff: University of Wales Press, 2008).

10 Laura D. Barefield, *Gender and History in Medieval English Romance and Chronicle* (New York and Oxford: Peter Lang, 2003), p. 13.

11 Valerie Flint, 'The *Historia Regum Brittaniae* of Geoffrey of Monmouth: parody and its purpose: a suggestion', *Speculum*, 54 (1979), 447–68, at p. 464.

12 Geoffrey of Monmouth, *HRB*, book 2, lines 22–5, pp. 32–3.

13 Geoffrey of Monmouth, *HRB*, book 6, lines 22–5, p. 340.

14 William Leckie, *The Passage of Dominion: Geoffrey of Monmouth and the Periodization of Insular History in the Twelfth Century* (Toronto, Buffalo and London: University of Toronto Press, 1981), p. 42.

15 Francis Ingledew, 'The Book of Troy and the genealogical construction of history: the case of Geoffrey of Monmouth's *Historia regum Britanniae*', *Speculum*, 69 (1994), 665–704, at p. 680.

16 Although whether the author(s) of the putative original Latin annals/chronicle, composed in the early twelfth century, that underlie the lost Latin chronicle that was translated as the *Brut*, knew Geoffrey's work is less clear – and of course if the original account of Nest's abduction was written soon after the event, it must have been independent of him.

17 Gillingham, 'Context and purposes', p. 101.

18 *Vita Griffini Filii Conani: The Medieval Latin Life of Gruffudd ap Cynan*, ed. and trans. Paul Russell (Cardiff: University of Wales Press, 2005).

19 *Vita Griffini Filii Conani*, p. 46.

20 David Moore, 'Gruffudd ap Cynan and the medieval Welsh polity' in K. L. Maund (ed.), *Gruffudd ap Cynan: A Collaborative Biography* (Woodbridge: Boydell and Brewer, 1996), pp. 1–59.

21 David E. Thornton, 'The genealogy of Gruffudd ap Cynan', in Maund (ed.), *Gruffudd ap Cynan*, pp. 79–108; see also relevant discussion in T. M. Charles-Edwards, *Early Irish and Welsh Kinship* (Oxford: Clarendon Press, 1993), pp. 220–4.

22 Moore, 'Gruffudd ap Cynan', p. 5.

23 K. L. Maund, 'Gruffudd, grandson of Iago', in David Bates, Julia Crick and Sarah Hamilton (eds), *Writing Medieval Biography, 750–1250: Essays in Honour of Professor Frank Barlow* (Woodbridge: Boydell Press, 2006), pp. 109–16, at p. 113.

24 *Vita Griffini Filii Conani*, ch. 24, pp. 76–7.

25 For medieval marriage see D. L. D'Avray, *Medieval Marriage: Symbolism and Society* (Oxford: Oxford University Press, 2005); Georges Duby, *Medieval Marriage: Two Models from Twelfth-Century France*, trans. Elborg Forster (Baltimore: Johns Hopkins University Press, 1991); idem, *Le Chevalier, la femme, et le prêtre* (Paris, 1981), trans. B. Bray, *The Knight, the Lady and the Priest: The Making of Modern Marriage in*

Medieval France (New York: Pantheon, 1983); A. E. Laiou (ed.), *Consent and Coercion to Sex and Marriage in Ancient and Medieval Societies* (Washington, DC: Dumbarton Oaks Research Library and Collection, 1993); C. N. L. Brooke, *The Medieval Idea of Marriage* (Oxford, 1989; new edn, Oxford: Clarendon Press, 1994); C. M. Rousseau and J. T. Rosenthal (eds), *Women, Marriage, and Family in Medieval Christendom: Essays in Memory of Michael M. Sheehan, C.S.B* (Kalamazoo, MI: Medieval Institute Publications, 1998); Michael M. Sheehan, *Marriage, Family, and Law in Medieval Europe: Collected Studies*, ed. James K. Farge (Toronto: University of Toronto Press, 1996), introduction by Joel T. Rosenthal.

26 Ingledew, 'Book of Troy', p. 677.

27 *Vita Griffini Filii Conani*, ch. 9 at p. 59.

28 *Vita Griffini Filii Conani*, ch. 11 at p. 61.

29 Williams, *When Was Wales?*, pp. 69–70. See P. Lynch, 'Court poetry, power and politics', in T. M. Charles-Edwards, Morfydd E. Owen and Paul Russell (eds), *The Welsh King and his Court* (Cardiff: University of Wales Press, 2000), pp. 167–90.

30 J. P. Clancy, *The Earliest Welsh Poetry* (London: Macmillan, 1970), p. 208, poem at pp. 133–4. The poem is also printed in J. P. Clancy, *Medieval Welsh Poems* (Dublin: Four Courts Press, 2003), p. 137.

31 Huw Meirion Edwards, 'Canu serch Hywel ab Owain Gwynedd', in Nerys Ann Jones (ed.), *Hywel ab Owain Gwynedd: Bardd-Dywysog* (Cardiff: University of Wales Press, 2009), pp. 88–110, is sceptical about direct continental influence this early, preferring to see Welsh love poetry as an independent manifestation of a broader European trend, and refers to his earlier work: *Dafydd ap Gwilym: Influences and Analogues* (Oxford: Clarendon Press, 1996), pp. 85ff.

32 *Gwaith Llywarch ap Llywelyn 'Prydydd y Moch'*, ed. Elin M. Jones with the assistance of Nerys Ann Jones (Cardiff: University of Wales Press, 1991), no. 14, provides a modern critical edition; and (at p. 137 of the Introduction to the poem) takes Nest to be identical with the 'daughter of Cynfelyn', line 9; if so, this would rule out a reference to Nest ferch Rhys ap Tewdwr. If the poem is, as the recent editors accept, addressed to Gwenllian ferch Hywel ap Iorwerth of Caerleon, then it is datable to the last quarter of the twelfth century, and thus long after Nest's time.

33 Clancy, *Earliest Welsh Poetry*, pp. 4–5.

34 The date of composition and the transmission of poetry into written forms is the subject of some debate: Clancy, *Earliest Welsh Poetry*, pp. 2–3; Nora K. Chadwick, *The Celtic Realms* (2nd edn, London: Weidenfeld and Nicolson, 1972); Patrick K. Ford, 'Performance and literacy in medieval Welsh poetry', *The Modern Language Review*, 100 (2005), 30–47.

35 Ceri Davies, *Welsh Literature and the Classical Tradition* (Cardiff: University of Wales Press, 1995), pp. 40–1, 49, 51.

36 Andrew Breeze, *Medieval Welsh Literature* (Dublin: Four Courts Press, 1997), p. 36.

37 '*Gwaith Meilyr Brydydd a'i ddisgynyddion*'; Clancy, *Earliest Welsh Poetry*, p. 121; *idem*, *Medieval Welsh Poems*, pp. 137–8; Breeze, *Medieval Welsh Literature*, pp. 36–7.

38 *Gwaith Cynddelw Brydydd Mawr*, ed. Nerys Ann Jones and Ann Parry Owen (2 vols, Cardiff: University of Wales Press, 1991–5), vol. I, no. 5; Clancy, *Medieval Welsh Poems*, pp. 141–4. Hywel ab Owain Gwynedd praises a girl: 'Fragile bright form, white supple, delightful', his 'chosen one' is 'tall and fair': *ibid.*, p. 134.

39 Brewer, 'Ideal of feminine beauty'; Eco, *Art and Beauty*, pp. 8–12.

40 *The Mabinogion*, trans. and ed. Sioned Davies (Oxford: Oxford University Press, 2007), p. 180.

41 Laura Radiker, 'Traditional and courtly themes in a medieval Welsh elegy to "G6ann Wargann Wery" ("A Fair Virgin, Meek and Mild")', *Proceedings of the Harvard Celtic Colloquium*, 24/25 (2004/5), 101–26.

42 *Gwaith Cynddelw Brydydd Mawr*, i. 59–63; Clancy, *Medieval Welsh Poems*, pp. 141–4.

43 *Gwaith Llywelyn Fardd I ac eraill o feirdd y ddeuddegfed ganrif*, ed. Kathleen Anne Bramley . . . [et al.]; under the supervision of Morfydd E. Owen (Cardiff: University of Wales Press, 1994), p. 143; Clancy, *Medieval Welsh Poems*, p. 134.

44 Jaeger, *Envy of Angels*, pp. 328–9.

45 Heller, 'Light as glamour', p. 935.

46 K. S. Whetter, *Understanding Genre and Medieval Romance* (Aldershot: Ashgate, 2008), pp. 20–32.

47 Humphrey Llwyd, *Cronica Walliae*, ed. Ieuan M. Williams (Cardiff: University of Wales Press, 2002), pp. 134–5; see chapter 4, above, for a full treatment of early modern sources.

Conclusion

This study of Nest and other high-status women in Wales in the high middle ages has shown the ways ideas about gender and power have been integral to narratives of Wales in both contemporary sources and interpretations of those sources. Such narratives were shaped by ideas about gender which interacted with ideas about conquest/imperialism. This was central to the way that Nest was constructed in *Brut y Tywysogion* and other sources, such as the writings of her grandson, Gerald of Wales. Later writers, such as Tudor antiquarians and eighteenth-century travel writers, utilised the narrative of Nest to inform their view of the past and the Norman conquest of Wales, and developed themes of love and beauty as key elements. The erotic charge of the narrative was fore-grounded as an explanatory device in which gender was key. This study of Nest has shown that placing women and gender at the heart of the analysis raises new questions about the construction of history. Ideas about gender, nation, conquest and imperialism affected the creation and portrayal of the Welsh medieval past in different genres at different periods. Thus a study of, for example, the ways that Nest was constructed in different sources has revealed the processes by which a narrative of Wales emerged which took account of the transformative changes wrought by conquest and its associated political development in Wales. The way that ideas about Nest developed is a map of how ideologies were themselves developing.

Nest was constructed within Welsh sources and historiography as a symbol of conflicted Welsh identity. Her actions at the scene of the abduction convey ideas about gender with its concomitant implicit assumption about the weakness and vulnerability of women. These stereotypes of the physical and mental weakness of women compared to men were inverted in the portrayal of Nest, since it was Nest who seized the initiative and faced the enemies of her husband Gerald of Windsor who fled the scene. This was implicitly woven into a narrative about the creation of a Welsh identity constructed and tested in the face of Norman activity. In order to contextualise Nest's example, the multiple and con-flicting portrayals of women in charters, chronicles, and literary and legal sources were analysed to suggest ways that such ideas appear in a wide range of sources.

It is has been suggested that complex questions concerning the inter-actions between gender, power and historiography can be addressed through an analysis which takes account of the imperatives of conquest and imperialism. Nationalist perspectives with their emphasis on violent and destructive conquest and reaction cannot adequately explain the multiple and competing forces which shaped society, and for the high middle ages do not explain the multiple and competing imperatives which shaped our sources, including, for example, gender. The tendency towards revisionism, with its focus on influence, has similarly tended to minimise the importance of gender constructions at the heart of the work of key writers and commentators on that history. Analysis of the portrayal of Nest suggests that her narrative was shaped and defined in different contexts, and was very much dependent on genre and contemporary imperatives. Her example, and others, such as that of Gwenllian, the wife of Rhys ap Gruffudd, suggest that writers utilised gendered ideas to convey ambiguity and conflict.

The portrayal of Nest in *Brut y Tywysogion* was part of a wider narrative of Wales developed through the twelfth and thirteenth centuries and was replicated and developed by later writers. The abduction narrative became associated with a romantic view of the Welsh medieval past in which the political context and shifting political alliances of the ruling dynasties were central. Historians have thus, following the lead of the medieval sources, cast the history of Wales within a framework which has necessarily emphasised the role of war in the broader questions of conquest, resistance and change. David Cannadine's analysis of a danger inherent in the 'new British History' – that it leads to a view of history which sees historical developments in the British Isles as a process by which the 'British became more British' – is perhaps applicable to the construct of the 'Age of the Princes'.[1] That is, Wales became 'more Welsh' as ideas about Wales as a nation emerged, and the association of the medieval period as one of 'the Princes' has served to limit the historiography of medieval Wales. It is further complicated by the way in which the labels 'Welsh' and 'Wales' (as expressed by a variety of terms in Latin and Welsh) partly replaced, but also continued to coexist with, long-established notions of the inhabitants of Wales as 'Britons'.[2] The importance of the emergence of Wales as a 'nation' has been a key driver of the historiography of Wales, and the problems encountered during this process have received some recognition.[3]

The historiography of medieval Wales has been enriched by work on the role of women in cultural, political and economic contexts as well as their roles in areas such as the formation and transmission of oral memory, religious benefaction and literary patronage throughout the medieval period. The historiography of medieval Wales can now move beyond the debates about the emergence of the nation and begin to consider how the importance of the national agenda has diverted attention away from the competing, multiple and complex messages in our sources. Nest of Deheubarth, as the Welsh 'Helen of Troy', has fulfilled a symbolic role in the historiography of medieval Wales, not only as a dynastic figure, but as an ambiguous and complex symbol of the multiple and competing interests which afflicted families and individuals. It has been argued that although the role of Welsh princesses or powerful noblewomen was only rarely acknowledged by Welsh contemporary sources on Wales in the high middle ages, their appearance in the sources reflects an acknowledgement that women had a role to play in shaping the complex changes in culture and society.

Nest's example suggests that her constructed role as 'Helen of Wales' was symbolic in later texts as an explanatory link in a broader narrative of war and conquest in south Wales with the narrative of the emergence of Britain in classical times. It was a way for commentators to explain a narrative which was conflicted and revealed a lack of unity in the Welsh elite who were just as ready to ally with their Norman neighbours as to rebel against them or to ally with each other. Her role in texts was as a catalyst for change, as a focus for explanations of defeat and a way for writers to come to terms with female agency. By giving the narrative a classical allusion it legitimised events and explained them by recourse to gender roles. The incorporation of romance elements in later explanations suggests that commentators, following the sources, felt it necessary to embroider and relate a dramatic tale of resistance and passion. It characterised Owain ap Cadwgan as a youthful, adventurous lover who sought his fair, beautiful lady, in a landscape which was fraught and contested.

The portrayal of the abduction narrative was contingent upon conventions of genre which therefore shaped the multi-layered nature of the narrative. Nest's position as ancestral figure and the link she represented to the royal dynasty of Deheubarth was stressed and her kinship with Owain was key. His role in the text as a dynamic romantic hero was a later interpretation, and Nest's role in directing Gerald of Windsor was key to the idea that she was a willing conspirator. The abduction revealed the fragility of the peace in Deheubarth, a peace that had been partly achieved through the marriage of Nest to Gerald of Windsor. This reveals the importance of the marriage as a symbol of union; its irruption was symbolic of the failure of Gerald's ability to control events. Thus his power as a lord was symbolically and practically shattered by the abduction.

Classical models of heroic men and women, including the classical stereotype of woman as a cause of war, informed the way that the abduction was represented; as such, it may obliquely reference the alleged Trojan descent from Brutus of the Welsh elite.[4] The portrayal was also affected by contemporary legal ideas and cultural norms concerning marriage and legitimacy, and thus different intellectual traditions framed the way that the episode was constructed. Therefore the varied and rich influences upon Welsh intellectual tradition can be detected in the account; this interacted with its conservatism and adaptability to create a dynamic portrayal. This resulted in the creation of an image of Owain as a heroic princely leader of a war-band of young 'hotheads' who nevertheless was able to strike a decisive blow against the Norman invaders. Although we may detect Powysian sympathies in this portrayal, it is nevertheless instructive that the sources portray an image of Nest that suggests her centrality to the political processes of south-west Wales. The ambiguity over her complicity is a direct reflection of distrust of her role and this is related to stereotypical distrust of women. Scholars have persisted in seeing the events as a romantically inspired affair. There are reasons why this might be the case in the sources. In the *Brut*, and many accounts springing from it, Nest's sexual conquest by Owain was romanticised since the portrayal of Owain in the *Brut* generally is positive, for example in the account of his reconciliation with Henry I and his knighthood later in the narrative. Later commentators glossed over Owain's part in the rape and abduction of Nest in an ongoing male-centred narrative in which they became subsumed in a narrative of heroic Welsh resistance to the Anglo-Normans. As such the abuse of a Welsh princess by the prince of another Welsh dynasty draws attention to the importance of personal actions and responsibility. The sexual relationship, her capture and subsequent actions for her children were interpreted to suggest compliance if not outright willingness to cuckold her husband. While commentators have noted the violence meted out on male members of ruling Welsh dynasties, descriptions of violence against women are rare. An acknowledgement that Nest's abduction may have been forced, and could have included rape, did not suit the purposes of later nationalist commentators who wanted to inculcate a romantic view of medieval Wales. Some writers in Welsh were ready to condemn examples of barbarous or immoral behaviour in the past as part of their moralising agenda for the improvement of the Welsh in the present, and this is evident in Gweirydd ap Rhys's account (1872–74) of Owain's abduction of Nest; more generally, however, there was no uniform view by Welsh historians – in either language – of patriotic disposition. In such a world women, and especially high-status Welsh women, were treated honourably by their fellow Welsh men. The *Brut* suggests that Nest's resistance to the destruction of her life was channelled to ensure her children's safety. Nest's abduction was constructed within the *Brut y Tywysogion* in a way which subverted normative forms of narrative of male action and resourcefulness. Gerald of Windsor, for example, as a Norman lord was parodied as a cuckolded husband whose dynamic and resourceful Welsh wife was honourable yet also central to the processes by which the balance of power was determined. Norman lordship, personified by Gerald, was impotent in the face of rash Owain who seized the initiative. Nest was no pawn, but neither was she a free agent, though she was able to make choices and influence how events would unfold.

The abduction narrative in the *Brut* serves to confirm the importance of women not just as pawns to be used by powerful men, but their centrality and ability to participate in subversion of the political order by their choices. It genders such portrayals by recourse to stereotypical and romance motifs which are obliquely deployed and resonate with gendered images. Thus Nest is the female who waits in confined, domestic space, a castle, for her 'rescuer', a young Welsh hothead, and she uses her voice to persuade her husband to leave the castle, which is the symbolic heart of his lordship. Owain's surprise attack thus strikes at the core of Anglo-Norman lordship. Nest thereby accepts her fate. The theme of the political subversion of women is evident in the writings of Gerald on Ireland and central to the *Song of Dermot and the Earl*. These texts are concerned with the axiomatic importance of individual choice to the conflict between the Anglo-Normans and native dynasties, and they placed sexual politics and gender norms as central causative elements in narratives of conquest.

Such evidence may be compared to charter evidence which provides a different view of women in twelfth-century Wales. This evidence can be set alongside a reading of Matthew Paris and Gerald of Wales, and of the lawbooks, evidence which is perhaps better known but which, read in isolation, poses problems. Read together, however, these sources suggest that in the high middle ages in Wales interaction in high politics by powerful women was driven from many perspectives. Contrary to the established view in much of the historiography, these findings suggest that political life in Wales was not necessarily to result in the dominance and subordination of the female high political elite, or of the Welsh. Charters suggest that there were different ways that women exerted power and influence and this was contingent upon a variety of factors, including marital and social status. Charters show that women of the elite were involved in different contexts in differing transactions. Some, such as Princess Joan, as a powerful wife and daughter of King John, or Senana, the wife of Gruffudd ap Llywelyn, appear in our sources and are suggestive of the ways that women could be involved in important political negotiations. Their examples provide some interesting contrasts with Nest. All three were important to the political processes as wives and all three supported their husbands in political contexts which were difficult and fraught. Yet Nest's narrative was enmeshed with an agenda which stressed Welsh resistance and challenge.

Nest's tale of resistance and sexual politics was a narrative which was rediscovered in the early modern period in the writings of Llwyd and Powel, and later in the histories of Owen. These developed in the context of other accounts of south Wales in which Norman activity was linked to a Welsh native nobility among whom politics could be destabilised by sexual passion. Such themes are evident in the presentation of the 'Winning of Glamorgan' by Stradling. The tale explains the Norman arrival in Glamorgan by recourse to contested eroticised themes and relays a pejorative view of the Welsh rulers of Deheubarth. The centrality of marriage to the political processes is evident in this view since a broken marriage agreement is key. Rice Merrick eroticises the portrayal of Nest's father in his depiction of his attempts to seduce the wife of the ruler of a neighbouring kingdom. The Norman conquest was indelibly linked with an attempted sexual conquest. Merrick suggests that this failed sexual conquest caused dispute, whereas in the Nest story we see the fulfilled sexual conquest of the wife of a Norman by a Welshman as a metaphor for the conquest of the kingdom, and the dispute over her body is nothing less than a dispute for legitimacy of political rule.

We might find parallels here with eighteenth-century colonial attitudes to colonised men as dangerous and unable to control their passions, sexually predatory, but also weak and not manly. Male weakness and lack of masculinity in a colonised population were central to the process of that population and its territory becoming a colony.[5] Such an approach to understanding conceptions of masculinity and attitudes to subjugated peoples may be seen to underpin the way that early modern writers sought to explain Norman success, and indirectly provide a prescription for Welsh reformation.

Modern theorists have debated what medieval chroniclers clearly knew: that the past informed the present, and they interpreted it according to their own notions of identity. Thus Nest's story, or narratives about other women, were repeated and, on occasion, reinterpreted because Welsh gendered identity in the past was felt to be the key to explaining Welsh identity in the present. Nest was positioned within the past in which her history was crucial to the narrative of Welsh identity. This debate was conducted within a context of a broader debate about Britishness and Englishness, as Wilson suggests, but also about Welshness within that broader debate. Such identities may not have been stable but they were constructed around a sense of a historical past which was romanticised and, crucially, gendered, and this interacted with social status. Thus Nest's abduction was an essential part of the narrative of Norman success in Wales and Welsh resistance. It featured women as conduits of instability through their sexual attractiveness which caused the Welsh male elite to respond inappropriately, with devastating consequences. This conquest was portrayed as sexual conquest, or rather women appear as objects of male desire, their bodies responsible for political catastrophe. We can see these themes revisited in the narrative of the conquest of Ireland as it developed from the early modern period and was revisited in later writings. Yet even here ambiguity remains, as Owain later reaches accommodation with Henry I; and the narratives of Nest's experience, especially on the crucial question of the nature of her response to Owain's aggression, and those of other women, consistently test the boundaries of gender norms. Thus in *Brut y Tywysogion* the experience of Nest is symbolic of the contested changes in political and social order from the dynasty of Rhys of Deheubarth, and of the enduring importance of marriage and family in contemporary politics, especially the politics of interaction and accommodation with change. Similarly the narrative of her sister-in-law Gwenllian is a tale of resistance and conflict where gender roles are challenged because of the extreme political context. In Wales therefore, and especially in south Wales, the overriding explanatory narratives of interactions with Normans and English related to women.

Early modern writers saw the abduction as an eroticised narrative with Nest's beauty a key explanatory feature. The classical context of female beauty as a cause of instability of catastrophe was a motif of ancient provenance, and Helen of Troy in particular provided a model which was utilised to provide a powerful message about the gravity and long-term political impact of the abduction in narratives of Wales which had the fate of the Welsh nation at their heart. Sixteenth-century interpretations, such as those of Humphrey Llwyd and Dr Powel, understood the legitimating function of beauty and thus the presentation of Nest was an integral element in the narrative.[6] The presentation of Nest in *Brut y Tywysogion* implicitly frames her as a great beauty when it states that Owain took action on hearing of her 'fame' as related by bards at the Christmas feast held by his father. The deployment of the motif of female beauty as a cause of war is localised to south-west Wales but this has a clear purpose. It is a key element in the portrayal of south-west Wales as the crucible of change and reaction in the first phase of Norman advances in the south. Later interpretations of Nest as a particularly great beauty were derived from early modern sources. The importance of beauty as a concept in the twelfth century is that it was a key element in the articulation of ideas about power, legitimacy and conduct: female beauty was a cause of instability in classical texts, and this was alluded to in the *Brut y Tywysogion* and reinterpreted later.

Beauty as a construct had specific purposes in texts which were dependent on socio-historical contexts as much as literary genre. Nest's beauty has functioned as a legitimating trope in narratives which are based on a static view of female beauty in a conception of medieval Wales which is both romanticised and sanitised. In the nineteenth century and subsequently this focus on beauty has played a particularly important role in the process by which the tawdry aspects of the abduction as a possible rape have been written out of accounts of the events in favour of a rose-tinted, nostalgic view of the past.

These themes of the activism of women, and of beauty and passion as expressive of social relations in a time of rapid change, are integral to the presentation of Welsh history in contemporary Wales. The importance of war as an agent of change and reaction are thus central to Nest's narrative, which also serves to remind that women, and gender, were contested sites of interpretation in contemporary texts. The narrative of her sister-in-law is dramatic and shocking, Nest's sums up a subtler but still more dramatic confrontation. The construction of Nest, and other women, in the historiography of Wales owes much to the power of early narratives which created an image of conflict and change in which gender and conquest were the central ideas. Nest has become associated with a romantic escapade in the modern imagination, and this construction is derived from readings of the *Brut*.

Her identity as a woman who is abducted is a motif of loss and retrieval. Nest, in order to satisfy the collective need of the Welsh to retrieve their lost past, loses her position as wife, her husband loses his wife, a wife who had provided a dynastic link to the dynasty of Deheubarth. The Welsh nation, symbolised by the youthful Owain, retrieves Nest who paradoxically symbolises both intersection and accommodation with the Normans and Welsh defiance. Owain is portrayed as separate from his father to suggest youthful resilience and the conflicted Welsh present.

Through the abduction the Welsh seize the initiative, reconfigure the political reality of the old kingdom of Deheubarth, test the strength of Norman lordship and do so through a narrative which is gendered, conflicted and ambiguous. The struggle for Nest's body was a struggle for the control of the Welsh nation. Hence the compilers of the *Brut* inscribed the abduction as a narrative of classically epic proportions; the ethnicity of the major protagonists was implicitly part of a dialogue about the fate of a conquered people; Owain's untamed sexual passion and impulsive nature represented a concern with the impact of a colonised people; the control of Nest was a metaphor for the control of the destiny of the self, the people, and control of the fertility of that people. That is why Gerald of Wales based his narratives about his kin and their conquest of Ireland and on Nest as an ancestral figure. The Anglo-Normans of south Wales, when combined with the dynasty of Deheubarth, had become transformed into a dynamic conquering people who in turn had shaped the destiny of another nation. Hitherto, discussions of the Norman impact on Wales have lacked an awareness of the gendered nature of sources whose concern with the conflicted nature of the Welsh polity and identity had caused them to place women at the symbolic heart of that destiny. Thus the abduction of Nest represented concerns with the conflicted nature of the Welsh nation who had come to terms with the Anglo-Normans. Nest was conflicted because the nation was conflicted; the narrative of integration and resilience central to concerns about the Welsh past and present.

With the advent of social history and more modern approaches to history throughout the twentieth century, including women's then gender history, economic, oral and postmodern approaches, the historiography of Wales has moved a long way from J. E. Lloyd's nationalistic views that the struggle of the nation was a central dynamic which shaped medieval Welsh history. Nevertheless it is still generally the case that historians are agreed that the impact of the Norman conquest was pivotal to the history of medieval Wales, and the narrative of Nest is an important element within that history. To ignore the abduction tale within a narrative of conquest is to minimise the importance of individual and communal responses to the Norman presence in Wales which were seen by contemporaries as deeply symbolic. Nest's abduction forms part of an unusually long and detailed entry in the *Brut*, a key source for medieval Wales. This suggests that the compilers of the *Brut* saw the events as pivotal and as such it was worthy of an extended narrative, and legitimate for later writers to include the episode in their interpretations of the Welsh medieval past.

The portrayal of the abduction of Nest in different genres at different periods suggests the appeal of a narrative about medieval Wales in which ideas about male and female relationships were central. The construction of a view of medieval Wales as it was affected by the activities of the Normans was key to this. Centrally, Nest and other women exemplify in modern interpretations a view of the Welsh medieval past which is framed within a construct of female subordination to the nation. This was intrinsic to the ordering and interpretation of the past. For example, Nest's marriage to the Norman Gerald of Windsor, the abduction and Owain's passion and culpability are definitive elements in the narrative, and this was taken up and replicated by interpreters of the *Brut* in the early modern period, and adapted and rewritten in the nineteenth century with the beginnings of the academic study of Wales in the writings of J. E. Lloyd and others. The narratives of other women of the elite, such as Joan, the daughter of King John, or Gwenllian, Nest's sister-in-law, wife of Gruffudd ap Rhys, also appear in a range of texts and are situated in the narrative of Wales as exceptions. They are viewed as powerful women who emerge in texts at critical points in a political narrative in the writings of eighteenth- and nineteenth-century travel writers, for example. Thus the portrayals of women such as Joan as a help-meet to her husband Llywelyn in his struggle to maintain independence in the face of a centralising royal crown in England, or Gwenllian who fought the Normans and lost at a critical moment in English history – Henry I had died and his nephew Stephen had seized the crown – are repeated in texts because their narratives are compelling and become part of the accepted canon of Welsh history which is derived from a narrow set of medieval texts, including the *Brut* and the writings of Gerald of Wales. Academic study of medieval Wales has inevitably focused upon important political and national themes and has also embraced the trends of medieval British historiography. In particular the historiography of the Welsh princes, and their military, political and social domination, has been a key element in discussions of medieval Wales. There has been an increasing interest in medieval Welsh women and their contribution to the history of Wales. It has been suggested that their role as contested sites of interpretation in different sources has been less well explored. The aim here is to suggest that there is much to be learned from an analysis which takes account of the ways that women of the elite such as Nest of Deheubarth had varying and mutable functions and symbolic aspects within texts. This has much to tell us about the importance of genre in shaping the portrayals of women which should be read in a context that takes account of gender, identity, conquest and imperialism, since these were key areas of concern for medieval and later writers. The present volume has focused on interpretations of Nest and has contrasted these with interpretations of other women from twelfth- and thirteenth-century Wales to suggest ways that readings of such women should be interpreted in a context which takes account of genre and historical contexts. The approach here has been to argue that an analysis of the way that the narrative appears at different periods in accounts of the Welsh medieval past has much to tell us about the gendered construction of the Welsh medieval past, and this has been a key trope in writings on Welsh resistance to the Normans in south-west Wales. Gender lies at the heart of this interpretation because Nest and her narrative are constructed around ideas of difference between men and women. Nest's actions are inscribed with symbolic significance because she is portrayed as a victim who helps her husband, but also a co-conspirator. The episode in full is concerned with the fate of Owain and events in Powys: the instabilities of Welsh political relationships are fully exposed by the events which unfold, with sexual politics at the heart of the dynamics of power. Nest represents the difficulties and choices made by Welsh medieval women who were caught in a fluid and divisive political context. Thus the portrayal of Nest, in different accounts, at different periods, in different genres, has much to tell us about conceptions of gender, nation, responses to conquest, ideologies of hierarchy, ethnicity and the interactions of gender with these.

Finally, the historiography of the Welsh princes is a dominant strand in writings on medieval Wales and serves to define modern interpretations of the Welsh medieval past. Cadw for example has recently launched a heritage project under the title of the Age of the Princes. It is a phrase which embodies ideas about chronology and the importance of war and politics in the Welsh medieval past. Scholars utilise the term since it is an embodiment of a certain phase of Welsh history where the princes of Welsh dynasties were predominant in Wales: it encapsulates ideas about diverse kingdoms with their own dynasties, and genders this process as male. This necessarily involves the creation of an analytical dichotomy. There is no equivalent concept of the Age of the Princesses in Welsh history. This is reflective of the role of war and conquest in shaping the contours of political history and the way that such forces are pivotal in the narrative of history as represented by the *Brut* and later writings. Thus this privileging of a male discourse about male activity is in itself reflective of the interest of medieval commentators, but is essentially a reductionist view of the Welsh medieval past which sets up a duality at the core of the discipline where gender is central to the analysis. Thus the narratives of individuals such as Nest have symbolic functions in texts which are imbued with conflicting resonances dependent on context. In the *Brut* Nest is symbolic of the change in political and social order from the dynasty of Rhys of Deheubarth, representing the enduring importance of marriage and family in contemporary politics as well as interaction and accommodation with political change. Similarly the narrative of her sister-in-law Gwenllian is a tale of resistance and conflict where gender roles are challenged because of the extreme political context. Such themes are integral to the presentation of Welsh history in contemporary Wales. Thus conquest and responses to it are the context of reaction, and this confirms that her narrative is symbolic of the importance of war as a dynamic, destructive and catalysing force.

Notes

1 David Cannadine, 'British History as a "new subject": politics, perspectives and prospects', in Alexander Grant and Keith J. Stringer (eds), *Uniting the Kingdom? The Making of British History* (London and New York: Routledge, 1995), pp. 12–28, at p. 26.
2 My thanks to Huw Pryce for this observation.
3 Gwyn A. Williams, *When was Wales? A History of the Welsh* (Harmondsworth: Penguin, 1985), p. 86; J. Beverley Smith, *Llywelyn ap Gruffudd: Prince of Wales* (Cardiff: University of Wales Press, 1998), p. 605.
4 See Ceri Davies, *Welsh Literature and the Classical Tradition* (Cardiff: University of Wales Press, 1995), pp. 39–44 for discussion of classical heroes and representations of classical motifs in *Brut y Tywysogion* and poetry.
5 Philippa Levine, *Gender and Empire* (Oxford: Oxford University Press, 2004), p. 6.
6 Humphrey Llwyd, *Cronica Walliae*, ed. Ieuan M. Williams (Cardiff: University of Wales Press, 2002), pp. 134–5.

Bibliography

Primary sources

MANUSCRIPT SOURCES

Aberystwyth, Llyfrgell Genedlaethol Cymru / The National Library of Wales (NLW)

MS 1406E Pembrokeshire Papers, 'A Tour thro' Pembrokeshire: Or a concise Account of Whatsoever in that County deserves the attention of the Traveller . . .'
MS 6680B Llawysgrif Hendregadredd
MS 9352A 'An account of three tours, by an English gentleman, accompanied by Mr and Mrs William (?) from Hereford . . . 1787'
MS 18943B 'Narrative of a tour through Wales by an anonymous English Gentleman setting out from Gloucester and returning to London after a journey of a thousand miles'
Cwrtmawr 1 (C) MS 199B 'Diary of a Journey into Wales A.D. 1789'
Cwrtmawr 393 C 'Walk through South Wales: an account of a tour made in October 1819 by William and Sampson Sandys, lawyers of London, with a number of sketches by WS'
Penrice and Margam charters

London, British Library

Additional MSS 10292–4

PRINTED PRIMARY SOURCES

The Acts of Welsh Rulers 1120–1283, ed. Huw Pryce with the assistance of Charles Insley (Cardiff: University of Wales Press, 2005).
Alderson, Bryan, *Nest: A Novel Based on the Life of the Twelfth Century Welsh Princes* (Haverfordwest: Hedgehog Publications, 2004).
Annales Cambriæ, ed. John Williams ab Ithel (Rolls Series, 20; London: Longman, Green, Longman, and Roberts, 1860).
Arnold, Matthew, *On the Study of Celtic Literature* (London: Smith, Elder and Co., 1867).
—— *The Complete Prose Works of Matthew Arnold*, III: *Lectures and Essays in Criticism*, ed. R. H. Super (Ann Arbor, MI: University of Michigan Press, 1962).
Baker, James, *A Picturesque Guide through Wales and the Marches* (2nd edn; Worcester: printed and sold by J. Tymbs; sold also by Robson; Ottridge; White; Rivingtons; Richardson; and at Taylor's architectural library, London, 1795).

Bell, Anne, *Daughter of the Dragon* (London: Hale, 1978).

Bingley, William, *A Tour round North Wales, Performed during the Summer of 1798: Containing not only the Description and Local History of the Country* . . . (London: sold by E. Williams (successor to the late Mr. Blamire); and J. Deighton, Cambridge. Printed by J. Smeeton, 1800).

Brady, Robert, *A Complete History of England from the First Entrance of the Romans under the Conduct of Julius Caesar unto the End of the Reign of King Henry III . . . : Wherein is Shewed the Original of our English Laws, the Differences and Disagreements between the Secular and Ecclesiastic Powers . . . and Likewise an Account of our Foreign Wars with France, the Conquest of Ireland, and the Actions between the English, Scots and Welsh . . .: All Delivered in Plain Matter of Fact, without any Reflections or Remarques by Robert Brady* (Savoy, London: printed by Tho. Newcomb for Samuel Lowndes . . . , 1685).

Brenhinedd y Saesson, or, The Kings of the Saxons, ed. T. Jones (Cardiff: University of Wales Press, 1971).

Brut y Tywysogion: Peniarth MS. 20 Version, ed. T. Jones (Cardiff: University of Wales Press, 1941).

Brut y Tywysogion, or, The Chronicle of the Princes, Peniarth MS. 20 Version, trans. T. Jones (Cardiff: University of Wales Press, 1952).

Brut y Tywysogion, or, The Chronicle of the Princes, Red Book of Hergest Version, ed. and trans. T. Jones (1955; 2nd edn, Cardiff: University of Wales Press, 1973).

Burton, Robert [i.e. Nathaniel Crouch], *Female Excellency, or, The Ladies of Glory Illustrated in the Worthy Lives and Memorable Actions of Nine Famous Women, who have been Renowned either for Virtue or Valour in Several Ages of the World . . .: The Whole Adorned with Poems and the Picture of each Lady* (London: printed for Nath. Crouch . . . , 1688).

—— *The History of the Principality of Wales: In Three Parts . . . Together with the Natural and Artificial Rarities and Wonders in the Several Counties of that Principality* (London: printed for Nathaniel Crouch, 1695).

Calendar of Entries in the Papal Registers Relating to Great Britain and Ireland: Papal Letters, i: *A.D. 1198–1304*, ed. W. H. Bliss (London: HMSO, 1893).

Camden, William, *Britain, or, A Chorographicall Description of the Most Flourishing Kingdomes, England, Scotland, and Ireland, and the Islands Adjoyning, out of the Depth of Antiquitie* (London: George Bishop and John Norton, 1610).

Campbell, E. C., *The History of Wales: Containing some Interesting Facts concerning the Existence of a Welsh Tribe among the Aborigines of America Arranged as a Catechism for Young Persons by a Lady of the Principality* (Shrewsbury: [printed by John Eddowes], 1833).

Capgrave, John, *The Chronicle of England*, ed. Francis Charles Hingeston (Rolls Series, 1; London: Longman, Brown, Green, Longmans, and Roberts, 1858).

Caradoc, of Llancarvan, d. 1147? *The Historie of Cambria, now called Wales: A Part of the Most Famous Yland of Brytaine, Written in the Brytish Language Aboue Two Hundreth Yeares Past: Translated into English by H. Lhoyd*

Gentleman: Corrected, Augmented, and Continued out of Records and Best Approoued Authors, by Dauid Powel Doctor in Diuinitie (London: printed by Rafe Newberie and Henrie Denham, 1584).

—— *The History of Wales Comprehending the Lives and Succession of the Princes of Wales, from Cadwalader the Last King, to Lhewelyn the Last Prince of British Blood . . . by William Wynne* (London: printed by Mary Clark, for the author, and are to be sold by R. Clavell, 1697).

Cartae et alia munimenta quæ ad domininum de Glamorgancia pertinent, vol. II: *MCXCVI – circ. MCCLXX*, ed. G. T. Clark (2nd edn, Cardiff: William Lewis, 1910).

The Charters of the Abbey of Ystrad Marchell, ed. G. C. G. Thomas (Aberystwyth: National Library of Wales, 1997).

The Charters of the Anglo-Norman earls of Chester, c. 1071–1237, ed. G. Barraclough (Record Society of Lancashire and Cheshire, 126, 1988).

Chronicon Angliae, ab anno Domini 1328 usque ad annum 1388, auctore monacho quodam Sancti Albani, ed. Edward Maunde Thompson (Rolls Series, 64; London: Longman, 1874).

Corn, C., *Pageant Pictorial* (Cardiff: E. Rees, 1909).

Curia Regis Rolls (20 vols, London: HMSO, 1922–2006).

Davis, Olwen, 'Princess Nest, the Helen of Wales', *Country Quest* (2007), 32–3.

The Deeds of the Normans in Ireland: La Geste des Engleis en Yrlande: A New Edition of the Chronicle Formerly Known as The Song of Dermot and the Earl, ed. Evelyn Mullally (Dublin: Four Courts Press, 2002).

[Derfel, R. J.], 'Cymru yn ei chysylltiad ag enwogion' [Wales in its relationship with heroes], *Y Traethodydd* (1855), 322–59.

Earldom of Gloucester Charters: The Charters and Scribes of the Earls and Countesses of Gloucester to A.D. 1217, ed. R. B. Patterson (Oxford: Clarendon Press, 1973).

Edwards, O. M., *A Short History of Wales* (London: T. Fisher Unwin, 1906).

Encyclopædia Cambrensis: Y Gwyddoniadur Cymreig: Duwinyddiaeth, Athroniaeth, a Henafiaethau (10 vols, Dinbych: Thomas Gee, 1858–79).

Evans, John, *Letters Written during a Tour through South Wales in the Year 1803 and at other Times Containing Views of the History, Antiquities and Customs of that Part of the Principality, and Interspersed with Observations on its Scenery, Agriculture, Botany, Mineralogy, Trade and Manufactures* (London: printed for C. and R. Baldwin, New Bridge-Street, 1804).

Evans, J. Gwenogfryn, with the cooperation of John Rhys, *The Text of the Book of Llan Dâv Reproduced from the Gwysaney Manuscript* (Oxford: J. G. Evans, 1893; facsimile edition, Aberystwyth: National Library of Wales, 1979).

Fenton, Richard, *A Historical Tour through Pembrokeshire* (London: Longman, Hurst, Rees & Orme, 1810).

Fuller, Thomas, *The History of the Worthies of England who for Parts and Learning have been Eminent in the Several Counties: Together with an Historical Narrative of the Native Commodities and Rarities in each County* (London: printed by J. G[rismond]., W. L[eybourne]., and W. G[odbid] for Thomas Williams, 1662).

Geoffrey of Monmouth, *The History of the Kings of Britain: An Edition and Translation of De Gestis Britonum (Historia regum Britanniae)*, Latin text ed. Michael D. Reeve, trans. Neil Wright (Woodbridge: Boydell Press, 2007).

—— *The Autobiography of Giraldus Cambrensis*, ed. H. E. Butler (London: Jonathan Cape, 1937).

—— *Expugnatio Hibernica: The Conquest of Ireland*, ed. A. B. Scott and F. X. Martin (Dublin: Royal Irish Academy, 1978).

—— *The Journey through Wales: and, The Description of Wales*, ed. Lewis Thorpe (Harmondsworth: Penguin, 1978).

Gwaith Llywarch ap Llywelyn 'Prydydd y Moch', ed. Elin M. Jones with the assistance of Nerys Ann Jones (Cardiff: University of Wales Press, 1991).

Handlist of the Acts of Native Welsh Rulers, 1132–1283, ed. K. L. Maund (Cardiff: University of Wales Press, 1996).

Hawtrey, G. P., and 'Rhoscomyl, Owen', *Book of Words* (Cardiff: Western Mail, 1909).

Henry of Huntingdon, *Historia Anglorum: The History of the English People*, ed. and trans. Diana Greenway (Oxford: Clarendon Press, 1996).

Heywood, Thomas, *The Exemplary Lives and Memorable Acts of Nine of the Most Worthy Women of the World: Three Iewes, Three Gentiles, Three Christians* (London: printed by Thomas Cotes, for Richard Royston, 1640).

Higden, Ranulph, *Polychronicon*, ed. Churchill Babington and Joseph Rawson Lumby (9 vols, Rolls Series, 41; London: Longman, Green, Longman, Roberts, and Green, 1865–86).

Jacobs, Carole, 'Journey-coat: a collection of poems inspired by Nest, Princess of Deheubarth, in eleventh-century west Wales' (unpubl. MA thesis, University of Wales, Trinity College, 2005).

Johnson, Richard, *The Nine Worthies of London Explaining the Honourable Exercise of Armes, the Vertues of the Valiant, and the Memorable Attempts of Magnanimious Minds. Pleasant for Gentlemen, not Vnseemely for Magistrates, and Most Profitable for Prentises. Compiled by Richard Iohnson* (London: by Thomas Orwin for Humfrey Lownes, 1592).

Jones, Glyn, *The Collected Poems of Glyn Jones*, ed. Meic Stephens (Cardiff: University of Wales Press, 1996).

Jones, John, *The History of Wales: Descriptive of the Government, Wars, Manners, Religion, Laws, Druids, Bards, Pedigrees, and Language of the Ancient Britons and Modern Welsh, and of the Remaining Antiquities of the Principality* (London: J. Williams, 1824).

Jones, Owen, Williams, Edward, and Owen, William, *The Myvyrian Archaiology of Wales Collected out of Ancient Manuscripts* (3 vols, London: printed by S. Rousseau for the editors and sold by Longman & Rees, 1801–7).

Jones, Theophilus, *A History of the County of Brecknock in Two Volumes* (Brecon: North, William and George, 1805–9).

Knight, Bernard, *Lion Rampant: The Story of Owain and Nest* (London: Hale, 1972).

Knighton, Henry, *Chronicon Henrici Knighton, vel Cnitthon, monachi Leycestrensis*, ed. Joseph Rawson Lumby (London: HMSO, 1889–95).

—— *Chronicle, 1337–1396*, ed. G. H. Martin (Oxford: Clarendon Press, 1995).

Landor, Robert Eyres, *The Earl of Brecon: A Tragedy in Five Acts; Faith's Fraud: A Tragedy in Five Acts; The Ferryman: A Drama in Five Acts* (London: Saunder's and Otley, 1841).

The Ledger Book of Vale Royal Abbey, ed. John Brownbill (Record Society of Lancashire and Cheshire, 68, 1914).

Leland, John, *The Itinerary in Wales of John Leland in or about the Years 1536–1539*, ed. Lucy Toulmin Smith (London: G. Bell and Sons, 1906).

Lipscomb, George, *Journey into South Wales, through the Counties of Oxford, Warwick, Worcester, Hereford, Salop, Stafford, Buckingham, and Hertford; in the Year 1799* (London: T. N. Longman & O. Rees, 1802).

The Llandaff Charters, ed. Wendy Davies (Aberystwyth: National Library of Wales, 1979).

Llwyd [sic], Humphrey, *Cronica Walliae*, ed. Ieuan M. Williams (Cardiff: University of Wales Press, 2002).

The Mabinogion, trans. and ed. Sioned Davies (Oxford: Oxford University Press, 2007).

Mackinley, Margaret, *The Pawns of Kings* (London: Hale, 1981).

Malkin, Benjamin Heath, *The Scenery, Antiquities and Biography of South Wales* (2 vols, London: Longman, Hurst Rees and Orme, 1807).

Map, Walter, *De nugis curialium: Courtiers' Trifles*, ed. and trans. M. R. James, rev. C. N. L. Brooke and R. A. B. Mynors (Oxford, 1983); repr. with corrections (Oxford: Clarendon Press, 1994).

Martin, Benjamin, *Introduction to the History of the Principality of Wales* (London, 1763).

Meredith, Gwenllian, 'Princess Nesta ferch Rhys ap Tewdwr of Deheubarth', *Cambria* (2009), 31–3.

The Merionith Lay Subsidy Roll, 1292–3, ed. Keith Williams-Jones (Cardiff: University of Wales Press, 1976).

Merrick, Rice, *Morganiae Archaiographia: A Book of the Antiquities of Glamorganshire*, ed. Brian Ll. James (South Wales Record Society, vol. 1, 1983).

Meyrick, S. R., *The History and Antiquities of the County of Cardigan Collected from the Few Remaining Documents which have Escaped the Destructive Ravages of Time, as from Actual Observation* (London: printed by T. Bensley, for Longman, etc., 1808).

Morton, H. V., *In Search of Wales* (London: Methuen, 1932).

Nicholson, George, *The Cambrian Traveller's Guide in Every Direction; Containing Remarks made during many Excursions, in the Principality of Wales and Bordering Districts, Augmented by Extracts from the Best Writers* (Stourport: George Nicholson, 1808; 2nd edn, London: Longman, Hurst, Rees, Orme & Brown; Sherwood, Neely, & Jones; and Baldwin, Cradock & Joy, 1813).

Orford, Margaret, *The Royal Mistress* (Swansea: Davies, 1976).

Owen, George, of Henllys, *The Description of Penbrokshire*, ed. H. Owen (4 vols, Honourable Society of Cymmrodorion, Cymmrodorion Record Series, 1, 1892–1936).

Owen, Geraint Dyfnallt, *Nest* (London: W. Griffiths a'i Frodyr, 1949).

—— *Dyddiaur'r Gofid: Yr ail I Nest* (London: W. Griffiths a'i Frodyr, 1950).

Paris, Matthew, *Chronica Majora*, ed. H. R. Luard (7 vols, Rolls Series, 57; London: Longman & Co., 1872–84).

Pennant, Thomas, *A Tour in Wales* (London: printed for Benjamin White, 1784).

Price, Thomas, *Hanes Cymru, a Chenedl y Cymry, o'r Cynoesoedd hyd at Farwolaeth Llewelyn ap Gruffydd; Ynghyd a Rhai Cofiaint Perthynol i'r Amseroedd o'r Pryd Hynny i Waered* (Crughywel: Thomas Williams, 1842).

Prichard, T. J. Llewelyn, *The Adventures and Vagaries of Twm Shon Catti, Descriptive of Life in Wales: Interspersed with Poems* (Aberystwyth: printed for the author by J. Cox, 1828).

—— *The Heroines of Welsh History: Comprising Memoirs and Biographical Notices of the Celebrated Women of Wales* (London: W. and F. G. Cash, 1854).

Rees, David Llewellyn, *The Modern Universal British Traveller: Or, a New, Complete, and Accurate Tour through England, Wales, Scotland, and the Neighbouring Islands* (London: printed for J. Cooke, 1779).

Rhoscomyl, Owen [Arthur Owen Vaughan], *Flame Bearers of Welsh History: Being the Outline of the Story of the 'Sons of Cunedda'* (Merthyr Tydfil: Welsh Educational Publishing Co., 1905).

Rhys, Gweirydd ap, *Hanes y Brytaniaid a'r Cymry: Yn Wladol, Milwrol, Cymdeithasol, Masnachol, llenorol, a Chrefyddol, o'r Amseroedd Boreuaf hyd yn Bresennol* (2 vols, London and Caerlleon: William Mackenzie, 1872–74).

Stawell, Mrs Rodolph, *Motor Tours in Wales and the Border Counties* (London: Hodder and Stoughton, 1908).

Taylor, J., *A Short Relation of a Long Journey, made Round or Ovall by Encompassing the Principalitie of Wales, from London. . . . This Painfull Circuit Began . . . the 13 of July . . . 1652, and was Ended . . . the 7 of September Following, being near 600 Miles. Whereunto is annexed an Epitome of the Famous History of Wales* (London, 1653).

Thompson, R. W., *An Englishman Looks at Wales* (Bristol: Arrowsmith, 1937).

Vita Griffini Filii Conani: The Medieval Latin Life of Gruffudd ap Cynan, ed. and trans. Paul Russell (Cardiff: University of Wales Press, 2005).

Warrington, William, *The History of Wales in Nine Books: With an Appendix* (London: printed for J. Johnson, 1786; 2nd edn 1788; 3rd edn 1791); 4th edn as *The History of Wales, in Nine Books: With an Appendix* (2 vols, Brecon: W. Williams, 1823).

William of Malmesbury, *Willelmi Malmesbiriensis monachi De gestis regum Anglorum Libri Quinque: Historiæ novellæ libri tres*, ed. William Stubbs (2 vols, Rolls Series, 90; London: HMSO, 1887, 1889).

Williams, Jane, *The Literary Women of England including a Biographical Epitome of all the Most Eminent to the Year 1700; and Sketches of the Poetesses to the*

Year 1850; with Extracts from their Works, and Critical Remarks (London: Saunders, Otley, & Co., 1861).

—— *History of Wales Derived from Authentic Sources* (London: Longmans, Green, and Co., 1869).

Woodward, B. B., *The History of Wales: From the Earliest Times, to its Final Incorporation with the Kingdom of England; with Notices of its Physical Geography, and Mineral Wealth; and of the Religion and Literature, Laws, Customs, Manners, and Arts of the Welsh* (London: Virtue and Co., 1853).

Wyndham, Henry Penruddocke, *A Gentleman's Tour through Monmouthshire and Wales, in the Months of June and July, 1774* . . . (London: printed for T. Evans, 1775; new edn 1881).

Yorke, Philip, *The Royal Tribes of Wales* (Wrexham: printed by John Painter, 1799).

Secondary sources

Aaron, Jane, *Nineteenth-Century Women's Writing in Wales: Nation, Gender and Identity* (2nd edn; Cardiff: University of Wales Press, 2010).

Anderson, Benedict, *Imagined Communities: Reflections on the Origin and Spread of Nationalism* (rev. edn, London and New York: Verso, 2006).

Andrews, Rhian M., 'The nomenclature of kingship in Welsh court poetry 1100–1300, part I: the terms', *Studia Celtica*, 44 (2010), 79–110.

—— 'The nomenclature of kingship in Welsh court poetry 1100–1300, part II: the rulers', *Studia Celtica*, 45 (2011), 53–82.

Appadurai, Arjun, *Modernity at Large: Cultural Dimensions of Globalization* (Minneapolis: University of Minnesota Press, 1996).

—— 'Disjuncture and difference in the global cultural economy', in Jane Evans Braziel and Anita Mannur (eds), *Theorising Diaspora: A Reader* (Oxford: Blackwell, 2003).

Ashe, Laura, *Fiction and History in England 1066–1200* (Cambridge: Cambridge University Press, 2007).

Austin, David, 'The context and the research design', in D. Austin (ed.), *Carew Castle Archaeological Project: 1992 Season Interim Report* (Lampeter: Department of Archaeology, University of Wales, 1993), pp. 5–9.

B., A., 'Notes on the antiquities and etymology of Eglwyseg, Denbighshire', *Archaeologia Cambrensis* (1865), 133–6.

—— 'Additional notes on Eglwyseg', *Archaeologia Cambrensis* (1865), 369–70.

Babcock, Robert S., 'Rhys ap Tewdwr, king of Deheubarth', *ANS*, 16 (1993), 21–35.

—— 'Imbeciles and Normans: the ynfydion of Gruffudd ap Rhys reconsidered', *Haskins Society Journal*, 4 (1993 for 1992), 1–9.

Barczewski, S. L., *Myth and National Identity in Nineteenth-Century Britain: The Legends of King Arthur and Robin Hood* (Oxford: Oxford University Press, 2000).

Barefield, Laura D., *Gender and History in Medieval English Romance and Chronicle* (New York and Oxford: Peter Lang, 2003).

Barrow, Julia, 'Editing St Davids episcopal acta 1085–1280', *The Carmarthenshire Antiquary*, 34 (1998), 5–10.

Bartlett, Robert, 'Medieval and modern concepts of race and ethnicity', *Journal of Medieval and Early Modern Studies*, 31 (2001), 39–56.

—— 'Rewriting saints' lives: the case of Gerald of Wales', *Speculum*, 58 (1983), 598–613.

—— *Gerald of Wales, 1146–1223* (Oxford: Clarendon Press, 1982).

—— 'Gerald of Wales [Giraldus Cambrensis, Gerald de Barry] (c.1146–1220x23), author and ecclesiastic', *ODNB*. 21. 925–8.

Bates, David, 'Charters and historians of Britain and Ireland: problems and possibilities', in Marie Therese Flanagan and Judith A. Green (eds), *Charters and Charter Scholarship in Britain and Ireland* (Basingstoke: Palgrave Macmillan, 2005), pp. 1–14.

Bates, David, Crick, Julia, and Hamilton, Sarah (eds), *Writing Medieval Biography, 750–1250: Essays in Honour of Professor Frank Barlow* (Woodbridge: Boydell, 2006).

Batten, Charles L., *Pleasurable Instruction: Form and Convention in Eighteenth-Century Travel Literature* (Berkeley, Los Angeles and London: University of California Press, 1978).

Beattie, Cordelia, 'Gender and femininity in medieval England', in Nancy Partner (ed.), *Writing Medieval History* (London: Hodder Arnold, 2005), pp. 153–70.

Beattie, Cordelia, and Fenton, Kirsten A. (eds), *Intersections of Gender, Religion and Ethnicity in the Middle Ages* (Basingstoke: Palgrave Macmillan, 2011).

Beddoe, Deidre, 'Williams, Jane [known as Jane Williams Ysgafell] (1806–1885), historian and writer', *ODNB*. 59. 218–20.

Bedos-Rezak, Brigitte, 'Medieval women in French sigillographic sources', in J. T. Rosenthal (ed.), *Medieval Women and the Sources of Medieval History* (Athens, GA and London: University of Georgia Press, 1990), pp. 1–36.

—— 'Women, seals and power in medieval France, 1150–1350', in M. Erler and M. Kowaleski (eds), *Women and Power in the Middle Ages* (Athens, GA and London: University of Georgia Press, 1998), pp. 61–82.

—— 'In search of a semiotic paradigm: the matter of sealing in medieval thought and praxis, 1050–1400', in Noel Adams, John Cherry and James Robinson (eds), *Good Impressions: Image and Authority in Medieval Seals* (London: British Museum, 2007), pp. 1–7.

Bergdolt, Klaus, *Wellbeing: A Cultural History of Healthy Living* (Cambridge: Polity, 2008).

Bitel, Lisa, 'Introduction: convent ruins and Christian profession: towards a methodology for the history of religion and gender', in Lisa M. Bitel and Felice Lifshitz (eds), *Gender and Christianity in Medieval Europe: New Perspectives* (Philadelphia: University of Pennsylvania Press, 2008), pp. 1–15.

Bohls, Elizabeth A., 'Age of peregrination: travel writing and the eighteenth-century novel', in Paula R. Backscheider and Catherine Ingrassia (eds), *A*

Companion to the Eighteenth-Century English Novel and Culture (Oxford: Blackwell, 2005), pp. 97–116.

—— *Travel Writing 1700–1830: An Anthology* (Oxford: Oxford University Press, 2005).

Bollard, John K., and Austin, David, 'Carew castle: the earliest documentary evidence', in D. Austin (ed.), *Carew Castle Archaeological Project: 1994 Season Interim Report* (Lampeter: Department of Archaeology, University of Wales, 1995), pp. 6–7.

Bowen, Lloyd, 'Representations of Wales and the Welsh during the civil wars and interregnum', *Historical Research*, 77 (2004), 358–76.

Bradshaw, Brendan, and Roberts, Peter (eds), *British Consciousness and Identity: The Making of Britain, 1533–1707* (Cambridge: Cambridge University Press, 1998).

Breeze, Andrew, *Medieval Welsh Literature* (Dublin: Four Courts Press, 1997).

Brewer, D. S., 'The ideal of feminine beauty in medieval literature, especially "Harley lyrics", Chaucer and some Elizabethans', *Modern Language Review*, 50 (1955), 257–69.

Brooke, C. N. L., *The Medieval Idea of Marriage* (Oxford, 1989; new edn, Oxford: Clarendon Press, 1994).

—— 'Map, Walter (d. 1209/10), royal clerk, raconteur, and satirist', *ODNB*. 36. 577–9.

Broun, Dauvit, *The Charters of Gaelic Scotland and Ireland in the Early and Central Middle Ages* (Cambridge: Department of Anglo-Saxon, Norse and Celtic, University of Cambridge, 1995).

Brown, Marjorie A., 'The feast hall in Anglo-Saxon society', in Martha Carlin and Joel T. Rosenthal (eds), *Food and Eating in Medieval Europe* (London and Rio Grande: Hambledon Press, 1999), pp. 1–28.

Brubaker, Leslie, and Smith, Julia M. H. (eds), *Gender in the Early Medieval World: East and West, 300–900* (Cambridge and New York: Cambridge University Press, 2004).

Bynum, Caroline Walker, 'Metamorphosis, or Gerald and the werewolf', *Speculum*, 73 (1998), 987–1013.

Cannadine, David, 'British History as a "new subject": politics, perspectives and prospects', in Alexander Grant and Keith J. Stringer (eds), *Uniting the Kingdom? The Making of British History* (London and New York: Routledge, 1995), pp. 12–28.

Capp, Bernard, 'Taylor, John [*called* the Water Poet] (1578–1653), poet', *ODNB*. 53. 930–5.

Carr, A. D., 'Hywel ab Owain Gwynedd (d. 1170), prince of Gwynedd and poet', also including 'Dafydd ab Owain Gwynedd (d. 1203)', *ODNB*. 29. 173–4.

—— 'Llywelyn ab Iorwerth [*called* Llywelyn Fawr] (c.1173–1240)' prince of Gwynedd, *ODNB*. 34. 180–5.

Cartwright, Jane, 'Virginity and chastity in medieval Welsh prose', in Anke Bernau, Ruth Evans and Sarah Salih (eds), *Medieval Virginities* (Cardiff: University of Wales Press, 2003), pp. 56–79.

Cavell, Emma, 'Aristocratic widows and the medieval Welsh frontier: the Shropshire evidence', *TRHS*, 6th ser., 17 (2007), 57–82.

Chadwick, Nora K., *The Celtic Realms* (2nd edn, London: Weidenfeld and Nicolson, 1972).

Charles, B. G., *George Owen of Henllys: A Welsh Elizabethan* (Aberystwyth: National Library of Wales Press, 1973).

Charles-Edwards, T. M., 'Nau Kynywedi Teithiauc', in Jenkins and Owen (eds), *Welsh Law of Women*, pp. 23–39.

—— *The Welsh Laws* (Cardiff: University of Wales Press on behalf of the Welsh Arts Council, 1989).

—— *Early Irish and Welsh Kinship* (Oxford: Clarendon Press, 1993).

Charles-Edwards, T. M., and Jones, Nerys Ann, 'Breintiau Gwŷr Powys: the liberties of the men of Powys', in Charles-Edwards, Owen and Russell (eds), *Welsh King and his Court*, pp. 191–223.

Charles-Edwards, T. M., Owen, M. E., and Russell, P. (eds), *The Welsh King and his Court* (Cardiff: University of Wales Press, 2000).

Charles-Edwards, T. M., and Russell, P., 'The Hendregadredd Manuscript and the orthography and phonology of Welsh in the early fourteenth century', *Cylchgrawn Llyfrgell Genedlaethol Cymru*, 28 (1994), 419–62.

Charles-Edwards, T. M., and Russell, Paul (eds), *Tair Colofn Cyfraith: The Three Columns of the Law in Medieval Wales: Homicide, Theft and Fire* (Bangor: Welsh Legal History Society, 2007).

Chibnall, M., *The Empress Matilda: Queen Consort, Queen Mother and Lady of the English* (Oxford: Blackwell, 1991).

—— *The Debate on the Norman Conquest* (Manchester: Manchester University Press, 1999).

Clancy, J. P., *The Earliest Welsh Poetry* (London: Macmillan, 1970).

—— *Medieval Welsh Poems* (Dublin: Four Courts Press, 2003).

Coates, Richard, 'Æthelflæd's fortification of *Weardburh*', *Notes and Queries,* 243 (1998), 8–12.

Colker, Marvin L., 'The "Margam Chronicle" in a Dublin manuscript', *Haskins Society Journal*, 4 (1993 for 1992), 123–48.

Courtney, Paul, 'The Norman invasion of Gwent: a reassessment', *JMH*, 12 (1986), 297–313.

Crane, David, *Walks through the History of Rural Llangollen* (Wrexham: Bridge Books, 2000).

Cressy, David, *Travesties and Transgressions in Tudor and Stuart England* (Oxford: Oxford University Press, 2000).

Crick, J. C., 'The British past and the Welsh future: Gerald of Wales, Geoffrey of Monmouth and Arthur of Britain', *Celtica*, 23 (1999), 60–75.

—— *The Historia Regum Britannie of Geoffrey of Monmouth*, 4: *Dissemination and Reception in the Later Middle Ages* (Cambridge: D. S. Brewer, 1991).

—— 'St Albans, Westminster and some twelfth-century views of the Anglo-Saxon past', *ANS*, 25 (2003), 65–83.

Crouch, David B., 'The slow death of kingship in Glamorgan', *Morgannwg*, 29 (1985), 20–41.

—— 'Robert, earl of Gloucester, and the daughter of Zelophehad', *JMH*, 11 (1985), 227–43.

—— 'The earliest original charter of a Welsh king', *BBCS*, 36 (1989), 125–31.

—— 'The last adventure of Richard Siward', *Morgannwg*, 35 (1991), 7–30.

—— 'The March and the Welsh kings', in Edmund King (ed.), *The Anarchy of King Stephen's Reign* (Oxford: Clarendon Press, 1994), pp. 255–89.

—— 'Robert, first earl of Gloucester (b. before 1100, d. 1147), magnate', *ODNB*. 47. 93–6.

—— 'Nest (b. before 1092, d. c.1130), royal mistress', *ODNB*. 40. 441–2.

—— *The Birth of Nobility: Constructing Aristocracy in England and France 900–1300* (Harlow: Pearson/Longman, 2005).

—— 'The transformation of medieval Gwent', in Ralph A. Griffiths, Tony Hopkins and R. C. Howell (eds), *Gwent County History*, vol. 2: *The Age of the Marcher Lords, c.1070–1536* (Cardiff: University of Wales Press on behalf of the Gwent County History Association, 2008), pp. 1–45.

Crump, J. J., 'Repercussions of the execution of William de Braose: a letter from Llywelyn ab Iorwerth to Stephen de Segrave', *BIHR*, 73 (2000), 197–212.

Davies, Ceri, *Welsh Literature and the Classical Tradition* (Cardiff: University of Wales Press, 1995).

Davies, Hywel, 'Wales in English travel writing 1791–8: the Welsh critique of Theophilus Jones', *WHR*, 23 (2007), 65–93.

Davies, John Reuben, *The Book of Llandaf and the Norman Church in Wales* (Woodbridge: Boydell, 2003).

Davies, R. R., 'Kings, lords and liberties in the March of Wales, 1066–1272', *TRHS*, 5th ser., 29 (1979), 41–61.

—— 'Law and national identity in thirteenth-century Wales', in R. R. Davies, Ralph Griffiths, Ieuan Gwynedd Jones and Kenneth Morgan (eds), *Welsh Society and Nationhood: Historical Essays Presented to Glanmor Williams* (Cardiff: University of Wales Press, 1984), pp. 51–64.

—— *Conquest, Coexistence and Change: Wales 1063–1415* (Oxford: Oxford University Press, 1987).

—— *The Age of Conquest: Wales 1063–1415* (Oxford: Oxford University Press, 1987; new edn 2000).

—— *Domination and Conquest: The Experience of Ireland, Scotland and Wales, 1100–1300* (Cambridge: Cambridge University Press, 1990).

—— 'The peoples of Britain and Ireland, 1100–1400, I: Identities', *TRHS*, 6th ser., 4 (1994), 1–20.

—— 'The peoples of Britain and Ireland, 1100–1400, III: Laws and customs', *TRHS*, 6th ser., 6 (1996), 1–23.

—— *The Matter of Britain and the Matter of England* (Oxford: Clarendon Press, 1996).

—— 'The peoples of Britain and Ireland, 1100–1400, IV: Language and historical mythology', *TRHS*, 6th ser., 7 (1997), 1–24.

Davies, Wendy, 'Charter-writing and its uses in early medieval Celtic societies', in Huw Pryce (ed.), *Literacy in Medieval Celtic Societies* (Cambridge: Cambridge University Press, 1998), pp. 99–112.

—— 'Looking backwards to the early medieval past: Wales and England, a contrast in approaches', *WHR*, 22 (2004), 197–221.

D'Avray, D. L., *Medieval Marriage: Symbolism and Society* (Oxford: Oxford University Press, 2005).

Doan, James, 'Sovereignty aspects in the role of women in medieval Irish and Welsh society', *Proceedings of the Harvard Celtic Colloquium*, 5 (1985), 87–102.

Dobson, Roger, 'Is this Welsh princess the first British woman author?', *The Independent*, 11 January 1997.

Duby, Georges, *Medieval Marriage: Two Models from Twelfth-Century France*, trans. Elborg Forster (Baltimore: Johns Hopkins University Press, 1991).

—— *Le Chevalier, la femme, et le prêtre* (Paris, 1981), trans. B. Bray, *The Knight, the Lady and the Priest: The Making of Modern Marriage in Medieval France* (New York: Pantheon, 1983).

Duffy, Seán, 'The 1169 invasion as a turning-point in Irish–Welsh relations', in Brendan Smith (ed.), *Britain and Ireland, 900–1300: Insular Responses to Medieval European Change* (Cambridge: Cambridge University Press, 1999), pp. 98–113.

Eales, Richard, 'Ranulf (III) [Ranulf de Blundeville], sixth earl of Chester and first earl of Lincoln (1170–1232)', *ODNB*. 46. 56–9.

Eco, Umberto, *Art and Beauty in the Middle Ages* (New Haven and London: Yale University Press, 1986).

Edwards, Huw Meirion, *Dafydd ap Gwilym: Influences and Analogues* (Oxford: Clarendon Press, 1996).

—— 'Canu serch Hywel ab Owain Gwynedd', in Nerys Ann Jones (ed.), *Hywel ab Owain Gwynedd: Bardd-Dywysog* (Cardiff: University of Wales Press, 2009), pp. 88–110.

Edwards, Hywel Teifi, 'Owen Rhoscomyl (1863–1919) a "Rhwysg Hanes Cymru"', *Transactions of the Honourable Society of Cymmrodorion*, 13 (2007), 107–33.

—— *The National Pageant of Wales* (Llandysul: Gomer, 2009).

Edwards, Robert R., 'Walter Map: authorship and the space of writing', *New Literary History*, 38 (2007), 273–92.

Emanuel, H. D., 'The historical study of the Welsh lawbooks', *TRHS*, 5th ser., vii (1962), 141–55.

Evans, Neil, 'Finding a new story: the search for a usable past in Wales, 1869–1930', *Transactions of the Honourable Society of Cymmrodorion*, new ser., 10 (2004), 144–62.

—— '"When men and mountains meet": historians' explanations of the history of Wales, 1890–1970', *WHR*, 22 (2004), 221–51.

Evans, J. Wyn., 'St David and St David's and the coming of the Normans', *Transactions of the Honourable Society of Cymmrodorion*, new ser., 11 (2004), 5–18.

Evans, D. Simon, *A Mediaeval Prince: The Life of Gruffudd ap Cynan* (Felinfach: Llanerch, 1990).

Fabricant, Carole, 'Eighteenth-century travel literature', in John Richetti (ed.), *The Cambridge History of English Literature 1660–1780* (Cambridge: Cambridge University Press, 2005), pp. 707–44.

Fairlamb, Neil, *The Viscount and the Baron: The Life and Times of Thomas James Warren Bulkeley 1752–1822 Viscount Bulkeley of Cashel and Baron Bulkeley of Beaumaris* (Carlisle: Bookcase, 2009).

Fenton, Kirsten, 'Gendering the First Crusade in William of Malmesbury's *Gesta Regum Anglorum*', in Beattie and Fenton (eds), *Intersections of Gender, Religion and Ethnicity*, pp. 125–39.

Field, Rosalind, 'The king over the water: exile-and-return revisited', in Corinne Saunders (ed.), *Cultural Encounters in the Romance of Medieval England* (Woodbridge and Rochester, NY: D. S. Brewer, 2005), pp. 41–53.

Fisher, Deborah C., *Princesses of Wales* (Cardiff: University of Wales Press, 2005).

Flanagan, M. T., *Irish Society, Anglo-Norman Settlers, Angevin Kingship: Interactions in Ireland in the Late Twelfth Century* (Oxford: Clarendon Press, 1989).

—— 'Mac Murchada, Diarmait [Dermot MacMurrough; *called* Diamait na nGall] (*c.*1110–1171)', *ODNB*. 35. 915–17.

Flint, Valerie, 'The *Historia Regum Brittaniae* of Geoffrey of Monmouth: parody and its purpose: a suggestion', *Speculum*, 54 (1979), 447–68.

Ford, Patrick K., 'Performance and literacy in medieval Welsh poetry', *The Modern Language Review*, 100 (2005), 30–47.

Foxley, Rachel, 'John Lilburne and the citizenship of "Free-Born Englishmen"', *The Historical Journal*, 47 (2004), 849–74.

Fradenburg, Louise Olga (ed.), *Women and Sovereignty* (Edinburgh: Edinburgh University Press, 1992).

Frame, R., *The Political Development of the British Isles, 1100–1400* (Oxford, 1990; rev. edn, Oxford: Clarendon Press, 1995).

Gillingham, J., 'The beginnings of English imperialism', *Journal of Historical Sociology*, 5 (1992), 302–409.

—— 'The English invasion of Ireland', in B. Bradshaw *et al.* (eds), *Representing Ireland: Literature and the Origins of Conflict, 1534–1660* (Cambridge: Cambridge University Press, 1993), pp. 24–42.

—— 'Foundations of a disunited kingdom', in Alexander Grant and Keith J. Stringer (eds), *Uniting the Kingdom? The Making of British History* (London and New York: Routledge, 1995), pp. 48–64; repr. in J. Gillingham, *The English in the Twelfth Century: Imperialism, National Identity and Political Values* (Woodbridge: Boydell, 2000), pp. 93–109.

—— 'The travels of Roger of Howden and his views of the Irish, Scots and Welsh', *ANS*, 20 (1998 for 1997), 151–69.

—— *The English in the Twelfth Century: Imperialism, National Identity and Political Values* (Woodbridge: Boydell, 2000).

—— 'Civilising the English: the English histories of William of Malmesbury and David Hume', *Historical Research*, 74 (2001), 17–43.

—— '"Slaves of the Normans"? Gerald de Barri and regnal solidarity in early-thirteenth-century England', in Pauline Stafford, Janet L. Nelson and Jane Martindale (eds), *Law, Laity and Solidarities: Essays in Honour of Susan Reynolds* (Manchester: Manchester University Press, 2001), pp. 160–71.

Golding, Brian, *Conquest and Colonisation: The Normans in Britain, 1066–1100* (rev. edn, Basingstoke and New York: Palgrave, 2001).

Goodich, Michael E., *Lives and Miracles of the Saints: Studies in Medieval Latin Hagiography* (Aldershot and Burlington: Ashgate/Variorum, 2004).

—— 'Biography, 1000–1350', in D. M. Deliyannis (ed.), *Historiography in the Middle Ages* (Leiden: Brill, 2003), pp. 353–85.

Gramich, Katie, *Women's Writing in Wales: Land, Gender, Belonging* (Cardiff: University of Wales Press, 2007).

Gransden, Antonia, *Historical Writing in England c. 550 to c. 1307* (London: Routledge and Kegan Paul, 1974).

Green, Judith A., *Henry I: King of England and Duke of Normandy* (Cambridge: Cambridge University Press, 2009).

Greenway, W., 'The Annals of Margam', *Transactions of the Port Talbot Historical Society*, 1 (1963), 19–31.

Griffiths, M., 'Native society on the Anglo-Norman frontier: the evidence of the Margam charters', *WHR*, 14 (1988–89), 179–216.

Griffiths, Ralph A., 'The rise of the Stradlings of St Donat's', *Morgannwg*, 7 (1963), 15–47.

—— 'The Norman conquest and the twelve knights of Glamorgan', *Glamorgan Historian*, 3 (1966), 153–69.

Gruffudd, Pyrs, Herbert, David T., and Piccini, Angela, 'In search of Wales: travel writing and narratives of difference, 1918–50', *Journal of Historical Geography*, 26 (2000), 589–604.

Hall, Stuart, 'Cultural identity and diaspora', in Nicholas Mirzoeff (ed.), *Diaspora and Visual Culture: Representing Africans and Jews* (London: Routledge, 2000).

Harding, Alan, '*Regiam Majestatem* amongst medieval law books', *The Juridical Review*, 29 (1984), 97–111.

Harris, B. E., Thacker, A. T., and Lewis, C. P., *A History of the County of Chester* (Victoria History of the Counties of England; 4 vols in 5, continuing, Oxford: Oxford University Press for the University of London Institute of Historical Research, 1979–2005).

Heal, Felicity, and Holmes, Clive (eds), *The Gentry in England and Wales, 1500–1700* (Basingstoke: Macmillan, 1994).

Hechter, Michael, *Internal Colonialism: The Celtic Fringe in British National Development* (2nd edn, New Brunswick, NJ and London: Transaction, 1999).

Heller, Sarah-Grace, 'Light as glamour: the luminescent ideal of beauty in the Roman de la Rose', *Speculum*, 76 (2001), 934–59.

Herendeen, Wyman H., 'William Camden (1551–1623), historian and herald', *ODNB*. 9. 603–14.

Hill, Christopher, *Intellectual Origins of the English Revolution Revisited* (Oxford: Clarendon Press, 1997; rev. edn of the text first pub. 1965).

Hilling, John B., *Cilgerran Castle, St Dogmaels Abbey, Pentre Ifan Burial Chamber* (Cardiff: Cadw – Welsh Historic Monuments, 1992; new edn 2000).

Holden, Brock, 'The making of the middle March of Wales, 1066–1250', *WHR*, 20 (2000), 207–26.

—— *Lords of the Central Marches: English Aristocracy and Frontier Society, 1087–1265* (Oxford: Oxford University Press, 2008).

Hopkins, T. J., 'Rice Merrick (Rhys Meurig) of Cottrell', *Morgannwg*, 8 (1964), 5–13.

Houghton, W. E., *The Victorian Frame of Mind 1830–1870* (New Haven: Yale University Press, 1957).

Houts, Elisabeth M. C. van, *Memory and Gender in Medieval Europe, 900–1200* (Basingstoke: Macmillan, 1999).

Howells, Brian (ed.), *Pembrokeshire County History*, vol. III: *Early Modern Pembrokeshire 1536–1815* (Haverfordwest: Pembrokeshire Historical Society, 1987).

Hughes, K. W., 'The Welsh Latin chronicles: *Annales Cambriae* and related texts', *Proceedings of the British Academy*, 59 (1973), 233–58.

Huws, Daniel, *Medieval Welsh Manuscripts* (Cardiff: University of Wales Press, 2000).

—— 'Twm Siôn Cati', *The Carmarthenshire Antiquary*, 45 (2009), 39–45.

Huws, Gwilym, 'Welsh language publishing 1919 to 1995', in Philip Henry Jones and Eiluned Rees (eds), *A Nation and its Books: A History of the Book in Wales* (Aberystwyth: National Library of Wales, 1998), pp. 341–53.

Ingledew, Francis, 'The Book of Troy and the genealogical construction of history: the case of Geoffrey of Monmouth's *Historia regum Britanniae*', *Speculum*, 69 (1994), 665–704.

Insley, Charles, 'Fact and fiction in thirteenth-century Gwynedd: the Aberconwy charters', *Studia Celtica*, 33 (1999), 235–50.

—— 'From *Rex Wallie* to *Princeps Wallie*: charters and state formation in thirteenth-century Wales', in J. R. Maddicott and D. M. Palliser (eds), *The Medieval State: Essays Presented to James Campbell* (London: Hambledon, 2000), pp. 179–96.

Ives, E. W., ' "Agaynst taking awaye of women": the inception and operation of the Abduction Act of 1487', in E. W. Ives, R. J. Knecht and J. J. Scarisbrick (eds), *Wealth and Power in Tudor England: Essays Presented to S. T. Bindoff* (London: Athlone Press, 1978), pp. 21–45.

Jack, I., *Medieval Wales* (London: Hodder and Stoughton for the Sources of History Ltd, 1972).

Jaeger, C. Stephen, *The Envy of Angels: Cathedral Schools and Social Ideals in Medieval Europe, 950–1200* (Philadelphia: University of Pennsylvania Press, 1994).

Jankulak, Karen, *Geoffrey of Monmouth* (Cardiff: University of Wales Press, 2008).

Jarman, A. O. H., and Hughes, Gwilym Rees (eds), *A Guide to Welsh Literature* (7 vols, Cardiff: University of Wales Press, 1976–2003).

Jenkins, Dafydd, 'Kings, lords and princes: the nomenclature of authority in thirteenth-century Wales', *BBCS*, 26 (1974–76), 451–62.

—— 'Property interests in the classical Welsh law of women', in Jenkins and Owen (eds), *Welsh Law of Women*, pp. 69–92.

—— 'Prolegomena to the law of court', in Charles-Edwards, Owen and Russell (eds), *Welsh King and his Court*, pp. 15–28.

Jenkins, Dafydd, and Owen, Morfydd E. (eds), *The Welsh Law of Women: Studies Presented to Professor Daniel A. Binchy on his Eightieth Birthday, 3 June 1980* (Cardiff: University of Wales Press, 1980).

Jenkins, Geraint H. 'Clio and Wales: Welsh remembrancers and historical writing 1751–2001', *Transactions of the Honourable Society of Cymmrodorion*, new ser., 8 (2001), 119–36.

—— 'Wales in the eighteenth century', in H. T. Dickinson (ed.), *A Companion to Eighteenth-Century Britain* (Oxford: Blackwell, 2002), pp. 392–402.

—— 'Evans, Theophilus (1693–1767) Church of England clergyman and author', *ODNB*. 18. 753.

Jenkins, Hugh, 'Shrugging off the Norman Yoke: Milton's History of Britain and the Levellers', *English Literary Renaissance*, 29 (1999), 306–25.

John, Angela, 'Lifers: modern Welsh history and the writing of biography', *WHR*, 25 (2010), 251–70.

Johns, Susan M., 'The wives and widows of the earls of Chester, 1100–1252: the charter evidence', *Haskins Society Journal*, 7 (1995), 117–32.

——'Poetry and prayer: women and the politics of spiritual relationships in the early twelfth century', *European Review of History – Revue européenne d'Histoire*, 8 (2001), 7–22.

—— *Noblewomen, Aristocracy and Power in the Twelfth-Century Anglo-Norman Realm* (Manchester: Manchester University Press, 2003).

Jones, Aled, and Jones, Bill, 'Empire and the Welsh press', in Simon J. Potter (ed.), *Newspapers and Empire: Ireland and Britain, c. 1857–1921* (Dublin: Four Courts Press, 2004), pp. 83–91.

Jones, John Gwynfor, *Concepts of Order and Gentility in Wales 1540–1640: Bardic Imagery and Interpretations* (Llandysul: Gomer, 1992).

—— *The Welsh Gentry 1536–1640: Images of Status, Honour and Authority* (Cardiff: University of Wales Press, 1998).

—— 'The Welsh gentry and the image of the "Cambro-Briton", c. 1603–25', *WHR*, 20 (2001), 615–55.

Jones, W. R., 'England against the Celtic fringe: a study in cultural stereotypes', *Journal of World History*, 13 (1971), 155–71.

Kearney, Hugh, *The British Isles: A History of Four Nations* (Cambridge: Cambridge University Press, 1989, 2nd edn 2006).

Kenny, Gillian, 'Anglo-Irish and Gaelic marriage laws and traditions in late medieval Ireland', *JMH*, 32 (2006), 27–42.

Keynes, Simon, 'King Alfred and the Mercians', in M. A. S. Blackburn and David N. Dumville (eds), *Kings, Currency and Alliances: History and Coinage of Southern England in the Ninth Century* (Woodbridge: Boydell, 1998), pp. 1–46.

Knox-Mawer, Howard, 'The house at World's End', *Country Quest*, 27 (1986), 28–9.

Laiou, A. E. (ed.), *Consent and Coercion to Sex and Marriage in Ancient and Medieval Societies* (Washington, DC: Dumbarton Oaks Research Library and Collection, 1993).

Latimer, P., 'Henry II's campaign against the Welsh in 1165', *WHR*, 14 (1988–89), 523–52.

Laws, Edward, *The History of Little England beyond Wales: And the Non-Kymric Colony Settled in Wales* (London and Tenby: George Bell and Sons, 1888).

Le Neve, John, *Fasti Ecclesiae Anglicanae IX, 1066–1300: The Welsh Cathedrals*, compiled by M. J. Pearson (London: University of London, School of Advanced Study, Institute of Historical Research, 2003).

Leask, Nigel, *Curiosity and the Aesthetics of Travel Writing, 1770–1840: 'From an Antique Land'* (Oxford: Oxford University Press, 2002).

Leckie, William, *The Passage of Dominion: Geoffrey of Monmouth and the Periodization of Insular History in the Twelfth Century* (Toronto, Buffalo and London: University of Toronto Press, 1981).

Levine, Philippa, *Gender and Empire* (Oxford: Oxford University Press, 2004).

Lewis, C. W., 'The literary tradition of Morgannwg', in T. B. Pugh (ed.), *Glamorgan County History*, vol. 3: *The Middle Ages: The Marcher Lordships of Glamorgan and Morgannwg and Gower and Kilvey from the Norman Conquest to the Act of Union of England and Wales* (Cardiff: University of Wales Press for the Glamorgan County History Committee, 1971), pp. 449–554.

—— 'Merrick, Rice [Rhys Meurug] (*c.* 1520–1587), landowner and antiquary', *ODNB*. 37. 906–7.

Lieberman, Max, 'Striving for Marcher liberties: the Corbets of Caus in the thirteenth century', in Michael Prestwich (ed.), *Liberties and Identities in the Medieval British Isles* (Woodbridge: Boydell, 2008), pp. 141–54.

—— *The March of Wales 1067–1300: A Borderland of Medieval Britain* (Cardiff: University of Wales Press, 2008).

—— *The Medieval March of Wales: The Creation and Perception of a Frontier, 1066–1283* (Cambridge: Cambridge University Press, 2010).

Livingstone, Amy, 'Noblewomen's control of property in early twelfth-century Blois-Chartres', *Medieval Prosopography*, 18 (1997), pp. 55–71.

Lloyd, J. E., *The Story of Ceredigion (400–1277)* (Cardiff: University of Wales Press Board, 1937).

—— *A History of Carmarthenshire* (2 vols, Cardiff: W. Lewis Ltd for the London Carmarthenshire Society, 1935).

—— *A History of Wales from the Earliest Times to the Edwardian Conquest* (2 vols, London, 1911; 3rd edn, London: Longmans, Green, 1939).

Lloyd, J. E., rev. David E. Thornton, 'Rhys ap Tewdwr (d. 1093), ruler in Wales', *ODNB*. 46. 619.

Lloyd, J. E., rev. Brynley F. Roberts, 'Price, Thomas [*pseud.* Camhuanawe] (1787–1848), historian', *ODNB*. 45. 317–18.

Lloyd, J. E., and Jenkins, R. T. (eds), *The Dictionary of Welsh Biography down to 1940* (London: Honourable Society of Cymmrodorion, 1959; based on first Welsh edition, as *Bywgraffiadur Cymreig hyd 1940*, London: Anrhydeddus Gymdeithas y Cymmrodorion, 1953).

Lloyd, Thomas, Orbach, Julian, and Scourfield, Robert, *Pembrokeshire* (The Buildings of Wales; New Haven and London: Yale University Press, 1994).

—— 'More written about than writing? Welsh women and the written word', in Huw Pryce (ed.), *Literacy in Medieval Celtic Societies* (Cambridge: Cambridge University Press, 1998), pp. 149–65.

Lloyd-Morgan, Ceridwen 'Women and their poetry in medieval Wales', in Carol M. Meale (ed.), *Women and Literature in Britain 1150–1500* (1993; 2nd edn, Cambridge: Cambridge University Press, 1996), pp. 183–203.

LoPrete, Kimberly A., *Adela of Blois: Countess and Lord (c.1067–1137)* (Dublin: Four Courts Press, 2007).

Ludlow, Neil, *Pembroke Castle: Birthplace of Henry Tudor* (Pembroke Castle Trust, n.d.).

Lynch, P., 'Court poetry, power and politics', in Charles-Edwards, Owen and Russell (eds), *Welsh King and his Court*, pp. 167–90.

McAll, Christopher, 'The normal paradigms of a woman's life in the Irish and Welsh law texts', in Jenkins and Owen (eds), *Welsh Law of Women*, pp. 7–22.

Mac Cana, Proinsias, *Branwen Daughter of Llŷr* (Cardiff: University of Wales Press, 1958).

Mc Elligott, Jason, 'Crouch, Nathaniel [*pseud.* Robert Burton] (c.1640–1725?), bookseller and writer', *ODNB*. 14. 465–6.

Maund, K. L., *Ireland, Wales and England in the Eleventh Century* (Woodbridge: Boydell, 1991).

—— (ed.), *Gruffudd ap Cynan: A Collaborative Biography* (Woodbridge and Rochester: Boydell and Brewer, 1996).

—— 'Owain ap Cadwgan: a rebel revisited', *Haskins Society Journal*, 13 (2004 for 1999), 65–74.

—— 'Gruffudd, grandson of Iago', in David Bates, Julia Crick and Sarah Hamilton (eds), *Writing Medieval Biography, 750–1250: Essays in Honour of Professor Frank Barlow* (Woodbridge: Boydell Press, 2006), pp. 109–16.

—— *Princess Nest of Wales: Seductress of the English* (Stroud: Tempus, 2007).

Mayer, R., 'Nathaniel Crouch, bookseller and historian: popular historiography and cultural power in late seventeenth-century England', *Eighteenth-Century Studies*, 27 (1993–94), 391–420.

Meddings, John, 'Friendship among the aristocracy in Anglo-Norman England', *ANS*, 22 (2000 for 1999), 187–204.

Meyer, Hannah, 'Gender, Jewish creditors and Christian debtors in thirteenth-century Exeter', in Beattie and Fenton (eds), *Intersections of Gender, Religion and Ethnicity*, pp. 104–24.

Miles, Dillwyn, 'George Owen (1552–1613), antiquary', *ODNB*. 42. 199–202.

Mittman, Asa Simon, 'The other close at hand: Gerald of Wales and the "Marvels of the West"', in Bettina Bildhauer and Robert Mills (eds), *The Monstrous Middle Ages* (Cardiff: University of Wales Press, 2003), pp. 97–112.

Moore, David, 'Gruffudd ap Cynan and the medieval Welsh polity', in K. L. Maund (ed.), *Gruffudd ap Cynan: A Collaborative Biography* (Woodbridge: Boydell and Brewer, 1996), pp. 1–59.

Morgan, Kenneth O., *Rebirth of a Nation: Wales, 1880–1980* (Oxford and Cardiff: Clarendon Press and University of Wales Press, 1981).

Morgan, Prys, *The Eighteenth Century Renaissance* (Llandybie: Christopher Davies, 1981).

—— 'Williams, Edward [*pseud.* Iolo Morganug] (1747–1826) Welsh-language poet and literary forger', *ODNB*. 59. 167–8.

Mortimer, Richard, 'Anglo-Norman lay charters, 1066–*c*. 1100: a diplomatic approach', *ANS*, 25 (2003), 153–75.

Nelson, J. L., 'Gender and genre in women historians of the early middle ages', in J. P. Genet (ed.), *L'Historiographie médiévale en Europe* (Paris: Éditions du CNRS, 1991), pp. 150–63.

—— *The Frankish World, 750–900* (London: Hambledon, 1996), pp. 183–98.

—— 'Family, gender and sexuality', in M. Bentley (ed.), *Companion to Historiography* (London and New York: Routledge, 1997; paperback edn 2002).

Neville, Cynthia J., 'Women, charters, and land ownership in Scotland, 1150–1350', *Journal of Legal History*, 26 (2005), 21–45.

—— 'Finding the family in the charters of medieval Scotland, 1150–1350', in E. Ewan and J. Nugent (eds), *Finding the Family in Medieval and Early Modern Scotland* (Aldershot: Ashgate Press, 2008), pp. 11–21.

Normington, Katie, *Gender and Medieval Drama* (Woodbridge: D. S. Brewer, 2004).

Oakley-Brown, Liz, and Wilkinson, Louise J. (eds), *The Rituals and Rhetoric of Queenship: Medieval to Early Modern* (Dublin: Four Courts Press, 2009).

'Our lost princess . . .', *The Leader* (15 September 2009), pp. 27–8.

Owen, Geraint Dyfnallt, 'Review of *The Golden Hive*', *WHR*, 3 (1966–67), 321–2.

Owen, Hywel Wyn, and Morgan, Richard, *Dictionary of the Place-names of Wales* (Llandysul: Gomer, 2007).

Owen, Morfydd E., 'Shame and reparation: woman's place in the kin', in Jenkins and Owen (eds), *Welsh Law of Women*, pp. 40–68.

Parsons, J. Carmi (ed.), *Medieval Queenship* (Stroud: Alan Sutton, 1994).

Patterson, Nerys, 'Honour and shame in medieval Welsh society', *Studia Celtica*, 16–17 (1981–82), 73–103.

Patterson, Robert B., 'The author of the "Margam annals": early thirteenth-century Margam Abbey's compleat scribe', *ANS*, 14 (1991), 197–210.

—— *The Scriptorium of Margam Abbey and the Scribes of Early Angevin Glamorgan: Secretarial Administration in a Welsh Marcher Barony, c. 1150–c. 1225* (Woodbridge: Boydell Press, 2002).

Patterson, W. B., 'Fuller, Thomas (1607/8–1661), Church of England clergyman', *ODNB*. 21. 159–63.

Perry, C. R., 'Morton, Henry Canova Vollam (1892–1979) travel writer and journalist', *ODNB*. 39. 419–20.

Phillips, Kim, 'Warriors, Amazons and Isles of Women: medieval travel writing and the construction of Asian femininities', in Beattie and Fenton (eds), *Intersections of Gender, Religion and Ethnicity*, pp. 183–207.

Pittock, Murray G. H., *Celtic Identity and the British Image* (Manchester: Manchester University Press, 1999).

Powell, Nia M. W., 'Genealogical narratives and kingship in medieval Wales', in Raluca L. Radelescu and Edward Donald Kennedy (eds), *Broken Lines: Genealogical Literature in Late-Medieval Britain and France* (Turnhout, Belgium: Brepols, 2008), pp. 175–202.

Prescott, Sarah, *Eighteenth-Century Writing from Wales: Bards and Britons* (Cardiff: University of Wales Press, 2008).

Pryce, Huw, 'The prologues to the Welsh lawbooks', *BBCS*, 33 (1986), 151–87.

—— 'In search of a medieval society: Deheubarth in the writings of Gerald of Wales', *WHR*, 13 (1987), 265–81.

—— *Native Law and the Church in Medieval Wales* (Oxford: Clarendon Press, 1993).

—— 'The origins and the medieval period', in Philip Henry Jones and Eiluned Rees (eds), *A Nation and its Books: A History of the Book in Wales* (Aberystwyth: National Library of Wales in association with Aberystwyth Centre for the Book, 1998), pp. 1–23.

—— 'A cross-border career: Giraldus Cambrensis between Wales and England', in Reinhard Schneider (ed.), *Grenzgänger* (Veröffentlichungen der Kommission für Saarländischen Landesgeschichte und Volksforschung, 33) (Saarbrücken: Kommissionsverlag SDV, 1998), pp. 45–60.

—— 'The Normans in Wales', part of the BBC Radio Wales Millennium History series, *The People of Wales* (1999).

—— 'Lawbooks and literacy in medieval Wales', *Speculum*, 75 (2000), 29–67.

—— 'The context and purpose of the earliest Welsh lawbooks', *Cambrian Medieval Celtic Studies*, 39 (2000), 39–63.

—— 'Medieval experiences: Wales 1000–1415', in Gareth Elwyn Jones and Dai Smith (eds), *The People of Wales* (Llandysul: Gwasg Gomer, 2000).

—— 'British or Welsh? National identity in twelfth-century Wales', *English Historical Review*, 116 (2001), 775–801.

—— 'Modern nationality and the medieval past: the Wales of John Edward Lloyd', in R. R. Davies and Geraint H. Jenkins (eds), *From Medieval to Modern Wales: Historical Essays in Honour of Kenneth O. Morgan and Ralph A. Griffiths* (Cardiff: University of Wales Press, 2004), pp. 14–29.

—— 'Culture, power and the charters of Welsh rulers', in Marie Therese Flanagan and Judith A. Green (eds), *Charters and Charter Scholarship* in Britain and Ireland (Basingstoke: Palgrave Macmillan, 2005), pp. 184–202.

—— 'The Normans in Welsh history', *ANS*, 30 (2008 for 2007), 1–18.

—— *J. E. Lloyd and the Creation of Welsh History: Renewing a Nation's Past* (Cardiff: University of Wales Press, 2011).

Prys-Jones, A. G., *The Story of Carmarthenshire*, vol. I: *From Prehistoric Times to the Beginning of the Sixteenth Century* (Llandybie: Christopher Davies, 1959).

Radiker, Laura, 'Traditional and courtly themes in a medieval Welsh elegy to "G6ann Wargann Wery" ("A Fair Virgin, Meek and Mild")', *Proceedings of the Harvard Celtic Colloquium*, 24/25 (2004/5), 101–26.

Reynolds, Susan, *Fiefs and Vassals: The Medieval Evidence Reinterpreted* (Oxford: Oxford University Press, 1994).

Richards, Gwenyth, *Welsh Noblewomen in the Thirteenth Century: An Historical Study of Medieval Welsh Law and Gender Roles* (Lewiston, NY: Edwin Mellen Press, 2009).

Richter, M., 'A new edition of the so-called *Vita Davidis Secundi*', *BBCS*, 22 (1966–68), 245–9.

—— 'Gerald of Wales: a reassessment on the 750th anniversary of his death', *Traditio*, 29 (1973), 379–90.

—— *Giraldus Cambrensis: The Growth of the Welsh Nation* (rev. edn, Aberystwyth: National Library of Wales, 1976).

—— 'The political and institutional background to national consciousness in medieval Wales', in T. W. Moody (ed.), *Nationality and the Pursuit of National Independence* (*Historical Studies*, 11; Belfast: Appletree Press, for the Irish Committee of Historical Sciences, 1978), pp. 37–55.

—— 'The interpretation of medieval Irish history', *Irish Historical Studies*, 24 (1985), 289–98.

Rigg, A. G., *A History of Anglo-Latin Literature 1042–1422* (Cambridge: Cambridge University Press, 1992).

Robbins, Keith, *Great Britain: Identities, Institutions and the Idea of Britishness* (Harlow: Longman, 1998).

Roberts, Brynley, *Gerald of Wales* (Cardiff: University of Wales Press on behalf of the Welsh Arts Council, 1982).

—— 'Oral tradition and Welsh literature: a description and survey', *Oral Tradition*, 3 (1988), 61–87.

Roberts, Gwyneth Tyson, *The Language of the Blue Books: Perfect Instrument of Empire* (Cardiff: University of Wales Press, 1998); reprinted as *The Language of the Blue Books: Wales and Colonial Prejudice* (Cardiff: University of Wales Press, 2011).

Roberts, Peter, 'Tudor Wales, national identity and the British inheritance', in Brendan Bradshaw and Peter Roberts (eds), *British Consciousness and Identity: The Making of Britain 1533–1707* (Cambridge: Cambridge University Press, 1998), pp. 8–42.

Roderick, A. J., 'Marriage and politics in Wales 1066–1282', *WHR*, 4 (1968–69), 3–20.

Rogers, Byron, 'Dateline, November 11th 1283 "The lost children"', *The Guardian*, 27 July 1991, p. 20.

—— *The Lost Children* (Tregynon, Newtown, Powys: Gwasg Gregynog, 2005).

—— *Me: The Authorised Biography* (London: Aurum Press, 2009).

Rousseau, C. M., and Rosenthal, J. T. (eds), *Women, Marriage, and Family in Medieval Christendom: Essays in Memory of Michael M. Sheehan, C.S.B* (Kalamazoo, MI: Medieval Institute Publications, 1998).

Saunders, Corinne, *Rape and Ravishment in the Literature of Medieval England* (Cambridge: D. S. Brewer, 2001).

Schweizer, Bernard, *Radicals on the Road: The Politics of English Travel Writing in the 1930s* (Charlottesville and London: University Press of Virginia, 2001).

Seaberg, R. B., 'The Norman conquest and the common law: the Levellers and the argument from continuity', *The Historical Journal*, 24 (1981), 791–806.

Searle, E., 'Women and the legitimisation of succession at the Norman conquest', *ANS*, 3 (1981 for 1980), 159–70.

Sheehan, Michael M., *Marriage, Family, and Law in Medieval Europe: Collected Studies*, ed. James K. Farge (Toronto: University of Toronto Press, 1996).

Smith, Anthony D., *Myths and Memories of the Nation* (Oxford and New York: Oxford University Press, 1999).

Smith, Bonnie G., *The Gender of History: Men, Women and Historical Practice* (Cambridge, MA and London: Harvard University Press, 1998).

Smith, Brendan, '"I have nothing but through her": women and the conquest of Ireland, 1170–1240', in Christine Meek and Catherine Lawless (eds), *Studies on Medieval and Early Modern Women: Pawns or Players?* (Dublin: Four Courts Press, 2007), pp. 49–55.

Smith, Dai, *Wales: A Question for History* (Bridgend: Seren, 1999).

Smith, J. B. (ed.), *Medieval Welsh Society: Selected Essays by T. Jones Pierce* (Cardiff: University of Wales Press, 1972).

Smith, J. Beverley, 'Land endowments of the period of Llywelyn ap Gruffudd', *BBCS*, 24 (1970–72), 77–93.

—— 'Castell Gwyddgrug', *BBCS*, 26 (1974), 74–7.

—— 'Dower in thirteenth-century Wales: a grant of the commote of Anhuniog, 1273', *BBCS*, 30 (1982–83), 348–55.

—— 'Magna Carta and the charters of the Welsh princes', *English Historical Review*, 99 (1984), 344–62.

—— 'Dynastic succession in medieval Wales', *BBCS*, 33 (1986), 199–232.

—— *Yr Ymwybod â Hanes yng Nghymru yn yr Oesoedd Canol: The Sense of History in Medieval Wales* (Aberystwyth: Coleg Prifysgol Cymru, 1991).

—— *Llywelyn ap Gruffudd: Prince of Wales* (Cardiff: University of Wales Press, 1998).

—— 'Historical writing in medieval Wales: the composition of *Brenhinedd y Saesson*', *Studia Celtica*, 42 (2008), 55–86.

Smith, Ll. Beverley, 'Dispute and settlements in medieval Wales: the role of arbitration', *English Historical Review*, 106 (1991), 835–60.

—— 'Towards a history of women in late medieval Wales', in Michael Roberts and Simone Clarke (eds), *Women and Gender in Early Modern Wales* (Cardiff: University of Wales Press, 2000), pp. 14–49.

—— 'On the hospitality of the Welsh: a comparative view', in Huw Pryce and John Watts (eds), *Power and Identity in the Middle Ages: Essays in Memory of Rees Davies* (Oxford: Oxford University Press, 2007), pp. 181–94.

Stacey, Robin C., 'Law and order in the very old West: England and Ireland in the early middle ages', in Benjamin Hudson and Vickie Ziegler (eds), *Crossed Paths: Methodological Approaches to the Celtic Aspect of the European Middle Ages* (Lanham: University Press of America, 1991), pp. 39–61.

—— 'King, queen and *edling* in the laws of the court', in Charles-Edwards, Owen and Russell (eds), *Welsh King and his Court*, pp. 29–62.

—— 'Divorce, medieval Welsh style', *Speculum*, 77 (2002), 1107–27.

Stafford, Pauline, *Unification and Conquest: A Political and Social History of England in the Tenth and Eleventh Centuries* (London and New York: Edward Arnold, 1989).

—— 'Women and the Norman conquest', *TRHS*, 6th ser., 4 (1994), 221–49.

—— *Queen Emma and Queen Edith: Queenship and Women's Power in Eleventh-Century England* (Oxford: Blackwell, 1997).

—— *Queens, Concubines and Dowagers: The King's Wife in the Early Middle Ages* (London, 1983; repr. London: Leicester University Press, 1998).

—— '"The annals of Æthelflæd": annals, history and politics in early tenth-century England', in Julia Barrow and Andrew Wareham (eds), *Myth, Rulership, Church and Charters: Essays in Honour of Nicholas Brooks* (Aldershot: Ashgate, 2008), pp. 101–16.

—— (ed.), *A Companion to the Early Middle Ages: Britain and Ireland, c.500–c.1100* (Chichester and Malden, MA: Wiley-Blackwell, 2009).

Stephenson, David, *The Governance of Gwynedd* (Cardiff: University of Wales Press on behalf of the History and Law Committee of the Board of Celtic Studies, 1984).

—— 'The laws of court: past reality or present ideal?', in Charles-Edwards, Owen and Russell (eds), *Welsh King and his Court*, pp. 400–9.

—— 'The "resurgence" of Powys in the late eleventh and early twelfth centuries', *ANS*, 30 (2008), 182–95.

—— 'Welsh chronicles' accounts of the mid-twelfth century', *Cambrian Medieval Celtic Studies*, 56 (2008), 45–57.

Stoyle, M., 'Caricaturing Cymru: images of the Welsh in the London press, 1642–6', in D. Dunn (ed.), *War and Society in Medieval and Early Modern Britain* (Liverpool: Liverpool University Press, 2000), pp. 162–79.

Strohm, Paul, 'Storie, spelle, geste, romaunce, tragedie: generic distinctions in the Middle English Troy narratives', *Speculum*, 46 (1971), 348–59.

Stuard, S. Mosher (ed.), *Women in Medieval Society* (Philadelphia: University of Pennsylvania Press, 1976).

Thompson, Carl, *The Suffering Traveller and the Romantic Imagination* (Oxford: Clarendon Press, 2007).

Thompson, K., 'Affairs of state: the illegitimate children of Henry I', *JMH*, 29 (2003), 129–51.

Thompson, Steven, *Unemployment, Poverty and Health in Interwar South Wales* (Cardiff: University of Wales Press on behalf of the History and Law Committee of the Board of Celtic Studies, 2006).

Thornton, David E., 'The genealogy of Gruffudd ap Cynan', in K. L. Maund (ed.), *Gruffudd ap Cynan: A Collaborative Biography* (Woodbridge and Rochester: Boydell and Brewer, 1996), pp. 79–108.

—— *Kings, Chronologies, and Genealogies: Studies in the Political History of Early Medieval Ireland and Wales* (Oxford: Unit for Prosopographical Research, Linacre College, 2003).

Thornton, Tim, 'Nationhood at the margin: identity, regionality and the English crown in the seventeenth century', in Len Scales and Oliver Zimmer (eds), *Power and the Nation in European History* (Cambridge: Cambridge University Press, 2005), pp. 232–47.

Tout, T. F., rev. Huw Pryce, 'Gruffudd ap Rhys (d. 1137), ruler in south Wales', *ODNB*. 24. 139–40.

'Towards a battlefields register for Wales', *Heritage in Wales*, 46 (Summer 2010), 5.

Turvey, Roger, 'King, prince or lord? Rhys ap Gruffydd and the nomenclature of authority in twelfth-century Wales', *The Carmarthenshire Antiquary*, 30 (1994), 5–18.

—— *The Welsh Princes: The Native Rulers of Wales, 1063–1283* (Harlow: Longman, 2002).

Vincent, N., 'Warin and Henry Fitz Gerald, the king's chamberlains: the origins of the FitzGeralds revisited', *ANS*, 21 (1998), 233–60.

Wada, Yoko, 'Gerald on Gerald: self-presentation by Giraldus Cambrensis', *ANS*, 20 (1998 for 1997), 223–47.

Walker, David, 'Windsor, Gerald of (d. 1116×36), a soldier and dynast', *ODNB*, lix. 708–9.

Walker, Sue Sheridan, 'Common law juries and feudal marriage customs in medieval England: the pleas of ravishment', *Illinois Law Review*, 3 (1984), 705–18.

Walters, D. B., 'The European legal context of the Welsh law of matrimonial property', in Jenkins and Owen (eds), *Welsh Law of Women*, pp. 115–31.

West, Francis James, 'The colonial history of the Norman conquest?', *History*, 84 (1999), 219–36.

Whetter, K. S., *Understanding Genre and Medieval Romance* (Aldershot: Ashgate, 2008).

Wickham, C., 'Medieval Wales and European history', *WHR*, 25 (2010), 201–8.

Wilkinson, Louise J., 'Joan, wife of Llywelyn the Great', in M. Prestwich *et al.* (eds), *Thirteenth Century England X* (Woodbridge: Boydell and Brewer, 2005), pp. 81–93.

Williams, Chris, 'Problematizing Wales: an exploration in historiography and postcoloniality', in Jane Aaron and Chris Williams (eds), *Postcolonial Wales* (Cardiff: University of Wales Press, 2005), pp. 3–22.

Williams, D. H., *The Welsh Cistercians* (2 vols, Caldey Island, Tenby: Cyhoeddiadau Sistersiaidd, 1984).

Williams, G. A., 'The succession to Gwynedd, 1238–47', *BBCS*, 20 (1962–64), 393–413.

Williams, Gwyn A., *When was Wales? A History of the Welsh* (Harmondsworth: Penguin, 1985).

Wilson, Kathleen, 'Empire, gender and modernity in the eighteenth century', in Philippa Levine (ed.), *Gender and Empire* (Oxford: Oxford University Press, 2004), pp. 14–45.

Winward, Fiona, 'Some aspects of women in *The Four Branches*', *Cambrian Medieval Celtic Studies*, 34 (1997), 77–106.

Wmffre, Iwan, *The Place-Names of Cardiganshire* (3 vols, Oxford: Archaeopress, 2004).

Wood, Juliette, 'The calumniated wife in medieval Welsh literature', *Cambridge Medieval Celtic Studies*, 10 (1985), 25–38.

—— 'Walter Map: the contents and context of *De nugis curialium*', *Transactions of the Honourable Society of Cymmrodorion* (1985), 91–103.

Index